GW00982484

Child-Centered
Play Therapy
Research

Child-Centered Play Therapy Research

The Evidence Base for Effective Practice

Edited by

Jennifer N. Baggerly
Dee C. Ray
Sue C. Bratton

WILEY

John Wiley & Sons, Inc.

This book is printed on acid-free paper.

Copyright © 2010 by John Wiley & Sons, Inc. All rights reserved.

Published by John Wiley & Sons, Inc., Hoboken, New Jersey.
Published simultaneously in Canada.

No part of this publication may be reproduced, stored in a retrieval system, or transmitted in any form or by any means, electronic, mechanical, photocopying, recording, scanning, or otherwise, except as permitted under Section 107 or 108 of the 1976 United States Copyright Act, without either the prior written permission of the Publisher, or authorization through payment of the appropriate per-copy fee to the Copyright Clearance Center, Inc., 222 Rosewood Drive, Danvers, MA 01923, (978) 750-8400, fax (978) 646-8600, or on the web at www.copyright.com. Requests to the Publisher for permission should be addressed to the Permissions Department, John Wiley & Sons, Inc., 111 River Street, Hoboken, NJ 07030, (201) 748-6011, fax (201) 748-6008.

Limit of Liability/Disclaimer of Warranty: While the publisher and author have used their best efforts in preparing this book, they make no representations or warranties with respect to the accuracy or completeness of the contents of this book and specifically disclaim any implied warranties of merchantability or fitness for a particular purpose. No warranty may be created or extended by sales representatives or written sales materials. The advice and strategies contained herein may not be suitable for your situation. You should consult with a professional where appropriate. Neither the publisher nor author shall be liable for any loss of profit or any other commercial damages, including but not limited to special, incidental, consequential, or other damages.

This publication is designed to provide accurate and authoritative information in regard to the subject matter covered. It is sold with the understanding that the publisher is not engaged in rendering professional services. If legal, accounting, medical, psychological or any other expert assistance is required, the services of a competent professional person should be sought.

Designations used by companies to distinguish their products are often claimed as trademarks. In all instances where John Wiley & Sons, Inc. is aware of a claim, the product names appear in initial capital or all capital letters. Readers, however, should contact the appropriate companies for more complete information regarding trademarks and registration.

The Association for Play Therapy graciously provided permission to reprint methods and results sections from the following articles: Fall, Navelski, & Welch, 2002; Foley, Higdon, & White, 2006; Garza, & Bratton, 2005; Glover & Landreth, 2000; Green, & Christensen, 2006; Jones & Landreth, 2002; Jones, Rhine, & Bratton, 2002; Packman & Bratton, 2003; Post, McAllister, Sheely, Hess, & Flowers, 2004; Ray, Blanco, Sullivan, & Holliman, 2009; Ray, Schottelkorb, & Tsai, 2007; Shen, 2002; Smith & Landreth, 2004; Tew, Landreth, Joiner, & Solt, 2002; Tyndall-Lind, Landreth, & Giordano, 2001; Yuen, Landreth, & Baggerly, 2002.

For general information on our other products and services please contact our Customer Care Department within the United States at (800) 762-2974, outside the United States at (317) 572-3993 or fax (317) 572-4002.

Wiley also publishes its books in a variety of electronic formats. Some content that appears in print may not be available in electronic books. For more information about Wiley products, visit our website at www.wiley.com.

Library of Congress Cataloging-in-Publication Data:
  Baggerly, Jennifer.
   Child-centered play therapy research : the evidence base for effective practice / Jennifer Baggerly, Dee C. Ray, Sue C. Bratton.
     p. cm.
   Includes index.
   ISBN 978-0-470-42201-4 (cloth)
  1. Play therapy. 2. Child psychotherapy. I. Ray, Dee C. II. Bratton, Sue C. III. Title.
   RJ505.P6B34 2010
   618.92′8914—dc22

                                                                                    2009046307

Printed in the United States of America

10 9 8 7 6 5 4 3 2 1

From Jennifer Baggerly,
I dedicate this book to my mother, Jean Louise Baggerly,
who is the wind beneath my wings, and to my daughter,
Katelyn Jean Baggerly, who also is learning to fly high.

From Dee Ray,
I dedicate this book to all play therapists who want
to research the difference they make in children's
lives but just have not had the chance yet.
We hope this book inspires you. I also dedicate
this book to my family who always inspires me
to continue trying to make a difference.

From Sue Bratton,
I dedicate this book to the play therapy pioneers whose
vision and unfailing dedication amaze and inspire me.
Specifically, I thank Garry Landreth, my mentor and
friend, for his innovative contributions to the research
and development of CCPT: Without you, this book truly
would not be possible! I also want to acknowledge the
many doctoral students as well as children and parents
who have graciously participated in our research: You
hold a special place in my heart! Finally, thank you,
David and Lauren, for your love and encouragement.
Without you, none of this would matter!

Contents

Foreword

P LAY THERAPY IS the most developmentally appropriate way to approach children in a counseling relationship, and it is in this safe, nurturing environment that children play out what they have experienced, their reactions and feelings about those experiences, what they need in their lives, and how they feel about themselves. Thus, play therapy is a complete therapeutic modality. I have long thought that play therapy is the most effective way we can help to make the world a safer place for children because in play therapy there will be no harm. Play therapy is a place that is absolutely safe, a place where the child is accepted as the person he is. In this kind of relationship, the creative- and growth-promoting potential of children emerges. We know experientially that this process occurs and have an accumulation of research-based studies that verify this fact.

The work of researchers in the field of play therapy has largely been overlooked, though, by the mental health profession. Although there are a multitude of published research studies, the general assumption of mental health professionals seems to have been, first, that play therapy is not effective and, second, that there probably hasn't been very much research. Consequently, the general population of mental health professionals has made little effort to find and become acquainted with existing play therapy research. Jennifer Baggerly, Dee Ray, and Sue Bratton have remedied this situation with the publication of this book, which pulls together significant research studies in the field of play therapy. A careful examination of 70 years of research, which has increased geometrically since the early 1940s, is a monumental undertaking, and the results are affirming, confirming, rewarding, supportive, encouraging, exciting, stimulating, and a significant contribution to the mental health field in general and the field of play therapy specifically. Does the use of play therapy and filial therapy result in changes in the behavior problems and adjustment of children? Yes, play therapy and filial therapy are effective as shown by the results of studies in this book.

The modalities of play therapy and filial therapy are no longer up-start "new kids on the block" as viewed by some. These modalities have matured into seasoned approaches. Likewise, the models, designs, and research methods used in play therapy research have become increasingly sophisticated and scientifically rigorous. Some of the most recent and best-designed play therapy and filial therapy research studies are included in this book.

Although the trend in the field of play therapy to become more scientific in measuring results has been necessary, the importance of the person of the child must never be overlooked. The person of the child is always more important than the child's presenting problem. And although I agree with and support the need for research, I hope we will never be able to measure the person of a child, because if we were able to do that, we would be in a position to control children, and I fear that. As you read this book, I can assure you that although there is a focus and emphasis on the measurement of behavior, there is an undercurrent of sensitivity to the child and an obvious concern for the emotional needs and welfare of children. Although we may never be able to measure the intangible dimensions in the play therapy relationship, it just may be that these are the most important elements in the play therapy process. There is still much to be done in studying the area of process to increase our knowledge of this important dimension.

Perhaps it is enough at this time to have this book in our hands that brings together in a clear and understandable way some of the most important studies in the field of play therapy and filial therapy. A light has been shined on our pathway.

Garry L. Landreth
Regents Professor
University of North Texas

Preface

"WHERE'S THE PLAY therapy research? I haven't seen any," was asked by several of my colleagues. Frankly, I feel aggravated by this question. I always have to bite my tongue, smile politely, and say, "Oh, there is a growing evidence-base of play therapy research. It is mostly published in the *International Journal of Play Therapy*. The most recent study is . . . " Then I proceed into a long lecture on play therapy research, to the point where my colleague becomes aggravated!

As the former research chair of the Association for Play Therapy and a play therapy researcher myself, I have answered this question about play therapy research in different formats through conference presentations, book chapters, university classes, and casual conversations. In fact, I have answered the question so often that I decided to follow one of my general rules—if you have to explain it more than two times, then write it down. Hence, the purpose of this book is to explain the most prominent play therapy research studies in this millennium, in a non-aggravating conversational tone with personal motivation by the researchers who actually conducted the studies.

Fortunately, I already knew most of the play therapy researchers from being a doctoral student at the University of North Texas and through my involvement with the Association for Play Therapy. Two of the most prominent play therapy researchers, Dr. Dee Ray and Dr. Sue Bratton, are my mentors and personal friends. Since they would be contributing a large amount of the chapters, it made sense to invite them to co-edit the book. Our common mentor, dissertation chair, and the "grandfather" of child-centered play therapy is Dr. Garry Landreth. He honored us by writing the foreword.

When reading this book, you will notice that all the research studies described are based on the child-centered play therapy (CCPT) theoretical orientation and filial therapy approach. This focus is because virtually all play therapy research studies that were published in a professional journal since the year 2000 were CCPT or filial therapy. Therefore, before describing the book contents, it will be helpful to provide a brief introduction to CCPT.

CCPT was popularized and operationalized by Virginia Axline (1947, 1964) who applied Carl Roger's (1942) non-directive therapeutic principles in her work with children. More recently, CCPT was promoted by the writings of Landreth (1993, 2001, 2002) and Guerney (1983) in North America, as well as West (1996) and Wilson and Ryan (2005) in Britain. CCPT is defined as "a dynamic interpersonal relationship between a child and a counselor trained in play therapy procedures who provides selected play materials and facilitates the development of a safe relationship for the child to fully express and explore self through the child's natural medium of expression, play" (Landreth, 2002, p. 16). The focus on the child's innate tendency to move toward growth and maturity and a deep belief in the child's ability to self-direct are the main tenets that set CCPT apart from other models of play therapy (Landreth & Bratton, 2006). The CCPT counselor allows the child to play freely with carefully selected toys. The play therapist initiates statements that reflect content and feeling (i.e., "you're angry at him"), encourage (i.e., "you worked really hard and you did it"), return responsibility to the child (i.e., "you can decide what color you want to use"), and if needed, set limits (i.e., the paint is not for throwing"). The typical CCPT counselor is trained to not ask questions, direct behavior, or interpret the child's words or actions. According to CCPT philosophy, these types of actions would serve to inhibit the child's expression and movement toward health.

The description of CCPT provided above and the description of filial therapy provided in chapter 15 will serve as a common set of procedures for most of the research studies explained in this book. In the first section of this book, Dee Ray and Sue Bratton provide an overview of play therapy research in the twenty-first century including Bratton et al.'s (2005) meta-analysis. The second section focuses on CCPT research. Specifically, 10 quantitative pre-test, post-test experimental control or comparison group studies are explained including research on self-efficacy (Marijane Fall), chronically ill children (Elizabeth Jones and Kara Carnes-Holt), child witnesses of domestic violence (Ashley Tynall-Lind), Chinese earthquake victims (Jean Shen), relationship stress (Dee Ray), children with aggressive behaviors (P. J. Blanco), ADHD (Dee Ray and Natalya Edwards), learning disabled preadolescents (Jill Packman and Ireon LeBeauf), Hispanic children (Yvonne Garza), and academic achievement (Brandy Schumann). Two single-case design studies are presented on ADHD (April Schottelkorb) and developmental levels of young children (April Brown). Finally, a qualitative study on children's perceptions of play therapy is described (Eric Green).

The third section describes filial therapy research published since the year 2000. Sue Bratton, Garry Landreth, and Dennis Lin provide an overview of Child Parent Relationship Therapy outcome research. Then, nine quantitative pre-test, post-test experimental control or comparison group studies are described including filial therapy with parents of chronically ill children (Kristi Tew), Native Americans (Geri Glover), Chinese parents (Tom Yuen), African American parents (Angela Sheely), Hispanic parents (Peggy Ceballos), high school students as therapeutic agents (Leslie Jones), teachers of deaf children (D. Michael Smith), teachers of at-risk children (Phyllis Post), and teachers of preschool children (Mary Morrison and Wendy Helker). A qualitative study of parents' voices in filial therapy is also presented (Yuehong Chen Foley). In the final chapter, Baggerly provides future research directions by identifying evidence-based standards and tips for designing your own play therapy research study.

Since this is an edited book, each chapter author's individual voice is preserved. Some are scientifically objective while others are deeply personal, thereby sustaining an important balance between the art and science in play therapy research. The authors were independently responsible for statistical analysis; and some studies were conducted prior to current standards regarding reporting of effect size, confidence intervals, and so forth. Thus, reporting of results vary. Readers will be able to see the progression of play therapy research and will be guided in contemporary standards for conducting their own research.

As you read this book, you will be ready to respond with confidence to your colleagues' questions about play therapy (PT) and filial therapy (FT) research. To school district administrators who want to know why children should be released from "instructional" time to attend play therapy, you will describe research studies by Fall (self-efficacy PT), Packman (learning disabled PT), Ray and Edwards (relationship stress PT), Blanco (aggression PT), Schumann (academic achievement PT), Schottelkorb (ADHD PT), Green (children's perceptions PT), Post (at-risk FT), M. Smith (deaf FT), Morrison and Helker (preschool FT), and L. Jones (high school therapeutic agents FT).

To community agency administrators who insist on empirically supported interventions, you will describe play therapy research studies by Shen (disaster PT), Brown (children's development PT), Ray

(ADHD PT), and Foley (parents' voices FT), as well as the studies mentioned above and below.

To judges, lawyers, and child protection case workers who want researched interventions for their abused clients, you will explain Tyndall-Lind's study (domestic violence PT).

To doctors and nurses who want research for their chronically ill patients, you will tell them about research studies by E. Jones (PT) and Tew (FT).

To multicultural advocates who want to know if your intervention is valid for culturally diverse children, you will explain research studies by Garza (Hispanic PT), Ceballos (Hispanic FT), Glover (Native Americans FT), Yuen (Chinese FT), and Sheely (African Americans FT).

To university professors who want to know your rationale and procedures for a research study, you will cite Ray and Bratton (current PT research and meta-analysis), Bratton and Landreth (current FT research), Ray and Schottelkorb (single-case design), and Baggerly (evidence-based standards and tips).

I hope this book will provide you with information and inspiration to respond graciously to questions about play therapy research and to conduct rigorous studies that contribute to play therapy's evidence base for effective practice!

Play and Research Well,
Jennifer N. Baggerly

REFERENCES

Axline, V. (1947). *Play therapy*. New York: Ballantine Books.

Axline, V. (1964). *Dibs: In search of self*. New York: Ballantine Books.

Bratton, S. C., Ray, D. C., Rhine, T., & Jones, L. (2005). The efficacy of play therapy with children: A meta-analytic review of treatment outcomes. *Professional Psychology: Research and Practice, 36,* 376–390.

Landreth, G. (1993). Child-centered play therapy. *Elementary School Guidance and Counseling, 28,* 18–28.

Guerney, L. (1983). Child-centered (non-directive) play therapy. In C. E. Schaefer & K. J. O'Connor (Eds.), *Handbook of play therapy* (pp. 21–64). New York: Wiley.

Landreth, G. (Ed.). (2001). *Innovations in play therapy: Issues, process, and special populations*. Philadelphia: Brunner-Routledge.

Landreth, G. (2002). *Play therapy: The art of the relationship* (2nd ed.). New York: Brunner-Routledge.

Landreth, G., & Bratton, S. (2006). *Child parent relationship therapy: A 10-session filial therapy model*. New York: Routledge.

Rogers, C. (1942). *Counseling and psychotherapy*. Boston: Houghton Mifflin.

West, J. (1996). *Client-centered play therapy* (2nd ed). London: Hodder Arnold.

Wilson, K., & Ryan, V. (2005). *Play therapy: A non-directive approach for children and adolescents* (2nd ed). Oxford, England: Elsevier.

ORIGINAL SOURCES FOR RESEARCH STUDIES

Fall, M., Navelski, L., & Welch, K. (2002).Outcomes of a play intervention for children identified for special education services. *International Journal of Play Therapy, 11*(2), 91–106.

Foley, Y. C., Higdon, L., White, J. F. (2006). A qualitative study of filial therapy: Parents' voices. *International Journal of Play Therapy, 15*, 37–64.

Garza, Y., & Bratton, S. (2005). School-based child centered play therapy with Hispanic children: Outcomes and cultural considerations. *International Journal of Play Therapy, 14*, 51–80.

Glover, G. J., & Landreth, G. L. (2000). Filial therapy with Native Americans. *International Journal of Play Therapy, 9*(2), 57–80.

Green, E., & Christensen, T. (2006). Children's perceptions of play therapy in school settings. *International Journal of Play Therapy, 15*(1), pp. 65–85.

Jones, E., & Landreth, G. (2002). The efficacy of intensive individual play therapy for chronically ill children. *International Journal of Play Therapy, 11*, 117–140.

Jones, L., Rhine, T., & Bratton, S. (2002). High school students as therapeutic agents with young children experiencing school adjustment difficulties: The effectiveness of a filial therapy training model. *International Journal of Play Therapy, 11*(2), 43–62.

Packman, J., & Bratton, S. (2003). A school-based group play/activity therapy intervention with learning disabled preadolescents exhibiting behavior problems. *International Journal of Play Therapy, 12*, 7–29.

Post, P., McAllister, M., Sheely, A., Hess, B., & Flowers, C. (2004). Child-Centered Kinder Training for Teachers of Pre-School Children Deemed At-Risk. *International Journal of Play Therapy, 13*(2), 53–74.

Ray, D., Blanco, P., Sullivan, J., Holliman, R. (2009). An Exploratory Study of Child-Centered Play Therapy with Aggressive Children. *International Journal of Play Therapy, 18*, 162–175.

Ray, D., Schottelkorb, A., & Tsai, M. (2007). Play therapy with children exhibiting symptoms of attention deficit hyperactivity disorder. *International Journal of Play Therapy, 16*, 95–111.

Shen, Y. (2002). Short-term group play therapy with Chinese earthquake victims: Effects on anxiety, depression, and adjustment. *International Journal of Play Therapy, 11*, 43–63.

Smith, D. M., & Landreth, G. (2004). Filial therapy with teachers of deaf and hard of hearing preschool children. *International Journal for Play Therapy, 13*(1) 13–33.

Tew, K., Landreth, G. L., Joiner, K. D., & Solt, M. D. (2002). Filial therapy with parents of chronically ill children. *International Journal of Play Therapy, 11*(1), 79–100.

Tyndall-Lind, A., Landreth, G., & Giordano, M. (2001). Intensive group play therapy with child witnesses of domestic violence. *International Journal of Play Therapy, 10*, 53–83.

Yuen, T., Landreth, G. L., & Baggerly, J. N. (2002). Filial therapy with immigrant Chinese families. *International Journal of Play Therapy, 11*(2), 63–90.

About the Editors

Jennifer N. Baggerly, PhD, LMHC-S, RPT-S, is an associate professor in the Counselor Education program at the University of South Florida and director of the Graduate Certificate in Play Therapy. She is on the Board of Directors of the Association for Play Therapy (APT) and the former chair of the APT research committee. She holds a doctorate in counseling education with a specialization in play therapy from the University of North Texas. Dr. Baggerly is a Licensed Mental Health Counselor Supervisor, a Registered Play Therapist Supervisor, and a Field Traumatologist. Dr. Baggerly's research projects and more than 40 publications include the effectiveness of play therapy with children who are homeless and counseling interventions for traumatized children.

Dee C. Ray, PhD, LPC, NCC, RPT-S, is an associate professor in the counseling program and director of the Child and Family Resource Clinic at the University of North Texas. Dr. Ray has published more than 40 articles, chapters, and books in the field of play therapy, and more than 15 peer-reviewed research publications specifically examining the effects of child-centered play therapy. Dr. Ray is the author of the *Child-Centered Play Therapy Treatment Manual* and former editor of the *International Journal of Play Therapy (IJPT)*. She currently serves on the editorial board for *IJPT* and the Research Committee for the Association for Play Therapy. She is the recipient of the 2008 Outstanding Research Award for Association for Play Therapy, the 2006 Outstanding Research Award for Texas Counseling Association, and the 2006 Nancy Guillory Award for Outstanding Service and Contribution to the Field of Play Therapy from the Texas Association for Play Therapy.

Sue C. Bratton, PhD, LPC, RPT-S is an associate professor of counseling and director of the Center for Play Therapy at the University of North Texas. She is a past president of the Association for Play

Therapy (APT), and currently serves on the APT Research Committee. She is the recipient of the 2007 APT Outstanding Research Award, the 2009 University of North Texas College of Education Faculty Excellence in Research Award, and the 2005 Nancy Guillory Award for Outstanding Service and Contribution to the Field of Play Therapy from the Texas Association for Play Therapy. Dr. Bratton is a frequent speaker at play therapy conferences both nationally and internationally, and has published more than 60 articles, chapters, books, videos, and other publications in the field of play therapy, including co-authorship of *Child Parent Relationship Therapy (CPRT): A 10-Session Filial Therapy Model*, the *CPRT Treatment Manual* and *The World of Play Therapy Literature*. Her research agenda focuses on investigating the effectiveness of CPRT and child-centered play therapy.

Contributors

Jennifer N. Baggerly, PhD,
    LMHC-S, RPT-S
Counselor Education
University of South Florida
Tampa, FL

P. J. Blanco, PhD
Counselor Education and
    Psychology
Delta State University
Cleveland, MS

Sue C. Bratton, PhD, LPC, RPT-S
Counselor Education
University of North Texas,
Denton, TX

April Garofano-Brown, PhD, LPC
Counselor Education
Georgia State University
Atlanta, GA

Peggy Ceballos, PhD
Counseling
University of North Carolina-
    Charlotte
Charlotte, NC

Kara Carnes-Holt, MS Ed, LPC,
    NCC, RPT-S
Counselor Education
University of North Texas
Denton, TX

Natalya A. Edwards
Counselor Education
University of North Texas
Denton, TX

Marijane Fall, EdD, LCPC,
    RPT-S (Deceased)
Counselor Education
University of Southern Maine
Gorham, ME

Yuehong Chen Foley, PhD, LPC,
    NCC
Gwinnett County Public Schools
Atlanta, GA
Grayson, GA

Yvonne Garza, PhD, LPC, RPT
Department of Educational
    Leadership and Counseling
Sam Houston State University
Huntsville, TX

Eric Green, PhD, LPCP, RPT-S
Private Practice
New Orleans, LA

Geri Glover, PhD, LPCC, RPT-S
Education Department
College of Santa Fe
Santa Fe, NM

Wendy P. Helker, PhD, LPC-S, NCC, RPT
Private Practice
Corinth, TX

Elizabeth Murphy Jones, PhD, LPC
Private Practice
Fort Worth, TX

Leslie Jones, PhD, LPC
Private Practice
Prosper, TX

Garry L. Landreth, EdD, LPC, RPT-S
University of North Texas
Denton, TX

Ireon LeBeauf
University of Nevada, Reno
Reno, NV

Yung-Wei Dennis Lin
University of North Texas
Denton, TX

Mary O. Morrison, PhD, LPC-S, NCC, RPT-S
Texas State University
San Marcos, TX

Jill Packman, PhD, LMFT, NCC, RPT-S
Department of Counseling and Educational Psychology
University of Nevada, Reno
Reno, NV

Phyllis Post, PhD, NCC, RPT
Department of Counseling
University of North Carolina-Charlotte
Charlotte, NC

Dee C. Ray, PhD, LPC, RPT-S
Counselor Education
University of North Texas
Denton, TX

April Schottelkorb, PhD, LPC, NCC, RPT-S
Boise State University
Boise, ID

Angela I. Sheely Moore, PhD, LPC, NCC
College of Education and Human Services
Montclair State University
Upper Montclair, NJ

Yih-Jiun Shen, EdD, NCC, CSC
Department of Educational Psychology
University of Texas-Pan American
Edinburg, TX

Brandy Schumann, PhD, LPC, RPT
Private Practice
McKinney, TX

David Michael Smith, PhD, LMFT, RPT-S
Community Reach Center
Fort Collins, CO

Kristi Tew, PhD
Private Practice
Southlake, TX

Ashley Tyndall-Lind, PhD, LPC-S, RPT-S
Dallas Children's Advocacy
  Center
Dallas, TX

Tom Yuen, PhD
City University of Hong Kong
Kowloon, Hong Kong

SECTION I

OVERVIEW OF PLAY THERAPY RESEARCH

CHAPTER 1

What the Research Shows About Play Therapy: Twenty-First Century Update

DEE C. RAY and SUE C. BRATTON

INTRODUCTION TO PLAY THERAPY RESEARCH

The field of mental health currently requires substantial evidence to support the use of interventions providing direct services to clients. Emphasis on evidentiary support of mental health interventions is not new. Many professional organizations, including the American Counseling Association (ACA), the American Psychological Association (APA), and the National Association of Social Workers (NASW), recognize the need for empirical support for practice (ACA, 2005; APA, 2002; NASW, 2008). Managed-care corporations often review interventions through panel evaluation of research and literature to help them make decisions regarding practitioner reimbursement. Over the last two decades, the field has observed the rise of the evidence-based movement of empirically supported treatments in which interventions are critiqued according to rigor of experimental research studies. Fortunately, play therapy research dates back more than 45 years, providing empirical support for even the harshest of critics. There are few interventions that can claim such a lengthy research history as well as a thriving body of current research.

We published our first review of play therapy research literature in 2000 in a simple article titled, "What the Research Shows About Play Therapy." We reviewed 82 play therapy research studies in the article, from 1942 to 1999. Bratton and Ray (2000) was our initial attempt to summarize and critique decades of play therapy research, including all studies that included the term *play therapy* and at least one aspect of experimental design, such as single-group pre- and post-assessment or stringent comparison of play therapy intervention to a control or comparison group. The purpose of Bratton and Ray (2000) was to explore the issues researched by historical and current play therapy literature and begin a review of methodological features of such studies. We later published findings applying precise methodology of meta-analysis review to 93 criteria-based controlled play therapy studies (Bratton, Ray, Rhine, & Jones, 2005). This chapter summarizes our earlier findings on play therapy research for the last century and reviews recent research from the first decade of the new millennium.

OVERVIEW OF OUTCOME RESEARCH FROM THE TWENTIETH CENTURY

To progress to the current century, we quickly review here the findings of Bratton and Ray (2000). Reviewing six decades of play therapy research, we found that play therapy research peaked in the decade of 1970, with a record 23 studies. Research leveled off in the 1980s and 1990s, resting at 16 to 17 studies in each decade. Most of the studies compared a play therapy intervention group with a control or comparison group, although we also included one group pre- and post-assessment designs. Play therapy interventions ranged from 2 to 100 sessions with a median number of sessions at 12. Participants ranged in age from 3 to 17 years. Although most interventions were designated as nondirective, many studies did not clearly identify the type or scope of play therapy orientation or treatment protocol. We focused on studies that were labeled *play therapy* and did not include studies involving parents or other treatment providers beyond therapists. The majority of studies included measurements of social maladjustment, with secondary priority in areas of intelligence, maladaptive school behavior, self-concept, and anxiety. Early play therapy research focused on intelligence and school achievement, while later years (1970s and 1980s) focused on social adjustment and self-concept.

Our review of twentieth-century research revealed positive effects of play therapy in the following areas: social maladjustment, withdrawn behavior, conduct disorder or aggression, maladaptive school behavior, emotional maladjustment, anxiety and fear, autism and schizophrenia, multiculturalism, self-concept, intelligence, reading, physical or learning disability, speech or language problems, sexual abuse and domestic violence, depression, post-traumatic stress, ADHD and locus of control, divorce, and alcohol or drug abuse. Not all studies noted significant changes on all dependent variables; and, because of the extensive amount of data collected, we reported only the statistics that were significant. While the majority of studies were limited by small sample size, findings were favorable in support of the effectiveness of play therapy with a wide range of mental health issues.

META-ANALYTIC RESEARCH ON PLAY THERAPY

Meta-analytic reviews of research have made it possible to overcome individual study limitations resulting from small sample size by combining study findings to compute an overall treatment effect. Two meta-analyses on play therapy outcomes have been published in the 2000–2009 decade and have contributed to the recognition of play therapy in the broader field of child psychotherapy (Bratton et al., 2005; LeBlanc & Ritchie, 2001). A few other meta-analyses and systemic reviews of child psychotherapy have reported favorable outcomes for play therapy; they included only a handful of play therapy studies, however, and made only minimal note of its effects (Allin, Walthen, & MacMillan, 2005; Beelmann & Schneider, 2003; Casey & Berman, 1985; Eyeberg, Nelson, & Bogs, 2008; Hetzel-Riggin, Brausch, & Montgomery, 2007; Wethington et al., 2008). LeBlanc and Ritchie (2001) conducted the first meta-analysis to focus exclusively on play therapy studies and reported a moderate treatment effect size (ES) of .66 standard deviations for the 42 controlled studies they included in their analysis. Their findings were consistent with effect sizes found in earlier child psychotherapy meta-analyses (Casey & Berman, 1985, ES = .71; Weisz, Weiss, Han, Granger, & Morton, 1995, ES = .71).

In our 2005 meta-analysis of six decades of play therapy outcome research (Bratton et al., 2005), our intent was to conduct a comprehensive review of controlled play therapy studies from the early pioneering work of Virginia Axline through the end of the century. We carefully reviewed 180 documents that appeared to measure the effectiveness of play therapy dated 1942 to 2000, resulting in 93 studies included in the final calculation of effect size. Studies that met the following criteria were included: use of a controlled research design, sufficient data for computing effect size, and the identification by the author of a labeled *play therapy* intervention. A play therapy intervention was further defined to include studies that examined the use of paraprofessionals (primarily parents) as well as professionals as the direct provider of the intervention. The majority of studies that fell into the paraprofessional category used filial therapy methodology. Consistent with earlier meta-analyses in child psychotherapy, we used Cohen's d (1988) guidelines (.20 = small; .50 = medium; .80 = large) to interpret treatment effect size. Overall ES for the 93 studies was calculated at .80 standard deviations, interpreted as a large treatment effect. This finding means that children receiving play therapy interventions performed .80 standard deviations above children who did not receive play therapy.

The average age of study participants was 7.0, reduced to 6.7 years when play therapy was conducted by paraprofessionals under the direct supervision of a professional trained in play therapy. This result contrasted meta-analytic findings conducted on a broad range of child psychotherapies that reported mean ages of 10.2 years (Kazdin, Bass, Ayers, & Rodgers, 1990) and 10.5 years (Weisz, Weiss, Han, Granger, & Morton, 1995). Brestan and Eyeberg (1998) reviewed studies focused on conduct-disordered children and also reported higher mean age (9.8 years) than the mean for play therapy studies. We believe the lower mean age of play therapy participants compared to other psychotherapeutic interventions for children is particularly meaningful in view of the national priority to identify effective early interventions that allow children to receive help when problems first arise (New Freedom Commission on Mental Health, 2003; Subcommittee on Children and Family, 2003; U.S. Public Health Service, 2000). The finding regarding age supports our belief that the developmental properties of play are responsive to children's maturational needs, allowing them to meaningfully participate in therapy at a young age. Because play therapy can be used successfully with younger children, it conceivably has the potential to prevent the development of more severe and costly mental health problems that can develop over time.

In the 2005 analysis, we were also interested in examining specific study characteristics to investigate their impact on play therapy outcome. Of the 93 studies coded for analysis, the largest number of studies (n = 36) were conducted in a school setting, followed by outpatient clinic (n = 34). The treatment effect for clinic-based investigations was consistent with the overall effect size for play therapy (ES = .81), while school-based studies demonstrated a treatment effect of .69 standard deviations. Studies conducted in residential or crisis settings produced significantly greater treatment effects (ES = 1.05) than those carried out in schools or clinics, indicating that the location in which play therapy is conducted affects treatment outcome. It is important to note, however, that the average number of sessions for play therapy in school settings was 8.4, approximately one-third the length of treatment in clinical settings (22.4 sessions). It is plausible that the lower number of sessions in schools might have accounted for the lower treatment effect. Because of inadequate staffing, school counselors and other school mental health professionals must often limit sessions per child so they can reach more students (Bratton, 2010). Hence, treatment length in school settings may be less likely to depend on the severity of the presenting issue and problem resolution than in other settings.

Additional findings indicated that play therapy had a moderate to large beneficial effect for internalizing (ES = .81), externalizing (ES = .79), and combined problem types (ES = .93). Treatment effects on outcomes for measures of self-concept, social adjustment, personality, anxiety, adaptive functioning, and family functioning, including quality of the parent-child relationship, were also reported in the moderate to large range. When play therapy was delivered by a parent or other caregiver (ES = 1.15), the effect size was larger than when delivered directly to the child by a mental health professional (ES = .72). This result was consistent with LeBlanc and Ritchie's (2001) findings and highlights the importance of including parents in treatment to increase the likelihood of a successful outcome. Both humanistic play therapy interventions (ES = .92) and nonhumanistic or behavioral play therapy approaches (ES = .71) were considered to be effective regardless of theoretical approach. The effect size reported for humanistic approaches, however, primarily defined as child-centered and non-directive play therapy, was in the large effect category, while the ES for the nonhumanistic group of interventions fell in the moderate category. This difference in effect may be attributed to a larger number of calculated humanistic studies (n = 73) compared to nonhumanistic studies (n = 12). Regardless, the findings for humanistic interventions is encouraging in light of the most recent survey of Association for Play Therapy members that indicated the majority of its members subscribed to the child-centered play therapy (CCPT) approach (Lambert et al., 2005).

The impact of treatment duration on outcomes was also of interest to us. Similar to LeBlanc and Ritchie's (2001) findings, optimal treatment effects were obtained in 35 to 40 sessions. It is important to note, however, that many studies with fewer than 14 sessions produced moderate to large treatment effects. Finally, age and gender were not found to be significant factors in predicting play therapy outcomes. Play therapy appeared to be equally effective across age and gender.

We were unable to compute an effect size for ethnicity because of the lack of specificity in the reporting of ethnicity in individual studies.

In summary, meta-analytic findings on play therapy (Bratton et al., 2005; LeBlanc & Ritchie, 2002) established play therapy's utility as a mental health intervention and further confirmed that its effect on children's outcomes was similar to other child interventions reported by contemporary meta-analytic researchers in the field of child psychotherapy (Casey & Berman, 1985; Kazdin, Bass, Ayers, & Rodgers, 1990; Weisz, Weiss, Han, Granger, & Morton, 1995). Showing that play therapy was comparable in treatment effect to other established and frequently used interventions was an important first step for the field in refuting critics that were skeptical of play therapy having any place within the broader field of child psychotherapy.

TWENTY-FIRST CENTURY OUTCOME RESEARCH

Over the last decade, play therapy research continues to thrive when measured by a number of studies (n = 25 so far, omitting filial therapy studies), experimental features applied to research, focused research questions on today's most pressing mental health issues, and rich description of methodology. Current publication of research has surpassed the record of play therapy studies published in the 1970s. This update is an attempt to review issues recently researched in the field of play therapy from 2000 to 2009. Criteria for inclusion included:

- *Play therapy* label is clearly used within the publication.
- Study was published in peer-review form in journal or book venue.
- Play therapy is a child-focused intervention and not parent or family intervention.
- Study utilized aspects of experimental design.

In contrast to the 2000 publication, we attempt to discern between rigorous and less rigorous research designs. Through the experience of meta-analysis, we discovered the need to differentiate levels of experimental research. Using Rubin's (2008) conceptual framework, we applied his evidentiary hierarchy for evidence-based practice to the identification of individual research studies and specifically categorized the studies into three labels, including experimental, quasi-experimental, and evidentiary. The *experimental* label describes studies meeting the most stringent criteria for research design, including random assignment of subjects, comparison to a control group or another treatment group, clear methodology and treatment descriptions, and attention to internal and external validity threats. The *quasi-experimental* label represents studies that use comparison or control groups with clear methodology and attention to internal and external validity threats but not random assignment. As evidenced by play therapy studies categorized as quasi-experimental, randomization is often difficult when designing an intervention-based research design for children. We used the *evidentiary* label as descriptive of studies that provide evidence of play therapy effectiveness through pre- and post-assessment and clear methodology but typically do not use a comparison or control group.

In summarizing the findings of the 25 studies reviewed for this chapter, we categorized 13 studies as experimental, 4 as quasi-experimental, and 8 as evidentiary. The most researched mental health issue related to recent literature is externalizing and disruptive behaviors, with 10 studies specifically demonstrating the positive effect of play therapy on children's disruptive behaviors. The second most researched dependent variable was parent-teacher relationship problems emphasizing the positive effect of play therapy in six studies. Evenly divided, internalizing problems, anxiety, and sexual abuse and trauma issues were explored in five studies. Other issues, such as multicultural populations, identified disability or medical condition, ADHD, language skills, moral reasoning, social behavior, homelessness, depression, and self-concept, were explored by one to three studies. Positive effect of play therapy can be seen in all research areas except sexual abuse, which provided mixed results in two studies.

The number of play therapy sessions ranged from 6 to 32 of those reported. The mean number of play therapy sessions was 13.57, and the median was 13, similar to our earlier report (Bratton & Ray, 2000). The mode was indeterminable because of equal representation of 10, 12, and 16 number of sessions reported among four studies each. Participants' ages ranged from 3 to 17 years old, with majority of studies starting at 4 years and capping the age below 12 years. Surprisingly, compared to earlier research, these studies reported participant number at a mean of $N = 45$ when two studies with more than 200 participants were eliminated as outliers. With a higher level of participants, results can be interpreted with more confidence in statistical analyses. As in our earlier report, we have organized studies by research topic in a chart format to allow play therapists to easily use information. Table 1.1 is presented to briefly describe research results

(continued on page 28)

Table 1-1

Play Therapy Research 2000–2009

Research Issue: Multiculturalism			
Authors	Research Classification	Participants	Findings
Garza & Bratton (2005)	Experimental	29 – Ages 5 to 11	Authors randomly assigned Hispanic children identified by teachers as demonstrating behavioral problems to an individual child-centered play therapy (CCPT) or guidance curriculum intervention. Each group received 30 minutes of the assigned intervention once per week for 15 weeks. Results demonstrated that children receiving play therapy showed statistically significant decreases in externalizing behavioral problems and moderate improvements in internalizing behavior problems as reported by parents.
Shen (2002)	Experimental	30 – Ages 8 to 12	Author randomly assigned child participants from a rural elementary school in Taiwan following an earthquake to a CCPT group or control group. All children were scored at high risk for maladjustment. The CCPT groups received ten 40-minute group play therapy sessions over four weeks. Results indicated the CCPT group demonstrated a significant decrease in anxiety, as well as a large treatment effect, and a significant decrease in suicide risk as compared to the control group.
Shen (2007)	Quasi-experimental	81 – 7th and 8th grades	Author assigned child participants from a public junior high school in Midwest Taiwan to one of three conditions: Gestalt-play group counseling, cognitive-verbal group counseling, or no intervention control group. The treatment groups received 10 sessions of 40-minute group counseling over five weeks. Both treatment groups demonstrated significant improvement in overall behavioral and

			emotional strengths, with the play therapy group demonstrating significant improvement on family involvement and cognitive verbal counseling significantly improving affective strength.
Research Issue: Externalizing Disruptive Behavior Problems			
Fall, Navelski, & Welch (2002)	Experimental	66 – Ages 6 to 10	Authors randomly assigned children identified with a special education label to six sessions of weekly 30-minute individual CCPT or a no-intervention control condition. Results demonstrated no difference between the groups in self-efficacy, but teacher ratings showed decreased problematic behavior and fewer social problems for the experimental group as compared to the control group.
Garza & Bratton (2005)	Experimental	29 – Ages 5 to 11	Authors randomly assigned Hispanic children identified by teachers as demonstrating behavioral problems to an individual CCPT or guidance curriculum intervention. Each group received 30 minutes of the assigned intervention once per week for 15 weeks. Results demonstrated that children receiving play therapy showed statistically significant decreases in externalizing behavior problems and moderate improvements in internalizing behavior problems as reported by parents.
Karcher & Lewis (2002)	Evidentiary	20 – Ages 8 to 17	Authors conducted a pre-test–post-test single group design for children in a residential psychiatric treatment facility. Participants were assigned according to primary diagnosis to the behavioral disorder or mood disorder group and received 15 to 18 biweekly sessions of pair counseling play therapy. Results indicated that reductions in problem behaviors were greatest for the behavioral disordered group. Results also demonstrated a decrease in externalizing behaviors, mediated by an increase in interpersonal understanding.

(continued)

Table 1-1
(continued)

Research Issue: Multiculturalism			
Authors	Research Classification	Participants	Findings
Muro, Ray, Schottelkorb, Smith, & Blanco (2006)	Evidentiary	23 – Ages 4 to 11	Authors conducted a repeated-measures single group design for children identified by teachers as exhibiting behavioral and emotional difficulties. Children participated in 32 sessions of individual CCPT across the duration of a school year. Ratings over three points of measure indicated statistically significant improvement on total behavioral problems, teacher-child relationship stress, and ADHD characteristics.
Packman & Bratton (2003)	Experimental	30 – Ages 10 to 12	Authors randomly assigned children who attended a school for learning differences and were identified as exhibiting behavioral difficulties to a group play therapy condition or a no-intervention control condition. The treatment group participated in a humanistically based play therapy intervention for one hour per week for 12 weeks. Results indicated treatment group demonstrated statistically significant improvement on internalizing and total problems with large effect sizes. Externalizing problems scores yielded a moderate effect, yet not statistically significant.
Ray (2008)	Evidentiary	202 – Ages 2 to 13	Author statistically analyzed archival data on children referred to a university counseling clinic and receiving weekly individual CCPT over a nine-year period. Children were assigned to data groups according to presenting problem and length of therapy as the independent variable and parent-child relationship stress as the dependent variable. CCPT

Study	Design	Sample	Results
			demonstrated statistically significant effects for externalizing problems, combined externalizing and internalizing problems, and nonclinical problems. Results also indicated that CCPT effects increased with the number of sessions, specifically reaching statistical significance at 11 to 18 sessions with large effect sizes.
Ray, Blanco, Sullivan, & Holliman (2009)	Quasi-experimental	41 – Ages 4 to 11	Authors assigned children identified by teachers as demonstrating aggressive behaviors to a CCPT condition or a wait-list control condition. Children in CCPT condition participated in 14 sessions of 30-minute individual play therapy conducted twice a week. Children in CCPT showed a moderate decrease in aggressive behaviors over children in the control group according to parent reports. Post hoc analysis revealed that children assigned to CCPT decreased aggressive behaviors statistically significantly and children assigned to control group demonstrated no statistically significant difference.
Schumann (2010)	Quasi-experimental	37 – Ages 5 to 12	Author assigned children identified by teachers as demonstrating aggressive behaviors to an individual CCPT condition or an evidence-based guidance curriculum condition. The CCPT condition received 12 to 15 weekly play therapy sessions, and the guidance condition received 8 to 15 group guidance sessions. Participation in either CCPT or evidence-based guidance curriculum resulted in significant decreases in aggressive behavior, internalizing problems, and externalizing problems.
Tyndall-Lind, Landreth, & Giordano (2001)	Quasi-experimental	32 – Ages 4 to 10	Authors compared a sibling group play therapy condition to an intensive individual play therapy condition and a control condition for children living in a domestic violence shelter. Sibling group CCPT consisted of 12 sessions of 45 minutes over 12 days. Results indicated

(continued)

Table 1-1
(continued)

Authors	Research Classification	Participants	Findings
Research Issue: Multiculturalism			
			that sibling group play therapy was equally effective to intensive individual play therapy. Children in sibling group play therapy demonstrated a significant reduction in total behavior, externalizing and internalizing behavior problems, aggression, anxiety, and depression and significant improvement in self-esteem.
Wang Flahive & Ray (2007)	Experimental	56 – Ages 9 to 12	Authors randomly assigned children identified with behavioral problems by teachers to a group sand tray therapy condition or a wait-list control condition. Children participating in sand tray received 10 weekly 45-minute sessions of group sand tray therapy. Results revealed statistically significant differences in total externalizing and internalizing problem behaviors according to teachers for children who participated in sand tray therapy. Parent reports also revealed statistically significant differences on externalizing behaviors.
Research Issue: Attention Deficit Hyperactivity Disorder			
Ray, Schottelkorb, & Tsai (2007)	Experimental	60 – Ages 5 to 11	Authors randomly assigned children meeting criteria for ADHD to a play therapy treatment condition or a reading mentoring active control condition. Children in both conditions participated in 16 individual

		30-minute sessions over eight weeks. The play therapy condition received individual CCPT. Results indicated that both conditions demonstrated statistically significant improvement on ADHD, student characteristics, anxiety, and learning disability. Children in CCPT demonstrated statistically significant improvement over reading mentoring children on student characteristics, emotional liability, and anxiety/withdrawal.
Research Issue: Internalizing Behavior Problems		
Baggerly & Jenkins (2009)	Evidentiary	36 – Ages 5 to 12	Authors conducted a pre-test–post-test single group design with children who were homeless. Children received 45-minute individual CCPT sessions once per week ranging from 11 to 25 sessions with an average of 14 sessions over the academic year. Results indicated that children demonstrated statistically significant improvements on the developmental strand of internalization of controls and diagnostic profile of self-limiting features.
Garza & Bratton (2005)	Experimental	29 – Ages 5 to 11	Authors randomly assigned Hispanic children identified by teachers as demonstrating behavioral problems to an individual CCPT or guidance curriculum intervention. Each group received 30 minutes of the assigned intervention once per week for 15 weeks. Results demonstrated that children receiving play therapy showed statistically significant decreases in externalizing behavior problems and moderate improvements in internalizing behavior problems as reported by parents.

(continued)

Table 1-1
(continued)

Research Issue: Internalizing Behavior Problems			
Authors	Research Classification	Participants	Findings
Packman & Bratton (2003)	Experimental	30 – Ages 10 to 12	Authors randomly assigned children who attended a school for learning differences and were identified as exhibiting behavioral difficulties to a group play therapy condition or a no-intervention control condition. The treatment group participated in a humanistically based play therapy intervention for one hour per week for 12 weeks. Results indicated treatment group demonstrated statistically significant improvement on internalizing and total problems with large effect sizes. Externalizing problems scores yielded a moderate effect, yet it was not statistically significant.
Tyndall-Lind, Landreth, & Giordano (2001)	Quasi-experimental	32 – Ages 4 to 10	Authors compared a sibling group play therapy condition to an intensive individual play therapy condition and a control condition for children living in a domestic violence shelter. Sibling group CCPT consisted of 12 sessions of 45 minutes over 12 days. Results indicated that sibling group play therapy was equally effective to intensive individual play therapy. Children in sibling group play therapy demonstrated a significant reduction in total behavior, externalizing and internalizing behavior problems, aggression, anxiety, and depression, and significant improvement in self-esteem.
Wang Flahive & Ray (2007)	Experimental	56 – Ages 9 to 12	Authors randomly assigned children identified with behavioral problems by teachers to a group sand tray therapy condition or a wait-list control condition. Children participating in sand tray received

			10 weekly 45-minute sessions of group sand tray therapy. Results revealed statistically significant differences in total externalizing and internalizing problem behaviors according to teachers for children who participated in sand tray therapy. Parent reports also revealed statistically significant differences on externalizing behaviors.
Research Issue: Anxiety			
Baggerly (2004)	Evidentiary	42 – Ages 5 to 11	Author conducted a pre-test–post-test single group design for children living in a homeless shelter. Children participated in 9 to 12 thirty-minute CCPT sessions once or twice a week. Results revealed significant improvement in self-concept, significance, competence, negative mood, and negative self-esteem related to depression and anxiety.
Ray, Schottelkorb, & Tsai (2007)	Experimental	60 – Ages 5 to 11	Authors randomly assigned children meeting criteria for ADHD to a play therapy treatment condition or a reading mentoring active control condition. Children in both conditions participated in 16 individual 30-minute sessions over eight weeks. The play therapy condition received individual CCPT. Results indicated that both conditions demonstrated statistically significant improvement on ADHD, student characteristics, anxiety, and learning disability. Children in CCPT demonstrated statistically significant improvement over reading mentoring children on student characteristics, emotional lability, and anxiety/withdrawal.
Reyes & Asbrand (2005)	Evidentiary	43 – Ages 7 to 16	Authors conducted a pre-test–post-test single group design with children who disclosed sexual abuse and were referred to a community-based agency. Children engaged in weekly 50-minute individual play therapy sessions over nine months and according to different theoretical orientations. Results indicated that trauma symptom severity, anxiety, depression, post-traumatic stress, and sexual distress in children decreased after six months of play therapy.

(*continued*)

Table 1-1
(*continued*)

Research Issue: Anxiety			
Authors	Research Classification	Participants	Findings
Shen (2002)	Experimental	30 – Ages 8 to 12	Author randomly assigned child participants from a rural elementary school in Taiwan following an earthquake to a CCPT group or control group. All children were scored at high risk for maladjustment. The CCPT groups received ten 40-minute group play therapy sessions over four weeks. Results indicated the CCPT group demonstrated a significant decrease in anxiety, as well as a large treatment effect, and significant decrease in suicide risk as compared to the control group.
Tyndall-Lind, Landreth, & Giordano (2001)	Quasi-experimental	32 – Ages 4 to 10	Authors compared a sibling group play therapy condition to an intensive individual play therapy condition and a control condition for children living in a domestic violence shelter. Sibling group CCPT consisted of 12 sessions of 45 minutes over 12 days. Results indicated that sibling group play therapy was equally effective to intensive individual play therapy. Children in sibling group play therapy demonstrated a significant reduction in total behavior externalizing and internalizing behavior problems, aggression, anxiety, and depression and significant improvement in self-esteem.
Research Issue: Depression			
Baggerly (2004)	Evidentiary	42 – Ages 5 to 11	Author conducted a pre-test–post-test single group design for children living in a homeless shelter. Children participated in 9 to 12 thirty-minute CCPT group play therapy sessions once or twice a week.

			Results revealed significant improvement in self-concept, significance, competence, negative mood, and negative self-esteem related to depression and anxiety.
Reyes & Asbrand (2005)	Evidentiary	43 – Ages 7 to 16	Authors conducted a pre-test–post-test single group design with children who disclosed sexual abuse and were referred to a community-based agency. Children engaged in weekly 50-minute individual play therapy sessions over nine months and according to different theoretical orientations. Results indicated that trauma symptom severity, anxiety, depression, post-traumatic stress, and sexual distress in children decreased after six months of play therapy.
Tyndall-Lind, Landreth, & Giordano (2001)	Quasi-experimental	32 – Ages 4 to 10	Authors compared a sibling group play therapy condition to an intensive individual play therapy condition and a control condition for children living in a domestic violence shelter. Sibling group CCPT consisted of 12 sessions of 45 minutes over 12 days. Results indicated that sibling group play therapy was equally effective to intensive individual play therapy. Children in sibling group play therapy demonstrated a significant reduction in total behavior, externalizing and internalizing behavior problems, aggression, anxiety, and depression and significant improvement in self-esteem.
Research Issues: Self-Concept and Self-Esteem			
Tyndall-Lind, Landreth, & Giordano (2001)	Quasi-experimental	32 – Ages 4 to 10	Authors compared a sibling group play therapy condition to an intensive individual play therapy condition and a control condition for children living in a domestic violence shelter. Sibling group CCPT consisted of 12 sessions of 45 minutes over 12 days. Results indicated that sibling group play therapy was equally effective to intensive

(continued)

Table 1-1
(continued)

	Research Classification	Participants	Findings
Research Issues: Self-Concept and Self-Esteem			
Authors			
			individual play therapy. Children in sibling group play therapy demonstrated a significant reduction in total behavior, externalizing and internalizing behavior problems, aggression, anxiety, and depression and significant improvement in self-esteem.
Baggerly (2004)	Evidentiary	42 – Ages 5 to 11	Author conducted a pre-test–post-test single group design for children living in a homeless shelter. Children participated in 9 to 12 thirty-minute CCPT group play therapy sessions once or twice a week. Results revealed significant improvement in self-concept, significance, competence, negative mood, and negative self-esteem related to depression and anxiety.
Research Issue: Social Behavior			
Fall, Navelski, & Welch (2002)	Experimental	66 – Ages 6 to 10	Authors randomly assigned children identified with a special education label to six sessions of weekly 30 minute individual CCPT or a no-intervention control condition. Results demonstrated no difference between the groups in self-efficacy, but teacher ratings showed decreased problematic behavior and fewer social problems for the experimental group as compared to the control group.

Research Issue: Moral Reasoning		
Paone, Packman, Maddux, & Rothman (2008)	Experimental	61 – Ages 13 to 16	Authors randomly assigned at-risk students to a talk therapy or activity therapy condition. Children in the talk therapy condition participated in 10 sessions of group talk therapy for 50 minutes per week. Children in the activity therapy condition participated in 10 sessions of developmentally appropriate group activity therapy for 50 minutes per week. Results indicated statistically significant development with a large effect size in moral reasoning for the activity therapy condition over the talk therapy condition.
Research Issue: Parent-Teacher Relationship		
Dougherty & Ray (2007)	Evidentiary	24 – Ages 3 to 8	Authors statistically analyzed archival data on children referred to a university counseling clinic and receiving weekly individual CCPT over a three-year period. Children were assigned to two data groups according to age (preoperational or operational) as the independent variable and parent-child relationship stress as the dependent variable. For both total stress and child domain scores, CCPT demonstrated statistically significant decreases in parent-child relationship stress with strong practical effects. Children in the concrete operations group experienced more change as a result of intervention than did children in the preoperational group.
Muro, Ray, Schottelkorb, Smith, & Blanco (2006)	Evidentiary	23 – Ages 4 to 11	Authors conducted a repeated-measures single group design for children identified by teachers as exhibiting behavioral and emotional difficulties. Children participated in 32 sessions of individual CCPT across the duration of a school year. Ratings over three points of measure indicated statistically significant improvement on total behavioral problems, teacher-child relationship stress, and ADHD characteristics.

(continued)

Table 1-1
(*continued*)

Research Issue: Parent-Teacher Relationship			
Authors	Research Classification	Participants	Findings
Ray (2007)	Experimental	93 – Ages 4 to 11	Author randomly assigned students who were identified as experiencing emotional and behavioral difficulties in the classroom into one of three treatment groups: play therapy only, play therapy and consultation, or consultation only. Children in the play therapy condition received 16 sessions of 30-minute individual CCPT over eight weeks. Teachers in consultation groups received one 10-minute person-centered consultation per week for eight weeks. Results demonstrated significant decreases in teacher-child relationship stress with large effects sizes in total stress for all three treatment groups.
Ray (2008)	Evidentiary	202 – Ages 2 to 13	Author statistically analyzed archival data on children referred to a university counseling clinic and receiving weekly individual CCPT over a nine-year period. Children were assigned to data groups according to presenting problem and length of therapy as the independent variable and parent-child relationship stress as the dependent variable. CCPT demonstrated statistically significant effects for externalizing problems, combined externalizing and internalizing problems, and nonclinical problems. Results also indicated that CCPT effects increased with the number of sessions, specifically reaching statistical significance at 11 to 18 sessions with large effect sizes.

Ray, Henson, Schottelkorb, Brown, & Muro (2008)	Experimental	58 – Ages Pre-K to 5th grade	Authors randomly assigned children identified by teachers as exhibiting emotional and behavioral difficulties into one of two treatment groups (short-term and long-term). Children in the short-term condition participated in 16 sessions of 30-minute individual CCPT over eight weeks. Children in the long-term condition participated in 16 sessions of 30-minute individual CCPT over 16 weeks. Results indicated that both intervention groups demonstrated significant improvement in teacher-student relationship stress. Post hoc analyses indicated that the short-term intensive intervention demonstrated statistical significance and larger effect sizes in overall total stress, teacher, and student characteristics.
Shen (2007)	Quasi-experimental	81 – 7th and 8th grades	Author assigned child participants from a public junior high school in midwest Taiwan to one of three conditions: Gestalt-play group counseling, cognitive-verbal group counseling, or no intervention control group. The treatment groups received 10 sessions of 40-minute group counseling over five weeks. Both treatment groups demonstrated significant improvement in overall behavioral and emotional strengths with the play therapy group demonstrating significant improvement on family involvement and cognitive verbal counseling significantly improving affective strength.
Research Issue: Sexual Abuse and Trauma			
Carpentier, Silovsky, & Chaffin (2006)	Experimental	291 – Ages 5 to 12	Authors randomly assigned children identified with sexual behavior problems into two treatment groups, including a cognitive behavioral condition (CBT) and a play therapy condition (PT). Both groups were compared to an archival data sample of children with disruptive behaviors but not sexual behavior problems. The CBT group

(continued)

Table 1-1
(continued)

Research Issue: Sexual Abuse and Trauma			
Authors	Research Classification	Participants	Findings
			was structured using behavior modification and psychoeducational principles. The PT group was less structured, using a combination of client-centered, psychodynamic, and directive methods. Ten-year follow-up data reported significantly fewer future sex offenses for the CBT group than for the play therapy group.
Reyes & Asbrand (2005)	Evidentiary	43 – Ages 7 to 16	Authors conducted a pre-test–post-test single group design with children who disclosed sexual abuse and were referred to a community-based agency. Children engaged in weekly 50-minute individual play therapy sessions over nine months and according to different theoretical orientations. Results indicated that trauma symptom severity, anxiety, depression, post-traumatic stress, and sexual distress in children decreased after six months of play therapy.
Scott, Burlingame, Starling, Porter, & Lilly (2003)	Evidentiary	26 – Ages 3 to 9	Authors conducted a pre-test–post-test single group design with children referred for possible sexual abuse. Children completed between 7 and 13 sessions of CCPT. Results indicated an increased sense of competency over the course of therapy. No improvement was reported in other group comparisons.
Shen (2002)	Experimental	30 – Ages 8 to 12	Author randomly assigned child participants from a rural elementary school in Taiwan following an earthquake to a CCPT group or control group. All children were scored at high risk for maladjustment.

			The CCPT groups received ten 40-minute group play therapy sessions over four weeks. Results indicated the CCPT group demonstrated a significant decrease in anxiety, as well as a large treatment effect, and a significant decrease in suicide risk as compared to the control group.
Tyndall-Lind, Landreth, & Giordano (2001)	Quasi-experimental	32 – Ages 4 to 10	Authors compared a sibling group play therapy condition to an intensive individual play therapy condition and a control condition for children living in a domestic violence shelter. Sibling group CCPT consisted of 12 sessions of 45 minutes over 12 days. Results indicated that sibling group play therapy was equally effective to intensive individual play therapy. Children in sibling group play therapy demonstrated a significant reduction in total behavior, externalizing and internalizing behavior problems, aggression, anxiety, and depression, and significant improvement in self-esteem.
Research Issue: Homeless			
Baggerly (2004)	Evidentiary	42 – Ages 5 to 11	Author conducted a pre-test–post-test single group design for children living in a homeless shelter. Children participated in 9 to 12 thirty-minute CCPT group play therapy sessions once or twice a week. Results revealed significant improvement in self-concept, significance, competence, negative mood, and negative self-esteem related to depression and anxiety.
Baggerly & Jenkins (2009)	Evidentiary	36 – Ages 5 to 12	Authors conducted a pre-test–post-test single group design with children who were homeless. Children received 45-minute individual CCPT sessions once per week ranging from 11 to 25 sessions with an average of 14 sessions over the academic year. Results indicated that children demonstrated statistically significant improvement on the developmental strand of internalization of controls and diagnostic profile of self-limiting features.

(continued)

Table 1-1
(*continued*)

Research Issues: Identified Disability and Medical Condition			
Authors	Research Classification	Participants	Findings
Danger & Landreth (2005)	Experimental	21 – Ages 4 to 6	Authors randomly assigned children qualified for speech therapy to one of two conditions, including group play therapy condition and regularly scheduled speech therapy session condition. Children assigned to the play therapy condition received 25 sessions of group CCPT concurrently with speech therapy over seven months. Results revealed that children in play therapy demonstrated increased receptive language skills and expressive language skills with large practical significance.
Fall, Navelski, & Welch (2002)	Experimental	66 – Ages 6 to 10	Authors randomly assigned children identified with a special education label to six sessions of weekly 30-minute individual CCPT or a no-intervention control condition. Results demonstrated no difference between the groups in self-efficacy but teacher ratings showed decreased problematic behavior and fewer social problems for the experimental groups as compared to the control group.
Jones & Landreth (2002)	Experimental	30 – Ages 7 to 11	Authors randomly assigned children diagnosed with insulin-dependent diabetes mellitus to an experimental or no-intervention control group. The experimental group participated in 12 sessions of CCPT over a 3-week camp. Both groups improved anxiety scores; the experimental group showed a statistically significant increase in diabetes adaptation over the control group.

Study	Design	Sample	Findings
Packman & Bratton (2003)	Experimental	30 – Ages 10 to 12	Authors randomly assigned children who attended a school for learning differences and were identified as exhibiting behavioral difficulties to a group play therapy condition or a no-intervention control condition. The treatment group participated in a humanistically based play therapy intervention for one hour per week for 12 weeks. Results indicated treatment group demonstrated statistically significant improvement on internalizing and total problems with large effect sizes. Externalizing problems scores yielded a moderate effect, yet not statistically significant.
Research Issue: Academic Achievement			
Blanco (2010)	Experimental	43 – 1st grade	Author randomly assigned first-graders labeled at risk by state academic standards to an experimental treatment group or wait-list control group. Children in experimental group participated in 16 sessions of 30-minute individual CCPT sessions over 8 weeks. Children in the CCPT treatment group demonstrated significant improvement on academic achievement composite score over children in the control group.
Research Issue: Language Skills			
Danger & Landreth (2005)	Experimental	21 – Ages 4 to 6	Authors randomly assigned children qualified for speech therapy to one of two conditions, including group play therapy condition and regularly scheduled speech therapy session condition. Children assigned to the play therapy condition received 25 sessions of group CCPT concurrently with speech therapy over 7 months. Results revealed that children in play therapy demonstrated increased receptive language skills and expressive language skills with large practical significance.

related to play therapy categorized by research issue. Hence, some studies are listed in multiple categories because of outcomes related to more than one area.

DISCUSSION

As can be seen in Table 1.1, the play therapy field is providing recent and relevant research to support its use with children. Among 13 experimental studies, typically regarded as the gold standard of research, 12 studies resulted in the positive effects of play therapy. Among the overall 25 studies, all but one resulted in positive effects, although some results were stronger than others. Unlike the earlier 2000 report, almost all studies (N = 23) provided a clear definition of play therapy treatment and the training of play therapists. Of the 25 studies, 18 used a child-centered play therapy treatment, 3 were identified as activity or sand tray with a humanistic or person-centered philosophy, 1 Gestalt, 1 Pair Counseling, and 2 were mixed and unclear. Consistent with the 2000 report, most research is being conducted using a child-centered play therapy approach typically aligned with the philosophies of Axline (1969) and Landreth (2002).

The identification and description of treatment protocol represents progress in conducting research in play therapy. Research conducted under the play therapy label but with a lack of clear structure related to theoretical conceptualization, however, is still a possible barrier to outcome. One example of this challenge emerged in review of this decade's research evidenced by Carpentier, Silovsky, and Chaffin (2006). In their study of children exhibiting sexual behavior problems, they compared a cognitive behavioral intervention with a play therapy intervention. The play therapy intervention was described as client-centered and psychodynamic principled with different materials and activities and topics introduced each week to the child. For play therapists who are trained in psychodynamic or child-centered principles, there is recognition that these two approaches are vastly different. The label of *play therapy* following psychodynamic principles is vague and open to interpretation by the reader or researcher. Child-centered play therapy, a well-defined approach to play therapy (Landreth, 2002), would not typically introduce any topic or activity in play therapy, nor would it advocate the use of different materials for each session. The failure to clearly define procedures or mention the use of a treatment protocol were important limitations to consider in drawing the conclusion that findings were due to the superiority of one treatment over the other. The use of a manualized protocol that showed how these distinct approaches were integrated would provide clarity. From a research perspective, the description of play therapy provided by Carpentier et al. is broad and ill-defined and could possibly mislead the reader into concluding that play therapy was ineffective, when in fact it may have been the lack of a well-defined treatment and omission of treatment integrity measures that produced the results. Such an example reminds researchers that adhering to stringent research methods, including manualization of valid play therapy approaches and the assurance of treatment integrity, is critical in conducting research of sufficient rigor to advance the field of play therapy.

Another observation of current and historical play therapy research is related to the choices of dependent variables by researchers and how those might be affected by cultural pressures. In the last decade, there has been a rise in research related to disruptive and externalizing behaviors. This trend coincides with the rise of behaviorism in the schools and the focus on external achievement-related status in American culture. Play therapy researchers have responded to this cultural phenomenon in an effort to stay relevant in the minds of parents and other authorities. Fortunately, outcomes related to externalized behavior are positive. However, considering that most play therapy research is conducted according to child-centered philosophy, which directly emphasizes the inner world of the child, one might question this focus on behavior. Also, it can be observed that research related to self-concept is in decline, so much so that only two studies reported positive effects. Surprisingly, only one study focused on social behavior as an individual dependent variable compared to its rank as the most studied variable in the 2000 report. And finally, research related to multicultural populations continues to be sparse, with only one study on Hispanic children in the United States and two on children in Taiwan. Most studies, however, reported on ethnicity (unlike the 2000 report) and revealed a diversity of ethnic identification among participants. Considering the diversity of urban settings, play therapy research would benefit from the exploration of specific populations.

Overall, play therapy research continues to show strong evidence to support its use among a variation of populations and presenting problems. The last decade revealed changes in research methodology that allow play therapy to compete among other child interventions as a viable treatment. Strikingly, current play therapy research appears to be conducted by play therapists who are well-trained in both methodology and play therapy, leading to designs that accurately explore effectiveness variables related to play therapy. Play therapy research will continue to be strengthened through the progress of treatment manualization and description, delivery by trained professionals, and focus on specific dependent variables relevant to mental health issues among child populations.

REFERENCES

Allin, H., Walthen, C., & MacMillan, H. (2005). Treatment of child neglect: A systematic review. *The Canadian Psychiatric Journal of Psychiatry, 50*(8), 497–504.

American Counseling Association. (2005). *ACA code of ethics.* Alexandria, VA: Author.

American Psychological Association. (2002). *Ethical principles of psychologists and code of conduct.* Washington, DC: Author.

Axline, V. M. (1969). *Play therapy.* New York: Ballantine Books.

Baggerly, J. (2004). The effects of child-centered group play therapy on self-concept, depression, and anxiety of children who are homeless. *International Journal of Play Therapy, 13,* 31–51.

Baggerly, J., & Jenkins, W. (2009). The effectiveness of child-centered play therapy on developmental and diagnostic factors in children who are homeless. *International Journal of Play Therapy, 18,* 45–55.

Beelmann, A., & Schneider, N. (2003). The effects of psychotherapy with children and adolescents: A review and meta-analysis of German-language research. *Zeitschrift für klinische Psychologie und Psychotherapie, 32*(2), 129–143.

Blanco, P. J. (2010). The impact of school-based child centered play therapy on academic achievement, self-concept, and teacher-child relationship stress. In J. Baggerly, D. Ray, & S. Bratton (Eds.), *Effective play therapy: Evidence-based filial and child-centered research studies* (pp. 125–144). Hoboken, NJ: John Wiley & Sons.

Bratton, S. C. (2010). Meeting the early mental health needs of children through school-based play therapy: A review of outcome research. In A. Drewes & C. Schaefer (Eds.), *School-based play therapy, Vol. 2.* Hoboken, NJ: John Wiley & Sons.

Bratton, S. C., & Ray, D. C. (2000). What the research shows about play therapy. *International Journal of Play Therapy, 9,* 47–88.

Bratton, S. C., Ray, D. C., Rhine, T., & Jones, L. (2005). The efficacy of play therapy with children: A meta-analytic review of treatment outcomes. *Professional Psychology: Research and Practice, 36,* 376–390.

Brestan, E., & Eyeberg, S. (1998). Effective psychosocial treatments of conduct-disordered children and adolescents: 29 years, 82 studies, and 5,272 kids. *Journal of Clinical Child Psychology, 27,* 180–189.

Carpentier, M., Silovsky, J., & Chaffin, M. (2006). Randomized trial of treatment for children with sexual behavior problems: Ten-year follow-up. *Journal of Consulting and Clinical Psychology, 74,* 482–488.

Casey, R., & Berman, J. (1985). The outcome of psychotherapy with children. *Psychological Bulletin, 98,* 388–400.

Cohen, J. (1988). *Statistical power analysis for the behavioral sciences* (2nd ed.). Hillside, NJ: Erlbaum.

Danger, S., & Landreth, G. L. (2005). Child-centered group play therapy with children with speech difficulties. *International Journal of Play Therapy, 14,* 81–102.

Dougherty, J., & Ray, D. C. (2007). Differential impact of play therapy on developmental levels of children. *International Journal of Play Therapy, 16,* 2–19.

Eyeberg, S., Nelson, M., & Boggs, S. (2008). Evidence-based psychosocial treatments for children and adolescents with disruptive behavior. *Journal of Child and Adolescent Psychology, 37*(1), 215–237.

Fall, M., Navelski, L., & Welch, K. (2002). Outcomes of a play intervention for children identified for special education services. *International Journal of Play Therapy, 11,* 91–106.

Garza, Y., & Bratton, S. C. (2005). School-based child centered play therapy with Hispanic children: Outcomes and cultural considerations. *International Journal of Play Therapy, 14,* 51–80.

Hetzel-Riggin, M., Brausch, A., & Montgomery, B. (2007). A meta-analytic investigation of therapy modality outcomes for sexually abused children and adolescents: An exploratory study. *Child Abuse and Neglect, 31*(2), 125–141.

Jones, E., & Landreth, G. L. (2002). The efficacy of intensive individual play therapy for chronically ill children. *International Journal of Play Therapy, 11,* 117–140.

Karcher, M., & Lewis, S. (2002). Pair counseling: The effects of dyadic developmental play therapy on interpersonal understanding and externalizing behavioral. *International Journal of Play Therapy, 11,* 19–41.

Kazdin, A., Bass, D., Ayers, W., & Rodgers, A. (1990). Empirical and clinical focus of child and adolescent psychotherapy research. *Journal of Consulting and Clinical Psychology, 58,* 729–740.

Lambert, S., LeBlanc, M., Mullen, J., Ray, D. C., Baggerly, J., White, J., et al. (2005). Learning more about those who play in session: The national play therapy in counseling practice project (Phase I). *International Journal of Play Therapy, 14*(2), 7–23.

Landreth, G. L. (2002). *Play therapy: The art of the relationship* (2nd ed.). New York: Brunner-Routledge.

LeBlanc, M., & Ritchie, M. (2001). A meta-analysis of play therapy outcomes. *Counseling Psychology Quarterly, 14*(2), 149–163.

Muro, J., Ray, D. C., Schottelkorb, A., Smith, M., & Blanco, P. (2006). Quantitative analysis of long-term child-centered play therapy. *International Journal of Play Therapy, 15,* 35–58.

National Association for Social Workers. (2008). *NASW code of ethics.* Washington, DC: Author.

New Freedom Commission on Mental Health. (2003). *Achieving the promise: Transforming mental health care in America. Final Report* (DHHS Publication No. SMA-03-3832). Rockville, MD: Department of Health and Human Services.

Packman, J., & Bratton, S. C. (2003). A school-based group play/activity therapy intervention with learning disabled preadolescents exhibiting behavior problems. *International Journal of Play Therapy, 12,* 7–29.

Paone, T., Packman, J., Maddux, C., & Rothman, T. (2008). A school-based group activity therapy intervention with at-risk high school students as it relates to their moral reasoning. *International Journal of Play Therapy, 17,* 122–137.

Ray, D. C. (2007). Two counseling interventions to reduce teacher-child relationship stress. *Professional School Counseling, 10,* 428–440.

Ray, D. C. (2008). Impact of play therapy on parent-child relationship stress at a mental health training setting. *British Journal of Guidance & Counselling, 36,* 165–187.

Ray, D. C., Blanco, P., Sullivan, J., & Holliman, R. (2009). An exploratory study of child-centered play therapy with aggressive children. *International Journal of Play Therapy, 18,* 162–175.

Ray, D. C., Henson, R., Schottelkorb, A., Brown, A., & Muro, J. (2008). Impact of short-term and long-term play therapy services on teacher-child relationship stress. *Psychology in the Schools, 45,* 994–1009.

Ray, D. C., Schottelkorb, A., & Tsai, M. (2007). Play therapy with children exhibiting symptoms of attention deficit hyperactivity disorder. *International Journal of Play Therapy, 16,* 95–111.

Reyes, C., & Asbrand, J. (2005). A longitudinal study assessing trauma symptoms in sexually abused children engaged in play therapy. *International Journal of Play Therapy, 14,* 25–47.

Rubin, A. (2008). *Practitioner's guide to using research for evidence-based practice.* Hoboken, NJ: John Wiley & Sons.

Schumann, B. (2010). Effectiveness of child-centered play therapy for children referred for aggression in elementary school. In J. Baggerly, D. Ray, & S. Bratton (Eds.), *Effective play therapy: Evidence-based filial and child-centered research studies* (pp. 193–208). Hoboken, NJ: John Wiley & Sons.

Scott, T., Burlingame, G., Starling, M., Porter, C., & Lilly, J. (2003). Effects of individual client-centered play therapy on sexually abused children's mood, self-concept, and social competence. *International Journal of Play Therapy, 12,* 7–30.

Shen, Y. (2002). Short-term group play therapy with Chinese earthquake victims: Effects on anxiety, depression, and adjustment. *International Journal of Play Therapy, 11,* 43–63.

Shen, Y. (2007). Developmental model using Gestalt-play versus cognitive-behavioral group with Chinese adolescents: Effects on strengths and adjustment enhancement. *Journal for Specialist in Group Work, 32,* 285–305.

Subcommittee on Children and Family (2003). *Promoting, preserving and restoring children's mental health.* Retrieved January 5, 2009, from http://www.mentalhealthcommission.gov/subcommittee/Sub_Chairs.html.

Tyndall-Lind, A., Landreth, G. L., & Giordano, M. (2001). Intensive group play therapy with child witnesses of domestic violence. *International Journal of Play Therapy, 10,* 53–83.

U.S. Public Health Service (2000). *Report of the Surgeon General's conference on children's mental health: A national action agenda.* Washington, DC: U.S. Public Health Service.

Wang Flahive, M., & Ray, D. C. (2007). Effect of group sand tray therapy with preadolescents. *Journal for Specialists in Group Work, 32,* 362–382.

Weisz, J., Weiss, B., Han, S., Granger, D., & Morton, T. (1995). Effects of psychotherapy with children and adolescents revisited: A meta-analysis of treatment outcomes studies. *Psychological Bulletin, 117,* 450–468.

Wethington, H., Hahn, R., Fuqua-Whitley, D., Sipe, T., Crosby, A., Johnson, R., et al. (2008). The effectiveness of interventions to reduce psychological harm from traumatic events among children and adolescents: A systematic review. *American Journal of Preventive Medicine, 35*(3), 287–313.

SECTION II

RESEARCH IN PLAY THERAPY

CHAPTER 2

Increased Self-Efficacy: One Reason for Play Therapy Success

MARIJANE FALL*

QUESTIONS AND IDEAS COME FROM PRACTICE

Melissa had not been to school for the last four months of the previous school year. Now she had already missed the first three weeks of her eighth-grade year. The principal asked me, the new school counselor, to call her home and see what could be done. Her mom answered the phone and said that she was glad I had called. Despite visits to several doctors, it was not clear what was wrong with Melissa. She had lost 30 pounds, was highly anxious, spent much time on the couch, and had visited a psychiatrist at the urging of her physician. No one had been able to help. When I asked her to bring Melissa to school to see me, she said Melissa did not want to come to school for fear she would get too anxious and be sick. After talking with Melissa, I arranged to see her at the school after school had closed for the day and the buses had left. My only surprise was that she came.

Melissa was sweet, a bright student, highly motivated, a cheerleader the previous year, very pretty, and a bit thin. She said she had always loved school before but she got stomach aches that were bad and she didn't want to have to stay in class and be sick. She worried that the students would make fun of her as they had done in the past. While she talked, we played with clay, pinching and poking, rolling, and dialoguing about figures depicting her and her classmates. I reflected her words, thoughts, feelings, and clay movements and tried to stay in

---

*Sadly, Marijane Fall died before this book was published. We honor her as a gracious and inspiring play therapist, researcher, and supervisor.

the present moment with her. Toward the end of our time, I said I wanted to see her again the next day at 9 A.M., a time when school was in session. She immediately said she just couldn't. I said I'd arrange for her mother to be available to take her home the minute she needed to go. My second surprise was when she arrived the next day at 9:00. Once again we chatted, and I noted her strengths whenever they were evident. For example, I said, "So, you just keep on trying even if your stomach hurts bad," "You were scared to come today but you did it," and "You wish you could stay in school because it would make your mom so happy." At the end of an hour, I asked her to stay for one period with a guarantee that she could leave at any time and go to the nurse's office where mom would meet her. She did it. Our relationship was off and running, and she began the journey back into her classes at school. Within a week, she was going to school for full days every day and continued in that pattern for the rest of the school year. Stories of severe bullying the previous year emerged. Three months later, she came to see me with a special card she had made. She said, "I never thought I could face school ever again. But you did. You didn't judge me, and I'm not sure what you did do. We just kinda played with clay, but I started to believe that I could really do it. And I did. I am so much stronger now, all because of that." My heart smiled.

The preceding example is one of the success of a student and the success of a process called child-centered play therapy. I was trained in this theoretical process and used it in schools and private practice. I knew the theory. I knew it worked. I knew what to do to make it work. Yet a part of me still wondered why it was so magical. Why did I feel so absolutely sure it would work? The question lingered for years.

Fast forward a few years. I was sitting at my computer working on a manuscript compiling data concerning the self-efficacy of school counselors (Sutton & Fall, 1995). As I wrote of the effects of self-efficacy and the components of a self-efficacy judgment, I had an "Aha" moment with more intensity than at any other time in my career. It appeared that all the components of a self-efficacy judgment that an individual makes about himself occurred when evidence was provided and would increase in a child-centered play therapy session! Furthermore, the effects of a higher level of self-efficacy were what I had seen demonstrated when children no longer needed to come to therapy. This was an answer to the question I had pondered. My belief in that moment was that one of the principal reasons children changed throughout child-centered play therapy sessions was that their self-efficacy increased significantly. (I still have that belief!) As soon as I finished the manuscript I had been working on, I wrote of the theoretical blending of child-centered play therapy and self-efficacy theory (Fall, 1994); and while there was not a groundswell of excitement over that publication, I remained excited. Authors are like that. My teaching in play therapy courses and presentations at national workshops reflected my excitement, and others soon joined in, wanting to prove it. Was it really true?

A good theory is just one person's musings, hopefully based to an extent in existing facts. The next step is to prove it. Submit it to a rigorous test and see what is true for that study and what needs to be revised. The next few pages tell of my efforts to examine child-centered play therapy, self-efficacy theory, and the success of children in play therapy. The most pivotal study examined the basic theoretical premise with a quantitative design (Fall, Balvanz, Johnson, & Nelson, 1999) and analyzed the recorded tapes in a qualitative design (Fall, 1997). A subsequent study used the same research design with a group of children labeled by the special education system (Fall, Nalvelski, & Welch, 2002) to see whether the results changed with this population. They did, but for a different reason from the one we expected. Validity and reliability of the self-efficacy scale used in all the studies was a follow-up to these three (Fall & McLeod, 2001) and includes a scale that is being used in many schools. As you read the summaries of these studies, remember the children you have worked with and remember Melissa. Does the theory pass the face-validity test of making sense? This examination begins with a brief background on self-efficacy and child-centered play therapy.

SELF-EFFICACY AND CHILD-CENTERED PLAY THERAPY THEORY

Self-efficacy is an individual's belief in personal ability to perform in ways that meet one's needs and serves as a mediator between past knowledge and skills and present behaviors (Bandura, 1997). Bandura first wrote of self-efficacy theory in 1977, and hundreds of studies have followed, especially concerning learning and career choice. He said these self-beliefs may enhance or impair both motivation and problem-solving efforts through affecting choices, motivation, and attribution of success. For example, children with a high self-efficacy level to learn new math believe they have many ways to help themselves learn if they run into a snag. They are motivated to persist at learning this information and attribute success or failure to their own efforts. Children with low self-efficacy to learn new math will sit back when they don't understand, will stop trying because they "know they can't learn," and will attribute this failure to everything else but self ("I'm not smart," "The teacher didn't explain," "It's stupid"). Bandura also postulated that self-efficacy judgments are formed by a synthesis of four main sources of information: mastery experiences of performance, vicarious experiences that provide for social comparison, verbal persuasion and social influences, and physiological responses (Bandura, 1997). This means that successful performance, seeing another person be successful, someone telling you can do it, and your autonomic nervous system saying you are okay are all contributors to higher self-efficacy.

Child-centered play therapy increases opportunities for all four sources of information that contribute to self-efficacy judgment (Fall, 1994). The idea that everything a child does in the play therapy session is successful is perhaps the most important source of the child's increased judgment of self-efficacy level. There is no judgment from another person, just the present moment following of the child's feelings, behaviors, and thinking. The second source of efficacy information, vicarious experiences that provide for social comparison, is present when the counselor models acceptance of the child's efficacy and the effective coping strategies. A therapist might say, "You did it. You made it go just where you wanted it." The child notes that the therapist accepts her as she is right now and passes no judgment, and she hears the verbal reinforcement for this behavior. We can imagine that the lack of judgment, the acknowledgment of who the child really is without judgment leads to self-acceptance ("If the therapist accepts me, perhaps I can accept myself") and management of anxiety or other conditions that would increase a physiological response in the body. In our example of Melissa, the therapist reflected her feelings, actions, and thoughts without judgment. She was okay exactly as she was. The counselor reinforced her strengths when they were in her present moment of thinking. For example, when she spoke of feelings of alienation and being bullied in school, the counselor reflected, "You kept trying and trying to be a good friend, even when they made fun of you. That was tough to do. You felt hurt and mad." This validation of her thoughts and feelings without redirection or admonishment to "get over it" left her free to be herself. The counselor gave verbal acknowledgment and therefore reinforcement of her thoughts, feelings, and actions through reflection. The anxiety became manageable. Her beliefs in her ability to be in school with people who made fun of her increased in strength and she was able to take some small, and then huge, steps of successful performance. I hope I've convinced you that this is worth investigating further. The next sections briefly tell of the first major study that researched the theoretical blending of self-efficacy and child-centered play therapy. The question asked by the study was, "Is there a difference between two groups of children—one group receiving six thirty-minute sessions of child-centered play therapy and one group receiving no treatment—as far as classroom learning behaviors and beliefs of self-efficacy?"

SELF-EFFICACY, CHILD-CENTERED PLAY THERAPY, AND CLASSROOM LEARNING BEHAVIORS

STUDY ONE

This empirical research study was a pre-test–post-test control group design so it could search for similarities between two groups of children. The experimental group received six weekly play therapy sessions of 30 minutes length each. The control group received no sessions. Full text of the study appears in the *Professional School Counseling* journal (Fall, Balvanz, Johnson, & Nelson, 1999).

Participants Sixty-two children ages five to nine in three school districts were randomly selected from a teacher-generated list of children whose coping behaviors in the classroom interfered with their learning. The students were stratified by teacher and grade level and randomly placed in either the control group that received no treatment or the experimental group that received the treatment of six sessions of 30 minutes duration of child-centered play therapy. The experimental group consisted of 15 boys and 16 girls, with 7 being in kindergarten, 5 in first grade, 10 in second grade, and 9 third-graders. The control group of 31 students was matched by grade level. Parents received information about the purpose and nature of the proposed six sessions and signed consent forms. All children were assigned a code reflecting the therapist name, the child's name, and the session number.

Instruments A demographic data form was filled out for all children. It consisted of the child's grade, age, gender, ethnicity, code name, and school. A classroom observation and two teacher rating instruments were also a part of the data collected for the study. The Self-Efficacy Scale for Children (S-ES) measures self-efficacy levels for children's beliefs in personal ability to perform in ways that meet their needs. Teachers rate children on nine items that reflect the child's self-efficacy for learning. Research shows that the scale is moderately reliable and valid and is useful for research purposes (Fall & McLeod, 2001). The Conners Teacher Rating Scale (CTRS), (Conners, 1986) was developed to measure children's classroom behaviors and has a test-retest reliability of .88 to .96 (Kramer & Conoley, 1992).

Observational data were collected one week before the start of counseling sessions and the week after the termination. Off-task behaviors in the classroom were recorded using momentary time sampling for a 20-minute period. Researchers were trained with videotapes of children and gained inter-rater reliability greater than 95 percent.

Procedures   All 62 children were pre- and post-tested on the Conners Teacher Rating Scale (Conners, 1986) for classroom behaviors, the Self-Efficacy Teacher Rating Scale (Fall & McLeod, 2001), and a 20-minute classroom observation by trained observers. Trained judges scored the three measures. The actual events of the study were in the following sequence: Weeks 1 and 8, teachers filled out the pre-tests for all students, and trained observers carried out the classroom observations.

During Weeks 2 through 7, the experimental group received a 30-minute session of child-centered play therapy each week. Three Caucasian female elementary school counselors with master's degrees in counseling, advanced training in child-centered play therapy, and clinical supervision for their work were the counselors for the play therapy sessions. The counselors followed standard child-centered play therapy procedures recommended by Landreth (2002) and described in Chapter 4 of this book. For example, the counselor informed the child, "You may use the toys in most any way you choose," and then responded to the child by reflecting feelings, meaning, and actions. Short responses that were developmentally appropriate were the goal. Sessions were recorded and transcribed by trained research assistants. All counselors met with the principal researcher before the study and received a list of sequential steps for gathering and recording data for the study. The control group received no treatment.

At the conclusion of Week 8, teachers responded to the question, "Have you seen any changes in this child's learning from six weeks ago?" The reader is referred to two journal articles for more focused detail on this procedure, participants, and results (Fall, Balvanz, Johnson, & Nelson, 1999; Fall, 1997).

Results and Discussion   There were several important results of this study. Statistical analyses with the three dependent variables—S-ES, CTRS, and classroom observation—included descriptive statistics, mixed ANOVA (analysis of variance) analysis, and follow up *t*-tests. The ANOVA analysis with one within-subjects variable, time (pre, post), and two between-subjects variables, group (control, experimental) and counselor (1, 2, 3) assisted in the interpretation. The major results are listed here.

- Teachers reported increased learning results for 67 percent of the children receiving the counseling intervention.
- There was a significant increase in self-efficacy as measured by the Self-Efficacy Teacher Rating Scale for the children receiving the counseling intervention. ANOVA of group by time resulted in $F(1, 56) = 11.34$, $p = .001$, and Partial $\eta^2 = .13$, indicating a medium effect size. There was a slight decrease in scores on the self-efficacy measure for children who did not receive the counseling intervention.
- The classroom behaviors as measured by the Conners Teacher Rating Scale improved for both groups of children, more so for the children who received the play therapy intervention. The improvement was not significant, however, at the $p < .05$ level as $F(1, 56) = 2.46$ and $p = .12$.
- The classroom observations of both groups of children were not significant, $F(1, m56) = 1.42$ and $p = .24$.

These results indicate that children in this study whose coping skills hindered personal learning were assisted with six sessions of child-centered play therapy of 30 minutes duration each. There are limitations that affect generalizability. Perhaps most important is the small number of subjects from each of three school districts and the variation in the districts themselves. The counselor from School District 2 was responsible for four schools and approximately 700 students. Counselors from Districts 1 and 3 were responsible for single schools of 350 and 240 students, respectively. Since this study started in February, many students whose classroom behaviors were not facilitative to learning had already been assisted in those two schools. Counselor 2 had responsibility for so many students that she did far more crisis work and less proactive work than the other two counselors. This counselor also had no office space, which would not allow a child to have the safety and consistency of a constant room.

A further limitation consisted of parents and teachers having some knowledge of the research study. This was a result of parents having to give permission for the testing and recording that was done and teachers referring students originally for the study and then seeing some students leave the classroom to see the counselor. Furthermore, teacher rating scales were used for two of the measures and could be influenced by teacher bias. A further uncontrolled factor relates to children's homes. Parents had seen a description of the study. This could have led to changes in the home and further changes in a child's behavior at school.

This examination of the theory of a relationship between self-efficacy and therapeutic sessions of child-centered play therapy continued my excitement that began with this experimental exploration. Yet the limitations always suggest more trails. Would the results change with a different population of children? Empirical research is strongest when studies increase in number. A qualitative study reported in the journals concluded that the very presence of a label, and the remedial actions attached to it in a school, can lead to secondary characteristics that adversely affect a child in a social situation (Johnson, McLeod, & Fall, 1997). We wondered if exploration of the original research question with the special education population would be helpful. We also speculated that a child-centered play therapy intervention could make a difference. The second study reported here, "Outcomes of a play counseling intervention for children identified for special education" (Fall, Navelski, & Welch, 2002), was an attempt to study self-efficacy and child-centered play therapy with children identified for special education services in a school.

STUDY TWO

This research consisted of repeating the procedure of the first study as closely as possible with the different population of elementary school-children identified for special education services in a school district. The pre-test–post-test control group experimental design had an additional feature of examining the anxiety level and social problems of these children as a follow-up to the Johnson, McLeod, and Fall (1997) research, since this could be done with the same instruments using one of the scales on the CTRS.

Participants   There were situational differences that emerged between the former study and this one. Perhaps most important, it was not possible to have the experimental and control groups stratified by teacher, case manager, and special education label because the population in the schools was not large enough for this. All children who received special education services in grades K–4 of a school district were identified by random selection for the control or experimental group. Since not all parents were willing for their children to participate, the final numbers were 30 children in the control group and 36 in the experimental group. Ages ranged from 6 to 10, with 10 first-graders, 19 second-graders, 19 third-graders, and 18 fourth-graders. Parents and teachers signed permissions for the students in the groups to participate. Labels from special education identifiers were speech and language (n = 27), behaviorally impaired (n = 7), autism (n = 1), ADHD (n = 3), multihandicapped (n = 3), LD (n = 22), and other (n = 3). Thirty children came from one school and 36 from the other school.

Two Caucasian female elementary school counselors delivered the play therapy intervention. Both had master's degrees, had advanced training in child-centered play therapy, and had received supervision for therapeutic interventions with children, including play therapy. Each counselor had been in the field as a school counselor for several years and was presently enrolled in a Certificate of Advanced Graduate Study program of 30 hours beyond the master's degree.

Instruments   The classroom observation used in the previous study was not duplicated because the results from the former study did not warrant time spent on this training and measure. The S-ES (Fall & McLeod, 2001), self-efficacy scale for children, and the CTRS-R-L (Conners, 1997) were used to measure the variables of self-efficacy and classroom behavior as in Study 1. The CTRS-R-L is the revised CTRS used in Study 1 and measures classroom behaviors (global index). It is a common assessment for classroom disruptive behaviors (Conners, 1997). The behavior index consists of 10 items. We also examined the social problems and anxious-shy scales of this instrument. The anxious-shy scale was used for the evaluation of anxiety and consists of six items with a .88 reliability. Reliability of the social problems scale is .61.

Procedures   The weekly schedule for the research study was as follows. During Week 1, the classroom teachers and case managers filled out the S-ES and the CTRS-R-L for all students. School counselors filled out the demographic data forms for all the students. During Weeks 2 through 7, the experimental group received an individual 30-minute child-centered play therapy session with the school counselor each week. The control group received no treatment. During Week 8, the classroom teachers and case managers filled out the S-ES and the CTRS-R-L for all students in the study.

Data Analysis   Means and standard deviations of variables were examined by time (pre- to post-test), by group (control and experimental), and by person completing the scale (teacher or case manager). Correlations were computed, and regressions examined the importance of variables to predict a change in score over time for the S-ES and the CTRS-R-L. These were all compiled with the SPSS data analysis system.

Results and Discussions   The results were complicated by a difference between teachers and case managers filling out the various scales.

- Children's self-efficacy increased for both experimental and control groups no matter who filled out the scale. The increase was less for the group receiving play therapy.
- Classroom behaviors that weren't conducive to learning decreased for the children receiving play therapy when rated by the teacher, but stayed about the same when rated by the case manager. Problematic classroom behaviors increased for the control group when scored by the teacher and decreased when scored by the case manager.
- Anxiety decreased for the children receiving play therapy when rated by the teacher and increased when rated by the case manager. The opposite was true for the children in the control condition: Teachers rated these students as increasing in anxiety, and the case managers reported decreasing anxiety.

We used multiple regression procedures to examine the difference in self-efficacy score over time when completed by the teacher and difference in classroom behavior, assignment to group, disability, age, and school. Significant results were obtained between group and disability, age and self-efficacy, and behavior and age. These variables accounted for 27 percent of the variance in the self-efficacy differential in score when completed by the teacher, $R2 = .27$, $F(4, 53) = 3.42$, $p < .01$, and Cohen's $f^2 = .37$, indicating a large effect size. Disability was the single best predictor of self-efficacy score. A second regression was run with the dependent variable of self-efficacy score differential when completed by case managers and self-efficacy score differential when completed by teachers. Age correlated with self-efficacy as rated by teacher and case manager, disability correlated with group condition, and school was the best predictor of the self-efficacy score. These variables accounted for 21 percent of the variance in self-efficacy score by the case manager, $R2 = .21$, $F(4, 53) = 2.70$, $p = .03$, and Cohen's

$f^2 = .27$, indicating a medium effect size. The increase in self-efficacy was not accounted for by the play therapy intervention. More statistical examination is available in the journal article (Fall, Navelski, & Welch, 2002).

While these results may seem confusing, we came to realize that there were many differences between this study and the former one and that the limitations of the first study were present here as well. One possible new difference may be that environmental conditions probably affect the children's classroom behaviors as well as the way these behaviors are rated. These were teacher rating scales. Teachers saw students in classrooms with many other students. Case managers saw students in quieter rooms, often with only one or two other students present. Children's behaviors change under such circumstances. Furthermore, teachers are comparing a student to many other students. Case managers compare students to a much smaller percentage of children. And last, children who require extra help as part of special education are frequently taught to look for cues from the case manager and to have strict regulations on their behavior. This is often necessary so as to assist them with learning. They were less self-directed, possibly because other people believed their handicap made them incapable of doing things on their own. These children were also different in the playroom. They did not use the toys with the same freedom but proceeded cautiously, always putting one toy away before touching another. These are all conditions that can affect the results of this study.

While the results of this study did not support a significant relationship between a child-centered play intervention and an increase in self-efficacy for children identified by the special education system, they pointed us in two interesting directions. First, the single best predictor of self-efficacy score was disability. So how a child views his ability to perform in ways that meet his needs was related to his special education label. While the reason behind this may be the condition itself, we were left wondering if the way we, as a society, treat the disability was perhaps at least a contributing factor. Second, it would appear that this population of children was affected by the freedom and self-responsibility of a child-centered play intervention. Both counselors reported that these children used the toys differently from nonlabeled children and were much slower in getting beyond the first stage of a play therapy intervention. In a learning situation, they are taught to use the cues of the case manager to not respond to their impulses. They are reinforced for this behavior. This helps them by patterning them in learning situations. Since this population of children is learning to get cues from an adult, children receiving special education may need more time in nondirective child-centered play therapy than their peers who are not part of the special education process. Since counselors seldom have time for long-term play therapy in a school, a cognitive behavioral or Adlerian play therapy might work best for children receiving special education and be less of a deviation from the way the rest of the school functions for them. This is important to find out. It could still appear important, however, that these children receive the beliefs in themselves that can emerge in child-centered play therapy as mentioned in the Johnson et al. study (1997). One way to assist with this would be to meet their need outside of the school system where a therapist could have more sessions and time with a child.

It is important to note other conditions that affect the integration of data from Study 1. First, since Study 2 was not stratified by teacher or case manager, children were in potentially very different learning and self-efficacy situations. We know that children can behave well with one teacher and not with another, and we were looking at behaviors that adversely affected their learning with the Conners scale. Furthermore, Bandura has said that self-efficacy level is specific to situations. As an example, that means that you might have high self-efficacy for learning a foreign language from a teacher that has a soft manner and lower self-efficacy from a very harsh, punitive teacher. In the first study, we controlled that by matching control and experimental conditions. This was not possible in Study 2. Since this variable was not controlled, the results might be very different from Study 1. The issues of matching control and experimental group are present in our second limitation as well. School was a predictor of self-efficacy score. We know that schools have different characteristics, different beliefs about how to work with students who may not be "square pegs for square holes," but instead learn and behave differently. A child may struggle in one school but be accepted as she is and flourish in another school.

Discussion of the Results of the Two Studies Together   Self-efficacy is an important variable that makes a difference in children's learning (Bandura, 1997). The theoretical blending of self-efficacy with child-centered play therapy (Fall, 1994) has been investigated by these two studies, with the primary outcome being that there is a relationship between an increase in self-efficacy and six sessions of 30 minutes of play therapy. Three hours of a counselor's time made a difference for children in schools. Does child-centered play therapy work? Yes. How does it work? One variable would appear to be an increase in self-efficacy.

Recommendations for the Future I believe self-efficacy is an important variable in the results of play therapy and is germane to all theories and interventions with children. However, child-centered play therapy has the conditions that align with all the elements that make up our personal self-efficacy judgment. More studies might concentrate on the effects of high and low self-efficacy and the conditions for increases and decreases before and after play therapy. Do other therapies also meet these conditions? How does self-efficacy increase in children from other cultural groups? The questions continue, and I hope the research does as well. This is too valuable to neglect.

In closing, I would like to relate the effects of the first study reported here. In one school in which the counselor had been the therapist for the play therapy in the study, the teachers voted that they needed to change the duties of the school counselor. There was such a learning difference in young students that participated in the research study experimental group that they voted to have all kindergarten children receive six sessions of child-centered play therapy during their first year in school. It would mean a reprioritizing of time for the counselor, but they could not afford to let children be without this beginning to their learning (L. Nelson, personal communication). Is there any better proof that play therapy works?

REFERENCES

Bandura, A. (1977). Self-efficacy: Toward a unifying theory of behavior change. *Psychological Review, 84*, 191–215.

Bandura, A. (1997). *Self-efficacy: The exercise of control.* New York: Freeman.

Conners, C. (1986). How is a teacher rating scale used in the diagnosis of attention deficit disorder? *Journal of Children in Contemporary Society, 19*, 33–52.

Conners, C. (1997). *Conners rating scales-revised.* New York: Multi-Health Systems.

Fall, M. (1994). Self-efficacy: An additional dimension in play therapy. *International Journal of Play Therapy, 3*(2), 21–32.

Fall, M. (1997). From stages to categories: A study of children's play in play therapy session. *International Journal of Play Therapy, 6*(1), 1–21.

Fall, M., Balvanz, J., Johnson, L., & Nelson, L. (1999). The relationship of a play therapy intervention to self-efficacy and classroom learning. *Professional School Counseling, 2*, 194–204.

Fall, M., & McLeod, E. (2001). Identifying children with low self-efficacy: Development of an instrument. *Professional School Counseling, 4*, 334–341.

Fall, M., Navelski, L., & Welch, K. (2002). Outcomes of a play intervention for children identified for special education services. *International Journal of Play Therapy, 11*(2), 91–106.

Johnson, L., McLeod, E., & Fall, M. (1997). Play therapy with labeled children. *Professional School Counseling, 1,* 31–34.

Kramer, J., & Conoley, J. (Eds.). (1992). *The eleventh mental measurements yearbook.* Lincoln, NE: Buros Institute of Mental Measurements.

Landreth, G. L. (2002). *Play therapy: The art of the relationship* (2nd ed.). New York: Brunner-Routledge.

Sutton, J., & Fall, M. (1995). The relationship of school climate factors to counselor self-efficacy. *Journal of Counseling and Development, 73.*

CHAPTER 3

The Efficacy of Intensive Individual Child-Centered Play Therapy for Chronically Ill Children

ELIZABETH MURPHY JONES and KARA CARNES-HOLT*

THE NEED FOR INDIVIDUAL PLAY THERAPY FOR CHRONICALLY ILL CHILDREN

An eight-year-old girl with chronic illness was sitting on the floor of the playroom drawing a picture during her first play therapy session. Our conversation revealed something important about her and many children with chronic illnesses.

CHILD: My grandmother told me this story of a bee and an elephant. They both got stuck in the mud.
THERAPIST: Hmm.
CHILD: They sat there and the bee said, "I can fly out of this mud," and the elephant said, "I'll never be able to get out of here." And the thing is, a bee is really too light to be able to fly out of mud, and elephants can easily get out because they are so strong.
THERAPIST: Really! So what happened?
CHILD: Well, the elephant just stays stuck and the bee flies right out!

*The authors would like to give special thanks to Katherine Purswell for her time and assistance with this chapter.

THERAPIST: Hmmm. So which one is most like you? The bee or the elephant?

CHILD: Oh, definitely the elephant. I can't do anything. (looking down)

This interaction illustrates the child's feelings of inadequacy and powerlessness in her world. Chronic illness can impede a child's normal developmental path and complicate the process of moving toward increased independence in adolescence (The Children's Hospital of Philadelphia, 2009). As suggested by numerous authors (Sartain, Clarke, & Heyman, 2000; Hoff et al., 2005; Hampel et al., 2005), children with chronic illness are required to give up a sense of control and mastery in their lives and bodies because of their medical condition. As one child expressed in play therapy, "There are so many things wrong with me, I just don't know where to start." This "damaged goods" misperception affects these children's emotional development, relationships with peers, and overall sense of control over their lives. As they seek to control and manage their lives, many children develop maladaptive behavior patterns, such as refusing to adhere to their medical treatment or acting out behaviors (Stuber, 1996).

According to the Centers for Disease Control and Prevention (2009) chronic diseases are now a leading health concern of the nation. It is estimated in the United States that 20 to 30 percent of children are living with a chronic illness (Brown et al., 2008). These children and families must endure financial strains, daily medical procedures, dependence on medical services and personnel, family tension, and uncertainty about the future (Brown et al., 2008; Patterson, 1988). In a meta-synthesis by Coffey (2006), parents of children with chronic illness were found to report pervasive worry and anxiety, a loss of freedom, and stressed relationships among family members. Although medical advances and technology have allowed children who might not have survived decades ago to live healthy, productive lives, chronically ill children and their families are faced with a host of rigorous demands and stressors associated with managing their illness in the face of societal neglect.

Despite such sobering statistics, opportunities for these children to lead normal, healthy lives have improved and the current focus is on improving the quality of their lives and preventing medical and psychological complications that often surface as a direct or indirect result of the child's illness. Advances in the area of disease prevention have focused on several areas, including the complications that occur as a result of the illness (Hinkle, 2004). While medical research strives to prevent and cure chronic illness, the medical community at large is working to reduce the number of physical, social, and psychological consequences of childhood disease. Home medical treatment, medical education, and social supports are used to help children and families cope with the challenges facing them and allow children with chronic illness to lead as normal a life as possible.

It has been shown that children with chronic illness are at increased risk for behavior difficulties, adjustment difficulties, and symptoms of anxiety and depression (Stuber, 1996). Because chronically ill children's psychological issues differ significantly from their physically healthy peers, researchers have challenged the use of standard psychological measures as insufficient in characterizing the experience of the chronically ill children and their families (Harris, Canning, & Kelleher, 1996). Future research should therefore be focused on the adjustment and coping of the child suffering from chronic illness, such as helping the child deal with anxiety and social adaptation (Drotar, 1993).

Diabetes is one of the most common diseases in school-aged children (National Diabetes Education Program, 2008). Insulin-dependent diabetes mellitus (IDDM) is a chronic condition that is typically diagnosed in childhood. IDDM (type 1) diabetes accounts for 5 to 10 percent of all diagnosed cases of diabetes and is the leading cause of diabetes in children of all ages; type 1 accounts for almost all diabetes in children under the age of 10 (National Diabetes Education Program). Because of the duration of IDDM, these children must learn to manage the disease for a lifetime. Because the complications associated with poorly managed diabetes usually manifest themselves later in life, children's cognitive developmental level makes it difficult to conceptualize the consequences of their current behavior. Given the gravity of IDDM and the daily demands of diabetes management, it is not surprising that children with diabetes are considered at risk for psychological and psychosocial difficulties.

As diabetic children are better able to manage the daily demands of diabetes treatment, including blood sugar testing, insulin injections, exercise, and dietary adherence, they tend to have improved metabolic control, which can significantly decrease their risk for medical complications associated with IDDM (Frey, Ellis, Templin, Naar-King, & Gutai, 2006). Daviss, Coon, Whitehead, Ryan, Burkley, and Macon (1995) found that compliance with medical treatment significantly affects diabetic control in children with IDDM. Children with healthier coping skills have been shown to have higher levels of adherence to their medical treatment (Jacobson et al., 1990). Jacobson et al. also found that children with IDDM tend to form adherence behaviors shortly after diagnosis, and these habits tend to persist overtime. It is therefore important that interventions aimed to prevent compliance problems among children with IDDM be directed toward younger children, to prevent adherence difficulties during adolescence.

Play therapy is developmentally appropriate for young children as "children express themselves more fully and more directly through self-initiated spontaneous play than they do verbally because they are more comfortable with play" (Landreth, 2002, p. 14). Children in play therapy learn to cope with problems through fantasy, metaphor, and reality testing within an emotionally safe environment. Children diagnosed with IDDM must live with a condition that they did not have the freedom to choose. In play therapy, children are allowed to choose their activities and direction of play, allowing them to feel more in control of their lives.

This purpose of this study was to examine the results of a series of child-centered play therapy sessions with children diagnosed with IDDM. The child-centered approach is grounded in "a deep and abiding belief in the child's ability to be constructively self-directing" (Landreth, 2002, p. 65). Children learn that they are responsible, independent, creative, and capable individuals. Hence, play therapy seems to be an appropriate intervention for young diabetic children, as adherence to a medical regime requires self-responsibility and self-direction. In addition, children with chronic illnesses must live with daily medical procedures and an illness that may often make their life seem out of control. As a result, these children may have feelings of anger, resentment, anxiety, and depression as they struggle with managing their disease. In this study, we were wondering how intensive child-centered play therapy would affect the levels of anxiety, depression, behavior problems, and overall adjustment to diabetes in children diagnosed with IDDM. Intensive play therapy was chosen because it provides both psychological and practical benefits for children. A format that allows children to experience the dynamics present in play therapy on a daily basis allows for the opportunity for concentrated and expedient intrapersonal change.

METHOD

PARTICIPANTS

Participants were selected from children attending Camp Sweeney, a summer camp for diabetic children in the United States. The camp served more than 600 children each summer. Children between the ages of 6 and 18 attend for three weeks. The children attending Camp Sweeney, all of whom are diagnosed with IDDM, are referred from various ethnic and socioeconomic backgrounds. No child diagnosed with IDDM is refused on the basis of financial need.

Two weeks before the camping term, the families of all children between the ages of 7 and 11 were contacted by mail to inform them of the purpose of the study and the opportunity to participate in it. A meeting was arranged with each child and parent who volunteered for the study, and risks and benefits of participation in the research study were discussed. In the order in which they volunteered for the study, 30 children were selected for the study on the basis of the following criteria:

- The child was between the ages of 7 and 11.
- The primary caretaker was able to speak, read, and write in English.
- The parent or legal guardian consented for the child to participate in the research study.
- The parent or legal guardian agreed to complete pre-testing, post-testing, and follow-up data.
- The child and the parent or legal guardian agreed for the child to participate in 12 play therapy sessions conducted by a trained play therapist during the camp term.

RESEARCH DESIGN

Children were randomly assigned to the experimental or control group on the first day of the camping term. Children in the experimental group began child-centered play therapy on the second day of the camp session, and they participated in 12 sessions during the three-week camping session. Because they were no longer at the diabetic summer camp, children in the control group did not receive play therapy after the completion of the experimental study. Any children in the control group who exhibited behaviors of concern or whose parents voiced concern about emotional difficulties were referred to an appropriate mental health professional in their community.

The experimental group comprised 9 boys and 6 girls, ages 7 to 11, with a mean age of 9.2 years. The control group comprised 8 boys and 7 girls, ages 7 to 11, with a mean age of 9.6. The population of the experimental group was 86.6 percent Caucasian, 6.7 percent African American, and 6.7 percent of Indian (country of India) descent. The population of the control group was 86.7 percent Caucasian and 13.3 percent Hispanic. Of the 15 children who participated in the experimental group, 14 received 12 play therapy sessions, and one child left camp before the study was completed. This child received 10 play therapy sessions and completed post-test data after returning home. Of the 30 children who participated in the study, 26 completed the 3-month follow-up questionnaires; three participants from the control group and one participant in the experimental group did not complete the questionnaire.

COLLECTION OF DATA

Parents were asked to complete pre-test data, including a demographic information sheet, the Filial Problems Checklist (FPC; Horner, 1974), and the Diabetes Adaptation Scale-Parent Form (DAS-Parent Form; Challen, Davies, Williams, Haslum, & Baum, 1988). Reliability coefficients of .83 for the FPC have been reported, demonstrating internal consistency within the measure. Because the follow-up data included self-report instruments for the child as well, all follow-up questionnaires were mailed to the child's home.

Before the first play therapy session, the children received an additional explanation of play therapy and the research study, and they had the opportunity to ask any questions of the play therapist. Each child was administered the Revised Children's Manifest Anxiety Scale (RCMAS; Reynolds and Richmond, 1985) and the Diabetes Adaptation Scale-Child Form (DAS-Child Form; Challen et al., 1988). Internal consistency reliability for the RCMAS is .83. DAS-Child Form alpha coefficients for the internal consistency have been reported at .78 to .82, and test-retest correlations were .74 and .88, which indicates a high level of internal consistency and test-retest reliability. Children had the instructions and questions read aloud to them as necessary. The children in the control group also completed pre-testing questionnaires during their rest hour on the second day of the camping session.

After the completion of 12 child-centered play therapy sessions, post-test data were collected. The children in both the experimental and control groups completed the RCMAS and the DAS-Child Form. The parents or legal guardians of children in both the experimental and control groups received the FPC and DAS-Parent Form post-test instruments to be completed two weeks after their child returned from camp.

Three months after the camp term ended, the children and the parents in the experimental and control groups were mailed the RCMAS and the DAS-Child Form. Written instructions were provided for the parents to read to the children before they completed the self-report instruments. The parents or legal guardians were asked to complete the FPC and the DAS-Parent Form.

The children in the experimental group received a total of 12 30-minute child-centered play therapy sessions during the three-week camp term, as the children's camping schedule allowed. As part of the camp, the children received therapeutic interventions provided by the camp, including small group discussions, medical education, and recreation. The children in the control group did not receive play therapy but participated in the therapeutic camping experiences provided by the diabetes camp.

The principles and procedures of child-centered play therapy were followed in the play therapy sessions, as outlined by Landreth (2002). The playroom was located in a small room in the hospital building on the camp grounds. In addition to the play materials recommended by Landreth (2002), the playrooms had play materials related to the medical issues faced by diabetic children, including a fully equipped doctor's kit, syringes, and blood glucose monitoring equipment.

Three play therapists conducted the play therapy sessions. They had taken an introductory course, an advanced course, and a practicum in play therapy. Two of the play therapists were doctoral students specializing in play therapy. One of these doctoral students had extensive experience working with children in a hospital setting. The third play therapist, employed as a school counselor providing play therapy in the schools, held a master's degree in counseling. The play therapists also received special education and training pertaining to the issues of diabetes, chronically ill children, and medical play. They were required to read a book describing the basic medical issues related to IDDM and the daily medical regime required for children with IDDM. The investigator (the first author) led a group discussion regarding the specific issues related to children with IDDM and the stressors facing these children and their families, as well as an orientation to the camp setting. Specific issues related to providing play therapy in the camp setting, such as confidentiality and scheduling, were discussed.

RESULTS AND DISCUSSION

ANALYSIS OF DATA

Following the collection of the pre-test, post-test, and follow-up questionnaires, the questionnaires were coded to maintain confidentiality. The questionnaires were hand scored, checked twice for errors, and the investigator keyed in the data using SPSS for Windows. An analysis of covariance (ANCOVA) was computed to test the significance of the difference between the experimental group and the control group on the post-test means and follow-up means for each hypothesis. In each computation, the specific post-test identified in each hypothesis was used as the dependent variable and the pre-test as the covariant. ANCOVA was used to adjust the group means in the post-test on the basis of the pre-test, thus statistically equating the control and experimental groups. Differences between the means were tested at the .05 level.

RESULTS

The results from this study, along with therapeutic observations, provide valuable information about the emotional and behavioral symptoms of children with IDDM as well as the effectiveness of play therapy for these children. As shown in Table 3.1, statistical trends indicate greater improvement of symptoms in a variety of areas in the experimental group compared to the control group.

Table 3-1

Pre- and Post-test Scores for Experimental and Control Groups

Measure	Experimental Group		Control Group				
	Pre-test M (SD)	Post-test M (SD)	Pre-test M (SD)	Post-test M (SD)	f	p	ES
FPC	33.40 (20.85)	29.14 (22.02)	24.73 (23.41)	15.92 (10.97)	.89	.36	.04
RCMAS	45.21 (12.53)	40.27 (12.20)	47.33 (11.04)	38.64 (14.41)	.42	.48	.02
DAS-C	74.36 (16.42)	79.07 (20.00)	79.93 (18.86)	77.93 (19.74)	1.03	.32	.04
DAS-P	38.93 (10.00)	36.77 (5.34)	43.00 (7.51)	43.47 (4.50)	6.88	.02	.22

M = Mean

(SD) = Standard Deviation

ANXIETY

Results from this study revealed that there was not a significant decrease in anxiety symptoms between the experimental and control groups at post-testing or at the three-month follow-up. In addition to a total anxiety score, scores on the RCMAS are divided into three subscales, including physiological anxiety, worry and oversensitivity, and social concerns and concentration. Although the experimental group showed improvement in all these areas, scores from the control group reflected improvement as well. It should be noted that the pre-test, post-test, and follow-up means of both the experimental and control groups of the RCMAS were within the normal range, indicating low levels of reported anxiety in both groups at pre-test and post-test. Although this might be expected for a preventative research study, it may have affected the lack of significance in these results.

Along with the ANCOVA, paired *t*-tests were performed on the RCMAS scores of the combined scores of the experimental and control groups, yielding significant results. On the RCMAS total anxiety score and the worry and oversensitivity subscale score, both groups showed a significant decrease in anxiety at the .05 level. These results point to the effectiveness of the camp experience to significantly decrease levels of anxiety in children with IDDM.

The play therapists involved with this study were also particularly moved by the high levels of stress and anxiety present in the play behaviors of the children in the experimental group. As one play therapist expressed, "These children are so high strung that it seemed difficult for them to relax and just *play*." Another play therapist stated, "Being with these children has changed me forever. They cope with so much every day—injections, insulin reactions, blood tests—it is so hard for them to just be normal kids."

Observations made in play therapy further explain the presence of anxiety symptoms for children with IDDM. One child in the experimental group appeared at the camp hospital each morning complaining of stomachaches. The medical staff could find no medical cause for these pains and asked the play therapist to "help him." In play therapy, the therapist reported that this child verbalized very little and was intent in his play activities. He seemed very anxious about something. In the first five play therapy sessions, he constructed an elaborate battle scene in the sandbox. Initially, he used play soldiers, but he began incorporating figures of nurses and doctors in his battles. During his play, he narrated occasionally, saying, "Here are the bad guys (nurses and doctors). They won't go away, they just keep coming back!" The child played out this theme repeatedly for five sessions. In the fifth session, the following conversation occurred:

CHILD: "Does your stomach ever have anxious, um, I mean, anxiousness?"
THERAPIST: "Hmm. Sounds like someone said something to you about anxiousness."
CHILD: "Yeah. What does that mean?"
THERAPIST: "In here, it can mean whatever you would like it to." (Child looked confused.) "What does it mean to you?"
CHILD: "That you are excited to do something?"
THERAPIST: "Ah. I think it can mean that. It can also mean that you feel worried or nervous sometimes."
CHILD: "Oh! I feel that."

In the days following this session, the play therapist observed that this child no longer appeared at the hospital to be examined by the medical staff. In addition, a medical student approached the play therapist and stated, "He certainly seems better. We don't see him anymore." It can be inferred that this child was experiencing anxiety related to his medical treatment and information provided by medical personnel. In the relationship with the child, the play therapist felt it was important to provide the child with information regarding the definition of the word *anxious*, as he had clearly heard this from the medical staff. In this instance, he seemed to be validated in his feelings while at the same time addressing these themes successfully in play.

BEHAVIOR PROBLEMS

Results on the Filial Problems Checklist (FPC) showed improvement in both the experimental and control groups on the post-test scores and increased improvement in the experimental group on the follow-up scores as compared to the control group. However, the difference between the mean scores on these measures was not significant at the .05 level. Follow-up results on this instrument were encouraging because it may indicate a statistical trend toward significance. A larger sample size may have increased the power of these results.

Further investigation of the parents' responses on the FPC yielded several general observations. Common to many of these children included internalizing behaviors such as "sulks, pouts," "difficulty falling asleep or sleeping," "cries easily," "headaches for no physical reason," and "stomach cramps, aches." Another predominant theme present in the children's behavior and the reports by their parents on the FPC pertained to peer relationships. When the parents met the investigator for the first time, many parents expressed concern about their children fitting in at school and fear that their children were excluded by their peers because of their diabetes. Parents reported that they believe negative peer relationships cause their children to become angry more often, irritable, and unsure of themselves. As one parent stated, "It makes me hurt inside when I see him carrying his big bag of [diabetes] supplies to school. He is so brave, but I know that he feels so bad because I see the other children look at him." A parent from the experimental group found encouragement from her child's increased confidence, writing, "I think he will really start off the school year more self-assured and confident."

All play therapists involved in the study provided qualitative information regarding improvement of behavioral symptoms in play therapy. In one case, a child's parent reported that the boy was extremely withdrawn at home, and his camp counselors stated that he was frequently excluded by his peers, primarily because of his nightly bedwetting. In the first play therapy session, this child did not establish eye contact with the play therapist, and he pulled his shirt over his head and appeared to hide inside his shirt. In response to the play therapist's reflection that he might not wish to be in the playroom, he responded, "I'd rather be jumping off a cliff than to be anywhere." Through his relationship with the play therapist, the child became increasingly interactive, although he remained primarily nonverbal. Outside the play sessions, this child was observed playing with other children and enjoying camp activities. During the final week of the camp session, his counselors reported that he was no longer wetting the bed at night. In his final play session he commented, "I like this place more than any place in the whole world." The play therapists reported other children gaining confidence in their own abilities and becoming more self-reliant. As one child said, "I used to not think I could do things like that, and now I can!"

DIABETES ADAPTATION AND ADHERENCE BEHAVIOR

The experimental group showed a significant increase ($p < .05$) in diabetes adaptation as indicated by the post-test scores on the Diabetes Adaptation Scale-Parent Form (DAS-Parent Form). Follow-up results noted minimal change in diabetes adaptation in both the experimental and control groups, suggesting that the long-term impact of this intervention was not sustained. The experimental and control groups both showed minimal change on the Diabetes Adaptation Scale-Child Form at post-test, suggesting that neither play therapy nor the camp experience significantly affected those children's attitude about their diabetes.

At follow-up, the experimental group reflected a minimal decrease in DAS-child form scores, while the control group scores decreased by a wider margin. On both the post-test and follow-up measures of the adherence scale of the DAS-Parent Form, the experimental group showed greater improvement than the control group, although this increase was not significant at the .05 level. Results on the adherence measure are promising, however, and a larger sample size may have provided increased statistical power. This is particularly important, considering the lack of assessment tools used for children with IDDM and the variability among research results regarding the factors affecting adherence.

DISCUSSION

The significant results of the post-test DAS-Parent Form total score suggest the possible effectiveness of play therapy as an effective intervention in increasing children's adaptation to diabetes. The implication is that children who are better adapted to their illness may be better able to cope with it. If children and their families adapt successfully to the difficulties presented in managing diabetes, they are likely to be more compliant with treatment and should experience increased overall health. It is important to note that the DAS-Parent Form, completed by the parent, reflects attitudes and emotional adjustment for the child, parent, and family. This instrument includes items pertaining to the family, such as "My child's diabetes causes problems for the whole family," items pertaining to the parent, such as "I feel overwhelmed with my child's diabetes," as well as to the child, such as "My child does blood sugars and takes his own shots without me nagging." Therefore, this instrument is a measure of the overall adjustment and adaptation of the child, parent, and family to the child's diabetes.

The lack of significance in the DAS-child form scores may be explained by the possibility of increased awareness by the children in the experimental group of their emotional difficulties and their attitude toward their diabetes. In play therapy, the play therapists observed that the children had a strong desire to discuss their feelings about their diabetes in play and in verbal exchanges with the therapist. This fact may be contributed to by the setting, as the children were attending a summer camp for children with diabetes, and they may have felt free to address issues pertaining to their diabetes. In addition, this desire to verbalize their feelings implies that children with diabetes have a strong need to express and explore their feelings about their diabetes. Often, children with chronic illness are encouraged by parents, medical, and adults at school to fit in and "behave like a normal kid." Such an attitude, though helpful in ways, ignores diabetic children's need to express their feelings regarding their diabetes and aspects related to it. In play therapy, these issues were readily addressed and accepted.

The play behaviors observed in one child illustrated his strong need to express his feelings regarding his diabetes. In play, he constructed a battle in the sandbox between a group of soldiers and "the enemy." In this scene, "the enemy" became various food items found in the play kitchen of the playroom. The boy arranged plastic slices of pizza, ice cream scoops, and french fries to attack the soldiers. He constructed this scene repeatedly for four play therapy sessions. In a subsequent play session, this child forcefully fed the play animals the food, shoving slices of pizza and vegetables down the hollow mouth of the alligators and sharks saying, "You have to eat, you have to eat!"

In the playroom, children were observed addressing issues of autonomy and self-reliance regarding their diabetes. One seven-year-old child entered the playroom and immediately began playing with the medical kit, examining the insulin syringe carefully and meticulously. For the duration of the session, he gave shots to the animals, the play therapist, and the dollhouse figures, and he become elated each time he completed the injection. The following day, this child was recognized at dinner for giving his injections independently for the first time. Clearly, he had been able to address his anxiety and apprehension about giving his insulin injections in play, and he was able to transfer this behavior to the world outside the playroom. By engaging in play behaviors that were related to this child's real-life experiences, he was able to experience himself in new ways, promoting new beliefs about his own potential and abilities. Very quickly, this child was able to apply these new learnings to his environment, allowing him to become more self-reliant in his world.

The experimental group showed a greater increase in the post-test and follow-up mean scores on the adherence scale of the DAS-parent form than the control group, although this increase was not significant at the .05 level. A larger sample size might have increased the statistical power of these results. The adherence scale on this instrument included items on the DAS-Parent Form pertaining to the child's adherence to her prescribed diet, exercise, and medical regime of blood tests and insulin injections, as well as the dynamics between the parent and child regarding the child's diabetic treatment. These results imply that play therapy may have been helpful in promoting the child's compliance behaviors in her medical treatment, as well as improving her attitude toward daily treatment.

The association between play therapy and diabetes treatment adherence may be seen in a variety of ways. In child-centered play therapy, the child is encouraged toward greater self-reliance, self-direction, creativity, and trust in his own inner resources. It is also generally believed that children are able to generalize these learnings from play therapy into the world outside the playroom.

The premise of this study was that the children who received play therapy would be able to learn in play therapy that they are capable, creative, self-directed individuals who can be trusted and relied upon. This new belief system would, in turn, affect their attitude and behavior toward their diabetes and medical regime. Observation and some statistical trends indicate that play therapy may have been an effective intervention to improve adherence in this way.

In terms of the play therapy conducted in this study, children in the experimental group were in a relationship with a play therapist that created an environment of trust, empathy, and unconditional acceptance to promote the natural process of growth within the child. A play therapy environment appears to allow the child to narrow the gap between her self-concept ("I am ill. There must be something wrong with me") and her real self ("I am trustworthy, creative, and capable. I am also a diabetic"). In this way, children may be increasingly self-accepting. This sense of acceptance may extend to their diabetes, as they may become more accepting of their disease and better able to cope with its demands.

CONCLUDING REMARKS

Some statistical trends in this study indicate that intensive play therapy may be an effective intervention for children diagnosed with IDDM in increasing their adherence to medical treatment. Qualitative observations and progress noted in play therapy reveal that young children with IDDM have the capability to address and resolve issues of anxiety and other emotional issues related to their diabetes in play therapy.

Providing play therapy in an intensive format in the summer camp setting was helpful to the children, as therapeutic changes seemed to occur more rapidly and the therapeutic relationship formed quickly and easily. Also, parents were eager for their children to receive play therapy, indicating the lack of preventative therapeutic services available to them and their awareness of a need for such services.

Future research should be conducted that will explore the qualitative aspects of play therapy for children with chronic illness. Their play behaviors tend to express different themes than play therapy with well children, and this area has not been explored. Research of this nature would contribute to an overall understanding of the emotional issues present for children with chronic illness. Future research should also focus on the emotional and behavioral symptoms present in young children with IDDM. Previous research studies have focused primarily on an adolescent population, as adherence difficulties tend to present for treatment at that time. A preventative approach might investigate emotional factors affecting young children to prevent more serious behavioral disorders in adolescence.

Further research should be conducted that uses other forms of play therapy for diabetic children. Providing weekly play therapy sessions over a longer period of time might yield more positive changes. Filial therapy may also provide a useful alternative for parents of children with diabetes, particularly those not living in areas where play therapy is accessible. Filial therapy might be provided in an intensive format as well, such as in the hospital setting.

Preventative approaches such as play therapy for children with IDDM are particularly important for this population as current behavior patterns and treatment adherence are highly correlated with long-term medical and psychological complications. By including play therapy as part of a multidisciplinary approach to diabetes treatment for young children, there is the potential to address these issues before they present difficulties for children and their families.

REFERENCES

Brown, R. T., Weiner, L., Kupst, M. J., Brennan, T., Behrman, R., Compas, B. E., et al. (2008). Single parents of children with chronic illness: An understudied phenomenon. *Journal of Pediatric Psychology*, 33(4), 408–421.

Centers for Disease Control and Prevention. (2009). *Chronic diseases: The power to prevent, the call to control.* Retrieved March 16, 2009, from http://www.cdc.gov/nccdphp/publications/AAG/chronic.htm.

Challen, A. H., Davies, A. G., Williams, R. J., Haslum, M. N., & Baum, J. D. (1988). Measuring psychosocial adaptation to diabetes in adolescence. *Diabetic Medicine, 5*(8), 739–746.

The Children's Hospital of Philadelphia. (2009). *Chronic illness and transplantation issues and the adolescent.* Retrieved March 23, 2009, from http://www.chop.edu/healthinfo/chronic-illness-and-transplantation-issues-and-the-adolescent.html.

Coffey, J. S. (2006). Parenting a child with chronic illness: A metasynthesis. *Pediatric Nursing, 32*(1), 51–59.

Daviss, W. B., Coon, H., Whitehead, P., Ryan, K., Burkley, M., & McMahon, W. (1995). Predicting diabetic control from competence, adherence, adjustment, and psychopathology. *Journal of the American Academy of Child and Adolescent Psychiatry, 34,* 1629–1636.

Drotar, D. (1993). Psychological perspectives in chronic childhood illness. In M. C. Roberts, G. P. Koocher, D. K. Routh, & D. J. Willis (Eds.), *Readings in pediatric psychology* (pp. 95–113). New York: Plenum Press.

Frey, M., Ellis, D., Templin, T., Naar-King, S., & Gutai, J. (2006). Diabetes management and metabolic control in school-age children with type 1 diabetes. *Children's health care, 35*(4), 349–363.

Hampel, P., Rudolph, H., Statchow, R., Laß-Lentzsch, A., & Peterman, F. (2005). Coping among children and adolescents with chronic illness. *Anxiety, Stress, and Coping, 18*(2), 145–155.

Harris, E. S., Canning, R. D., & Kelleher, K. J. (1996). A comparison of measures of adjustment, symptoms, and impairment among children with chronic medical conditions. *Journal of the American Academy of Child and Adolescent Psychiatry, 35,* 1025–1032.

Hinkle, A. S., Prokou, C., French, C., Kozlowski, A. M., Constine., L. S., Lipsitz, S. R., et al. (2004). A clinic-based comprehensive care model for studying late effects in long-term survivors of pediatric illness. *Pediatrics, 11*(4), 1141–1145.

Hoff, A. L., Mullins, L. L., Page, M. C., Carpentier, M. Y., Chaney, J. M., et al. (2005). The relationship of control-related beliefs to depressive symptomatology among children with type 1 diabetes and asthma: A disease-specific approach. *Children's Health Care, 34*(4), 261–272.

Horner, P. (1974). *Dimensions of child behavior as described by parents: A monotonicity analysis.* Unpublished master's thesis, The Pennsylvania State University, University Park.

Jacobson, A. M., Hauser, S. T., Lavori, P., Wolfsdorf, J. I., Herskowitz, R. D., Miley, J. E., et al. (1990). Adherence among children and adolescents with insulin-dependent diabetes mellitus over a four-year longitudinal follow-up, I: The influence of patient coping and adjustment. *Journal of Pediatric Psychology, 15*(5), 11-526.

Landreth, G. L. (2002). *Play therapy: The art of the relationship.* New York: Brunner-Routledge.

National Diabetes Education Program. (2008). *Overview of diabetes in children and adolescents.* Retrieved March 16, 2009, from http://www.ndep.nih.gov/diabetes/youth/youth_FS.htm.

Patterson, J. (1988). Chronic illness in children and the impact on families. In C. Chilman, E. Nunnally, & F. Cox (Eds.), *Chronic illness and disability* (pp. 69–107). Newbury Park, CA: Sage.

Reynolds, C. R., & Richmond, B. O. (1985). *Revised children's manifest anxiety scale.* Los Angeles: Western Psychological Services.

Sartain, S. A., Clarke, C. L., & Heyman, R. (2000). Hearing the voices of children with chronic illness. *Journal of Advanced Nursing, 32*(4), 913–921.

Stuber, M. L. (1996). Psychiatric sequelae in seriously ill children and their families. *The Psychiatric Clinics of North America, 19,* 481–493.

CHAPTER 4

Intensive Sibling Group Play Therapy with Child Witnesses of Domestic Violence*

ASHLEY TYNDALL-LIND

INTRODUCTION

By the time Robyn (five years old) and Christopher (seven years old) arrived at the family violence shelter, they had determined that adults were not trustworthy, love meant hurting one another, and caring relationships were too frightening to consider. They had been taught early on that *no one* could know of the brutality that occurred in their home on a daily basis and that they must be strong or at least die trying. Robyn's helplessness, insecurity, and secrecy coupled with Christopher's demand for absolute control of his surroundings were classic characterizations of children coping with domestic violence. Christopher was the *perfect child* who carried the burden of keeping the peace in the family, while Robyn was identified as the overly emotional, needy child who served as the scapegoat. Their roles in the family allowed the violence to seem strangely tolerable and somewhat predictable for many years.

Until one Thanksgiving afternoon, Robyn and Christopher were unable to effectively cope with the near-lethal maternal beating that they witnessed. Unable to stop their father's tirade, they were left to sit

*The authors express appreciation to Katherine Purswell for editing help.

with the seemingly lifeless body of their unconscious mother as they cried for help from neighbors. The police and the ambulance arrived, and the children ultimately came to the domestic violence shelter, where the average length of stay is a mere 14 days.

During my first play therapy session with them, Robyn and Christopher demonstrated a high degree of anxiety, fear, and psychic distress that is not uncommon for children who have experienced extreme trauma. They engaged in abreactive spontaneous play as they played out the sequence of crisis events surrounding the violent beating of their mother. Since these children were siblings, the play flowed remarkably well; each child automatically knew what to say, how to react, and what should happen next. There was no need to explain the details to me. When they entered the room, they immediately agreed that they would play house.

CHRISTOPHER: "Okay, you be the Mommy and *I'm* the Daddy!"
THERAPIST: "Oh, you know just what you want to do."
ROBYN: "I'm gonna make dinner" (as she raced over to the kitchen).
CHRISTOPHER: "Where are my car keys? (as he rummaged through the shelves). Oh, here they are . . . rumm . . . rummm." (Christopher raced off in his make-believe car. But he returned very quickly after departing.)
CHRISTOPHER: "I'm soooo hungry. Aren't you finished cooking yet?!" (Christopher spoke with an agitation in his voice.)
THERAPIST: "Christopher, you seem frustrated because you want to eat *now.*"
ROBYN: "Just a minute." (Robyn was nervously fidgeting with the pots.)
CHRISTOPHER: "Just a minute!?" (Christopher angrily pranced up to the stove where Robyn was nervously working and pushed the pot and vegetables on the floor and began to yell.)

The reenactment of the trauma dominated every session, but in each session they played slightly different outcomes. These outcomes ranged from death of their mother after the beating to a harmonious family life in which the parents used problem-solving skills to avoid the conflict. The repetitive theme suggested that both children needed to understand the crisis from a variety of different vantage points.

Clearly, these children and the 30 to 40 other children residing at the domestic violence shelter needed therapeutic intervention immediately. Yet, they would be at the shelter for only 14 days. What therapeutic intervention would give these children enough comfort to make progress in this short amount of time? Intensive sibling group play therapy seemed to be the best answer; there was little research, however, to support this intervention with siblings. It was Robyn and Christopher that helped propel intensive sibling play therapy research to the top of the priority list.

CHILD WITNESSES OF DOMESTIC VIOLENCE

Many children living with domestic violence never have the opportunity to find refuge at a domestic violence shelter. The issue is shrouded by secrecy; it is consequently difficult to accurately assess the number of children affected by domestic violence. The most recent estimates indicate that 15.5 million American children live in households in which intimate partner violence has occurred within the past year (McDonald, Jouriles, Ramisetty-Mikler, Caetano, & Green, 2006). Of those children, seven million have been exposed to severe partner violence (McDonald et al., 2006). Children exposed to family violence are profoundly affected and have a compromised ability to cope with daily life stressors.

Because children do not fully understand the dynamics of domestic violence, they may come to view power, control, aggression, and violence as the only means of getting one's needs met. Also, they may adopt coping strategies that include identification with the abuser. It is not uncommon for child witnesses of domestic violence to abuse peers, animals, and even caregivers. Children who externalize their emotions related to domestic violence may demonstrate hyperactivity and conduct problems (Jouriles, Wolfe, Garrido, & McCarthy, 2006). Alternately, some children embrace the victim role, becoming passive and withdrawn in their interactions with other people. Children who internalize their emotions are more prone to anxiety, depression, and suicidal ideation. Overall, it is difficult for these children to control emotional expression or to delay gratification (McKay, 1994).

Children from the same family can have completely different coping strategies and will present clinically with varying concerns. Eth and Pynoos (1994) noted a number of factors that influence the child's reaction to domestic violence, including proximity to the violent incident, duration of the experience, nature of the threats and injuries, and the existence of protective factors. Research into family environments and resiliency of children suggests that, despite the burden of parental psychopathology, family discord, or chronic poverty, most children identified as resilient have had the opportunity to establish a close bond with at least one person (UCLA, 2008). In many of the cases represented in this study, sibling pairs identified the presence of a brother or sister as a comfort in times of intense family stress. To my surprise, during and after this research, even in sibling dyads that appeared to be adversarial, the presence of a sibling during frightening times has been consistently reported to be helpful in managing fear.

Despite the presence of a sibling, the potential for traumatic reactions and poor coping strategies is highly likely among child witnesses of domestic violence (Jouriles et al., 2006). Without intervention, these children are ill-equipped to manage the challenges present in day-to-day relational exchanges.

INTENSIVE SIBLING GROUP PLAY THERAPY

Treatment duration and time between sessions are the primary factors associated with varying therapeutic intensity. The concept of intensive therapy has been explored since the 1970s, when Gestalt therapeutic weekends became popularized. Furthermore, psychiatric hospitals have long valued the benefit of intensive treatment in managing traumatic reactions (Gantt & Tinnin, 2007). Using intensive play therapy interventions with traumatized children has also been shown to have merit with varying types of traumatic events. Hoffman and Rogers (1991) used intensive play therapy in their work with traumatized children who had been displaced from their homes because of an earthquake. The groups met on a daily basis for four days for four to six hours and included children between the ages of 2 and 12. Positive outcomes included increased sense of control, mastery over the crisis, decreased anxiety, and an understanding of the traumatic episode.

More specifically, Kot, Landreth, and Giordano (1999) found that child witnesses of domestic violence showed significant improvement in self-concept, reduced externalizing behaviors, and improved behavior overall after intensive individual play therapy. After reviewing these studies, I was curious to explore whether there would be an enhanced treatment effect with the inclusion of siblings who experienced the same family violence.

Play therapy as a treatment modality has long been recognized as an effective strategy for working with relational issues (Axline, 1955; Gil, 1994). The therapeutic relationship is the primary curative tool when working with child witnesses of domestic violence. The primary goal of play therapy with child witnesses of domestic violence is to establish a corrective therapeutic relationship that optimizes trust, safety, and mutual respect. Within the context of a respectful relationship, children can begin to understand what happened to them in an age-appropriate way. Play therapy accomplishes this task in numerous ways. Specifically, the play therapy room allows the child to engage with a caring, stable, significant adult who provides the child with a safe therapeutic environment (Gil, 1991; Klem, 1992). Since child witnesses of domestic violence have experienced unpredictable life circumstances, this safe, predictable, and stable environment is a primary therapeutic agent in itself. Also, the toys allow the child to enter into a setting that is comforting and appealing to their natural way of interacting. This environment is nonthreatening and allows the child to work through difficulties at his own pace by manipulating the toys that are symbolic of the event. Symbolic play provides the child with a sense of safety by providing distance from the traumatizing event (Allan & Berry, 1987; Cattanach, 1995; Klem, 1992). Many child witnesses of domestic violence believe that the violence is their fault. Play therapy enables children to work through these concepts and to practice what-if scenarios that would be too risky to act out in their day-to-day lives.

Group play therapy has additional benefits when working with this population. Group interventions have been hailed as the treatment of choice when working with child witnesses of domestic violence (Ragg & Webb, 1992; Peled & Davis, 1994). Peled and Davis (1995) found that child witnesses of domestic violence who participated in group therapy while residing in family violence shelters were able to break the secret, could define abuse, distinguish among forms of abuse, and state that the abuse was not their fault. Specifically, sibling groups allow children to practice new behaviors within the family unit before using these new skills outside the therapeutic arena. Siblings serve as a catalyst and a sounding board for each other (Saravay, 1991). These groups have the added advantage of enhanced group cohesiveness because siblings have typically experienced similar traumatic events within the family of origin, resulting in extremely trusting and bonded relationships. Siblings have been found to be more comfortable in acknowledging and reaffirming loving and nonthreatening relationships, which allows children to experience deeper therapeutic explorations and catharsis (Frey-Angel, 1989). Finally, generalizability of therapeutically derived catharsis is greater when two children begin to shift the family dynamic during nontherapeutic encounters.

The therapeutic concepts of intensive treatment, play therapy, and sibling group design, when practiced together, are a combination that has the potential to meet the therapeutic needs of children like Robyn and Christopher.

METHOD
PARTICIPANTS AND DATA COLLECTION

Children ages 4 to 10 residing in domestic violence shelters in a large metropolitan area were provided with an option to participate in the study on a volunteer basis with informed consent from the legal guardian. The children were required to meet the following criteria to be eligible for participation:

- Must be between the ages of 4 and 10.
- Must have the full consent of the legal guardian.
- Must agree to participate in 12 sessions of sibling group play therapy.
- Must be a resident of one of the domestic violence shelters involved in this study.
- Those assigned to intensive sibling group play therapy must have a sibling who was concurrently residing in the shelter.
- Siblings must be no more than three years apart in age to be assigned to the intensive sibling group treatment.

The experimental group, consisting of 10 child witnesses of domestic violence, received 12 intensive sibling play therapy sessions within a two-week period, in addition to basic shelter services. Data collected for the intensive sibling group play therapy intervention were closely matched with and compared with results from a previously existing study evaluating intensive individual play therapy conducted by Kot et al. (1999). The results from both studies were statistically analyzed to evaluate the effectiveness of intensive sibling group play therapy in relation to intensive individual play therapy and a wait-list control group. The comparison group, from the Kot et al. study, consisted of 11 child witnesses of domestic violence and received 12 intensive individual play therapy sessions within a three-week period, in addition to basic shelter services. Finally, the control group, consisting of 11 child witnesses of domestic violence, received no treatment intervention; rather, they received only basic shelter services. Demographics of the children are shown in Table 4.1.

Table 4-1
Demographics of Children in the Studies

	Gender	Mean Age	Ethnicity
Individual	6 girls	6.9	46% Caucasian
Play Therapy	5 boys		27% Hispanic
			27% African American
Sibling Group	6 girls	6.2	60% Caucasian
Play Therapy	4 boys		20% Hispanic
			20% African American
Control Group	7 girls	5.9	70% African American
	4 boys		15% Hispanic
			15% Caucasian

MEASURES

All three groups completed the Joseph Pre-School and Primary Self-Concept Screening (JPPSST) (Joseph, 1979) as pre-test and post-test measures of self-concept. The JPPSST uses two sets of gender-specific pictures depicting polar opposite positive and negative situations. For example, one set of cards depicts a child alone in a corner versus a group of children playing together. The examiner asks the child to identify which situation in each set of pictures is most like herself. The JPPSST is appropriate for use with children ranging in age from 3 years 6 months to 9 years 11 months (Joseph, 1979).

The Child Behavior Checklist (CBCL) (Achenbach, 1991) was used to measure behaviors of a child as reported by the parents. The CBCL is a well-established and recognized instrument for the identification of behavior and emotional difficulties in children from the ages of 4 to 18. It is a self-administered, 120-item checklist that requires a fifth-grade reading level to complete and takes approximately 20 minutes to complete. It involves rating the existence of behavioral symptoms from zero to two, with zero indicating that the behavior is not true for this child and two indicating that the behavior is often seen in this child. All three groups completed the CBCL as pre- and post-measures.

PROCEDURE

Before initiating intensive play therapy sessions, mothers of the children in the individual play therapy group, sibling play therapy group, and control group completed the CBCL and the children completed the JPPSST. The children in the individual play therapy group and in the sibling play therapy group received 12 45-minute sessions of play therapy within a period of 12 days to 3 weeks. The playrooms were similarly equipped with play materials as outlined by Landreth (2002). Play therapy was provided by two master's and three doctoral level counselors who were specifically trained in play therapy.

In addition to the intensive play therapy intervention, all three groups also received three to four educational and recreational group sessions per week. These sessions focused on family violence awareness, sexual abuse prevention, feelings, and self-esteem. The group activities included arts and crafts, paper and pencil worksheets, and outdoor activities. The children in the control group received no other intervention.

Following the completion of the 12 play therapy sessions or at the end of two weeks for the control group, the researchers administered the post-test battery of instruments to each of the experimental, comparison, and control groups. The post-testing procedure followed the same procedures used in pre-testing.

RESULTS

Analysis of covariance (ANCOVA) was used to test the significance of the differences between groups on self-concept and behavior. In each case, the post-test specified in each of the hypotheses was used as the dependent variable and the pre-test as the covariant. ANCOVA was used to adjust the means on the post-test on the basis of the pre-test, thus statistically equating the individual play therapy, sibling play therapy, and control groups. Significance of difference between means was tested at the .05 level.

The individual play therapy group was found to score significantly higher than the control group in post-test self-concept scores: $F(1, 22) = 48.956$, $p < .001$. The mothers of the children in the individual play therapy group reported at post-test that their children exhibited significantly fewer externalizing behavior problems: $F(1, 22) = 4.388$, $p < .05$, and fewer total behavior problems as measured by the Child Behavior Checklist.

The sibling play therapy group scored significantly higher than the control group at post-test on self-concept scores: $F(1, 21) = 18.91$, $p = .000$. The mothers of the children in the sibling play therapy group reported at post-test that their children exhibited significantly fewer externalizing behavior problems: $F(1, 21) = 13.71, p = .002$, and fewer total behavior problems: $F(1, 21) = 11.67, p = .003$, as measured by the Child Behavior Checklist. The mothers of the children in the sibling play therapy group also reported at post-test that their children exhibited significantly fewer aggressive behaviors: $F(1, 21) = 11.01$, $p = .004$, and anxious or depressed behaviors: $F(1, 21) = 5.04, p = .038$. Results did not reach significance in internalizing behavior problems for the experimental group or the comparison group.

Overall, it was demonstrated that sibling play therapy group and individual play therapy group were effective in addressing behaviors of child witnesses of domestic violence. Both intensive individual play therapy and intensive sibling play therapy group demonstrated greater benefit than no intervention. In some cases, those who were in the control group showed regression without intervention.

DISCUSSION

SELF-CONCEPT

The experimental group showed a significant increase ($p < .001$) in self-concept as indicated by the Joseph Pre-School and Primary Self-Concept Screening Test. These findings are extremely robust and, therefore, imply a high degree of generalizability to the larger population. Also, these findings carry particular meaning given the fact that children in the control group showed a significant decline in self-concept without any therapeutic intervention. The implications of continued poor self-concept are central to long-term social and interpersonal difficulties for child witnesses of domestic violence.

BEHAVIOR PROBLEMS

Subjects in the experimental group demonstrated a significant ($p < .05$) decrease in total behavior problems at the time of post-testing. The total score encompasses the scores on all eight subscales of the CBCL:

1. Withdrawn
2. Somatic complaints
3. Anxious or depressed
4. Social problems
5. Thought problems
6. Attention problems
7. Delinquent behavior
8. Aggressive behavior

Results specific to improved total behavioral difficulties, as perceived by the children's mothers, are particularly noteworthy because mothers who are experiencing significant distress have a tendency to judge their children using excessively harsh standards, which may be a reflection of a greater sensitivity to their children's behaviors due to personal distress (Hughes & Barad, 1983). This implies that any changes noted by the mothers have a potential to be an underestimation of the actual behavior change exhibited by the child.

AGGRESSIVE BEHAVIORS

The significant ($p < .01$) reduction in externalizing behaviors for the experimental group at the time of post-testing indicates that the children were perceived to exhibit less aggression and fewer behaviors such as lying, cheating, and swearing. Of particular importance to the discontinuation of violent behaviors is the reduction of aggressive behaviors at post-test. There are several explanations for the dramatic decrease in aggression in the experimental group. Pynoos and Eth (1994) state that the expression of aggression in fantasy tends to decrease tension in traumatized children. This implies that the level of aggression in child witnesses of domestic violence may be a function of the level of interpersonal distress that the child is experiencing. A decrease in aggressive behaviors may be indicative of an internal resolution and a decrease in distress experienced by the child who received treatment. It should be noted that children in the control group showed an increase in aggressive behavior without an effective outlet for feelings of tension. Frick-Helms (1997) suggests that aggressive behaviors erupt when the child assumes responsibility, feels guilty, and believes that he or she deserves punishment for the traumatic event. According to this explanation, as the child works through these issues in the playroom, aggressive behaviors decrease.

The family environment is perceived as the key factor to understanding the etiology and maintenance of aggressive behavior. The idea of intergenerational transmission of violent family behavior underscores the need for positive interventions that incorporate siblings or other family members who have the opportunity to develop and practice new ways of behaving while in the safe environment of the therapy room. Improved relational style of siblings, with a decrease in aggression being a central component, has far-reaching implications in regard to breaking the cycle of violence.

With this in mind, clinicians may want to consider broader parameters for screening child witnesses of domestic violence. The results from this study imply that even extremely aggressive siblings have the potential to show drastic reductions in the expression of hostility. For example, an extremely aggressive sibling dyad, John (10 years old) and Brian (8 years old), volunteered for sibling group play therapy services as participants in the experimental group of this study. Given alternate circumstances, these two children may have been screened out of a group intervention because of excessive aggressive tendencies. Although maintaining the therapeutic environment was a more demanding challenge for the therapist, the boys were able to work through episodes of intensely reactive behaviors. Both boys demonstrated extremely positive therapeutic results at post-testing. Initially, sibling interactions included frequent unprovoked hitting, kicking, scratching, and biting. The unpredictability of these interactions was reflective of the chaos experienced in their family life before entering the shelter. Upon the termination of services, John and Brian showed a significant decrease in aggressive behavior, and attacks that were initially impulsive and second nature took on a more restrained and playful characteristic. With improved coping skills, the boys routinely explored alternative measures to solving conflict before resorting to aggressive means.

JOHN: "I'm going to paint!" (as he raced over to the easel; painting his house was his newfound passion).
BRIAN: "Painting is for sissies!"
THERAPIST: "You think that calling Brian a sissy will make him choose not to paint. Sounds like you might prefer that he play with you."
JOHN: "If you're going to be mean to me, I'd rather paint!" (as he aggressively splashed red paint on the easel).

John began to use art as a method of communicating how he felt and how well he was interfacing with the world. This medium enhanced his ability to get out aggressive feelings in an appropriate way and increased his positive interactions with his brother and others in his environment outside of the therapeutic hour.

ANXIOUS AND WITHDRAWN BEHAVIORS

A high pre-test anxiety level is not uncommon among children residing in safe hiding. Initial play therapy sessions are often marked by play behaviors characteristic of increased arousal and high levels of anxiety indicative of the child's pre-shelter situation. Many children are pre-occupied with safety and self-preservation, which is representative of concern regarding maintaining safety from the perpetrator. Play themes, in these circumstances, revolve around shielding oneself from harm and gaining mastery and control over an otherwise frightening situation. Many children engage in elaborate play with weapons and shields or they established secret, protected hiding places for themselves. These types of play behaviors allow children to restructure their reality so as to experience control and psychological safety, thereby decreasing high levels of anxiety (Frick-Helms, 1997). One would expect a slight reduction in anxiety as the child's safety in the community increases with protective orders, safety plans, and distance from the abuser. It should be noted, however, that despite legal and factual changes, safety measures are often ineffective in maintaining the safety of the family. Children seem to have a keen understanding of their realities regardless of the implied safety offered by external sources. The perceived safety is often played out thematically during sessions.

One specific example of the therapeutic change in anxiety involved a child, Nathan (nine years old), who created a super-durable magnetic tank with special protective powers. The metallic tank had the ability to withstand any amount of violent attacks from dinosaurs and magical-destructive demons and it could even withstand nuclear bombs. In addition to the protective powers of this tank was a secret hiding place under 10 tons of sand on the side of a mountain in the desert. No one was allowed to know where the tank went to rest every night. On a daily basis, however, the metallic tank retrieved all of the solders that were honored members of its force (his brother) and retreated to the secret hiding place. This play served to reduce the overwhelming anxiety that this child was experiencing.

NATHAN: Come on troops, it's time to retreat. You never know who's hiding out there. Let's get a little rest and get back at it in the morning." (Nathan used his most grown-up army voice to call in the troops.)

THERAPIST: "You're getting tired and you want your men to be in a safe place."

NATHAN: "Wait! What's that? Troops . . . Stand firm!" (Nathan whispered in a nervous voice).

THERAPIST: "You want to check out every noise. It's scary out there, but you know where to find safety now."

While residing in the shelter, the play created a feeling of safety and control during feelings of intense vulnerability and fear in reality. Nathan went on to create an internal shield that required no hiding place. At conclusion, therapeutic reduction of anxiety and therapeutic resolution of his internal protective strength showed preparation for termination.

RECOMMENDATIONS

Although there were no significant differences between intensive sibling group play therapy and intensive individual play therapy, there are several statistical trends worth noting. Additional research with a larger sample may reveal variability in treatment effect, giving these trends more statistical power. As indicated by the change in pre-test and post-test scores on the CBCL, children who participated in intensive sibling group play therapy showed more positive change than those who participated in intensive individual play therapy on the following subscales: total behavior problems, internalizing behaviors, externalizing behaviors, anxious or depressed, aggressive behavior, delinquent behaviors, somatic complaints, social problems, and with-drawn behavior. Conversely, the attention problems subscale showed a larger decrease as measured by the change in CBCL pre-test and post-test scores after intensive individual play therapy. Additional research is necessary to refine our understanding of the most appropriate applications of sibling interventions versus individual interventions. For example, group play therapy has the potential to be more helpful with issues related to emotional and social difficulties, while intensive individual play therapy has the potential to be most helpful with attention difficulties and thought problems.

The findings in this study are consistent with previously reported results evaluating the impact of positive sibling relationships on management of stressful life events. There are two primary aspects of the design of the intensive sibling group play therapy intervention that may have contributed to the number of statistically significant findings and may have enhanced the therapeutic effects exemplified in the group process: siblings as therapeutic partners and daily therapy sessions.

Additional research is necessary to parcel out treatment effects: daily therapy versus sibling involvement. It is important to have a clear understanding of which dynamic has the greater impact on child witnesses of domestic violence. This study is consistent with previous research findings that have found therapeutic benefits to providing sibling group play therapy (Frey-Angel, 1989). The sibling context may expedite the therapeutic process with regards to issues related to family dynamics.

REFERENCES

Achenbach, T. M. (1991). *Manual for the child behavior checklist and 1991 profile.* Burlington, VT: University Associates Psychiatry.

Allan, J., & Berry, P. (1987). Sand play. *Elementary School Guidance and Counseling, 21*(4), 301–307.

Axline, V. M. (1955). Group therapy as a means of self-discovery for parents and children. *Group Psychotherapy, 8*, 152–160.

Cattanach, A. (1995). *Play therapy with abused children.* London: Jessica Kingsley.

Center for Mental Health in Schools at UCLA. (2008). *A technical assistance sampler on protective factors (resiliency).* Los Angeles, Author.

Eth, S., & Pynoos, R. (1994, November). Children who witness the homicide of a parent. *Psychiatry, 57*, 287–311.

Frey-Angel, J. (1989). Treating children of violent families. *Social Work with Groups, 12*, 95–107.

Frick-Helms, S. (1997). Boys cry louder than girls: Play therapy behaviors of children residing in shelters for battered women. *International Journal of Play Therapy, 6*(1), 73–91.

Gantt, L. M., & Tinnin, L. W. (2007). Intensive trauma therapy of PTSD and dissociation: An outcome study. *The Arts in Psychotherapy, 34*(1), 69–80.

Gil, E. (1991). *The healing power of play: Working with abused children.* New York: Guilford.

Gil, E. (1994). *Play in family therapy.* New York: Guilford.

Hoffman, J., & Rogers, P. (1991). A crisis play group in shelter following the Santa Cruz earthquake. In N. B. Webb (Ed.), *Play therapy with children in crisis: A casebook for practitioners* (pp. 379–395). New York: Guilford.

Hughes, H. M., & Barad, S. J. (1983). Psychological functioning of children in battered women's shelter: A preliminary investigation. *American Journal of Orthopsychiatry, 53*, 525–531.

Joseph, J. (1979). *Joseph pre-school and primary self-concept screening test.* Chicago: Stoelting.

Jouriles, E., Wolfe, D. A., Garrido, E., & McCarthy, A. (2006). Relationship violence. In D. A. Wolfe & E. J. Mash (Eds.), *Behavioral and emotional disorders in adolescents: Nature, assessment, and treatment* (pp. 621–641). New York: Guilford.

Klem, P. R. (1992). The use of the dollhouse as an effective disclosure technique. *International Journal of Play Therapy, 1*, 69–73.

Kot, S., Landreth, G., & Giordano, M. (1999). Intensive play therapy with child witnesses of domestic violence. *International Journal of Play Therapy, 7*, 17–36.

Landreth, G. L. (2002). *Play therapy: The art of the relationship* (2nd ed.). Muncie, IN: Accelerated Development, Inc.

McDonald, R., Jouriles, E., Ramisetty-Mikler, S., Caetano, R., & Green, C. (2006). Estimating the number of American children living in partner-violent families. *Journal of Family Psychology, 20*, 137–142.

McKay, M. (1994). The link between child abuse and domestic violence. *Child Protection Leader, 7*, 1–2.

Peled, E., & Davis, D. (1994). *Group work with children of battered women: A practitioner's manual.* Thousand Oaks, CA: Sage.

Peled, E., & Davis, D. (1995). *Group work with child witnesses of domestic violence: A practitioner's manual.* Thousand Oaks, CA: Sage.

Peled, E., Jaffe, P. J., & Edleson, J. (Eds.) (1995). *Ending the cycle of violence: Community response to children of battered women.* Thousand Oaks, CA: Sage.

Pynoos, R. S., & Eth, S. (1994). Children who witness the homicide of a parent. *Psychiatry: Interpersonal and Biological Processes, 57*, 287–306.

Ragg, D. M., & Webb, C. (1992). Group treatment for the preschool child witness of spouse abuse. *Journal of Child and Youth Care, 7*, 1–19.

Saravay, B. (1991). Short-term play therapy with two pre-school brothers following sudden parental death. In N. B. Webb (Ed.), *Play therapy with children in crisis: A casebook for practitioners* (pp. 177–201). New York: Guilford.

CHAPTER 5

Effects of Postearthquake Group Play Therapy with Chinese Children

YIH-JIUN SHEN

A FTER A 7.3-MAGNITUDE earthquake struck midwestern Taiwan, the massive corpses not only putrefied the air but also traumatized survivors' hearts. In the house of Ja-Lin, an 11-year-old boy, the seven people who died were his cousins' whole family. They came to visit and stayed overnight for an early celebration on the upcoming Moon Festival, a traditional family reunion holiday in the Chinese culture. When most people slept deeply at 1:50 in the morning of September 21, 1999, the unexpected calamity struck one part of his house where his cousins' family slept. Physically, Ja-Lin was not injured in this so-called *921 Earthquake*. The ironically striking contrast between the joy of family reunion and the sorrow of the relatives' sudden death, however, severely traumatized him. The originally bashful and quiet boy was suddenly changed into a hyper-talkative one. Although the air was full of the foul smell of the dead bodies, he walked on the street in his village with an odd smile, whereas most people's facial expressions were sad and frightened. Ja-Lin was one of the numerous frightened youngsters whose personality and behavior were changed by the unbearable tragedy. To see if children who experienced earthquake trauma were able to be assisted effectively by child-centered play therapy in group settings within a limited time, I conducted my research with the child survivors in an elementary school. I found their anxiety and suicidal risk were significantly decreased after play therapy treatments compared to children receiving no treatment. Details about the study are reported in this chapter.

PREVALENCE AND IMPACT OF EARTHQUAKES ON CHILDREN

Major earthquakes that are measured 6.0 magnitude and above on the Richter scale have taken tens of millions of lives and victimized countless school-aged children around the world (*The World Almanac and Book of Facts 2009*, 2009). In the past two decades, for instance, more than 69,000 people perished in China in 2008, 80,000 people in Pakistan and India in 2005, 26,000 people in Iran in 2003, 20,000 people in India in 2001, 17,000 people in Turkey in 1999, and 40,000 people in Iran in 1990. Particularly in 2004, the 9.1 magnitude earthquake in Indonesia and the subsequent tsunamis killed more than 226,000 people in 11 countries. Following the 2004 South Asia earthquake and tsunamis, the United Nations Children's Fund (UNICEF, 2004) reported that children were likely to account for more than one third of the deaths. Most notably, in 2008 and 2005, more than 19,000 and 17,000 schoolchildren died in China and Pakistan, respectively, while schools collapsed after the 8.0 and 7.6 magnitude jolts powerfully shook these countries (Revkin, 2008; "More than 19,000 Students Died," 2008; Wisner, 2005). School-aged children are one of the most vulnerable among various populations (Norris, Byrne, Diaz, & Kaniasty, 2002; Tucker, 2004).

Because of deadly school collapses, primarily caused from unsafe construction of school buildings, along with other risk factors (for example, proximity to the epicenter, prior earthquake experiences), an enormous amount of young children have been either killed or traumatized (Revkin, 2008; Şahin, Batıgün, & Yılmaz, 2007; Wisner, 2005). Compared with adults, school-aged survivors are more likely to suffer from impairments, including psychological distresses, after the disasters (Norris et al., 2002). The 15 million surviving children after the 8.0 magnitude quake in China, for example, were reported awaiting psychological rehabilitation desperately (Chiu, 2008). Unlike other natural disasters (for example, hurricanes, snowstorms, tornados) whose occurrences are more predictable, major earthquakes remain one of the most destructive catastrophes, despite the efforts of seismologists, meteorologists, and governments to detect and predict the quakes (Shen, 2002; Tucker, 2004). In the aftermath of catastrophic earthquakes, following the rescuing of lives from debris, supplying basic needs, and preventing contagious diseases, the most urgent task is to provide psychological rehabilitation services for survivors (Chiu, 2008; National Child Traumatic Stress Network and National Center for PTSD, 2006; Shiu, 2008).

Why do young survivors need psychological treatments after the disaster? Despite the impression that some child victims do not manifest any pathological symptoms, most longitudinal studies found negative impacts of a disaster on children (Kiliç, Özgüven, & Sayil, 2003; Shen, 2010; Vernberg, La Greca, Silverman, & Prinstein, 1996; Wolmer, Laor, Dedeoglu, Siev, & Yazgan, 2005). The severity and duration of the effects may vary because of personal factors (for example, individual vulnerability, level of functioning, previous trauma experiences, personal injuries) and environmental factors (for example, degree of exposures, aftermath placement and care, parental reactions, parent-child relationships, domestic violence) (Gordon, Farberow, & Maida, 1999; Kiliç et al., 2003; Wolmer et al., 2005). Regardless of the risk factors, children's postdisaster vulnerability has been recognized in several dimensions.

The multifaceted reactions include cognitive, affective, somatic, behavioral, and neurobiological (Galante & Foa, 1986; Norris, et al., 2002, 2010; Shen, 2002). The negative cognitive effects may be manifested in memory, learning, and school performance. Affectively, children may experience anger, fear, grief, guilt, low self-efficacy, anxiety, depression, phobias, or irritability. Physically, they may suffer from headaches, stomachaches, enuresis, palpitations, or nightmares. Behaviorally, the youngsters may become hyperactive, aggressive, regressive, withdrawn, pessimistic, or unfocused. Commonly observed reactions may include fear of being alone, suicidal thoughts, and psychological disorders, such as posttraumatic stress disorder (PTSD) and acute stress disorder (ASD) (Chou et al., 2003; Eksi, Peykerli, Saydam, Toparla, & Braun, 2008; Hsu, Chong, Yang, & Yen, 2002; Kiliç et al., 2003). From the view of neurobiology, the communications between the left and right cerebral hemispheres of traumatized children are impeded (Norris, et al., 2002). These reactions—the survivors' tentative coping mechanisms—may interact with youngsters' emerging personalities, inhibiting maturation process and even hindering normal functioning later in life (Eksi et al., 2008; Kiliç et al., 2003).

School-based interventions, which mobilize the social support system during the postdisaster upheaval, are fairly suitable for the aforementioned children because they are most familiar with the school environment, where normalcy can be rebuilt (Gordon et al., 1999;

Wolmer et al., 2005). Among the few studies that have demonstrated the effectiveness of school intervention programs following major earthquakes, Goenjian, Walling, Steinberg, Karayan, Najarian, and Pynoos (2005) reported that school children who received brief trauma-and-grief-focused psychotherapy after the 1988 Armenian earthquake showed significantly reduced PTSD symptoms when compared to an untreated control group. In the three-year follow-up of a brief teacher-as-clinical-mediator program after the 1999 earthquake in Turkey, Wolmer et al. (2005) found that teachers rated children who received treatment with significantly higher adaptive functioning in academic performance, social behavior, and general conduct in comparison to those without treatment. After an earthquake in Italy, Galante and Foa's (1986) intervention for elementary school students demonstrated a significant reduction in posttraumatic symptoms after seven monthly sessions and in earthquake fears after one academic year's treatment. The results of the study, which systematically applied play-and-art media, illustrated the effectiveness of play interventions in small group settings for children traumatized by earthquakes.

Moreover, research has shown the effectiveness of play therapy in reducing children's anxiety, depression, and adjustment. In studying child witnesses of domestic violence, Tyndall-Lind, Landreth, and Giordano (2001) found significant reduction of anxiety, depression, and other behavioral and psychological problems following two weeks of intensive child-centered group play therapy, compared with child witnesses receiving no treatments. In the study of Reyes and Asbrand (2005), the levels of anxiety, depression, and posttraumatic stress among sexually abused children were significantly decreased after six months of play therapy. Brandt (2001) and Rennie (2003) also found that children with adjustment problems exhibited significant behavioral improvement after 7 to 12 sessions of weekly child-centered play therapy in comparison to those who had no treatment. Among these studies, only Tyndall-Lind et al. (2001) applied play therapy in group settings.

Although many have advocated the usefulness of child-centered play therapy with traumatized children, empirical data demonstrating its efficacy in group settings, particularly following calamitous earthquakes, are still lacking (Shen, 2010; Wethington et al., 2008). The report of Galante and Foa (1986) was an important initiative; however, neither the theoretical orientation of the play intervention was presented nor was there a control group taken into account of the developmental effects used in their study. Besides, none of the aforementioned research examined the interventional effectiveness with Chinese children. Furthermore, although both individual and group interventions can be effective with traumatized children, intensive short-term group counseling may be especially appropriate because it allows school-based mental health providers to serve large numbers of victims in the shortage of manpower, resources, and time after disasters (Shen, 2002, 2010). The effectiveness of such intervention needs to be demonstrated. Therefore, I examined the following research questions:

- How effective is short-term child-centered group play therapy in reducing the anxiety of the Chinese children who experienced the 7.3 magnitude quake in Taiwan?
- How effective is the approach in mitigating the depression of these children?
- How effective is the approach in improving the life adjustment of the affected children as perceived by their parents?

METHOD

I implemented a pretest-posttest design with an experimental group receiving the treatment and a control group receiving no treatment. Parents completed assessments within two weeks of the initial and final treatment. Children completed assessments the day before and the day after the treatment.

Participants

In midwestern Taiwan, 30 students in a rural elementary school participated in this study. The area was hit by the 921 Earthquake and more than 1,000 aftershocks months later. The major quake killed nine students and damaged three of the five buildings in the school. Many students and families had to transfer and move to other areas. A total of 65 out of 244 parents with children from third through sixth grade consented to participate and completed the *Children's Mental Health Checklist* (CMHC; see Gordon et al., 1999). The CMHC identified 30 high-risk students, who were 8 to 12 years old. These participants were 10 third-graders (4 boys and 6 girls), 8 fourth-graders (4 boys and 4 girls), 8 fifth-graders (3 boys and 5 girls), and 4 sixth-graders (3 boys and 1 girl). The 30 children were randomly assigned to an experimental or a control group with 15 in each group.

The experimental group comprised 5 third-graders (3 boys and 2 girls), 4 fourth-graders (2 boys and 2 girls), 3 fifth-graders (1 boy and 2 girls), and 3 sixth-graders (2 boys and 1 girl).

INSTRUMENTS

I administered four measures. The first two were individually passed to a parent via his or her child; the others were group-administered in the school. These measures, originally designed for American children, were administered in Taiwan's official language, Mandarin Chinese, because no existing instruments were available to measure postearth-quake symptoms in Chinese children. The initial psychometric prop-erties reported herein were derived from U.S. populations and the present Taiwanese sample.

Children's Mental Health Checklist (CMHC)   The 25-item yes-or-no CMHC was originally developed in response to the Loma Prieta earthquake in California in 1989 (see Gordon et al., 1999). Each parent checks on situations that could pose psychological harmfulness to his or her child. Psychometric information of CMHC is not available, but this measure served as a critical tool to initially identify child earth-quake survivors needing psychological assistance.

Filial Problem Checklist (FPC)   The 108-item FPC allows parents to indicate the life adjustment of their children (Horner, 1974). Areas of interests include behavior, psychological circumstances, inter-personal relationships, somatic problems, eating, sleeping, and school performance. Parents rate items on a Likert scale (1 = *It is true, but not really a problem*; 2 = *The problem is mild*; and 3 = *It is a severe problem*). The FPC generates a total score only. Psychometric information of the FPC is not available in previous studies, but it has been used in many studies to measure parental views after the children underwent child-centered group play therapy (Landreth & Lobaugh, 1998). The pretest and posttest of the present study yielded a .99 Alpha coefficient reliability, respectively.

Revised Children's Manifest Anxiety Scale (RCMAS)   The 37-item true-or-false RCMAS measures children's self-reported anxiety, including the subscales of physiological anxiety (anxiety manifested by physiological symptoms, for example, fatigue, nausea, sleep difficulties), worry or oversensitivity, and social concerns or concentration (Reynolds & Richmond, 1985). A lie subscale is included to measure respondent bias. Concerning the reliability, most Alpha coefficients of the RCMAS exceed .80. The test-retest reliability coefficients range from .68 to .98. The subscales' Alpha coefficients range from .60s to .80s. The scale correlates at .67 and .65 (for females and males, respectively) with the trait scale of the *State-Trait Anxiety Inventory for Children*, whose validity was substantially supported by research data on validity (Reynolds & Richmond; Spielbereger, Edwards, Lushene, Montuori, & Platzek, 1973). The Cronbach's Alpha coefficients, based on the pretests of the present study, were .94 for the total scale and ranged from .67 to .92 for the subscales; based on the posttests, the Alpha coefficients were .95 for the total scale and ranged from .82 to .92 for the subscales.

Multiscore Depression Inventory for Children (MDI-C)   The 79-item MDI-C measures children's self-reported depression, including the subscale of anxiety, self-esteem, sad mood, instrumental helplessness, social introversion, low energy, pessimism, and defiance (Berndt & Kaiser, 1996). MDI-C also includes an item testing children's suicide risk. An infrequency score is included to measure respondent malingering. The face validity of MDI-C is considered excellent because this is the first depression inventory that is written in children's own words. The Alpha coefficient reliabilities of MDI-C range from .92 to .96, with coefficients of subscales ranging from .64 to .89. MDI-C also has a .92 test-retest reliability and a .84 correlation with the *Child Depression Inventory* (Kovacs, 1981) on validity (Berndt & Kaiser). The Cronbach's Alpha coefficients, based on the pretests of the present study, were .96 for the total scale and ranged from .60 to .89 for the subscales; based on the posttests, they were .96 for the total scale and ranged from .62 to .90 for the subscales.

PROCEDURE

According to participants' genders and grades, I classified the 15 children in the experimental group into five subgroups. In a makeshift playroom in the school, a school counselor with graduate-level child-centered play therapy training provided the children with the treatments. Child-centered play therapy procedures as described by Guerney (1994) and Landreth (2002) were implemented. Each subgroup received 40-minute group play therapy treatments two to three times per week for a total of 10 sessions.

RESULTS

I analyzed my data collected through the analysis of covariance (ANCOVA), multivariate analysis of covariance (MANCOVA), and a two-independent-samples t test to examine the difference between the experimental and control groups. Because the norms of RCMAS and MDI-C were not established based on the children in Taiwan, I analyzed raw scores rather than standard scores. The null hypothesis for the adjusted posttest mean was tested with an F distribution with an Alpha level of .05. The covariate for the ANCOVA was the pretest score; the dependent variable was the posttest score. Before applying ANCOVAs and MANCOVAs, equal variance and homogeneity of regression were examined to ensure that these assumptions were met. The social introversion subscale on MDI-C was the only one that did not meet the homogeneity-of-regression assumption. Hence, a two-independent-samples t test was applied. ANCOVAs were used to compare the adjusted posttest scores for the RCMAS, MDI-C, and FPC. ANCOVAs also tested the subscores of MDI-C and the item on suicide risk. MANCOVAs tested the subscores of the RCMAS. In the experimental group and the control group, one student did not complete the posttests on RCMAS and MDI-C. In addition, four parents whose children were in the control group did not complete the posttests on FPC. The missing data were replaced with the group means.

As presented in Table 5.1, the results of ANCOVA on the student-reported RCMAS indicated that the overall anxiety in the experimental

Table 5-1
Descriptive and Influential Statistics of the RCMAS, MDI-C, and FPC Total Scores as Dependent Variables by Each Condition in ANCOVA

Measure		Pretest		Posttest		ANCOVA		
		M	SD	M	SD	Adjusted M	$F(1, 27)$	η_p^2
RCMAS total score	E	18.00	7.97	13.41	7.78	12.98	10.17*	.27
	C	17.07	8.61	16.94	9.06	17.37		
MDI-C total score	E	35.00	14.29	29.67	13.53	32.09	0.30	
	C	41.20	21.51	36.47	20.01	34.06		
FPC	E	93.33	76.60	69.33	67.06	72.88	0.92	
	C	104.87	76.99	93.36	66.48	89.81		

Note: RCMAS = Revised Children's Manifest Anxiety Scale; MDI-C = Multiscore Depression Inventory for Children; FPC = Filial Problem Checklist; E = experimental group; C = control group.
*$p < .01$

group was significantly reduced in comparison to the control group. According to Cohen (1977), the overall treatment effect ($\eta_p^2 = .27$) was large. As presented in Table 5.2, the results of the post hoc contrasts on MANCOVA showed that based on the students' RCMAS reports, the levels of physiological anxiety and worry or oversensitivity in the experimental group were significantly decreased in comparison to the control group. Both of the treatment effects ($\eta_p^2 = .30$ and $\eta_p^2 = .14$, respectively) were large. As presented in Table 5.3, the results of ANCOVA on the student-reported suicide risk showed a significant reduction in the experimental group in comparison to the control group.

There were no significant differences between experimental and control groups' pretest to posttest changes on the overall depression, as reported by students on the MDI-C, and on the life adjustment, as reported by parents on the FPC (see Table 5.1). Specifically, there were no significant differences on changes for social concerns or concentration, as reported by students on the RCMAS (see Table 5.2), and for anxiety, self-esteem, sad mood, instrumental helplessness, low energy, pessimism, and defiance, as reported by students on the MDI-C (see Table 5.3). However, a significant difference in suicide risk was shown. The result of the *t* test on the social introversion subscale of MDI-C further indicated no significant difference between the experimental and the control groups.

DISCUSSION

The results of this study point to the effectiveness of child-centered short-term group play therapy with Chinese elementary school students who experienced a devastating earthquake in Taiwan. Response bias or malingering was not found, as indicated by the lie subscale of the RCMAS and the infrequency score of the MDI-C. Hence, the students should have provided unbiased and accurate reports, and the internal validity of the study could be assumed. As measured by the RCMAS, children's anxiety in general, physiological anxiety, and worry or oversensitivity were significantly reduced after play therapy treatment; the reduction of the children's anxiety related to social concerns or concentration, however, was not significant. It appears that the significant reduction of physiological anxiety and worry or oversensitivity reflect the precise measure of RCMAS on children's posttraumatic symptoms. As measured by the MDI-C, children's depression in general, anxiety, self-esteem, sad mood, instrumental

Table 5-2

Descriptive and Influential Statistics of the RCMAS Subscores as Dependent Variables by Each Condition in MANCOVA

Measure		Pretest M	SD	Posttest M	SD	MANCOVA $F(3, 23)$	η_p^2	ANCOVA Follow-up Adjusted M	$F(1, 27)$	η_p^2
RCMAS						3.14^a	.29			
Physiological anxiety	E	7.20	2.34	4.87	2.39			4.11	11.66**	.30
	C	5.53	3.18	5.27	3.39			6.03		
Worry/oversensitivity	E	7.00	4.28	5.50	4.14			5.63	4.22*	.14
	C	7.33	3.94	7.36	3.86			7.22		
Social concerns/concentration	E	3.87	2.13	2.84	2.25			2.88	3.67	
	C	4.00	2.36	4.24	2.41			4.19		
Lie^b	E	3.73	2.28	3.08	2.25	—		—	—	
	C	3.53	2.30	3.35	2.84	—		—	—	

Note: RCMAS = Revised Children's Manifest Anxiety Scale; E = experimental group; C = control group.

a Wilks's $\wedge$ = .04

b Measuring response bias.

* $p < .05$

** $p < .01$

Table 5-3
Descriptive and Influential Statistics of the MDI-C Subscores as Dependent
Variables by Each Condition in ANCOVA

Measure		Pretest		Posttest		ANCOVA		
		M	SD	M	SD	Adjusted M	$F(1, 27)$	η_p^2
Anxiety	E	6.60	2.75	4.75	2.82	4.83	2.06	
	C	6.80	3.65	5.82	3.40	5.74		
Self-esteem	E	3.27	2.15	2.76	2.13	3.07	1.32	
	C	4.13	2.72	4.16	2.84	3.86		
Sad mood	E	4.07	2.68	3.66	2.74	4.01	0.16	
	C	5.07	3.35	4.06	3.22	3.70		
Instrumental helplessness	E	4.47	2.62	3.72	2.60	4.23	1.28	
	C	6.00	3.23	5.78	3.53	5.27		
Social introversion	E	1.80	1.74	2.02	2.17	—	—	
	C	3.13	1.96	2.48	1.64	—		
Low energy	E	3.93	1.91	3.44	2.06	3.52	0.10	
	C	4.13	2.88	3.77	2.88	3.69		
Pessimism	E	4.53	2.20	3.94	1.71	4.09	0.10	
	C	5.20	2.86	4.41	1.96	4.26		
Defiance	E	5.93	2.74	5.16	2.95	5.25	0.02	
	C	6.20	3.21	5.49	3.56	5.39		
Suicide risk[a]	E	0.40	0.51	0.01	0.05	0.02	6.28*	.19
	C	0.53	0.52	0.34	0.48	0.33		
Infrequency score[b]	E	2.73	2.15	4.26	1.28	—		
	C	3.87	1.92	3.39	1.64	—		

Note: MDI-C = Multiscore Depression Inventory for Children; E = experimental group; C = control group.
[a]One item rather than a subscale.
[b]Measuring response malingering.
*$p < .05$

helplessness, social introversion, low energy, and pessimism did not show significant improvement after play therapy treatments; children's suicide risk, however, was significantly reduced.

Generally, these findings support Galante and Foa's findings (1986) that children's postearthquake symptoms can be significantly reduced by interventions that infuse play media in small group settings. The findings also support previous investigations indicating the possibilities of applying school-based interventions after severe earthquakes

(Goenjian et al., 2005; Wolmer et al., 2005). The results further support the arguments of Sweeney and Homeyer (1999) and Tyndall-Lind et al. (2001) for the feasibility of intensive short-term group play therapy.

Importantly, the results support Axline's argument (1947) for the enormous power of child-centered play therapy on children with limited power to change their environments. When the environment overwhelms one's ability of self-awareness and self-direction, child-centered play therapy allows the situation and feelings to be openly expressed, yet nonjudgmentally identified, and unconditionally accepted. The following sample dialog illustrates the process experienced by three participants, 10-year-old Wendy and Ming and 9-year-old Yu, in the study:

WENDY: We got an earthquake (aftershock) again last night.
YU: (Overhearing the funeral music off campus) My younger brother died.
MING: (Picking up a doll) This is a *Mountain People*.
YU: (Raising her voice abruptly) Why did you curse my mother?
COUNSELOR: It occurred to Yu that your brother died because of the furious earthquake, and you don't like the term Ming used because you think he is humiliating your mother.

The counselor recognized Yu's feelings and thoughts. The sense of being understood and accepted empowered Yu to gradually adjust her oversensitivity. (Note: *Mountain People*, implying a certain degree of condescension, is an out-of-date term for *Native Taiwanese*.)

In addition to the general effects discussed above, the following sections will discuss the specific effects of the treatment on anxiety, depression and suicide risk, and life adjustment. Other related issues will also be addressed later.

ANXIETY

The findings of current study support previous investigations indicating the effectiveness of play therapy on reducing children's fears and anxiety (Reyes & Asbrand, 2005; Tyndall-Lind et al., 2001). The enjoyment experienced by children during play therapy also seems to have reduced anxiety or worry over what others think. For example, consider the behavior of Wendy, Ming, and Yu, who did not know each other before their first session.

COUNSELOR: (After entering the playroom) You can play with many things you want here.

WENDY: Wow! There are a lot of toys!

MING: (Walked around the playroom and touched several items.)

YU: (Looking at the counselor) Can I play with the dollhouse?

COUNSELOR: Yu, you can play with things you like.

The children were permitted to play freely and were becoming acquainted with each other.

By session eight, they chased each other and ran into the playroom with cheerful smiles.

MING: Wait for me! Don't run so fast!

YU: You can't catch me!

WENDY: My mom said, ''If you spent your time there just for play, you should not participate in the program anymore.'' But I will complete the program (Shen, 2002, p. 54).

COUNSELOR: You guys really enjoyed this program. Wendy, your mom does not want you to play in school any more, but you are confident about what you are doing.

Wendy was one of the children who experienced the conflict between the expectations of her mother (prioritizing academic achievement over play therapy) and that of her teacher (encouraging students' participation in play therapy). By this session, Wendy had developed the inner strength to honestly express her thoughts and was confident in her choice, thereby lowering her internal anxiety.

DEPRESSION AND SUICIDE RISK

On the one hand, the results of this study do not support the previous findings regarding the effectiveness of the play therapy treatments for children's depression (Reyes & Asbrand, 2005; Tyndall-Lind et al., 2001). On the other hand, the results of the current study indicated a significant decrease of children's suicidal risk. It should be noted that this finding is based on one item on the MDI-C (see Table 5.1). Although there is no subscale measuring suicidal ideation, the reaction is likely to happen among children who have experienced catastrophic earthquakes and is thus worthy of investigation. Instead of a real action plan, the responses of children to the item ''I have a suicide plan" were interpreted as their thoughts in this study. The surviving children's views about self and life were significantly improved after the treatment, perhaps because of the esteem-building component in child-centered play therapy. The following synopsis demonstrates how the counselor strengthened children's esteem during the third session:

YU: (Looking at Ming and Wendy in the room) Let's play the dinner time. Ming is the father, I am the mother, and Wendy is the daughter. You guys will come home for dinner in just a few minutes.

COUNSELOR: (Recognizing Yu's leadership) Yu knows what role each of you should play.

YU: (Looking at the counselor) I can't get the dinner ready!

COUNSELOR: You want to prepare a nice dinner for your family, but you are afraid that you won't be able to get everything ready.

YU: (Looking at the counselor) Can you do it for me?

COUNSELOR: It really frustrates you, and you want my help.

YU: Yah! Can you help me?

COUNSELOR: You just want me to help. Tell me which part and how you want me to do it.

YU: (Starting to organize the table quietly) Guys, dinner is ready!

COUNSELOR: You are able to do it yourself, and you feel accomplished.

Overall, compared with children in the control group who played outside the playroom, those who were in the experimental group significantly decreased their anxiety and suicidal thoughts after the therapeutic play. It appears that the climate fostered in the treatment process may be a factor contributing to the improvement. When a sense of permissive safety and warm acceptance is established, a calming influence occurs. The feelings of trust and stability consistently rise in the counselor-client relationship and further facilitate the child survivor's self-awareness, self-acceptance, and ability to better relate to others. For example, after completing the play therapy program, some children wrote notes to the counselor:

WENDY: You are leaving this week. ☹ It is a little bit hard for me. Thank you for taking care of us these days and providing me with psychological rehabilitation.

YU: I am very sorry that I raised my voice in the playroom. You are leaving, but I feel somewhat hard to detach myself. Come back to see us. THANK YOU.

MING: (Instead of writing, he drew a picture of an airplane with a person standing by an airport to reflect the image that the counselor was leaving for another country.)

LIFE ADJUSTMENT

With respect to children's life adjustment, the results of this study do not support the previous findings (Brandt, 2001; Rennie, 2003) revealing the improvement of life adjustment in children who received child-centered play therapy. The discrepancy might be attributed to the insufficient collaboration of the parents in the study, who became less observant because of their necessary focus on fulfilling their family's basic needs following the major quake and numerous aftershocks. Because of the parents' unavailability in the chaos, the parent who had completed the pretest might not be the one who completed the posttest. Moreover, children's postdisaster recovery could be further complicated if they had other ongoing problems in life (for example, child abuse, parental divorce) (Shen, 2002).

OTHER RELATED ISSUES

It is critical to examine the measures in a cross-cultural view. Although not statistically significant, the results of the social concerns or concentration subscale of the RCMAS and the social introversion subscale of the MDI-C indicated a decline in socialization (see Table 5.1). Some of the concepts of the scale are in conflict with Chinese norms, however. Based on the manuals, positive answers to the items "I love playing with friends" and "I enjoy playing" imply children's ability in socialization. In contrast, these statements may be interpreted as inappropriate or immature in Chinese students. Once Chinese children reached school age they are discouraged from playing because academic emphasis is prioritized over mental health concerns (Shen, 2002). The low rate (25%) of parental consent for children's participation might well echo the majority parents' resistance to recognizing or unawareness of their children's psychological needs (for example, having fun) or unfamiliarity with Western interventions (play therapy).

Further fighting against the cultural norm (discouraging the play behavior) for them to receive play therapy, these children might have given positive answers to the scale items "I feel someone will tell me I do things the wrong way" or "A lot of people are against me." According to the instrument manual, positive implies an inability.

In contrast, these children might indeed have the strength to live up to the expectations of others, such as the teachers and administrators who encouraged students to participate in play therapy. These items might have wrongly measured the children, and thus the validity of the two subscales could be uncertain.

I also observed that there was less resistance to child-centered play therapy among children under age 11. The observation was especially true for boys. Children of ages 11 or 12 are entering what Piaget termed *formal operational stage,* at which time they tend to enjoy task-oriented activities more than free play (Shen, 2002). The efficacy of play therapy might have been affected by the high percentage (40%) of fifth- and sixth-graders in this study. The age factor might also explain why children's depression and life adjustment were not reduced in the experimental group relative to the control group.

LIMITATIONS AND RECOMMENDATIONS

There are several limitations of this study and recommendations for future studies. The generalization of the findings might be limited by the small sample; recruiting participants from several schools should be considered. The participants' gender and age could influence the program results; how these two factors may affect the effectiveness of the program warrants future inquiries. The collection of quantitative data on parental perceptions was limited; qualitative studies may obtain the perceptions of children's changes in greater depth. A child-centered approach was the only theoretical orientation applied; future research should add comparison groups using various theoretical approaches. The application of Western instruments might have weakened the validity of this study; it is urgent to develop psychological measures appropriate for Chinese children, for whom adequate mental health measures do not exist.

In this study's findings, the application of a 4-week short-term model applying child-centered play therapy with Chinese children should be underscored. Mental health professionals are encouraged to educate Chinese teachers, and especially parents, about the importance of interventions and the rationale for applying play therapy. School counselors and other mental health professionals should be encouraged to provide Chinese children with short-term interventions and to alleviate the parents' concerns that longer-term treatment may interfere more with children's learning.

In conclusion, this study's results support child-centered group play therapy as a useful tool to help Chinese children suffering from anxiety and suicidal ideation, an important indicator of depression, after a devastating disaster. The findings point to the potential of applying a Western psychotherapy to promote the well-being of children in a non-Western culture.

REFERENCES

Axline, V. M. (1947). *Play therapy: The inner dynamics of childhood*. Boston: Houghton Mifflin.

Berndt, D. J., & Kaiser, C. F. (1996). *Multiscore depression inventory for children*. Los Angeles: Western Psychological Services.

Brandt, M. A. (2001). An investigation of the efficacy of play therapy with young children (Doctoral dissertation, University of North Texas, 1999). *Dissertation Abstracts International*, *61*, 2603.

Chiu, C. (2008, May 29). Fifteen million children in the disaster area are awaiting psychological rehabilitation urgently. *Sina*. Retrieved May 30, 2008, from http://chinanews.sina.com/news/2008/0530/07072729589.html.

Chou, Y.-J., Huang, N., Lee, C.-H., Tsai, S. L., Tsay, J.-H., Chen, L.-S., et al. (2003). Suicides after the 1999 Taiwan Earthquake. *International Journal of Epidemiology*, *32*, 1007–1014.

Cohen, J. (1977). *Statistical power analysis for the behavioral sciences*. New York: Academic Press.

Eksi, A., Peykerli, G., Saydam, R., Toparla, D., & Braun, K. L. (2008). Vivid intrusive memories in PTSD: Responses of child earthquake survivors in Turkey. *Journal of Loss and Trauma*, *13*, 123–155.

Galante, R., & Foa, D. (1986). An epidemiological study of psychic trauma and treatment effectiveness for children after a natural disaster. *Journal of the American Academy of Child Psychiatry*, *25*, 357–363.

Goenjian, A. K., Walling, D., Steinberg, A. M., Karayan, I., Najarian, L. M., & Pynoos, R. (2005). A prospective study of posttraumatic stress and depressive reactions among treated and untreated adolescents five years after a catastrophic disaster. *American Journal of Psychiatry*, *162*, 2302–2308.

Gordon, N. S., Farberow, N. L., & Maida, C. A. (1999). *Children and disasters*. Philadelphia: Brunner/Mazel.

Horner, P. (1974). *Dimensions of child behavior as described by parents: A monotonicity analysis*. Unpublished doctoral dissertation, The Pennsylvania State University, University Park.

Hsu, C. C., Chong, M.-Y., Yang, P., & Yen, C.-F. (2002). Posttraumatic stress disorder among adolescent earthquake victims in Taiwan. *Journal of the American Academy of Child and Adolescent Psychiatry*, *41*, 875–881.

Kiliç, E. Z., Özgüven, H. D., & Sayil, I . (2003). The psychological effects of parental mental health on children experiencing disaster: The experience of Bolu Earthquake in Turkey. *Family Process, 42*, 485–495.

Kovacs, M. (1981). Rating scales to assess depression in school-aged children. *Acta Puedopsychiatrica, 46*, 305–315.

Landreth, G. L. (2002). *Play therapy: The art of the relationship* (2nd ed.). New York: Brunner-Routledge.

Landreth, G. L., & Lobaugh, A. F. (1998). Filial therapy with incarcerated fathers: Effects on parental acceptance of child, parental stress, and child adjustment. *Journal of Counseling and Development, 76*, 157–165.

More Than 19,000 Students Died During Wenchuan Earthquake. (2008, November 21). *Rusnews.CN*. Retrieved March 1, 2009, from http://big5 .rusnews.cn/guojiyaowen/guoji_anquan/20081121/42341266.html.

National Child Traumatic Stress Network and National Center for PTSD. (2006). *Psychological first aid: Field operations guide* (2nd ed.). Retrieved August 20, 2009, from http://ncptsd.va.gov/ncmain/ncdocs/manuals/ smallerPFA_2ndEditionwithappendices.pdf.

Norris, F. H., Byrne, C. M., Diaz, E., & Kaniasty, K. (2002). The range, magnitude, and duration of effects of natural and human-caused disasters: A review of the empirical literature. *National Center for PTSD*. Retrieved March 8, 2009, from http://www.ncptsd.va.gov/ncmain/ncdocs/fact _shts/fs_range.html?opm=1&rr=rr48&srt=d&echorr=true.

Rennie, R. L. (2003). A comparison study of the effectiveness of individual and group play therapy in treating kindergarten children with adjustment problems (Doctoral dissertation, University of North Texas, 2000). *Dissertation Abstracts International, 63*, 3117.

Revkin, A. C. (2008, May 14). Earthquake in China highlights the vulnerability of schools in many countries. *New York Times*. Retrieved March 1, 2009, from http://www.nytimes.com/2008/05/14/world/14codes.html?_r=2& sq=&st=nyt&oref=slogin&scp=1&pagewanted=print.

Reyes, C. J., & Asbrand, J. P. (2005). A longitudinal study assessing trauma symptoms in sexually abused children engaged in play therapy. *International Journal of Play Therapy, 14*(2), 25–47.

Reynolds, C. R., & Richmond, B. O. (1985). *Revised children's manifest anxiety scale*. Los Angeles: Western Psychological Services.

Şahin, N. H., Batıgün, A. D., & Yılmaz, B. (2007). Psychological symptoms of Turkish children and adolescents after the 1999 earthquake: Exposure, gender, location, and time duration. *Journal of Traumatic Stress, 20*, 335–345.

Shen, Y. J. (2002). Short-term play therapy with Chinese earthquake victims: Effects on anxiety, depression, and adjustment. *International Journal of Play Therapy, 11*(1), 43–63.

Shen, Y. J. (2010). Trauma-focused group play therapy in the school. In A. A. Drewes & C. E. Schaefer (Eds.). *School-based play therapy* (2nd ed.). Hoboken, NJ: John Wiley & Sons.

Shen, Y. J., & Sink, C. A. (2002). Helping elementary-age children cope with disasters. *Professional School Counseling, 5*, 322–330.

Shiu, Y. Y. (2008, May 18). Sichuan Earthquake rescuing medical group returned to Taiwan, and the disaster area needs disinfection and immunization urgently. *NOW News.* Retrieved May 18, 2008, from http://tw.news.yahoo.com/article/url/d/a/080518/17/zhpf.html.

Spielbereger, C. D., Edwards, C. D., Lushene, R. E., Montuori, J., & Platzek, D. (1973). *State-trait anxiety inventory for children.* Palo Alto, CA: Consulting Psychologists Press.

Sweeney, D. S., & Homeyer, L. E. (1999). Group play therapy. In D. S. Sweeney & L. E. Homeyer (Eds.), *The handbook of group play therapy* (pp. 3–14). San Francisco: Jossey-Bass.

Tucker, B. E. (2004). At the turning point for global earthquake safety. Paper presented at the second annual dinner of geohazards international dinner, Washington DC. Retrieved March 1, 2009, from http://geohaz.org/contents/publications/BET_DC_speech_for_website6.pdf.

Tyndall-Lind, A., Landreth, G. L., & Giordano, M. A. (2001). Intensive group play therapy with child witnesses of domestic violence. *International Journal of Play Therapy, 10*(1), 53–83.

United Nations Children's Fund (UNICEF). (2004, December 28). *Children account for one third of tsunami dead.* Retrieved March 6, 2009, from http://www.unicef.org/emerg/disasterinasia/index_24659.html.

Vernberg, E. M., La Greca, A. M., Silverman, W. K., & Prinstein, M. J. (1996). Prediction of posttraumatic stress symptoms in children after Hurricane Andrew. *Journal of Abnormal Psychology, 105*, 237–248.

Wethington, H. R., Hahn, R. A., Fuqua-Whitley, D. S., Sipe, T. A., Crosby, A. E., Johnson, R. L., et al. (2008). The effectiveness of interventions to reduce psychological harm from traumatic events among children and adolescents: A systematic review. *American Journal of Preventive Medicine, 35*, 287–313.

Wisner, B. (2005). The right to safety: Building safe schools for children. *UN Chronicle, 42*(4), 59–60.

Wolmer, L., Laor, N., Dedeoglu, C., Siev, J., & Yazgan, Y. (2005). Teacher-mediated intervention after disaster: A controlled three-year follow-up of children's functioning. *Journal of Child Psychology and Psychiatry, 46*, 1161–1168.

The World Almanac and Book of Facts 2009. (2009). Pleasantville, NY: World Almanac Books.

CHAPTER 6

Play Therapy Effect on Relationship Stress

DEE C. RAY and NATALYA A. EDWARDS

CHILD RELATIONSHIPS WITH PARENTS AND TEACHERS

Relationships between children and their primary adult figures provide a foundation for child development and, possibly, emotional and behavioral adjustment. Extensive research indicates that the quality of parent and teacher relationships is correlated with children's conduct disorders, social aggression and other externalizing problems, attention problems, internalizing problems, anxiety, depression, self-esteem, and academic problems (Abidin, Jenkins, & McGaughey, 1992; Boutelle, Eisenberg, Gregory, & Neumark-Sztainer, 2009; Deater-Deckard, 2005; Hamre & Pianta, 2001; Herber, 1998; Ladd & Burgess, 2001; Pianta, Steinberg, & Rollins, 1995; Pianta & Stuhlman, 2004). Theorists conjecture, with substantial evidence, that parent-child interactions show reciprocity, thereby creating a circle of continued effect on attitudes, relationship, and behavior between parent and child (Abidin, 1995; Boutelle et al., 2009; Deater-Deckard, 1998). A similar cycle can be observed in teacher-child relationships (Abidin, Greene, & Konold, 2004). In other words, when adults and children interact, the child's behavior and attitudes, the adult's behavior and attitudes, and the quality of the relationship will act together to produce continued effects on each of these relationship variables.

When children exhibit behavioral problems, parents or teachers may react in a negative manner, damaging the relationship, which may possibly worsen the child's behavior. Ackerman, Brown, and Izard

105

(2003) found that children demonstrating externalizing behaviors from first to third grades who experienced harsh parenting behaviors or parent maladjustment continued to show a clinical level of externalizing problems. Hughes, Cavell, and Jackson (1999) measured levels of aggression in children from first to third grades and found that the quality of the teacher-student relationship predicted children's trajectories of aggressive behaviors. Hamre and Pianta (2001) revealed that negativity in the teacher-child relationship, as early as kindergarten, predicted academic and behavioral problems in middle school. When studying both parent and teacher relationship effects on school adjustment, Murray (2009) concluded that parent relationship quality was highly correlated with student-rated school engagement, school competence, and standardized reading scores, while teacher relationship quality was highly correlated with student-reported engagement, grades in language arts and mathematics, and mathematical achievement. Murray's results highlight the importance of quality in both parent and teacher relationships in the academic success of children.

INDIVIDUAL CHILD-CENTERED PLAY THERAPY AND CHILD RELATIONSHIPS

Literature on child relationships with parents and teachers emphasizes the importance of each individual within the relationship. With such an emphasis on both the adult and the child, it seems logical that mental health professionals would concentrate on systemic interventions to improve relationships. We, too, agree that interventions with adults in collaboration with child interventions are the most effective way to affect the relationship. In practice, however, it is our experience that adults involved in children's caretaking or education are often unavailable or unwilling to participate in intervention. As counselors in schools, we interacted on a daily basis with children whose parents did not return phone calls or refused to participate in problem solving in any way. In one phone call, a parent said, "I'm tired of dealing with all of his problems. You do something about it. I won't be up there anymore." And for children who often display behavioral problems, teachers become frustrated and respond by ignoring or negatively interacting with the child, sometimes refusing to try any longer with possible solutions.

Accepting the premise that adults may refuse intervention, the theory that a change in a child's behavior will result in improving his or her relationships with parents and teachers became intriguing and hence, a research agenda was born. When adults are unavailable for counseling, can a child-only intervention help with behavior and improve a child's relationships with adults? The purpose of this chapter is to present a case study and summarize findings of three research studies on parent-child relationship stress and teacher-child relationship stress conducted in recent years that explore the effects of individual child-centered play therapy (CCPT) on children's relationships.

Case Study

The following is a case example of a six-year-old African American girl, Tamika, who was brought to play therapy by her grandmother, Stacie. Stacie was assigned as legal guardian for Tamika and her sister Anna, age three, after their mother was charged with drug trafficking and prostitution. At the time of treatment, the girls' father was incarcerated for assault and had not been in contact with his children for a year.

Stacie noted during the intake interview that within the past six months, Tamika had started exhibiting significant behavioral problems both at home and at school. According to her teacher's report, Tamika had become increasingly withdrawn, played more frequently alone, and on several occasions started fights with her classmates. Stacie also noted that Tamika had started throwing tantrums at home when she did not get her way. Her behavior problems also included biting, hitting, and screaming at her grandmother. Although she was close to her younger sister, consistent with recent behavior, Tamika would occasionally hit Anna without provocation. When asked about any significant event or major change within the past six months, Stacie noted that her daughter, Yvonne, was about to have her third child and had revealed the news to Tamika.

Stacie was employed full time and was the sole provider for her grandchildren. Because of her hectic schedule and no available child care, she was unable to participate in parent consultations. Conversations with the therapist were often conducted by phone (in 15-minute intervals). It was therefore difficult for the therapist to provide Stacie with additional support and receive timely updates on Tamika's experiences at home and school.

During her first few play sessions, Tamika participated in exploratory play. Throughout this period, she did not verbally communicate with the play therapist and often played alone behind the

(continued)

puppet theater. Through basic CCPT techniques (for example, reflecting nonverbal behavior, reflecting content, reflecting feeling, esteem building, and encouragement), the therapist facilitated an environment of permissiveness, allowing Tamika the freedom to make choices. During her fourth session, Tamika began to talk to the therapist and invite her to participate in her play.

By her fifth play therapy session, Tamika entered into mastery play, which focused on reenacting classroom lessons and identifying various sea and land animals. She drew a picture at the end of this session. She told the therapist when she was finished, "This is my father, my mother, my sister, and me." All characters were standing smiling and holding hands. Subsequent sessions would end with Tamika drawing the same picture. Each time she would tell the therapist, "This is my father, my mother, my sister, and me." During this phase of therapy, Tamika frequently involved the therapist in her play. For example, she would ask the therapist to play specific characters in her stories and puppet play.

During one of their 15-minute telephone conversations, Stacie told the therapist that her third grandchild, Jason, was born, and she was also given custody of him. When asked about Tamika's reaction, Stacie said that Tamika appeared to be happy and was very caring toward her little brother. She also said that Tamika was being more cooperative at home and the frequency of her tantrums had decreased.

In the sixth through tenth sessions, the therapist noticed a gradual but steady change in Tamika. Her affect changed from negative and sad to happy and pleased. Her play themes became more elaborate; she was able to play out story sequences and her play had direction. Reports from Stacie continued to reflect improvements at home and school. Tamika had become more involved in caring for her younger siblings. She had also become less aggressive and more playful toward her grandmother. Tamika's teacher also reported that she had become less withdrawn and less aggressive toward other children.

At the end of the eleventh play therapy session, Tamika sat at the table and drew a picture. It resembled her usual drawing, but there was one difference—there was an additional character. When she was finished, Tamika told the therapist, "This is my father, my mother, my sister, me, and my grandmother." When the session was over, the therapist walked Stacie, Tamika, Anna, and Jason to the car. As Stacie got the children into the car, she leaned over to the therapist and whispered, "Thank you for giving me my granddaughter back."

This case provides some anecdotal support for the effectiveness of individual CCPT even where there is a lack of parent-teacher involvement. Tamika was able to use the play therapy sessions to work through her feelings about herself and her relationships with others. Of significance, and as indicated by her drawings, was her ability to integrate her view of family, her desire to be with her parents, and the reality of her grandmother's place in her life. Through CCPT, she was able to transfer her growth in therapy to her relationship with her peers, teacher, and grandmother. The following describes three research studies, which also indicate that individual CCPT has the potential to positively influence child behavior as well as adult-child relationships.

THREE RESEARCH STUDIES ON CHILD RELATIONSHIP STRESS
WITH PARENTS AND TEACHERS

There were several common features related to CCPT for all three studies, including structure and protocol of play therapy treatment, training of play therapists, and treatment integrity. Each is explained in the following and applies to all three studies that are presented.

CHILD-CENTERED PLAY THERAPY

In all relationship studies, play therapy was facilitated according to the principles of CCPT. CCPT is designed to provide specific therapist responses to the child during play therapy. Procedures for CCPT are based on Landreth's (2002) general guidelines and can be found in current form in Ray (2009). Playrooms were equipped with a variety of specific toys to facilitate a broad range of expression. A specific list of toys is suggested in Landreth (2002).

PLAY THERAPISTS

Play treatment for all studies was conducted by master's and doctoral students in a counselor education graduate training program. All play therapists successfully completed at least two courses in play therapy and participated in individual and triadic supervision with a counseling faculty member certified in play therapy or an advanced doctoral student.

TREATMENT INTEGRITY

All play therapy sessions were video-recorded for the purpose of supervision. Supervisors ensured that the basic principles of CCPT were being followed and enacted in play sessions. For teacher-child relationship studies, a checklist of CCPT responses was used during supervision to more concretely assess the alignment of therapist responses to CCPT protocol.

STUDY 1: IMPACT OF PLAY THERAPY ON PARENT-CHILD RELATIONSHIP STRESS AT A MENTAL HEALTH TRAINING SETTING

PARTICIPANTS

Data were obtained from archival files of 202 child clients at a community counseling clinic on a university campus covering a period of nine years (study originally published in Ray, 2008). All clients were between 2 and 13 years old with a mean near 6 years (M = 5.96; SD 2.32). Most clients were nine years old or younger (92.5 percent). Of the 202 participants, 79 were females and 119 were males with missing gender data on four. Ethnicity of children was reported as African American (n = 1), Asian (n = 1), Caucasian (n = 160), Hispanic/Latino (n = 11), Native American (n = 4), biracial (n = 17), and other (n = 3), with missing ethnicity data on five participants. Household living situation was reported as 19 in a blended family, 5 in a father-only family, 66 in a mother-only family, 65 in a two-parent family, 12 in a relative's family, 10 in an adoptive family, 14 in other, with missing household information on 11.

INSTRUMENTS

Parenting Stress Index   The purpose of the Parenting Stress Index (PSI; Abidin, 1995) is to identify parent-child systems that are under significant stress and at risk for development of problematic parent or child behavior. The PSI can be used with parents of children ranging in age from one month to 12 years. Clinical scores are determined at or above the 85th percentile. Abidin recognized three major source domains of stressors, which include child characteristics, parent characteristics, and situational life stress. Hence, the PSI reports in three domains including child domain, parent domain, and life stress. The parent and child domains are combined to present an overall total stress score.

Child Behavior Checklist   Because of the time length of the study, both the Achenbach (1991) and the revised Achenbach and Rescorla Child Behavior Checklists (CBCL, 2001) were used. Two age-specific versions of the CBCL exist: CBCL for children ages 1½ to 5 (Achenbach & Rescorla, 2000) and CBCL for ages 6 to 18 (Achenbach & Rescorla, 2001). Achenbach and Rescorla (2000) ensured the comparability of the two versions by summarizing that t-scores of internalizing, externalizing, and total problems scales between the instruments could be used with no loss of differentiation. The CBCL was developed to measure problematic child behaviors as identified by the parent. CBCL reports clinical behaviors according to three domains of externalizing, internalizing, and total behavior that are composed of eight syndrome scales: anxious and depressed, withdrawn and depressed, somatic complaints, social problems, thought problems, attention, aggression, and rule-breaking behavior.

PROCEDURES

Upon intake to the clinic, a parent or guardian of the child was administered the PSI, the CBCL, and a child background form. The assigned play therapist provided the parent or guardian with an informed consent regarding treatment procedures and a data collection protocol that notified parents that the clinic would request the completion of instruments at unidentified times during treatment for the purpose of tracking counseling progress. The consent form also informed parents that such instruments might be used for research purposes. The play therapist then facilitated CCPT with the child on a weekly basis until the parent and the counselor mutually decided upon termination based on completion of therapeutic goals or the parent prematurely terminated. Each play therapy session was between 40 and 50 minutes in length. Post-testing of the PSI and CBCL was administered upon the therapist's notification from the parent that therapy would be terminated or upon the end of a university academic semester. Because the data for this study were provided from archival data collected during the course of serving a clinical population, there was no control for time of post-test administration of the instrument or length of treatment. Measurements were initially administered by play therapists for purposes of understanding the extent of problem behaviors reported by parents and subsequently administered for the purposes of determining progress of treatment. Only data collected by the same therapist were used, signifying the length of play therapy for each client was conducted by the same therapist.

For the purpose of this study, the CBCL was used to distinguish between presenting behavioral concerns for children so that group placement could be made to examine the effect of CCPT on differing symptoms. Children who scored at or above 70 on the externalizing problems subscale, the clinical cut-off score according to Achenbach and Rescorla (2001), but scored below 70 on the internalizing problems subscale were categorized as externalizing group. Children who scored at or above 70 on the internalizing problems subscale but scored below 70 on the externalizing subscale were categorized as internalizing group. Participants who scored at or above 70 on both externalizing and internalizing subscales were categorized as combined group. Children who scored below 70 on both subscales were categorized as a nonclinical group. The CBCL was administered before play therapy and used only to categorize participants to establish comparison groups. Post-testing on the CBCL was not conducted.

The two main purposes of this study were to explore the effect of CCPT on parent-child relationship stress when children are divided by behavioral problem groups and the effect of CCPT on parent-child relationship stress according to length of treatment. This study involved two hypotheses. Hypothesis 1: From pre-test to post-test, children identified as externalizing, internalizing, combined, and nonclinical types who participated in CCPT will demonstrate statistically significant differences in the improvement of parent-child relationship stress as demonstrated by total stress, child domain, and parent domain scores on the PSI. Hypothesis 2: From pre-test to post-test, children who participated in CCPT for different lengths of therapy will demonstrate statistically significant differences in the improvement of parent-child relationship stress as demonstrated by total stress, child domain, and parent domain scores on the PSI.

RESULTS

The following results apply to the behaviorally differentiated data analyses group, including externalizing, internalizing, combined externalizing and internalizing, and nonclinical.

PSI Total Stress Results of the ANOVA on total stress revealed a statistically significant main effect for time, $F(1, 195) = 13.20, p <. 001$ (partial $\eta^2 = .06$); a statistically significant main effect for group, $F(3, 195) = 17.24, p < .001$ (partial $\eta^2 = .21$); and no statistical significance for interaction effect, $F(3, 195) = .24, p = .87$ (partial $\eta^2 = .004$). Post hoc paired samples *t*-tests were conducted for each behavioral group. To help address the risk of an inflated experiment-wise Type I error, the alpha level employed for the post hoc analyses was .025 (Armstrong & Henson, 2005). These analyses indicated improvement for all four groups, with statistically significant gains for the externalizing and nonclinical groups, with $t(36) = 2.64, p = .01$ and $t(90) = 2.33, p = .02$, respectively. The effect for the externalizing group was large ($\eta^2 = .16$) according to Cohen's (1988) guidelines (.01 = small, .06 = moderate, .14 = large). The effect for the nonclinical group was moderate ($\eta^2 = .05$).

The internalizing group did not demonstrate statistical significance, $t(23) = 1.52, p = .14$; this group demonstrated a moderate-to-large effect size, however ($\eta^2 = .09$). Finally, the combined group did not demonstrate statistical significance, $t(46) = 1.38, p = .18$; yet this group also demonstrated a small-to-moderate effect size of $\eta^2 = .04$.

PSI Child Domain Results of the ANOVA on the child domain revealed a statistically significant main effect for time, $F(1, 197) = 13.84, p < .001$ (partial $\eta^2 = .07$); a statistically significant main effect for group, $F(3, 197) = 26.32, p < .001$ (partial $\eta^2 = .29$); and no statistical significance for interaction effect, $F(3, 197) = 1.59, p = .19$ (partial $\eta^2 = .02$). Post hoc paired samples *t*-tests were conducted for each behavioral group. These analyses indicated improvement for all four groups, with statistically significant gains for the externalizing and combined groups, with $t(36) = 2.44, p = .02$ and $t(46) = 2.96, p = .005$, respectively. The effect for the externalizing group was large ($\eta^2 = .14$), while the effect for the combined group was small ($\eta^2 = .03$).

PSI Parent Domain Results of the ANOVA on parent domain did not reveal a statistically significant main effect for time, $F(1, 195) = 3.54, p = .06$ (partial $\eta^2 = .02$); or a statistically significant interaction effect, $F(3, 195) = .78, p = .50$ (partial $\eta^2 = .01$). ANOVA revealed a significant main effect for group, $F(3, 195) = 4.49, p = .005$ (partial $\eta^2 = .07$). Post hoc paired samples *t*-tests were conducted for each behavioral group and revealed that all four groups improved from pre-test to post-test, although none of the four groups showed significant gains.

The following results apply to the length of treatment analyses in which data were divided into four groups: 3 to 7 sessions, 8 to 10 sessions, 11 to 18 sessions, and 19 to 74 sessions.

PSI Total Stress   Results of the ANOVA on total stress revealed a statistically significant main effect for time, $F(1, 194) = 12.75$, $p < .001$ (partial $\eta^2 = .06$); and a statistically significant interaction effect, $F(3, 194) = 4.53$, $p = .004$ (partial $\eta^2 = .07$). There was no statistically significant difference between groups, $F(3, 194) = 1.86$, $p = .14$ (partial $\eta^2 = .03$).

Post hoc paired samples *t*-tests were conducted for each session number group. These analyses indicated differences in improvement across session number groups. Session number group 3 to 7 demonstrated an increase in scores from pre-test to post-test with a negative t score of $t(44) = -.71$, $p = .48$. Session number group 8 to 10 demonstrated a decrease in scores from pre-test to post-test but did not reach significance, $t(44) = .1.01$, $p = .32$. Session number group 11 to 18 demonstrated a statistically significant decrease in scores on total stress from pre-test to post-test, $t(56) = 3.13$, $p = .003$, with a large effect size ($\eta^2 = .15$). Session number group 19 to 74 also demonstrated a statistically significant decrease in scores on total stress from pre-test to post-test, $t(50) = 3.77$, $p < .001$, with a large effect size ($\eta^2 = .22$).

PSI Child Domain   Results of the ANOVA on child domain revealed a statistically significant main effect for time, $F(1, 196) = 12.70$, $p < .001$ (partial $\eta^2 = .06$); and statistical significance for interaction effect, $F(3, 196) = 3.92$, $p = .01$ (partial $\eta^2 = .06$). There was not a statistically significant main effect for group, $F(3, 196) = .55$, $p = .65$ (partial $\eta^2 = .01$). Post hoc paired samples *t*-tests were conducted for each session number group. Findings on each group mirrored results on the total stress session number group analysis. Session number group 3 to 7 demonstrated an increase in scores from pre-test to post-test with a negative t score of $t(44) = -.19$, $p = .85$. Session number group 8 to 10 demonstrated a decrease in scores from pre-test to post-test but did not reach statistical significance, $t(46) = .77$, $p = .45$. Session number group 11 to 18 demonstrated a statistically significant decrease in scores on the child domain from pre-test to post-test, $t(56) = 2.71$, $p = .009$, with an approximate large effect size ($\eta^2 = .12$). Session number group 19 to 74 demonstrated a significant decrease in scores on the child domain from pre-test to post-test, $t(50) = 3.61$, $p = .001$, with a very large effect size ($\eta^2 = .25$).

PSI Parent Domain Results of the ANOVA on parent domain did not reveal a statistically significant main effect for time, $F(1, 194) = 2.22, p = .14$ (partial $\eta^2 = .01$); or a statistically significant main effect for group, $F(3, 194) = 2.53, p = .06$ (partial $\eta^2 = .04$); or a statistically significant interaction effect, $F(3, 194) = 1.29, p = .28$ (partial $\eta^2 = .02$). Post hoc analyses were not conducted because of a lack of significant findings.

SUMMARY

CCPT demonstrated a statistically significant general positive effect for the total stress and child domain scores of the PSI. Results confirmed that CCPT had a significant beneficial effect for children categorized with externalizing behavioral problems, combined internalizing and externalizing behavioral problems, and children whose parents sought counseling services but were not exhibiting clinical problems. Results appeared to validate that individual CCPT appears to affect the child factor of the parent-child relationship, which subsequently positively affects the total stress of the parent-child relationship. In contrast, CCPT appeared to have little impact on the parent characteristics of the parent-child relationship. The results of this study also revealed that upon the completion of 3 to 7 sessions of play therapy, mean scores worsened because of child behavior. Yet, demonstrative beneficial effects began from 8 to 10 sessions, with statistically significant results demonstrated from 11 sessions and beyond.

STUDY 2: TWO COUNSELING INTERVENTIONS TO REDUCE TEACHER-CHILD RELATIONSHIP STRESS

PARTICIPANTS

Teachers from three low-income schools referred children who demonstrated emotional and behavioral difficulties in the classroom (study originally published in Ray, 2007). A total of 93 students and 59 teachers were randomly assigned to one of three treatment groups. Students were between pre-kindergarten and fifth grade with 68 males and 25 females. Student ethnicity breakdowns were as follows: 12 African Americans, 38 Hispanics, 39 Caucasians, and 4 biracial.

INSTRUMENTS

Index of Teaching Stress The purpose of the Index of Teaching Stress (ITS; Abidin, Greene, & Konold, 2004) is to measure stress that a teacher experiences in the relationship with a specific student. The ITS recognizes the independent factors that correlate highly with the quality of the teacher-child relationship, including behavioral characteristics of the student, the teacher's perception of the teaching process, and the teacher's perception of support from others who interact with the child. The ITS includes 90 Likert-scale items and is standardized for use with teachers of students in preschool through twelfth grade. ITS produces a total stress score and three domain scores, consisting of attention deficit hyperactivity disorder, student characteristics, and teacher characteristics. The attention deficit hyperactivity disorder domain measures the teacher's stress level associated with the child's behaviors that are commonly associated with ADHD. The student characteristics domain measures the teacher's stress related to the student's temperament and behaviors. The teacher characteristics domain measures the teacher's stress as related to self-perception and expectation regarding teaching the particular student. The total stress score is a sum of the three domain scores. (Abidin et al., 2004).

PROCEDURES

Once informed consents and pre-testing ITS data were obtained, children were randomly assigned to one of three treatment groups. Treatment conditions included a play therapy–only condition (PT), which consisted of 16 sessions of play therapy over eight weeks. Each student received two sessions per week of 30-minute individual CCPT sessions. The second condition was a consultation-only group (CO), which consisted of eight consultation sessions with a counselor consultant. Each teacher of the assigned students received 10 minutes of person-centered consulting per week over the eight weeks, totaling eight sessions. The third condition was a combined play therapy and consultation treatment group (PTC). All consultants had completed a master's program in counseling or psychology. Students assigned to this group received two sessions per week of 30-minute CCPT sessions totaling 16 sessions. Teachers of students assigned to this condition received 10-minute consultation sessions each week for eight weeks, totaling eight sessions. At the end of condition length, teachers completed ITS data.

RESULTS

ITS Total Stress   Results of the ANOVA on total stress revealed a statistically significant main effect for time, $F(1, 90) = 20.16$, $p < .01$

(partial $\eta^2 = .18$); no statistically significant main effect for group, $F(2, 90) = .40$, $p = .67$ (partial $\eta^2 = .01$); and no statistically significant interaction effect, $F(2, 90) = .68$, $p = .51$ (partial $\eta^2 = .02$). Because the change was fairly consistent across all three groups, the interaction effect was negligible. The effect size of .18 as the main effect for time indicates a large effect size, according to Cohen's (1988) guidelines. There was no significant difference between groups; hence, no further simple effects analysis was necessary.

ITS ADHD Domain   Results of the ANOVA on the ADHD domain revealed a statistically significant main effect for time, $F(1, 90) = 24.27$, $p < .01$ (partial $\eta^2 = .21$); no statistically main effect for group, $F(2, 90) = .30$, $p = .74$ (partial $\eta^2 = .01$); and no statistical significance for interaction effect, $F(2, 90) = 2.67$, $p = .08$ (partial $\eta^2 = .06$). Again, the effect size for main effect for time (.21) was in the large category.

ITS Student Characteristics Domain   Results of the ANOVA on the student characteristics domain revealed a statistically significant main effect for time $F(1, 90) = 17.97$, $p < .01$ (partial $\eta^2 = .17$); no statistically main effect for group, $F(2, 90) = 1.82$, $p = .17$ (partial $\eta^2 = .04$); and no statistical significance for interaction effect, $F(2, 90) = 1.00$, $p = .37$ (partial $\eta^2 = .02$). The effect size for main effect for time (.17) was in the large category.

ITS Teacher Characteristics Domain   Results of the ANOVA for the teacher characteristics domain revealed a statistically significant main effect for time $F(1, 90) = 11.41$, $p = .01$ (partial $\eta^2 = .11$); no statistically significant main effect for group, $F(2, 90) = .42$, $p = .66$ (partial $\eta^2 = .01$); and no statistically significant interaction effect, $F(2, 90) = .23$, $p = .79$ (partial $\eta^2 = .01$). The effect size for main effect for time (.13) was in the moderate category.

SUMMARY

The three treatment groups, PT, CO, and PTC all yielded statistically significant reductions in teacher stress response to student characteristics, student behaviors associated with ADHD, and teacher characteristics. Results produced a large effect size for three of the scores: total stress, ADHD, and student characteristics, indicating practical significance of the findings. Play therapy and consultation, alone and combined, appeared to positively affect the teacher-child relationship. There was no statistical difference between groups, signifying that the treatments had a statistically equal effect on teacher-child relation-ship stress. However, statistical differences were noted across time, which could indicate that the passage of time alone was a possible variable in determining significant change. Alternately, the design of the current study was based on previous literature that a play therapy intervention yields a large positive effect over no intervention (Bratton, Ray, Rhine, & Jones, 2005).

STUDY 3: EFFECT OF SHORT- AND LONG-TERM PLAY THERAPY SERVICES ON TEACHER-CHILD RELATIONSHIP STRESS

PARTICIPANTS

Teachers from four low-income elementary schools referred students who demonstrated emotional and behavioral difficulties in the class-room, such as emotional outbursts, disruptive or aggressive behaviors, extreme moodiness, or constant verbal or behavioral interruptions (study originally published in Ray, Henson, Schottelkorb, Brown, & Muro, 2008). A total of 58 students from pre-kindergarten to fifth grade were assigned to one of two treatment groups. Gender and ethnicity breakdowns were: 40 male, 18 female; 4 African American, 24 Hispanic, 26 white, 4 biracial.

INSTRUMENTS

Index of Teaching Stress   Description of the ITS (Abidin et al., 2004) was provided in the previous summary.

PROCEDURES

Once informed consents and pre-testing ITS data were obtained, children were randomly assigned to one of two treatment groups. Children assigned to the short-term group (ST) participated in 16 sessions of CCPT over eight weeks. They received two sessions per week of 30-minute individual CCPT sessions. Children assigned to the long-term group (LT) participated in 16 sessions of CCPT over 16 to 20 weeks. The LT students received 30 minutes of individual CCPT once per week. Teachers completed an ITS at the end of each condition.

RESULTS

ITS Total Stress   Results of the between-within subjects ANOVA on total stress revealed a statistically significant main effect for time, $F(1, 56) = .927$, $p = .04$ (partial $\eta^2 = .07$); no statistically significant main effect for group, $F(1, 56) = .09$, $p = .77$ (partial $\eta^2 < .01$); and no statistically significant interaction effect, $F(1, 56) = .95$, $p = .10$ (partial $\eta^2 = .05$). Results demonstrated an average decrease in scores for both groups. The eight-week group also demonstrated greater average improvement. Although this interaction effect was not statistically significant, it did yield a moderate effect size, which may be of practical significance (see, for example, Cohen, 1994; Henson, 2006; Thompson, 2002). In this study, both the main effect for time and the interaction yielded effects in the moderate range, although only the former was statistically significant.

Given the moderate effect noted for the interaction, a post hoc paired samples t-test was conducted for each group on pre- and post-test scores of ITS total stress. Using a reduced alpha to help control for Type I error, these analyses indicated a statistically significant improvement for the ST intensive play therapy group ($t(25) = 3.21$, $p < .01$). The effect size for the ST group was in the large category ($\eta^2 = .29$) according to Cohen's (1988) guidelines. The LT group did not demonstrate statistical significance ($t(31) = .28$, $p = .78$) and had a very small effect size ($\eta^2 < .01$). The statistically significant time effect observed was primarily due to the reduction in scores in the ST group, although the differences between the ST and LT groups were not dramatic enough to yield a statistically significant interaction.

ITS ADHD Domain   Results of the combined between-within subjects ANOVA on the ADHD domain revealed no statistically significant main effect for time, $F(1, 56) = .96$, $p = .16$ (partial $\eta^2 = .04$); no statistically significant main effect for group, $F(1, 56) = .18$, $p = .68$ (partial $\eta^2 < .01$); and no statistically significant interaction effect, $F(1, 56) = .99$, $p = .72$ (partial $\eta^2 < .01$). The effect sizes for time, between groups, and interaction of groups were all in the small range.

The post hoc paired samples t-tests confirmed that there was little improvement for either the ST ($t(25) = 1.22$, $p = .23$, $\eta^2 = .05$) or the LT group ($t(31) = .80$, $p = .43$, $\eta^2 = .02$). The effect sizes for both groups were generally small and not substantial enough to warrant interpretation. These results suggest that the gains noted in the total stress scores come primarily from the student characteristics and teacher characteristics domains.

ITS Student Characteristics   Results of the combined between-within subjects ANOVA on the student characteristics domain revealed a statistically significant improvement for time, $F(1, 56) = .90$, $p = .02$ (partial $\eta^2 = .10$); no statistically significant main effect for group, $F(1,$

56) $= .05$, $p = .83$ (partial $\eta^2 < .01$); and no statistically significant interaction effect, $F(1, 56) = .99$, $p = .38$ (partial $\eta^2 = .01$). The effect size of .10 as main effect for time indicates a moderate-to-large effect size, although in this case, the effect for the interaction was small.

Post hoc paired samples t-tests were conducted for each group on pre- and post-test scores of ITS student characteristics domain so they could clarify the time effect noted. The ST intensive play therapy group decreased from pre- to post-test ($t(25) = 3.34$, $p < .01$) with a substantial effect ($\eta^2 = .31$). The LT group did not demonstrate statistical significance ($t(31) = .99$, $p = .33$) and had a small effect size ($\eta^2 = .03$). Again, the time effect observed is mainly due to the improvement in the ST group, although the group differences across time were not large.

ITS Teacher Characteristics Results of the combined between-within subjects ANOVA on teacher characteristics domain revealed no statistically significant main effect for time, $F(1, 56) = .98$, $p = .30$ (partial $\eta^2 = .02$); no statistically significant main effect for group, $F(1, 56) = .02$, $p = .89$ (partial $\eta^2 < .01$); and no statistically significant interaction effect, $F(1, 56) = .94$, $p = .06$ (partial $\eta^2 = .06$). The effect size for time and group was in the small range. The interaction effect size was interpreted in the moderate range.

Post hoc paired samples t-tests indicated statistically significant improvement for the ST group with a large effect ($t(25) = 2.32$, $p = .02$, $\eta^2 = .17$) and a small increase in problems with no statistical significance for the LT group ($t(31) = -.62$, $p = .54$, $\eta^2 = .01$).

SUMMARY

Both interventions resulted in a statistically significant effect across time from pre-test to post-test, with no statistically significant difference between interventions. When looking specifically at short-term intensive treatment in post hoc analysis, the ST intensive treatment group demonstrated statistically significant reductions with large effect sizes for overall teacher-child relationship stress, child characteristics, and teacher characteristics. Long-term treatment yielded a reduction in overall teacher-child relationship stress, child characteristics, and ADHD, but not to a level of statistical significance found in post hoc analyses and with smaller effect sizes. This study explored the format of providing CCPT in a school environment, and it lends preliminary support for short-term intensive CCPT as equally effective to long-term

CCPT in reducing teacher-child relationship stress, with some strong indications that short-term CCPT may be more effective.

DISCUSSION

The original research agenda motivating these studies was the question, "When adults are unavailable for counseling, can a child-only intervention help with behavior and improve a child's relationships with adults?" Each of the three studies outlined in this chapter emphasized an individually oriented approach to intervention, namely individual CCPT. In all three studies, adults reported that child behavior improved and relationship stress decreased. The findings of these studies align with the anecdotal evidence presented in the case study. In that example, individual CCPT was also employed, and the caregiver reported improved child behavior as well as enhanced adult-child relationships.

CCPT is designed to foster self-direction, growth, and integration (Bratton, Ray, & Landreth, 2008). A major premise is that a child's behavior is an outworking of self-concept. Therefore, children learn during CCPT to develop a more positive view of self and increase self-responsibility and self-acceptance (Landreth, 2002). The child is provided with the freedom to make choices and be responsible for those choices. As self-concept improves and self-control develops, the child is able to transfer this growth from the therapeutic setting to the outside world. This includes interactions with significant adults, such as parents and teachers.

In CCPT, the therapist recognizes the important role that parents and teachers play in children's lives and therefore aims to maintain regular parent-teacher consultations. These meetings allow the play therapist to continue to build a relationship with parents and teachers, provide additional support, and receive updates on the child's progress at home and school. Parents and teachers, however, are often unwilling or unable to participate in the play therapy process. This precludes adult-specific interventions, and the individual CCPT sessions become the basis for treatment.

This chapter has provided some evidence that CCPT appears to have a positive impact on child behavior and adult-child relationships even when there is a lack of parent-teacher involvement. This supports the reciprocity inherent in adult-child relationships. As mentioned, child behavior, adult behavior, and perceived relationship quality interact and continually affect each of these relationship components. The research and anecdotal data suggest that even when parent and teacher consultations are not possible, CCPT creates an environment in which children can experience self-direction, self-acceptance, and integration. They can then transfer new learning from the therapeutic context to their relationships with adults.

REFERENCES

Abidin, R. R. (1995). *Parenting stress index* (3rd ed.). Lutz, FL: Psychological Assessment Resources.

Abidin, R. R., Greene, R., & Konold, T. (2004). *Index of teaching stress: Professional manual*. Lutz, FL: Psychological Assessment Resources.

Abidin, R. R., Jenkins, C., & McGaughey, M. (1992). The relationship of early family variables to children's subsequent behavioral adjustment. *Journal of Clinical Child Psychology, 21,* 60–69.

Achenbach, T. M. (1991). *Manual for the child behavior checklist: 4–18 and 1991 profile*. Burlington, VT: University of Vermont Department of Psychiatry.

Achenbach, T. M., & Rescorla, L. A. (2000). *Manual for the ASEBA preschool forms and profiles*. Burlington, VT: University of Vermont, Research Center for Children, Youth, & Families.

Achenbach, T. M., & Rescorla, L. A. (2001). *Manual for the ASEBA school-age forms and profiles*. Burlington, VT: University of Vermont, Research Center for Children, Youth, & Families.

Ackerman, B., Brown, E., & Izard, C. (2003). Continuity and change in levels of externalizing behavior in school of children from economically disadvantaged families. *Child Development, 74,* 694–709.

Armstrong, S., & Henson, R. (2005). Statistical practices of IJPT researchers: A review from 1993–2000. *International Journal of Play Therapy, 14*(1), 7–26.

Boutelle, K., Eisenberg, M., Gregory, M., & Neumark-Sztainer, D. (2009). The reciprocal relationship between parent-child connectedness and adolescent emotional functioning over 5 years. *Journal of Psychosomatic Research, 66,* 309–316.

Bratton, S. C., Ray, D. C., & Landreth, G. L. (2008). Play therapy. In M. Hersen & A. Gross (Eds.), *Handbook of clinical psychology, Vol. II: Children and adolescents*. Hoboken, NJ: John Wiley & Sons.

Bratton, S. C., Ray, D. C., Rhine, T., & Jones, L. (2005). The efficacy of play therapy with children: A meta-analytic review of treatment outcomes. *Professional Psychology: Research and Practice, 36,* 376–390.

Cohen, J. (1988). *Statistical power analysis for the behavioral sciences* (2nd ed.). Hillside, NJ: Erlbaum.

Cohen, J. (1994). The earth is round (p < .05). *American Psychologist, 49,* 997–1003.

Deater-Deckard, K. (1998). Parenting stress and child adjustment: Some old hypotheses and new questions. *Clinical Psychology: Science & Practice, 5,* 314–332.

Deater-Deckard, K. (2005). Parenting stress and children's development: Introduction to the special issue. *Infant and Child Development, 14,* 111–115.

Hamre, B., & Pianta, R. (2001). Early teacher-child relationships and the trajectory of children's school outcomes through eighth grade. *Child Development, 72,* 625–638.

Henson, R. K. (2006). Effect size measures and meta-analytic thinking in counseling psychology research. *The Counseling Psychologist, 34,* 601–629.

Herber, K. (1998). Single mothers, stress, and perception of their child's behavior (Doctoral dissertation, Oklahoma State University, 1997). *Dissertation Abstracts International, 58*/08, 4523.

Hughes, J., Cavell, T., & Jackson, T. (1999). Influence of the teacher-student relationship on childhood conduct problems: A prospective study. *Journal of Clinical Child Psychology, 28,* 173–184.

Ladd, G., & Burgess, K. (2001). Do relational risks and protective factors moderate the linkages between childhood aggression and early psychological and school adjustment? *Child Development, 72,* 1579–1601.

Landreth, G. L. (2002). *Play therapy: The art of the relationship* (2nd ed.). New York: Brunner-Routledge.

Murray, C. (2009). Parent and teacher relationships as predictors of school engagement and functioning among low-income urban youth. *Journal of Early Adolescence, 29*(3), 376–404.

Pianta, R., Steinberg, M., & Rollins, K. (1995). The first two years of school: Teacher-child relationships and deflections in children's classroom adjustment. *Development and Psychopathology, 7,* 295–312.

Pianta, R., & Stuhlman, M. (2004). Teacher-child relationships and children's success in the first years of school. *School Psychology Review, 33,* 444–458.

Ray, D. C. (2007). Two counseling interventions to reduce teacher-child relationship stress. *Professional School Counseling, 10*(4), 428–440.

Ray, D. C. (2008). Impact of play therapy on parent-child relationship stress at a mental health training setting. *British Journal of Guidance & Counselling, 36*(2), 165–187.

Ray, D. C. (2009). *Child-centered play therapy treatment manual.* Royal Oak, MI: Self-Esteem Shop.

Ray, D. C., Henson, R., Schottelkorb, A., Brown, A., & Muro, J. (2008). Effect of short- and long-term play therapy services on teacher-child relationship stress. *Psychology in the Schools, 45*(10), 994–1009.

Thompson, B. (2002). What future quantitative social science research could look like: Confidence intervals for effect sizes. *Educational Researcher, 31*(3), 25–32.

CHAPTER 7

Impact of School-Based Child-Centered Play Therapy on Academic Achievement, Self-Concept, and Teacher-Child Relationships

PEDRO J. BLANCO

OR THE PAST several years I have had the opportunity to work both as a school-based play therapist and as a counselor within an agency. While both have advantages and disadvantages, I found myself drawn to the children within the schools I served. I often met with children who did not have any source of support, guidance, or nurturance outside of the school setting. As the summer approached each year, I referred many of these children to continue receiving services, only to find that counseling was not often a priority of the child's family. It is with this realization that I concluded that for many of these lost children, the services at school were their saving grace. This led me in my attempt to find an avenue that could support these children who needed developmentally appropriate emotional support.

Lacking emotional support, many of these children continued to struggle to meet academic milestones. I discovered the priority of schools was to educate all attending students. However, if schools are expected to meet academic needs of all students, then they must also address emotional needs of all students. It is in this way the interdependent relationship between the child's emotional needs and his academic performance can be fully realized. Literature confirms that development of a child's understanding of emotions can improve academic achievement (Zins, Wessberg, Wang, & Walberg, 2004). Because of a strong correlation between emotional development and academic success, development of a solid mental health program within the school is necessary to help promote academic achievement (New Freedom Commission on Mental Health, 2003).

The purpose of this study was to concentrate improving academic progress by using a mental health program intended to address the developmental needs of children. Specific mental health components have been correlated with academic progress, including self-concept and student-teacher relationship. Children who develop a higher self-concept have been found to have more fulfilling personal relationships, a lower incidence of problem behaviors, and an increase in their academic achievement (Elias et al., 1997). Other authors suggested a developed self-concept is necessary for children to succeed academically (Romasz, Kantor, & Elias, 2004). Research has also found the quality of the student-teacher relationship affects children's social, emotional, and academic development (Greene, Abidin, & Kmetz, 1997; Hamre & Pianta, 2001; Ladd & Burgess, 2001; Pianta & Stuhlman, 2004).

Child-centered play therapy (CCPT) is one possibility for providing a mental health program in public schools. Use of play in therapy allows school-age children to naturally express emotions and experiences (Moustakas, 1959; Landreth, 2002). Meta-analytic results provided empirical evidence demonstrating the effectiveness of play therapy with children, revealing that play therapy offers increased support for children's emotional health (Bratton, Ray, Rhine, & Jones, 2005). Children who received CCPT have demonstrated improved self-confidence, development of positive interpersonal relationships, and an increased sense of autonomy (Brandt, 1999; Newcomer & Morrison, 1974; Post, 1999; Quayle, 1991; Ray, 2007; Shmukler & Naveh, 1985). These studies revealed play therapy may help foster self-concept and adult-child relationships in school-age children. Landreth (2002) suggested that because of the unique relationship established in CCPT, the child perceives the playroom and the therapist as safe; the therapist in the playroom will accept and reflect the child's emotional expressions, thereby allowing the child to become more empowered and accepting of herself.

METHOD

PARTICIPANTS

Participants consisted of first-grade children identified as at risk by state standards and within four low-income elementary schools. To participate in the study, children needed to meet the following criteria:

- The student must be in first grade.
- The student must be younger than eight years old for the duration of the study.
- The student must be labeled as at risk by the school district.
- The student has parental or guardian consent.
- The student agrees to participate in the study.
- The student is fluent in the English language.
- The student's parent or guardian can consent to participation in the study.
- The student's teacher agrees to participate in the study.
- The student is not receiving play therapy or counseling anywhere else during the duration of the study.

Participating schools identified and tracked progress of students labeled as at risk according to district criteria. The school counselors contacted the parents of each child who were labeled as at risk and informed them of the study and obtained informed consent. Upon gaining informed consent, the researcher then contacted teachers of the participating children to gain informed consent for their participation.

Qualified participants (n = 43) were randomly assigned by school site to the experimental group (n = 21) or the no-treatment wait-list control group (n = 22). In School 1, the parents of 14 first-grade students identified as academically at risk provided consent for treatment. One of these students (placed in the experimental group) moved to School 3 and was provided services at her new school. Because there were different teachers, no teacher data were recorded for this child. In School 2, the parents of eight first-grade students identified as academically at risk consented to treatment. For School 3, 10 students made up the participants. In School 4, the parents of 11 first-grade students identified as academically at risk provided consent for treatment. Two of these students, both from the control group, dropped out of the study. One student in foster care was placed in another foster home, and the other student was placed in an alternative education program for disruptive behavior. Their data are not included in the results or demographics of this study.

Participants were administered the Young Children's Achievement Test (YCAT) and the Pictorial Scale of Perceived Competence and Social Acceptance for Young Children (PSPCSAYC). Both of these instruments were proctored by doctoral-level counseling students during the school day at each identified school. Teachers were asked to complete the Student-Teacher Relationship Scale (STRS) for each identified child. These administered instruments served as the pre-test battery for all subjects before the start of the play therapy sessions. Children who completed all instruments were randomly assigned to the experimental or the control group.

Instruments

The Young Children's Achievement Test (YCAT; Hresko, Peak, Herron, & Bridges, 2000) is a comprehensive assessment that measures early academic achievement levels and can be used to monitor the student's progress. The YCAT assesses an overall achievement score in academic areas from the combination of five subtests. The results from the five subtests make up the child's early achievement composite. This composite scale reflects the child's school-related achievement across the major areas of academic tasks. Hresko, Peak, Herron, and Bridges (2000) further indicated the *early achievement composite* is the best indicator of the child's overall academic abilities.

The Pictorial Scale of Perceived Competence and Social Acceptance for Young Children (PSPCSAYC; Harter and Pike, 1984) measures a child's perceived competence and perceived social acceptance among four domains. The PSPCSAYC can be used as a guide to monitor the child's perception of self over time. Although not indicated in the manual, previous research summed and averaged each subscale to create a global self-concept score that is used in data analysis (Jerome, Fujiki, Brinton, & James, 2002; Wright, Boschen, & Jutai, 2005).

The Student-Teacher Relationship Scale (STRS; Pianta, 2001) measures teachers' perceptions of their relationships with young students aged four to eight among three domains. The STRS is a short assessment that accurately assesses the student-teacher relationship and is often used as a preventative measure. The STRS also can be used to monitor the student-teacher relationship over different intervals. The STRS assesses the overall perception of the teacher's relationship with his student from the combination of three subtests and measures the degree to which the teacher perceives his relationship with a particular student as positive and effective. The combination score is referred to as the *total scale*, an overall score, and is the best indicator of measurement of the Student-Teacher Relationship Scale (STRS).

PROCEDURES

After testing was completed, each subject in the experimental group received two 30-minute individual child-centered play therapy sessions per week for a period of eight weeks. These sessions were held at the individual student's school in a fully equipped playroom and were facilitated by doctoral-level counseling students or master's level practitioners. The subjects in the wait-list control group did not receive treatment during this time. Upon completion of the play therapy sessions, the students were readministered the Young Children's Achievement Test (YCAT) and the Pictorial Scale of Perceived Competence and Social Acceptance for Young Children (PSPCSAYC) Teachers also completed the Student-Teacher Relationship Scale (STRS) at this time. These completed assessment instruments served as the post-test battery for the subjects.

EXPERIMENTAL GROUP PROCEDURES

Children placed in the experimental group completed 16 30-minute CCPT sessions based on the procedures and principles previously defined by Landreth (2002). Children entered a room in which play materials were provided to allow the child to express herself. All therapists were required to conduct treatment using CCPT principles, including both nonverbal and verbal skills outlined by Ray (2009):

- Maintaining a leaning forward, open stance
- Appearing to be interested
- Remaining comfortable
- Having a matching tone with the child's affect
- Having appropriate affect in responses
- Frequent interactive responses
- Behavior tracking responses
- Responding to verbalizations with paraphrases
- Reflecting the child's emotions
- Facilitating empowerment through returning responsibility
- Encouraging creativity

- Self-esteem boosting statements
- Relational responses

These skills are used to convey that the therapist understands the child's world, and send the message of, "I am here, I hear you, I understand, and I care" (Landreth, 2002, pp. 205–206). All therapists had completed at least 42 hours in a graduate-level counseling program, including an introduction to play therapy, an advanced play therapy course, and one clinical course in play therapy. All therapists received one hour of weekly play therapy supervision during the course of the study to ensure that each therapist was following CCPT protocol. At that time the play therapists, with their supervisors, were required to review their video-recorded play therapy sessions. The play therapist's supervisor ensured that the play therapist was following CCPT protocol through the use of the play therapy skills checklist (Ray, 2009). Furthermore, a randomized check of video recordings was conducted by the researcher and research assistants trained in CCPT to ensure that the play therapy sessions were conducted by CCPT.

DATA ANALYSIS

Following the completion of the study, the researcher and the research team scored the pre-test and post-test data by using hand scoring on the Young Children Achievement Test, the Pictorial Scale of Perceived Competence and Social Acceptance for Young Children, and the Student-Teacher Relationship Scale, according to their prospective manuals. The YCAT, PSPCSDYC, and STRS were administered before treatment and at the end of treatment. An increase in scores on the YCAT, PSPCSDYC, and STRS scales indicated improvement in the targeted measures. A two-factor repeated measures split-plot analysis of variance (SPANOVA) (time × treatment group) was performed on each dependent variable (achievement, self-concept, and student-teacher relationship) to determine if the experimental group that received 16 sessions of CCPT performed differently from the control group across time, which was a particular interest for this study.

Wilks's lambda was used to interpret results. Significant differences between the means across time were tested at the .05 alpha level. An effect size was computed for each analysis using the eta-squared statistic (η^2) to assess the practical significance of findings. Partial eta squared effect sizes were calculated to assess treatment effect and recognize the magnitude of difference attributed to treatment between the two groups and practical significance (Kazdin, 1999). Cohen's guidelines (1988) were used to interpret η^2 effect size: .01 = small, .06 = medium, and .14 = large. Only interpretations for moderate-to-large effect sizes are reported. Results for clinical significance are also reported.

RESULTS

EARLY ACHIEVEMENT COMPOSITE TOTAL SCALE OF THE YCAT

Results of a two-factor repeated measures analysis of variance indicated that the dependent variable, early achievement composite, revealed a statistically significant interaction effect of time (pre-test, post-test) x treatment group (experimental, control); [Wilks's lambda = .56, $F(1, 39) = 5.23$, $p = .03$, (partial $\eta^2 = .12$)], statistically significant main effect for time [$F(1, 39) = 30.14$, $p < .01$ (partial $\eta^2 = .44$)]; and no statistically significant main effect for group [$F(1, 39) = .10$, $p = .75$ (partial $\eta^2 < .01$)]. These results indicate that when grouped together, children in the CCPT group and the control group obtained statistically significant higher scores on the early achievement composite subscale of the YCAT from pre-test to post-test. Furthermore, results from the ANOVA interaction effect and further analysis of means indicate that the children who attended CCPT obtained a statistically significantly higher score on the early achievement composite from pre-test to post-test when compared to the control group from pre-test to post-test. The effect size of .44 for change over time indicates a large effect size, and the effect size of .12 for interaction indicates a moderate effect size according to Cohen's (1988) guidelines.

Because main effects and interaction effect were significant, a paired samples *t*-test was calculated for each treatment condition to explore group performance. Results of a paired samples *t*-test indicated that the early achievement composite for the treatment group revealed a statistically significant difference from pre-test to post-test, $t(20) = -5.07$, $p < .01$, ($\eta^2 = .56$). Results of a paired samples *t*-test demonstrated that the early achievement composite for the control group also revealed a statistically significant difference from pre-test to post-test, $t(19) = -2.53$, $p = .02$, ($\eta^2 = .25$). While both groups, treatment and control, demonstrated large effect sizes, results indicated that the treatment group had an effect size that was twice as large as the control group.

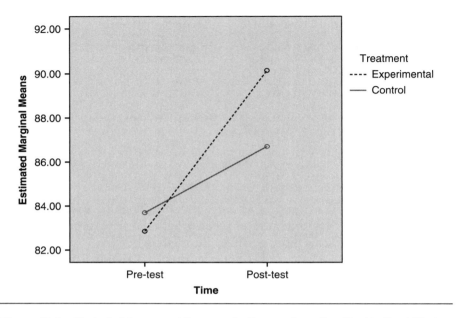

Figure 7.1   Early Achievement Composite Scores from Pre-Test to Post-Test

GLOBAL SELF-CONCEPT SCORE OF THE PSPCSAYC

Results of the split plot ANOVA indicated that the dependent variable, global self-concept, revealed no statistically significant interaction effect [Wilks's lambda = .99, $F(1, 39) = 1.21$, $p = .28$ (partial $\eta^2 = .03$)]; no statistically significant main effect for time [$F(1, 39) = .27$, $p = .62$ (partial $\eta^2 = .01$)]; and no statistically significant main effect for group [$F(1, 39) = .54$, $p = .61$ (partial $\eta^2 = .01$)].

Table 7-1

Mean Scores on the Early Achievement Composite on the Young Children's Achievement Test (YCAT)

	Experimental Group n = 21		Control Group n = 20	
	Pre-test	Post-test	Pre-test	Post-test
Mean	82.86	90.14	83.70	86.70
Standard Deviation	13.71	12.50	12.31	14.85

Note: An increase in mean scores indicates an improvement in achievement.

Table 7-2
Summary of Split-Plot Analysis of Variance for Early Achievement Composite of the YCAT According to Group Assignment

Source	df	SS	MS	F	p	partial η^2
			According to Group Assignment			
			Between Subjects			
Intercept	1	603998.72	603998.72	1777.54	<.01	.98
Group	1	34.62	34.62	.1	.75	<.01
Error 1	39	339.75	339.75			
			Within Subjects			
Time	1	541.88	541.88	30.14	<.01*	.44
Time × Group	1	94.08	94.08	5.23	.03*	.12
Error 2	39	701.43	17.99			
Total	41	653.95				

TOTAL SCORE OF THE STRS

Results of the split-plot ANOVA indicated the dependent variable, total score, revealed no statistically significant interaction effect of time (pre-test, post-test) × treatment group (experimental, control); [Wilks's lambda = .97, F(1, 39) = 1.02, p = .32, (partial η^2 = .03)]; no statistically significant main effect for time [F(1, 39) = 3.85, p = .06 (partial η^2 = .09)]; and no statistically significant main effect for group [F(1, 39) < .01, p = .97 (partial η^2 < .01)]. The effect size of .09 for change over time indicates a moderate effect size. These results indicate that the children who attended CCPT were not statistically different on the total score of the STRS from pre-test to post-test, when compared to the control group.

CLINICAL SIGNIFICANCE

Clinical significance according to Kazdin (2003) is the real-life benefit that treatment offers the client. To further explore the impact of CCPT on the improvement of academic achievement with at-risk first-graders, their individual pre and post scores for the dependent variable were examined. Specifically, clinical significance was determined by detecting the number of experimental children (n = 21) who moved from being considered at risk for academic failure at pre-test to a normal range of functioning following treatment.

ACADEMIC ACHIEVEMENT OUTCOMES

To determine clinical significance, children's early achievement composite scores (EAC) from the YCAT were examined to evaluate improvement of a child's academic achievement from pre- to post-test. As a result of the treatment, 36 percent of the 14 experimental group children (n = 5) moved from at risk of academic failure to one of normal functioning following their participation in CCPT, compared to 29 percent of the 14 in the control group (n = 4). Of the nine remaining children in the experimental group, four showed marked improvement (over 10 point increases), and three showed moderate improvement (5 point increases), whereas for the nine remaining control group children, none showed marked improvement (over 10 point increases), and one showed moderate improvement (5 point increase). Furthermore, no children from the experimental group showed moderate decline (5 or more point decrease), compared to one child in the control group. These results demonstrate the clinical significance of CCPT on improving academic achievement with first-grade at-risk children.

SELF-CONCEPT OUTCOMES

To determine clinical significance, children's global self-concept scores (GSC) from the PSPCSAYC were examined to evaluate the improvement of a child's self-concept from pre- to post-test. GSC scores below two are considered to be low self-concept, while scores between three and four are considered to be high self-concept. Scores in between two and three are considered to be at the normal range (Harter & Pike, 1984). For the control group (n = 20), a total of 14 identified as having a high self-concept, 5 were in the normal range, and 1 was at the low range at pre-test. At post-test, 15 children identified as having a high self-concept, 4 were in the normal range, and 1 was at the low range. Similar findings were also found for the experimental group. At pre-test, 15 of the experimental group children (n = 21) identified as having a high self-concept, and the remaining 6 were in the normal range. No change was observed at post-test because all children remained in the same range.

STUDENT-TEACHER RELATIONSHIP OUTCOMES

To determine clinical significance, children's total scale scores from the STRS were examined to evaluate improvement of student-teacher relationship from pre- to post-test. Total scale score percentiles below

25 indicate significant low levels of a positive relationship (Pianta, 2001). Following the study, 33 percent of the 12 experimental group children (n = 4) moved from a significantly low level of a positive relationship with their teacher to one of normal functioning following their participation in CCPT, compared to 11 percent of the 9 in the control group (n = 1). These results demonstrate the clinical significance CCPT may have on improving student-teacher relationships with first-grade at-risk children.

Case Study

The following case study is presented so as to further highlight the process behind the use of CCPT and its effect on academic achievement. Billy was a six-year-old first-grade Caucasian male who was labeled at risk because he had not performed satisfactorily on a readiness test at the beginning of first grade. He was randomly selected to be a participant in the experimental group. Upon meeting Billy, his teacher asked to speak to me in the hallway. Billy's teacher informed me in the hallway that Billy often appeared unmotivated, distracted in the classroom, and frequently failed to complete assignments. After listening to his teacher's concerns, I met Billy, introduced myself, and invited him to the playroom. He was initially very quiet and hesitant in the playroom, slowly, cautiously, walking around exploring the room.

In the early stages of the therapeutic relationship, I attempted to establish a safe place for Billy to express himself. In all of my early interactions with Billy, he appeared solemn and void of emotion and often had difficulty being engaged in focused play, as if he were hesitant to make a full-hearted effort. Billy appeared to be a boy who for some reason was fearful of trusting himself and his abilities.

As treatment progressed, Billy began to engage in long sequences of soothing play. He preferred to slowly run his hands through the sandbox, run small cars through the sandbox, or paint lines of different colors. He still remained very quiet in the playroom, making only short responses to my reflections, such as ''Uh, huh'' and ''Yeah.'' Until one day, while he was running the cars

(continued)

through the sandbox, he turned to me and told me that his father lived in a different city. I responded with a reflection of feeling, "You really miss him." He shrugged his shoulders, a common physical movement for him, and quietly went back to the sandbox. He later verbalized that he wished he could see him more. I responded, "You think about him a lot and want to see him." This sharing became the catalyst for Billy in the playroom. After being free to express his emotions of fear and sadness in an accepting environment, it appeared that Billy became open to exploring his strengths and weakness. At the end of the session, he requested to run to the door of the school. (Our playroom was located in a portable room adjacent to the school.) It was at that moment that I saw Billy smile.

After that session, running to and from the playroom, each time faster than the previous, became a pattern until the end of the study. In session, Billy began to try different things out in the playroom. He created castles out of blocks, he played musical instruments, dressed up as the sheriff and arrested Bobo (bop bag), threw darts at the dartboard, and bowled. Billy appeared eager to go to the playroom and highly engaged in his mastery-like play. He appeared more confident in his abilities in the playroom and more comfortable with himself.

Upon termination, Billy's teacher reported that his academic performance and previous difficulties had improved. Before intervention, at pre-test, Billy was scored at 70 (the poor range for academic success) on early achievement composite of the YCAT, indicating that he was well below his peers and the likelihood of him completing first grade without assistance was slim. At post-test, he scored at 93 (the average range for academic success), placing him at level with his peers in academic performance. Both the self-concept and student-teacher relationship instruments used in this study yielded no change for Billy.

DISCUSSION

This study investigated the effectiveness of CCPT on at-risk first-grade students' academic achievement, self-concept, and student-teacher relationships. Specifically, this study examined the effect of CCPT treatment on increasing the child's early achievement composite as measured by the YCAT, the global self-concept scale of the PSPCSDYC, and the total scale of the STRS. Treatment outcomes for children's early achievement composite for the YCAT and global self-concept score for the PSPCSDYC were measured by child performance and self-report. The total scale outcomes on the STRS were measured through the teachers' reports of their relationship with the identified child. A total of 41 identified students completed the study. Of the three dependent variables, one was reported at the .05 level of significance, indicating an improvement in academic achievement with the experimental group when compared to a wait-list control group. Effect sizes indicated very large improvement on academic achievement for children participants in play therapy over children in a control group. Analysis of clinical significance also revealed favorable effect of play therapy on academic achievement and the student-teacher relationship. No differences were found for self-concept.

ACADEMIC ACHIEVEMENT

Results of this study help to highlight the benefit of CCPT with students at risk of academic failure. As previously reported, the YCAT assesses the early academic achievement levels of young children by the use of an overall achievement score identified as the early achievement composite, the best indicator of the child's overall academic abilities (Hresko et al., 2000).

Results indicated that from pre-test to post-test, students who participated in the CCPT treatment group scored statistically significantly higher ($p < .05$) on the early achievement composite of the YCAT when compared to students who were placed on a wait-list no-treatment control group. In post hoc analyses, the treatment effect size for the CCPT intervention was twice as large as the control for the early achievement composite, indicating the practical significance of the study's findings. Based on the mean scores from pre-test to post-test on the early achievement composite, the experimental group had a 7.28-point increase in their mean score compared to a 3 point increase for the control group. Helpful clinical significance of findings for CCPT treatment indicates that 36 percent of the children improved from at risk of academic failure to one of normal functioning following their participation of CCPT. These results provide a foundation for future controlled studies measuring the impact CCPT may have on academic achievement. Although is it noted that both groups improved over time, children participating in play therapy demonstrated statistically significant improvement over children in the control group.

As early as Axline (1947), implications for education using basic principles of CCPT have been made. She suggested children cannot be productive students while in the midst of emotional turmoil. Several of the eight basic principles developed by Axline are further outlined to explore their possible impact on lifting emotional barriers so children become more available to learn. Principles such as accepting the child for who he is at the current moment and recognizing the child's feelings may contribute to learning. By displaying this acceptance, children are free of expectations placed upon them. This allows children to develop a better sense of their current abilities in safety, without the anxiety of performance, unlike the classroom. This nonevaluative environment gives the child freedom to express feelings without judgment.

Axline (1947) reports, "It is the permissiveness to be themselves, the understanding, the acceptance, the recognition of feelings, the clarification of what they think and feel that helps children retain their self-respect; and the possibility of growth and change are forthcoming as they all develop insight" (p. 140).

Furthermore, perhaps providing this warm, caring, safe environment is a precondition for children to become eager to learn.

Self-Concept

As previously reported, the PSPCSAYC assesses the child's perceived level of self-concept by the use of an overall score total score that was calculated and identified as the global self-concept score, "a valid estimation of the child's self-perceptions" (Jerome et al., 2002, p. 704).

Results indicated that from pre-test to post-test, students who participated in the CCPT treatment group did not score statistically significantly higher ($p < .05$) on the global self-concept score of the PSPCSAYC when compared to students who were placed on a wait-list control group and did not receive CCPT. Upon further analyzing data for clinical significance, a majority of children both in the control and experimental group reported having high initial and post levels of self-concept. Because scores were high at pre-test, a statistical ceiling effect may have been created that did not allow for an accurate measure of change.

Another explanation is the difficulty involved in assessing self-concept at a young age. Jerome et al. (2002) reported young children ages five to seven, when using the PSPCSAYC, "tend to think about themselves in absolutes and are usually unrealistically positive in their self-evaluations" (p. 701). Harter (1999) further adds that children at this age are still developing a sense of their own abilities and have difficulties comparing their abilities to others in an accurate way. This may explain why many of the children in this study reported high levels of self-concept, as all children in the study were under the age of eight. Furthermore, the length of the study, eight weeks, may not have been sufficient to see a shift in self-concept, as it appears to be fairly static.

Several findings also indicate academic achievement may come before self-esteem, leading to an improved self-concept. Similar to findings in this study, historical research suggests fostering academic achievement in elementary school-age children can increase the self-concept scores of children (Helmke & van Aken, 1995; Marsh & Yueng 1997; Skaalvik & Hagtvet, 1990). Results of this study may provide further support for previous studies, in that the improvement to academic achievement may further lead to an improved self-concept over time. Marsh and Yueng (1997) suggested improving the child's achievement ability may lead to a higher self-concept with elementary-age children. Perhaps CCPT offered academically at-risk children freedom to perform at a heightened ability, resulting in further academic achievement. After successful academic experiences, it is theorized that children will develop positive self-concepts. Because of these findings, further academic achievement longitudinal controlled studies measuring the impact CCPT may have on self-concept should be conducted, perhaps using an instrument that is more sensitive to young children's view of self.

STUDENT-TEACHER RELATIONSHIPS

As previously reported, the STRS assesses a teacher's perception of her relationships with individual students by the use of an overall score identified as the total scale, the best indicator of student-teacher relationships (Pianta, 2001). Results indicated from pre-test to post-test that students who participated in the CCPT treatment group did not score statistically significantly higher ($p < .05$) on the total scale of the STRS when compared to students who were placed on a wait-list control group and did not receive CCPT.

Upon further analyzing data for clinical significance, teachers of 53 percent of children in the study (n = 21) reported having a significantly low level of positive relationship with students at pre-test. These findings are surprising, as the students referred for the study were referred as being academically at risk, not for emotional or behavioral difficulties often found in significantly low levels of a positive relationship reported by the teachers on the STRS. Twenty-five percent of children are typically reported by their teachers as having significantly low levels of a positive relationship (Pianta, 2001).

Of the 21 students identified as having significantly lower levels of a positive teacher relationship, 66 percent were male (n = 14). One must wonder what impact these initially perceived negative relationships and gender may have had on the study, as demographically, the experimental group contained 16 male participants compared to 10 in the control group. Fagot (1994) found that boys tend to have more behavioral and academic problems than girls, which, in turn, negatively affects student-teacher relationships. Crosnoe, Kirkpatrick-Johnson, and Eder (2004) further report a gender effect in the bond between teachers and students, expressing that minority male students may be less likely to bond with teachers. Pianta (2001) found teachers reported higher total scale scores for girls than boys, indicating teachers perceived more positive relationships with girls on the STRS. With that in mind, however, 33 percent of the 12 experimental group children (n = 4) moved from a significantly low level of a positive relationship with their teachers to one of normal functioning following their participation in CCPT, compared to 11 percent of the nine in the control group (n = 1). Surprisingly, by the end of treatment, five male students in the experimental group moved from low positive relationships to one of normal functioning, indicating CCPT effectiveness in diminishing effects of possible gender bias.

Several previous studies have indicated that student-teacher relationships help with the development of social and academic skills (Birch & Ladd, 1997; Lynch & Cicchetti, 1997; Pianta & Stuhlman, 2004). The child's relationships with his teacher have been viewed as affecting the child's emotional and academic development to promote the enhancement of academic success with at-risk students, suggesting student-teacher relationships for at-risk children can be an effective means to ensure academic success (Burchinal, Peisner-Feinberg, Pianta, & Howes, 2002; Hamre & Pianta, 2005). The possibility of providing at-risk children CCPT as an intervention to enhance teacher-student relationships is a fairly new phenomenon. Ray (2007) found CCPT and consultation could be effective interventions in reducing the stress of teacher-student relationships. Further longitudinal controlled studies measuring the impact of CCPT with academically at-risk children on student-teacher relationships are highly recommended.

RECOMMENDATIONS FOR FURTHER RESEARCH

Based upon the limitations and findings of this study and previous studies, several recommendations for future research are suggested:

- The present study is confined to reporting the effects of CCPT over an eight-week period. A follow-up study to investigate the long-term impact of CCPT on academic achievement, student-teacher relationships, and especially self-concept is recommended.
- The present study focused on first-grade children labeled academically at risk of school failure. It is recommended to investigate possible effects of CCPT on academic achievement, student-teacher relationships, and self-concept with differing ages within the elementary school system. It is suggested to target a younger population to continue to investigate the possible preventative intervention between CCPT and academic achievement.
- The present study focused on children who were labeled academically at risk of school failure. It is recommended to investigate possible effects of CCPT on academic achievement, student-teacher relationships, and self-concept with children who have and have not been identified with behavioral and/or emotional difficulties.
- The present study had a relatively small sample size of 41 participants. Replicating the study with a larger sample size could allow for greater generalizability.
- The present study excluded children from bilingual education because of instrument limitations. Future research investigating the impact CCPT has on academic achievement, self-concept, and student-teacher relationships with these children could be done using different instruments.
- Lastly, the present study did not include a treatment comparison group. Future research should investigate the impact CCPT has in comparison to other treatment interventions, such as curriculum guidance in relation to academic achievement, self-concept, and student-teacher relationships.

REFERENCES

Axline, V. M. (1947). *Play therapy*. New York: Ballantine Books.
Birch, S., & Ladd, G. (1997). The teacher-child relationship and children's early school adjustment. *Journal of School Psychology*, 35(1), 61–79.

Brandt, M. (1999). An investigation of the efficacy of play therapy with young children (Doctoral dissertation, University of North Texas, Denton, 1999). *Dissertation Abstracts International, A61*(07), 2603.

Bratton, S. C., Ray, D. C., Rhine, T., & Jones, L. (2005). The efficacy of play therapy with children: A meta-analytic review of treatment outcome. *Professional Psychology: Research and Practice, 36*(4), 376–390.

Burchinal, M., Peisner-Feinberg, E., Pianta, R., & Howes, C. (2002). Development of academic skills from preschool through second grade: Family and classroom predictors of developmental trajectories. *Journal of School Psychology, 40*(5), 415–436.

Cohen, J. (1988). *Statistical power analysis for the behavioral sciences* (2nd ed.). New York: Academic Press.

Crosnoe, C., Kirkpatrick-Johnson, M., & Elder, G. (2004). Intergenerational bonding in school: The behavior and contextual correlates of student-teacher relationships. *School of Education, 77*, 60–81.

Elias, M., Zins, J., Weissberg, R., Frey, K., Greenberg, M., Haynes, N., et al. (1997). *Promoting social and emotional learning: Guidelines for educators.* Alexandria, VA: Association for Supervision and Curriculum Development.

Fagot, B. (1994). Peer relations and the development of competence in boys and girls. *New Directions in Child Development, 65*, 53–65.

Greene, R., Abidin, R., & Kmetz, C. (1997). The index of teaching stress: A measure of student-teacher compatibility. *Journal of School Psychology, 35*, 239–239.

Hamre, B., & Pianta, R. (2001). Early teacher-child relationships and the trajectory of children's school outcomes through eighth grade. *Child Development, 72*, 625–638.

Hamre, B., & Pianta, R. (2005). Can instructional and emotional support in the first-grade classroom make a difference for children at risk of school failure? *Child Development, 76*(5), 949–967.

Harter, S. (1999). *The construction of the self: A developmental perspective.* New York: Guilford.

Harter, S., & Pike, R. (1984). The pictorial scale of perceived competence and social acceptance for young children. *Child Development, 55*, 1969–1982.

Helmke, A., & van Aken, M. (1995). The causal ordering of academic achievement and self-concept of ability during elementary school: A longitudinal study. *Journal of Educational Psychology, 87*(4), 624–637.

Hresko, W., Peak, P., Herron, S., & Bridges, D. (2000). *Examiner's manual for the young children's achievement test.* Austin, TX: Pro-Ed.

Jerome, A., Fujiki, M., Brinton, B., & James, S. (2002). Self-esteem in children with specific language impairment. *Journal of Speech, Language, and Hearing Research, 45*, 700–714.

Kazdin, A. (1999). The meaning and measurement of clinical significance. *Journal of Counseling and Clinical Psychology, 67*, 332–339.

Kazdin, A. (2003). Clinical significance: Measuring whether interventions make a difference. In A. Kazdin (Ed.), *Methodological issues & strategies in clinical research* (3rd ed.) (pp. 691–710). Washington, DC: American Psychological Association.

Ladd, G., & Burgess, K. (2001). Do relational risks and protective factors moderate the linkages between childhood aggression and early psychological and school adjustment? *Child Development, 72*, 1579–1601.

Landreth, G. L. (2002). *Play therapy: The art of the relationship* (2nd ed.). Levittown, PA: Accelerated Development.

Lynch, M., & Cicchetti, D. (1997). Children's relationship with adults and peers: An examination of elementary and junior high school students. *Journal of School Psychology, 35*(1), 81–99.

Marsh, H., & Yeung, A. (1997). Causal effects of academic self-concept on academic achievement: Structural equation models of longitudinal data. *Journal of Educational Psychology, 89*(1), 41–54.

Moustakas, C. (1959). *Psychotherapy with children: The living relationship.* New York: Harper and Brothers.

New Freedom Commission on Mental Health. (2003). *Achieving the promise: Transforming mental health care in America: Final report.* DHHS Pub. No. SMA-03-3832. Rockville, MD: Department of Health and Human Services.

Newcomer, B., & Morrison, T. (1974). Play therapy with institutionalized mentally retarded children. *American Journal of Mental Deficiency, 78*, 727–733.

Pianta, R. (2001). *STRS student-teacher relationship scale professional manual.* Lutz, FL: Psychological Assessment Resources.

Pianta, R., & Stuhlman, M. (2004). Teacher-child relationships and children's success in the first years of school. *School Psychology Review, 33*, 444–458.

Post, P. (1999). Impact of child-centered play therapy on self-esteem, locus of control, and anxiety of at-risk 4th-, 5th-, and 6th-grade students. *International Journal of Play Therapy, 8*, 1–18.

Quayle, R. (1991). The primary mental health project as a school-based approach for prevention of adjustment problems: An evaluation (Doctoral dissertation, Pennsylvania State University, 1991). *Dissertation Abstracts International, 52*, 1268.

Ray, D. C. (2007). Two counseling interventions to reduce teacher-child relationship stress. *Professional School Counseling, 10*, 428–440.

Ray, D. C. (2009). *Child-centered play therapy treatment manual.* Royal Oaks, MI: Self-Esteem Shop.

Romasz, T. E., Kantor, J. H., & Elias, M. J. (2004). Implementation and evaluation of urban school-wide social-emotional learning programs. *Evaluation and Program Planning, 27*, 89–103.

Shmukler, D., & Naveh, I. (1985). Structured vs. unstructured play training with economically disadvantaged preschoolers. *Imagination, Cognition, and Personality, 4*(3), 293–304.

Skaalvik, E., & Hagtvet, K. (1990). Academic achievement and self-concept: An analysis of causal predominance in a developmental perspective. *Journal of Personality and Social Psychology 53*(2), 292–307.

Wright, F., Boschen, K., & Jutai, J. (2005). Exploring the comparative responsiveness of a core set of outcome measures in a school-based conductive educational programme. *Child: Care, Health & Development* 31(3) 291–302.

Zins, J., Weissberg, R., Wang, M., & Walberg, H. (Eds.). (2004). *Building academic success and emotional learning: What does the research say?* New York: Teachers College Press.

CHAPTER 8

Play Therapy with Children Exhibiting ADHD

DEE C. RAY

PLAY THERAPY IMPACT ON CHILDREN WITH ATTENTION DEFICIT HYPERACTIVITY DISORDER

Several years ago, I was taking a graduate-level child psychopathology course in my doctoral program. At the time, I had been trained in play therapy for a couple of years and was facilitating play therapy in both clinical and school settings. As I read my assigned textbook, I came across a statement claiming that research showed play therapy was not effective with children diagnosed with attention deficit hyperactivity disorder (ADHD). The statement was surprising and listed two citations. I quickly found those two references to read the studies that disproved the use of play therapy with children who have ADHD. Interestingly, both references were practice/theoretical articles in which the authors stated that play therapy was not effective with children with ADHD. Yet, in these articles, there was no reference to research, only the authors' opinions. Being new to the academic world, I was shocked that such a strong statement would be published in a mainstream textbook with absolutely no credibility to defend itself. I have since experienced that these types of statements are commonplace in the field and learned to always question the written word, in both textbook and peer-reviewed form.

As I read that play therapy was not effective with children experiencing ADHD symptoms, I was facilitating quite a bit of play therapy with children demonstrating ADHD symptoms. And I was finding that it was working. The children with whom I worked entered play therapy with an inability to concentrate or focus, even on the simplest forms of play. Although they were 6 or 7 years old, they could not carry out play scenes for any length of time. They were often hyperactive and moved around the room quickly, touching everything in the room for just seconds at a time. I found them almost painful to observe because they clearly emotionally struggled with their own inability to finish a thought or process. Their frustration levels were high with low tolerance for their own lack of focus. And some even became more aggressive with play materials as their frustration grew during the session. In an adult analogy, I saw them similar to writers who sit down to write but end up with half-sentences and phrases in no particular order and give up altogether because of frustration.

Through the play therapy process, I provided an environment that would reflect the child's attentive process, "You'd like to finish that but there are so many other things you want to do," emotional struggle with the process, "You're really frustrated and moving on to something else," and provide acceptance of process, "Sometimes, in here, it's hard to stay with one thing when there are so many other things around you." Through providing these conditions and facilitative responses, children who demonstrated ADHD symptoms lowered their anxiety related to their frustration level and learned to accept themselves and their way of processing. I have not conducted qualitative research to test this personal theory of how play therapy works with ADHD children, but this is my experience. In time, I would observe play scenes lengthen to full stories from beginning to end. Of course, because of ADHD proclivities, there were distractions during a storyline but play therapy seemed to help them come back and carry through to the end. Outside of the playroom, I assessed child behavior through behavioral measurements and relationship inventories. Parents reported children being less annoying, less volatile, and concentrating better in school.

As a new play therapist, I experienced the benefits of play therapy with children demonstrating ADHD; but as a new researcher, it took some time to design a way to quantify such benefits. The study presented in this chapter represents years of play therapy and research experience. Along with a team of researchers (Ray, Schottelkorb, & Tsai, 2007), I was able to empirically observe the effects of play therapy on children with ADHD for more than four months. We asked the question, "Does child-centered play therapy

(CCPT) have an impact on teacher-child relationship stress and ADHD symptom exhibition when facilitated with children exhibiting attention deficits?''

BRIEF LITERATURE REVIEW

Students exhibiting difficulties with attention and behavior may qualify for a diagnosis of attention-deficit hyperactivity disorder (ADHD), which is one of the most frequent diagnoses of childhood (American Psychiatric Association, 2000). The behaviors associated with ADHD—inattention, hyperactivity, and impulsivity—have been found to cause significantly more stress for teachers as compared to teaching students without ADHD (Greene, Beszterczey, Katzenstein, Park, & Goring, 2002).

Greene et al. (2002) examined the level of stress for teachers of students with and without ADHD. This study reported that teachers experienced more stress with students with ADHD as compared to students without ADHD. Additionally, students with ADHD that had coexisting difficulties with social impairments and oppositional or aggressive behaviors were significantly more stressful to teach than students with ADHD only. The student-teacher interactions for students with ADHD were significantly more negative than interactions for students without ADHD. It appears that students with ADHD, particularly students that have additional difficulties with social and oppositional or aggressive behaviors, may experience more negative student-teacher interactions.

Many interventions have been used with children identified with ADHD, such as the use of psychotropic medication, behavioral interventions in the schools, and parent education (DuPaul & Stoner, 2004). Many practitioners use different interventions in the school and clinic settings, which they claim to be effective in improving the behavioral symptoms of children with ADHD. One such intervention, play therapy, has not been established as an efficacious treatment for children with ADHD (DuPaul & Stoner, 2004) but has been utilized with children and been found to be effective in improving children's externalizing and internalizing behavioral problems (Bratton, Ray, Rhine, & Jones, 2005). This study intended to explore empirical evidence regarding the use of CCPT in ameliorating the symptoms of ADHD. Details and results of this study were originally published in Ray et al. (2007).

METHOD

PARTICIPANTS

Participants were 60 students from three elementary schools in the southwestern United States. The researchers requested that teachers at each of the elementary schools identify students who exhibited attention problems and hyperactivity in the classroom. Teachers notified the school counselors of identified students. The school counselors obtained informed consent for participation in the study from parents and presented the informed consents to the researchers. All three schools served students from pre-kindergarten to fifth grade. All three were considered Title 1 schools targeted by the state for schoolwide assistance because of high percentages of children qualifying for free or reduced lunch. Because of playroom space and availability, 16 children were selected for the study from School 1, 26 children were selected from School 2, and 18 children were selected from School 3. Overall, 48 males and 12 females participated in the study.

Children at each school were randomly assigned to one of two research groups. Initially, 34 children were assigned to the play therapy intervention, and 33 children were assigned to a reading mentoring condition. Over the course of the study, seven children moved out of the schools, three in the play therapy group and four in the reading mentoring group. The final participant number of 60 represented 31 in the play therapy group and 29 in the reading mentoring group. Of the males, 26 were assigned to the play therapy treatment group (PT), and 22 were assigned to a reading mentoring group (RM). Of the females, 5 were assigned to the PT group, and 7 were assigned to the RM group. Participants were between 5 and 11 years old and between kindergarten and fifth grade. Ethnicity breakdowns were as follows: 10 African American (5 PT, 5 RM); 21 Hispanic (10 PT, 11 RM); 28 Caucasian (15 PT, 13 RM), and 1 biracial (PT). According to parent report, 15 participants (9 PT, 6 RM) received medication for ADHD symptoms during the duration of the study.

INSTRUMENTS

Index of Teaching Stress (ITS; Abidin, Greene, & Konold, 2004)   The purpose of the ITS is to measure the stress a teacher experiences in the relationship with a specific student. The ITS is based on the belief that the relationship between a teacher and a student is primary to the academic and personal success of the student. The ITS assesses the independent factors that correlate highly with the quality of the teacher-child relationship, including behavioral characteristics of the student, the teacher's perception of the teaching process, and the teacher's perception of support from others who interact with the child. The ITS includes 90 Likert-scale items and is standardized for use with teachers of students in preschool through twelfth grade.

The ITS produces a total stress score and three domain scores, consisting of attention deficit hyperactivity disorder, student characteristics, and teacher characteristics. The attention deficit hyperactivity disorder domain measures the teacher's stress level associated with the child's behaviors that are commonly associated with ADHD. The student characteristics domain measures the teacher's stress related to the student's temperament and behaviors. The teacher characteristics domain measures the teacher's stress as related to self-perception and expectation regarding teaching the particular student. The total stress score is a sum of the three domain scores (Abidin et al., 2004).

The ADHD domain consists of 16 items that factored together to form a unique source of relationship stress. The student characteristics domain is furthered divided into four areas specific to the teacher's response to student behavior, including the student's level of emotional lability and low adaptability (ELLA), anxiety or withdrawal (ANXW), low ability or learning disability (LALD), and aggressive conduct disorder (AGCD). The ELLA subscale measures the extent that the student's moodiness and emotional reactions create stress for the teacher. The ANXW subscale examines the amount of student anxiety and teacher dependence. The LALD subscale provides a score representing the impact on the teacher of student's special learning needs and disabilities. The AGCD subscale measures the amount of stress the teacher experiences because of the student's antisocial behavior.

The teacher characteristics domain is also composed of four scales that include the teacher's sense of competence and need for support, loss of satisfaction from teaching, disruption of the teaching process, and frustration working with parents. For the purpose of this study, the researchers chose to specifically analyze the ADHD domain, student characteristics domain, and the subscales of the student characteristics domain, which included emotional lability and low adaptability, anxiety or withdrawal, low ability or learning disability, and aggressive conduct disorder of the ITS. Because the play therapy and reading mentoring conditions were specifically targeted to the students and because previous research (Ray, 2007; Muro, Ray, Schottelkorb, Smith, & Blanco, 2006) demonstrated a negligible effect of intervention on teachers, researchers chose not to analyze the teacher characteristics domain and total score on the ITS.

Conners Teacher Rating Scale-Revised: Short Form (CTRS-R:S) (Conners, 2001)   The CTRS-R:S is an assessment completed by teachers to assess problematic behaviors of children and adolescents most commonly associated with ADHD. The assessment is normed to be used with children between the ages of 3 and 17 years. CTRS-R:S consists of 28 questions that are rated on a four-point frequency scale. The shortened version of the form is recommended for use when administration time is limited and when multiple administrations are planned to be used (Conners, 2001). The teacher version of this form provides four sub-scales: oppositional, cognitive problems and inattention, hyperactivity, and an ADHD index score. The ADHD index score is considered the best indicator of attention difficulties associated with a diagnosis of ADHD (Conners, 2001).

Demographic Data   The teachers completed demographic data on each student. Teachers indicated the student's age, grade, ethnicity, and school. Furthermore, researchers requested medication data from parents of each participant to indicate whether the child was receiving medication for ADHD and for what time period.

PROCEDURE

Upon receiving the informed consent from each student's parent, teachers completed an ITS, CTRS-R:S, and demographic form on each student. Instruments were scored, and those participants who were scored in the clinical range (61 or above) on the ADHD Index of the CTRS-R:S were qualified for the study. Qualifying participants were randomly assigned to one of two experimental conditions: play therapy or reading mentoring. All participants were matched according to school and grade level, and then by using a table of random numbers, children were assigned to an experimental condition (Shadish, Cook, & Campbell, 2002). Teachers provided informed consent because of their completion of the ITS. Teachers were blind to the treatment assignment of the students. Students were scheduled to participate in 16 weeks of treatment. Because of typical school scheduling difficulties such as field trips, standardized testing, winter break, and occasional absences, the study required 22 weeks to be completed. At the end of 22 weeks, each teacher completed an ITS and CTRS-R:S on each participating student as a post-measure. Also at post-test administration, parents were administered a questionnaire regarding medication usage during the time of the study. The following paragraphs describe each experimental condition.

Play Therapy (PT)   Thirty-one students were assigned to the PT group, which consisted of 16 sessions of play therapy scheduled over 16 weeks. Each student received one session per week of 30-minute individual child-centered play therapy (CCPT) sessions. All play therapists had successfully completed at least two courses in play therapy and participated in direct individual or triadic supervision with a counseling faculty member certified in play therapy. Play therapists included seven doctoral-level counseling students and three advanced master's students. Play therapists were required to review their videotaped play therapy sessions with their supervisors on a weekly basis. Supervisors ensured that the CCPT protocol was being followed and enacted in the play sessions through the use of the play therapy skills checklist (PTSC; Ray, 2009). Supervisors rated responses on the PTSC, confirming that each response fell into a CCPT category. Play therapists were not allowed to discuss the student with the teacher during the study.

Play therapy sessions were conducted in specially equipped playrooms in each of the school settings. Playrooms were equipped with a variety of specific toys to facilitate a broad range of expression, following Landreth's (2002) general guidelines. CCPT is designed to provide specific therapist responses to the child during play therapy. These response sets are clarified in detail in Landreth (2002) and Ray (2009), and both include nonverbal skills and verbal skills.

Reading Mentoring (RM)   To qualify as an experimental study, we designed an active control group as a comparison group, the reading mentoring (RM) group. The RM served two purposes from a research perspective. First, the RM group provided some level of intervention for children experiencing problems, which was requested by the school's administration. I have found in my experience that schools are not supportive of traditional control groups because of the ethical implications of not providing a child help when it is needed. Secondly, the RM group helped control for the research internal validity threat of maturation in which we needed to address if children were getting better just due to the passage of time. The RM group was not intended to be an evidence-based comparison group but an active control group.

Twenty-nine students were assigned to the reading mentoring group, which consisted of 16 sessions of reading scheduled over 16 weeks. Each student received one 30-minute session of individual reading mentoring per week. Reading mentors were trained by one of the researchers to establish continuity of the mentoring procedures. Mentors were instructed to choose age-appropriate books for the assigned child from the university reading program library. In each session, the mentor provided a choice to the child regarding the child reading to the mentor or the mentor reading to the child. Mentors helped children with pronouncing words when the child was challenged by the reading selection. Mentors were encouraged to focus on reading and to not initiate discussions with the child. Mentors were also trained in limit-setting procedures in preparation for possible discipline issues. Four undergraduate students served as reading mentors.

Data Analysis

We developed two specific data research questions to answer the broader research question. They were (1) Was there an overall change from mean pre-test score to mean post-test score on student characteristics of teacher-child relationship stress after application of the interventions? and (2) Was there a change across time that depended on which intervention the child received? Data analysis intended to answer the research questions using a combined between-within subjects ANOVA (that is, split plot analysis) (Tabachnick & Fidell, 2001). Analyses were run separately with the ITS ADHD domain, student characteristics domain, emotional lability and low adaptability (ELLA) subscale, anxiety or withdrawal (ANXW) subscale, low ability or learning disability (LALD) subscale, and aggressive conduct disorder (AGCD) subscale as dependent variables. A separate split plot analysis was run with the ADHD index of the CTRS-R:S. In each combined between-within subjects ANOVAs, the required assumption of sphericity was assumed, given that there were only two points of measurement. It was decided that if statistically significant differences were found with a meaningful effect size between groups, simple effects post hoc analyses would be conducted as needed. Effect size was reported according to partial eta squared and was interpreted according to Cohen's (1988) guidelines of .01 as a small effect, .06 as a moderate effect, and .14 as a large effect. When post hoc analysis was conducted, a modified alpha level of .025 was employed to control for Type 1 error (Armstrong & Henson, 2005).

RESULTS

ITS ADHD DOMAIN

Table 8.1 presents the ITS and CTRS-R;S ADHD index means, standard deviations, and sample sizes on the pre-test and post-test for both treatment groups. Results of the ANOVA on ADHD domain revealed a statistically significant main effect for time, $F(1, 58) = 12.89, p < .01$ (partial $\eta^2 = .18$); no statistically significant main effect for group, $F(1, 58) = .77$, $p = .38$ (partial $\eta^2 = .01$); and no statistically significant interaction effect, $F(1, 58) = .69, p = .41$ (partial $\eta^2 = .01$). Because the change was fairly consistent across both groups, the interaction effect was negligible. The effect size of .18 for change over time indicates a large effect size according to Cohen's (1988) guidelines. There was no significant difference between groups; hence, no further simple effects analysis was necessary.

Table 8-1
Pre- and Post-Test Means and Standard Deviations for ITS and
CTRS-R:S ADHD Index

Dependent Variable	Play Therapy n = 31				Reading Mentoring n = 29			
	Pre		Post		Pre		Post	
	M	SD	M	SD	M	SD	M	SD
ADHD Domain	51.39	13.52	43.65	11.86	47.38	13.46	42.55	13.70
Stu Char Domain	70.58	21.49	60.13	16.92	58.45	21.55	58.07	21.17
ELLA	26.39	11.12	22.52	9.03	19.34	8.65	20.31	10.38
ANXW	19.23	7.03	15.87	5.07	16.21	7.50	15.97	6.34
LALD	12.65	6.08	10.32	5.06	12.59	5.60	11.55	5.59
AGCD	13.29	5.38	11.74	4.68	10.31	4.94	10.24	5.34
CTRS-R:S ADHD Index	67.65	7.15	64.61	12.04	68.45	9.75	61.17	12.10

Note: ITS = Index of Teaching Stress; ADHD = Attention Deficit Hyperactivity Disorder; Stu Char = Student Characteristics; ELLA = Emotional Lability/Low Adaptability; ANXW = Anxiety/Withdrawal; LALD = Low Ability/Learning Disability; AGCD = Aggressive/Conduct Disorder; CTRS-R:S = Conners Teacher Rating Scale-Revised: Short Form
Table originally published in Ray et al. (2007).

ITS Student Characteristics

Results of the ANOVA on the student characteristics domain revealed a statistically significant main effect for time, $F(1, 58) = 6.07$, $p = .02$ (partial $\eta^2 = .10$); no statistically main effect for group, $F(1, 58) = .2.21$, $p = .14$ (partial $\eta^2 = .04$); but a statistically significant interaction effect, $F(1, 58) = 5.26$, $p = .03$ (partial $\eta^2 = .08$). The effect size for time (.10) and the effect size for interaction (.08) were in the moderate category.

Because a statistically significant interaction effect was found, further post hoc analyses were conducted through paired sample t-tests to explore differences. Between pre- and post-testing, paired samples t-test revealed a statistically significant difference for student characteristics for the PT group [$t(30) = 3.56$, $p < .01$]. The effect size was large ($\eta^2 = .30$). Between pre- and post-testing for the RM group, paired samples t-test revealed no significant difference for student characteristics [$t(28) = .12$, $p = .91$]. The effect size was negligible ($\eta^2 < .01$).

ITS Emotional Lability and Low Adaptability (ELLA) Subscale

Results of the ANOVA on the ELLA subscale revealed no statistically significant main effect for time $F(1, 58) = 2.42$, $p = .13$ (partial $\eta^2 = .04$); no statistically significant main effect for group, $F(1, 58) = 3.81$, $p = .06$ (partial $\eta^2 = .06$); but a statistically significant difference for interaction effect, $F(1, 58) = 6.70$, $p = .01$ (partial $\eta^2 = .10$). The effect size for interaction (.10) was in the moderate category.

Because an interaction effect was found, further post hoc analyses were conducted through paired sample t-tests to explore differences. Between pre- and post-testing, paired samples t-test revealed a statistically significant difference for ELLA subscale for the PT group [$t(30) = 2.89$, $p < .01$]. The effect size was large ($\eta^2 = .21$). Between pre- and post-testing for the RM group, paired samples t-test revealed no significant difference for ELLA subscale [$t(28) = -.75$, $p = .46$]. The effect size was small ($\eta^2 = .02$).

ITS Anxiety or Withdrawal (ANXW) Subscale

Results of the ANOVA for the ANXW subscale revealed a statistically significant main effect for time $F(1, 58) = 7.71$, $p < .01$ (partial $\eta^2 = .12$); no statistically significant main effect for group, $F(1, 58) = .88$, $p = .35$ (partial $\eta^2 = .02$); but a statistically significant interaction effect, $F(1, 58) = 5.78$, $p = .02$ (partial $\eta^2 = .09$). The effect size for time (.12) and interaction effect (.09) were in the moderate category.

Because a statistically significant interaction effect was found, further post hoc analyses were conducted through paired sample t-tests to explore differences. Between pre- and post-testing, paired samples t-test revealed a statistically significant difference for ANXW subscale for the PT group [$t(30) = 4.32$, $p < .01$]. The effect size was large ($\eta^2 = .38$). Between pre- and post-testing for the RM group, paired samples t-test revealed no significant difference for ANXW subscale [$t(28) = -.23$, $p = .82$]. The effect size was negligible ($\eta^2 < .01$).

ITS LOW ABILITY OR LEARNING DISABILITY (LALD) SUBSCALE

Results of the ANOVA on LALD subscale revealed a statistically significant main effect for time, $F(1, 58) = 9.90$, $p < .01$ (partial $\eta^2 = .15$); no statistically significant main effect for group, $F(1, 58) = .19$, $p = .67$ (partial $\eta^2 < .01$); and no statistically significant interaction effect, $F(1, 58) = 1.46$, $p = .23$ (partial $\eta^2 = .03$). Because the change was fairly consistent across both groups, the interaction effect was negligible. The effect size of .15 for change over time indicates a large effect size. Because of a lack of significant difference between groups, no further simple effects analysis was necessary.

ITS AGGRESSIVE CONDUCT DISORDER (AGCD) SUBSCALE

ANOVA on AGCD subscale revealed no statistically significant main effect for time, $F(1, 58) = 2.01$, $p = .16$ (partial $\eta^2 = .03$); no statistically significant main effect for group, $F(1, 58) = 3.58$, $p = .06$ (partial $\eta^2 = .06$); and no statistically significant interaction effect, $F(1, 58) = 1.68$, $p = .20$ (partial $\eta^2 = .03$). There was no significant difference between groups; hence, no further simple effects analysis was necessary.

CONNERS ADHD INDEX

Split plot ANOVA revealed a statistically significant main effect for time between pre- and post-test on the Conners ADHD Index, $F(1, 58) = 12.54$, $p < .01$ (partial $\eta^2 = .18$); no statistically significant main effect for group, $F(1, 58) = .34$, $p = .56$ (partial $\eta^2 < .01$); and no statistically significant interaction effect, $F(1, 58) = 2.13$, $p = .15$ (partial $\eta^2 .04$). The effect size of .18 for change over time is interpreted as a large effect. There was no significant difference between groups; hence, no further simple effects analysis was necessary.

DISCUSSION

In summary, results revealed that on the ADHD domain, student characteristics domain, ELLA, ANXW, LALD, and AGCD subscales of the ITS, mean difference scores were larger for children participating in play therapy than for children participating in a reading mentoring intervention. Statistically significant differences were found between the two groups on the student characteristics domain and ELLA and ANXW subscales, indicating that children participating in play therapy were significantly less stressful to their teachers in personal characteristics, specifically emotional distress, anxiety, and withdrawal difficulties. Regarding symptoms associated with ADHD, a statistically significant effect for time coupled with a large effect size on both the ADHD domain of the ITS and the ADHD index of the CTRS-R:S indicate children who participated in either play therapy or reading mentoring exhibited a significantly positive change in symptoms over the time of the study with no difference between the groups. The absence of a statistically significant difference between groups signifies that both conditions had an equal effect on ADHD symptoms. However, statistical differences were noted across time, which could indicate that the passage of time alone was a possible variable in determining significant change. An alternate likely explanation for the change over time is the effectiveness of the interventions, a supposition that is based on previous literature that a play therapy intervention yields a large positive effect compared to no intervention (Bratton et al., 2005).

This is the first research project to investigate the effect of CCPT on children exhibiting specific symptoms assessed as ADHD. Results of this study are promising in light of positive time effects for CCPT with symptoms related to ADHD, but even more promising is the effect of CCPT on challenges that are co-morbid with the symptoms of ADHD. Significant differences were found between children participating in play therapy and those who participated in reading mentoring on emotional issues such as frequent crying, explosive anger, difficulty in calming, perseveration, resistance to change, apprehension, fear, extreme tension, and emotional withdrawal (Abidin et al., 2004). Teachers reported significantly less stress related to these issues for children who received play therapy over children who received reading mentoring.

Behavioral problems associated with ADHD, such as inattention and oppositional behavior, can be suggestive of other internal problems that co-exist with ADHD. Some of these conditions are conduct disorder, oppositional-defiant disorder, learning disabilities, mood disorders, anxiety disorders, and sleep disorders (Kronenberger & Meyer, 2001). Baxter and Rattan (2004) examined the anxious and depressed behaviors of 86 male students between the ages of 9 and 11 who were diagnosed with ADHD. In their examination of parent-, teacher-, and self-report measures, Baxter and Rattan found that the students with ADHD were significantly more likely to have anxiety and depression when compared to the normative population. The authors recommended that professionals working with children with ADHD must consider co-morbid conditions when designing treatment interventions.

Case Study

The following is one case example among the 31 CCPT participants. Mark was a 7-year-old African American boy in second grade. Mark's teacher indicated on Mark's paperwork that he was "extremely ADHD" and could not finish his school assignments, nor could he sit still for more than a couple of minutes at a time. He was a constant disruption in the classroom, and Mark's teacher scored within the clinical range on stress related to student characteristics on the ITS.

In Mark's first three sessions, he fluttered from toy to toy in the playroom. He picked up or touched every play material in the room during the session. The typical play therapy interaction during these sessions was as follows:

MARK: (picks up gun) What's this?
PLAY THERAPIST (PT): You're wondering what . . .
MARK: (quickly picks up handcuffs and interrupts) What's this?
PT: You're not sure . . .
MARK: (quickly picks up glue and interrupts) How do you get this out?
PT: It's kinda hard to . . .
MARK: (interrupts) Yeah, but I can do it. (Mark struggles to open and when it doesn't work, he throws it on the ground. He crosses room to pick up a ball.)
PT: That didn't work like you . . .
MARK: (interrupts, holding ball) I can play football.

(continued)

In these first sessions, the play therapist struggled to finish sentences and concentrated on providing an environment in which Mark was accepted in his movement from toy to toy.

An excerpt from the fourth session:

MARK: (opens doll house) What's this?

PT: You're checking that out.

MARK: Yeah, it's a house. It's like mine.

PT: So, it seems just like yours.

MARK: (He points to one of the rooms with a bed) Yep, this is my room.

PT: Sound like you like that one.

MARK: (opens doll house garage) I'm going to put a car in there. (He crosses the room to get a car. He picks up the car but then notices a tractor and picks it up. He runs it through the sandbox.)

PT: Looks like you decided to do something else.

MARK: Look how it picks up the sand.

Fifteen minutes later, after PT has given a five-minute warning and Mark has played with many other items, PT announces that their time is up.

MARK: (gets up to walk out but notices the dollhouse) I'm going to put the car in the garage.

PT: You'd really like to put the car in the garage now, but our time is up for today. You can do that next time.

MARK: (crosses room to get car and places it in garage). No, I'm doing it now. (Mark and PT walk out.)

In this fourth session, Mark has shown the first signs of a thought or play scene that appears to have a focus. His short time focused on the dollhouse and intention to complete his action at the end of the session indicate that he is experiencing some process related to the dollhouse that he was distracted from early in the session.

In the fifth through tenth sessions, Mark extends his time with the dollhouse. Each session, he spends a few more minutes organizing the house, talking about each room, and picking out family figures to go in the house. He moves the figure he has labeled as his room to room each time.

In the eleventh session, Mark spends 10 minutes organizing the dollhouse and placing a mother, grandmother, sister, and his figure in the house.

MARK: (he moves his figure from room to room) I want to see what's going on here.

PT: You're wondering what's going on in all of the other rooms.

MARK: (he moves from room to room) Yep, and here and here and here.

PT: You want to know what's going on everywhere at the same time.

MARK: Yep, when I go here (moves to mother figure), she yells, "Get out." When I go here (moves to grandmother figure), she yells, "Get out." When I go here (moves to sister figure), she hits me.

PT: It sounds like they don't like you knowing what's going on.

MARK: No, they don't. They want me to stay here (his figure in a room alone), but I don't like it. I'm really bored. I want to go outside.

PT: So, you'd really rather be outside.

MARK: But mom says it's too dangerous. I have to stay inside.

PT: So, you seem stuck in one boring place.

MARK: (his affect brightens) But I can do other stuff. (He moves all the furniture around in his room.)

PT: You figured out a way to not be bored.

In this session, Mark makes several points of progress clear. First, he is able to hold a conversation with the therapist in which both finish their sentences and communicate with each other. Second, he is able to stay with one play storyline for a lengthy period of time. Third, Mark shows awareness that his behavior is annoying to others and leaves him lonely. And finally, he demonstrates the development of a possible coping skill by giving himself an idea of another acceptable thing to do to meet his needs. Other play behaviors have also improved, including his ability to develop games to play with the therapist; his sticking with things that are hard, such as opening containers; and other extended storylines in his play.

At the end of the study, Mark's teacher reported through assessments that he now scored in the nonclinical range of student characteristics on the ITS and a four-point drop on his Conners ADHD index score. Mark's case indicates that as children are able to provide focus and completion to their play storylines, they can possibly transfer this same skill to other settings.

LIMITATIONS

Several limitations were noted in this study. The most obvious limitation is the lack of a no-treatment control group. Although this was a limitation of the design, findings further exacerbate this limitation by demonstrating no significant differences between groups on the specific symptoms of ADHD. The possibility exists that children demonstrated positive significant change based on time alone. However, other studies indicate that with no intervention, problem relationships with teachers actually increase over time (Hamre & Pianta, 2001; Pianta, Steinberg, & Rollins, 1995; Pianta & Stuhlman, 2004). The likelihood that a control group with no intervention would have improved ADHD symptoms over time is weak, but possible.

Another limitation of this study was the use of self-report measures that were completed only by teachers. Diagnostic criteria for ADHD clearly requires the exhibiting of symptoms in two or more settings (American Psychiatric Association, 2000). By limiting assessment to teachers, only one setting was represented in this study. Self-report measures used in this study might have been influenced by the perceptions of teachers and perhaps might not be indicative of behavior that can be measured through objective observers or raters. However, Abidin (1992) argued that behavioral observations are not adequate in measuring belief systems of caretakers on children and that self-report measures are more practical to this end.

CONCLUSION

ADHD is the most common diagnosis of childhood, with well-documented evidence that problematic long-term effects may result. Thus, interventions that occur in the early school years may reduce the impact of ADHD for children in the short and the long term. Although some parent and teacher interventions have proven to be effective with this population, counseling interventions for these children are lacking. Child-centered play therapy is one intervention that has a minimal amount of research with this specific population, none of which has rigorous research designs.

The results of the present study indicated that among 60 elementary-age students qualifying with reported symptoms of ADHD who were placed in a play therapy or reading mentoring condition, both groups exhibited significantly less ADHD behaviors following 16 sessions of treatment. Between groups, those children who participated in play therapy exhibited significantly fewer problems in the areas of emotional instability, anxiety, and withdrawal, as well as overall problem student characteristics. Results offer CCPT as a promising intervention for children exhibiting ADHD behaviors, especially with co-morbid difficulties such as emotional outbursts and anxiety.

I personally found these results very interesting because they reflected my clinical experiences in play therapy with children demonstrating ADHD symptoms. It is noted that there was no difference between groups on the Conners ADHD index. Both groups significantly improved over time, which could possibly lead to the conclusion that time and some attentive intervention will help alleviate attention and hyperactive symptoms. The difference was found with the teacher's overall perception of the child, however, along with anxiety and emotionality challenges. Children who participated in CCPT were growing, in a sense, more likable or relatable to teachers. The co-morbid symptoms that often occur with ADHD such as emotional outbursts or impulsivity related to anxiety decreased, which allowed teachers to experience the children as less stressful. I also interpret this finding with some validity because the teachers knew the children left the room for 30 minutes but they were not aware to which condition children were assigned, and we requested that they not ask the children. The finding that children become more relational as a result of CCPT is one that was consistent with my clinical experience with parents. On a case-by-case basis, not generalizable by research standards, parents have reported that they experience more joyful times with their children after participation in CCPT, less marked by emotional volatility. CCPT appears to provide children exhibiting ADHD symptoms with an environment that allows for full acceptance of their processing abilities, which, in turn, allows children to accept their own abilities and unique ways of working. Such acceptance of self is key to increasing an internal sense of self-concept, decreasing the need to externalize negative self-feelings onto significant relationships.

REFERENCES

Abidin, R. R. (1992). The determinants of parent behavior. *Journal of Clinical Child Psychology*, *21*, 407–412.

Abidin, R. R., Greene, R., & Konold, T. (2004). *Index of Teacher Stress: Professional manual*. Lutz, FL: Psychological Assessment Resources.

American Psychiatric Association. (2000). *Diagnostic and statistical manual of mental disorders* (4th ed.). Washington, DC: Author.

Armstrong, S., & Henson, R. (2005). Statistical practices of *IJPT* researchers: A review from 1993–2000. *International Journal of Play Therapy*, *14*(1), 7–26.

Baxter, J., & Rattan, G. (2004). Attention deficit disorder and the internalizing dimension in males, ages 9–0 through 11–1. *International Journal of Neuroscience, 114*, 817–832.

Bratton, S. C., Ray, D. C., Rhine, T., & Jones, L. (2005). The efficacy of play therapy with children: A meta-analytic review of treatment outcomes. *Professional Psychology: Research and Practice, 36*, 376–390.

Cohen, J. (1988). *Statistical power analysis for the behavioral sciences* (2nd ed.). Hillside, NJ: Erlbaum.

Conners, C. K. (2001). *Conners Rating Scales-Revised: Technical manual.* North Tonawanda, NY: Multi-Health Systems, Inc.

DuPaul, G. J., & Stoner, G. (2004). *ADHD in the schools: Assessment and intervention strategies* (2nd ed.). New York: Guilford.

Greene, R., Beszterczey, S., Katzenstein, T., Park, K., & Goring, J. (2002). Are students with ADHD more stressful to teach? *Journal of Emotional and Behavioral Disorders, 2*, 79–90.

Hamre, B., & Pianta, R. (2001). Early teacher-child relationships and the trajectory of children's school outcomes through eighth grade. *Child Development, 72*, 625–638.

Kronenberger, W. G., & Meyer, R. G. (2001). *The child clinician's handbook* (2nd ed.). Needham Heights, MA: Allyn & Bacon.

Landreth, G. L. (2002). *Play therapy: The art of the relationship* (2nd ed.). New York: Brunner-Routledge.

Muro, J., Ray, D. C., Schottelkorb, A., Smith, M., & Blanco, P. (2006). Quantitative analysis of long-term play therapy. *International Journal of Play Therapy, 15*, 35–58.

Pianta, R., Steinberg, M., & Rollins, K. (1995). The first two years of school: Teacher-child relationships and deflections in children's classroom adjustment. *Development and Psychopathology, 7*, 295–312.

Pianta, R., & Stuhlman, M. (2004). Teacher-child relationships and children's success in the first years of school. *School Psychology Review, 33*, 444–458.

Ray, D. C. (2007). Two counseling interventions to reduce teacher-child relationship stress. *Professional School Counseling, 10*, 428–440.

Ray, D. C. (2009). *Child-centered play therapy treatment manual.* Royal Oaks, MI: Self-Esteem Shop.

Ray, D. C., Schottelkorb, A., & Tsai, M. (2007). Play therapy with children exhibiting symptoms of attention deficit hyperactivity disorder. *International Journal of Play Therapy, 16*, 95–111.

Shadish, W., Cook, T., & Campbell, D. (2002). Experimental and quasi-experimental designs for generalized causal inference. Boston: Houghton Mifflin.

Tabachnick, B., & Fidell, L. (2001). *Using multivariate statistics* (4th ed.). Boston: Allyn and Bacon.

CHAPTER 9

A School-Based Group Activity Therapy Intervention with Learning-Disabled Preadolescents Exhibiting Behavior Problems*

JILL PACKMAN and IREON LEBEAUF

Motivation and Rationale for Study

When I worked with preadolescents in school settings, I was acutely aware of students who caused frequent trouble for teachers, parents, and administrators. Adults often complained that these problem students didn't understand social cues. For these students, their difficulties were compounded by the inherent struggles of simply being a preadolescent (Ormrod, 2009). They are not quite an adolescent but do not want to be considered a child. Adults are often confused by their behavior. When in stressful situations, preadolescents often regress to childlike behavior. This stage in development is particularly difficult for preadolescents struggling with social-emotional, behavioral, and cognitive difficulties. My goal in doing this research was to see if group activity and play therapy could have a beneficial effect on issues faced by preadolescents.

---

*Please note: The first author of this chapter, Jill Packman, was involved in the original research. The second author, Ireon LeBeauf, joined the project at a later date. Therefore, when in the text the first person is used, it is in reference to the first author's experiences during and before the research project began.

After the attacks at Columbine High School in 1999, many people were asking why such a tragic event happened and if it would happen again. Then the terrorist attacks of September 11, 2001, further increased people's fears and bewilderment. The subsequent war on terrorism caused children to be exposed to more brutality and violence than ever before. Many parents express concerns for their children to me. Children were building structures and knocking them down, throwing things, and generally being more destructive than usual. Parents kept asking, "Is this normal behavior, or do I need to be concerned about something bigger?" Further concerns were expressed in United States society in 2001 when the Surgeon General emphasized the serious lack of children's mental health services. The shortage of services was described as a mental health crisis. "Growing numbers of children are suffering needlessly because their emotional, behavioral, and developmental needs are not being met" (U.S. Public Health Service, 2001, p. 3).

After reading these comments, I became even more dedicated to working with children to help them develop coping and expressive skills. And where better to meet the needs of children than in a school? All children attend school; they are essentially a captive audience. Teachers are often concerned about children with behavioral problems both from a social-emotional and an academic perspective. Play therapy is accepted as an effective way to work with children, yet little to no research had been done with preadolescents (Landreth, 2002). And, from my perspective, preadolescents were in dire need. While adults talk about their challenges, repeating the story over and over until it feels resolved, children often do not have the language skills to do this. Play therapy is a widely accepted developmentally appropriate way for children to cope with their challenges. Play is the language of children; and toys are their words (Landreth, 2002). When people look at preadolescents, however, they immediately assume they can talk about what is bothering them. In my experience, while preadolescents appear old enough to talk, they often answer questions with a shrug and "I don't know."

Younger children may embrace the playroom immediately; on the other hand, preadolescents are skeptical of anything that looks juvenile (Ormrod, 2009; Paone, Packman, Maddox & Rothman, 2008), including the play therapy room (Ginott, 1994). In 1945, Slavson introduced the idea of a developmentally appropriate type of therapy for preadolescents (Bratton & Ferebee, 1999; Krall & Irvin, 1973; Schiffer, 1969). Preadolescents are in the concrete operational stage of cognitive development, meaning that they are beginning to use abstract thought (Piaget, 1977). Words are abstract concepts. Using play, which is more concrete, and verbal processing matches the development of preadolescents and is a way to bridge the gap between the concrete and the abstract (Ginott, 1994).

Groups are the ideal place for preadolescents to learn from one another. In upper elementary grades (fourth through sixth) preadolescents become acutely more aware of what their peers think (Bratton & Ferebee, 1999). Additionally, socioemotional growth is characterized by inferiority versus industry (Erikson, 1980). Industry includes learning the rules and playing with others in a self-directed way. While these two things will not eliminate feelings of inferiority, which include low self-esteem, a sense of incompetence, depression, anxiety, withdrawal, and difficulty with peer, sibling, and parental relationships, a sense of industry facilitates appropriate interactions with others. Because school is the preadolescents' social world, underdeveloped social skills can affect not only learning but also teacher and peer interactions and the ability to make friends (Johnson, 1988; Ormrod, 2009; Yasutake & Bryan, 1995). Group activity therapy provides preadolescents with opportunities to learn social and coping skills in a safe and developmentally appropriate environment. When these groups are conducted in the school, the benefits are increased because the preadolescents are learning with a group of peers they already have relationships with and in an environment they already know.

Preadolescents with learning difficulties feel different because they struggle academically and believe they are inferior to their peers. Difficulties include awkwardness, feeling lonely, depression, anxiety, and isolation. They also cope with low self-esteem because of academic and social failures (Yasutake & Bryant, 1995). Children with learning disabilities often have difficulty reading and interpreting social and facial cues of others. This leaves them acting incongruent and not understanding how they are perceived by those around them. Children and preadolescents with learning disabilities often exhibit a range of behaviors, including impulsivity, aggression, depression, withdrawal, and anxiety. These behaviors serve to further isolate them from their peers and from other adults, causing the social awkwardness to increase. Group activity therapy helps preadolescents deal with these problematic behaviors as well as taking into account cognitive developmental and social-emotional needs.

RESEARCH DESIGN

The proliferation of play therapy research in recent years has been formidable, yet a dearth of information focused on the preadolescent child. Not only are preadolescents often overlooked in play therapy research, learning-disabled preadolescents are nonexistent as a target population. In an effort to illuminate the concerns of a marginalized group, I decided to focus my research on learning-disabled, behaviorally challenged preadolescents in a special needs school setting. The research design was quasi-experimental; I used a pre-test–post-test control group design to determine the effects of group play and activity therapy on fourth- and fifth-grade preadolescents with learning disabilities exhibiting behavior problems.

PARTICIPANTS

There was a total of 24 participants in the study. All of the participants included in the study had been diagnosed with a specific learning disability and attended a special needs school. The school specializes in the education of children with learning differences. The school identifies learning differences as occurring "in people with average to superior intelligence and become apparent when a person has difficulty cognitively processing information because of a disorder in auditory, visual, or motor skills. As a result, language, math, reading, and writing are often below potential, causing frustration and low self-worth" (The Winston School, 2003). Specifically, the treatment group in the study consisted of 10 males and 2 females. In the treatment group, there were 4 fourth-graders and 8 fifth-graders. The treatment group was Caucasian with the exception of one African American student. While racial diversity was lacking in the sample, the unspoken subculture that learning-disabled students and their families engage in on a daily basis provided the cultural context for my research.

INSTRUMENTATION

Learning-disabled students oftentimes exhibit behavioral difficulties differently across academic and social environments. The instruments used in this research study provided a holistic view of student behavior across settings. The Behavior Assessment System for Children-Parent Rating Form (BASC-PRF) by Reynolds and Kamphaus (1992) provides parents, teachers, and children the opportunity to rate behavior at home and at school. The instrument is designed to determine a composite score, the Behavioral Symptom Index (BSI), and two scales: clinical and adaptive. Items from these scales are further categorized as either internalizing or externalizing behaviors. This study focused on the adaptive scale, which measures positive behaviors such as social skills, leadership, adaptability, and study skills.

Additionally, I chose the Child Behavior Checklist-Parent Report Form (CBCL-PRF) developed by Achenbach and Edelbrock (1991); it consists of a parent, teacher, and self-report version. This instrument measures perceived social ability, behavioral functioning, and behavior problems as indicated by the child, parent, or teacher. The selected assessments along with the recording of qualitative observations pro- vided me with a three-dimensional thrust to my research; I was able to ascertain robust information about the participants across observers and across home and school settings.

DATA COLLECTION

Before treatment, parents completed a Behavior Assessment System for Children-Parent Report Form (BASC-PRF) and the Child Behavior Checklist-Parent Report Form (CBCL-PRF). Following the treatment, post-test data were collected from parents. The same procedures were used to collect pre- and post-test data. Qualitative data were also recorded so I could analyze the clinical significance of the treatment. Qualitative data were also acquired from the comment section of CBCL-PRF as well as comments from the parents', teachers', partic- ipants', and the researcher's observations. Immediately following each session, I logged significant verbalizations and happenings. Additional subjective information was gathered through face-to-face interviews with each teacher and all parents that were available. I asked the following two questions in the interview to solicit spontaneous feed- back: "Do you have any questions or feedback for me?" and "Is there anything else you would like me to know?"

INTERVENTION PROTOCOL

The experimental group of preadolescents participated in 12 sessions of developmentally appropriate group therapy for one hour a week. Although the literature suggests that activity groups meet for 90 minutes (Bratton & Ferebee, 1999; Kottman, Strother, & Deniger, 1987), one-hour time blocks were used because of the school schedule. The activity groups followed the principles laid out by Bratton and Ferebee (1999), using humanistic theory. This theory believes that people strive for mastery and growth, self-understanding, self-direction, and socialization. It also emphasizes the importance of the therapeutic relationship and the need for belonging and being part of a group (Bratton & Ray, 2000; Task Force for the Development of Guidelines for the Provisions of Humanistic Psychosocial Services, 1997). The group activity therapy provided three different opportunities for the preadolescents to practice skills: semi-structured activities (10 to 15 minutes), self- or group-directed time (15 to 20 minutes), and a snack time (10 to 15 minutes).

During the semi-structured activity time, I would introduce an activity that served as a catalyst for self-exploration. The activity broke the ice and encouraged the preadolescents to engage. The purpose of the activity was not to focus on a completed product or to direct the preadolescents' play, but rather to facilitate group cooperation and cohesion (Ginott, 1994), comfort of the students by encouraging them to interact, and anxiety reduction for those who were timid about joining in the group and who tend to be withdrawn (Bratton & Ferebee, 1999; Hillman, Penczar, & Barr, 1975; Paone et al., 2008).

The self-directed, group-directed time provided opportunities for group members to practice decision-making skills, test limits, and explore their world and how they are perceived (Landreth, 2002). Also, during self-directed play, preadolescents gain a sense of power, when they may feel otherwise feel powerless, and self-control. Through their own exploration, preadolescents develop an internal locus of control. In the group, the preadolescents' current relationship skills become evident (Schachter, 1974). When they came to the surface, I was able to facilitate awareness and understanding within and between group members. With this new understanding, preadolescents can choose to modify their behavior so that their peers more readily accept them (Ginott, 1975).

Snack time has a special significance. Schiffer (1969) recognized this significance, as snack time is a time when children share spontaneously from both in and out of the session. Snack time also provides a transition, providing closure and allowing the students to prepare to go back to class. After checking with parents for food allergies and to respect any dietary restrictions, a variety of snacks was offered to the students. When possible, students were allowed to participate in the preparation of the snack. For example, preadolescents decorated cookies or mixed their own punch.

The control group did not receive specialized interventions during the study. I did provide large-group activity therapy to the control group, however, after the data were collected.

DESCRIPTION OF PLAY THERAPIST

The activity groups were conducted by the researcher. At the time of the research, I was in the final year of my doctoral program and had advanced training and supervision in play therapy, group therapy, group play therapy, and group activity therapy. I am a white female, who was in my mid-thirties at the time.

DATA ANALYSIS

To determine the effect of group play and activity therapy on preadolescents, a pre-test–post-test experimental control group design was used. Analysis of covariance (ANCOVA) was performed on all appropriate data. An a priori alpha level of .05 was established as a criterion for determining statistical significance. Cohen's d effect size was calculated to determine the practical significance of the results.

RESULTS

Specific pre-test and post-test means as well as ANCOVA results for this study can be found in Packman and Bratton (2003).

TOTAL BEHAVIOR

The group play and activity therapy had a large treatment effect on the behaviors of the experimental group as measured by the BASC ($d = .91$). Also, a large treatment effect was found on the total scores on the CBCL-PRF ($d = .82$). The overall composite scores for the BASC yielded statistical significance ($p = .05$), while the CBCL did not indicate statistical significance ($p = .08$).

INTERNALIZING PROBLEMS

The internalizing problems scale of the BASC yielded a large effect size ($d = 1.03$), as did the internalizing problems scale of the CBCL ($d = .90$). Also, statistical significance was found on the internalizing problems scale of the BASC and CBCL ($p = .03$ and $p = .05$, respectively). These improved behaviors of preadolescents are consistent with other play therapy studies that use humanistic play therapy techniques (Brandt, 1999; Tyndall-Lind, 1999; Kot, Landreth, & Giordano, 1998). Similar to results in these studies, preadolescents in the treatment group decreased mean scores on the internalizing problems scale, while those in the control group showed no change or a slight increase in mean score.

Post hoc analysis of the subscales was conducted to determine the specific areas in which the preadolescents experienced improvement in their internalizing behavior. It was determined that scores of the BASC and CBCL found statistical and practical significance on the anxiety and depression subscales of the BASC ($p = .01$, $d = .92$, respectively) and the anxious and depressed subscale of the CBCL ($p = .08$, $d = .98$, respectively). Students participating in group play and activity therapy showed a decrease in anxiety and depression. The somatic complaints measures of both of the instruments, while not statistically significant at the 0.05 level, demonstrated a moderate treatment effect (BASC $d = .54$, CBCL $d = .53$), indicating that those who participated in the groups were less likely to complain of stomachaches, headaches, and nausea. Analysis of the attention problems subscale of the CBCL showed a moderate treatment effect ($d = .56$), indicating that the students participating in the group play and activity therapy sessions showed an increase in their ability to remain on task, exercise self-control, and improve their school work.

EXTERNALIZING PROBLEMS

The externalizing composite scores of the BASC and CBCL showed less improvement, but the treatment effect of both were noteworthy. The BASC yielded a medium effect size ($d = .53$), and the CBCL yielded a moderate-to-large effect size ($d = .78$). These effect sizes indicate that participants in the treatment decreased externalizing behavior such as aggression and delinquent actions. No statistical significance was found on the BASC ($p = .24$) or on the CBCL externalizing behavior scale ($p = .09$).

Further analysis of the externalizing subscales was done to determine specific areas of improvement. These results revealed that preadolescents in the experimental group were less overactive, more patient, and more socially courteous of others (waiting their turn, not interrupting). Also, a large ($d = 1.04$) effect size on the delinquent behavior subscale of the CBCL indicated that students who participated in the play and activity groups were more aware and sensitive to the feelings of others, less likely to lie to get out of trouble, found appropriate ways to deal with dissatisfaction, and made better choices in friends, while those in the control group demonstrated a gain in delinquent behavior as determined by parent ratings on the BASC and CBCL. A moderate-to-large effect size was also found on the aggression subscale of the CBCL ($d = .71$), indicating a meaningful decrease in teasing, arguing, destroying property, fighting, and being mean in general for the students in the experimental group as compared to those in the control group.

SUBJECTIVE OBSERVATIONS

Internalizing Behavior Problems   The findings on the internalizing subscales of the BASC and CBCL are supported by teacher and parent comments and my recorded qualitative observations. Anxious behavior, along with withdrawal and isolation, caused many preadolescents to have difficulty forming relationships with teachers and peers. I observed several children move from anxiety and withdrawal to confidence and engaging behavior.

For example, in Session 1, Don rarely smiled and seemed uncomfortable with the boisterous actions of the other group members. Choosing to be silent and observe the two other group members, Brian and John actively engaged with one another, with Brian exhibiting particularly aggressive behavior. I used reflections to facilitate an understanding of each group member's intentions as well as their verbal and nonverbal responses to each other.

During Session 1, a group of boys were sword fighting during the group-directed playtime. Don, a quiet child, would flinch each time the swords came near. I would reflect that Don was overwhelmed by all the activity in the playroom. At the end of the session, as the group was leaving the room, Brian looked at Don and said, "I know I was kind of overwhelming." During the next session, Brian chose to modify his aggressive behavior with more marked improvements by Session 4. This change, along with the therapist's support and understanding of Don's needs, and the influence of the group allowed Don to feel more comfortable with himself and the other group members. Don then became more engaged in the group activities. In Session 4, the group played a game where they took turns buying things and setting up forts. In this session, Brian continually instructed Don how he thought things should be used. Don participated but acquiesced to Brian's directions. By Session 6, however, Don began to state his needs: "No, Brian, I like it the way I'm doing it." He was no longer anxious and withdrawn, but rather was engaging, smiled frequently, and was able to express his desires. Also, Brian was able to accept Don's assertiveness, and the group played together harmoniously.

This example was substantiated by Don's teachers, who reported that after completing the groups he was, "more outgoing and interacted more in class" as well as more able to laugh and share his sense of humor. Don's mother also reported that he was more outgoing with children in the neighborhood and more able to stand up for himself. Don's mother further noted that he no longer participated or sanctioned when his friends acted in ways that he did not agree with. Brian's teachers also stated that he was showing more responsibility for his work and more respect for other's opinions. Parents and teachers for several students reported similar results.

Through group play and activity therapy the students were able to, through an internal locus of control, exhibit less impulsivity. After a particularly rowdy session in which the preadolescents played tag with pieces of paper propelled through straws, the preadolescents seemed interested in continuing this activity in the classroom. As the group was leaving, they began to put paper and straws into their pockets. I stated, "Guys, I know you would like to take that stuff back to your classroom, but the items in the room are for staying in the room," then walked to the door. The students followed, opened the door, and began walking back to class. About half way down the hall, one of the students dramatically grinned and exclaimed, "I can't do it!" From his pockets, he removed paper and a straw. I matched the students' affect and reflected, "Even though you could have snuck those out, you just couldn't do it." The student returned the items to the room. Through his own sense of responsibility and control, the preadolescent was able to respect the limit and leave the items in the room.

Externalizing Behavior Problems   Among students diagnosed with attention deficit disorder (ADD), there was a marked increase in positive behaviors. Some of the treatment group students became more patient and used their energy constructively to accomplish goals. During the course of the intervention, I observed the students learning to delay gratification and beginning to take turns. One popular activity for all groups was basketball. While there were several balls in the room, there was only one hoop; and often, all group members wanted to play at the same time. The preadolescents quickly learned that if they impulsively threw the balls all at once, it was difficult for anyone to get the ball in the hoop. In every group, by the midpoint, participants were able to negotiate a solution that allowed cooperative attainment of goals. After treatment, teachers reported that the students were less impulsive and more patient in class and games or in the lunch line. Several parents also made similar comments: "He's less frustrated and more patient when we go places," and "She's able to save her energy for playing outside instead of running through the house."

I also observed improved social interactions between the students during the group activity sessions. Children who were not accepted by the other group members were able to modify their interactions, allowing them access to their desired peer group. Preadolescents stated that the group setting gave them the opportunity to meet and get to know people they would not have met otherwise. These students stated that they had also begun to interact in the lunchroom and on the playground. Teachers observed similar new friendships develop, stating that the students that went to the group together were associating with one another more. Parents reported that their preadolescents seemed to be making new friends and approaching children with ease.

DISCUSSION

This was the first study using group activity therapy with learning-disabled preadolescents. It supports group activity therapy as an effective and appropriate intervention with learning-disabled preado-lescents. Overall, findings show that the treatment had a positive effect on the behavior of the preadolescents by revealing statistically signifi-cant effects on total behavior on the BASC and internalizing behavior on both the BASC and CBCL. More important to clinicians, practical significance was indicated with the treatment having a large effect size on four of the six scales (BASC: BSI and internalizing behavior, and CBCL: total score and internalizing behavior), a moderate-to-large effect size on one (CBCL externalizing behavior), and a medium effect size on one (BASC externalizing behavior). The overall effect size for this study was computed ($d = .83$) and is consistent with the body of play therapy outcome studies ($d = .80$) and better than the body of play therapy outcome studies in which professionals were the therapeutic agents ($d = .73$) (Ray et al., 2001). Also, the effect size is consistent with child psychotherapy research ($d = .78 - .70$) (Kazdin, Ayers, Bass, & Rodgers, 1990).

These positive results as well as parent, teacher, and researcher observations support the use of group play and activity therapy in schools. Preadolescence is a difficult time, and preadolescents with a learning disability have added challenges. Group activity therapy can have a profound effect on the behavior, coping, and interacting skills of preadolescents diagnosed with a learning disability.

By using group, the school counselor can meet the needs of more students in less time. When group activity therapy takes place in the school, teachers are likely to observe changes more quickly because the group members are also in class together. So they are practicing skills with the very students they may be having trouble with. Behaviors learned in the group are more likely to be seen in the lunchroom, classroom, and playground.

This project's results were consistent with other research on play therapy. Specifically, positive results justify the use of group activity therapy in schools with preadolescents. Parents, teachers, the researcher's observations, and the students themselves agreed that the groups were effective. One important piece of information from this study is the necessity to identify and treat depression and anxiety in preadolescents. Depression and anxiety in adults are diagnosed and treated in the United States with regularity. The signs of depression and anxiety in children are often ignored or misdiagnosed. It is especially important to treat childhood depression and anxiety because many times the instigators of school violence are described as loners who are withdrawn. By identifying symptoms early and using developmentally appropriate interventions, practitioners can be catalysts in assisting the client in a lifetime of meaningful interactions in lieu of facing the inter- and intrapersonal ramifications brought on by years of living with anxiety and depression.

RECOMMENDATIONS FOR FURTHER RESEARCH AND PRACTICE

After completing this research, there are several areas that still need to be researched. For example, the sample size of this study was small, and it would be ideal to replicate this project using more students. Doing this would increase knowledge and increase the power of the statistical findings. Additionally, a follow-up study would allow us to know if the improved behavior was maintained. Including training for parents and teachers would provide consistency for the students to continue to improve their learned skills. Filial therapy research supports that parents and teachers can be effective therapeutic agents in children's lives. By teaching these techniques to those who interact with the children, the children's school and home experience would be consistent with the positive environment of the groups.

CONCLUSION

The current review of the literature suggests that this study is the first treatment-outcome study designed to focus on a humanistic and developmentally sensitive group activity therapy model of intervention for learning-disabled preadolescents. The statistical and practical significance of these results as well as the comments of parents, teachers, the researcher, and the students indicate that group activity therapy is an effective intervention in reducing behavior problems of learning-disabled preadolescents. Therefore, school mental health professionals are encouraged to implement group play and activity therapy with preadolescents.

REFERENCES

Achenbach, T. M., & Edelbrock, C. (1991). *Manual for the child behavior checklist.* Burlington, VT: University of Vermont Department of Psychiatry.

Brandt, M. (1999). *Investigation of play therapy with young children.* Unpublished doctoral dissertation, University of North Texas, Denton, TX.

Bratton, S. C., & Ferebee, K. (1999). The use of structured expressive art activities in group activity therapy with preadolescents. In D. S. Sweeney & L. E. Homeyer (Eds.), *Group play therapy: How to do it, how it works, whom it's best for* (pp. 192–214). San Francisco, CA: Jossey-Bass.

Bratton, S. C., & Ray, D. C. (2000). What the research shows about play therapy. *International Journal of Play Therapy, 9*(1), 47–88.

Erikson, E. H. (1980). *Identity and the life cycle.* New York: Norton (originally published 1959).

Ginott, H. (1975). Group play therapy with children. In G. Gazda (Ed.), *Basic approaches to group psychotherapy and group counseling* (2nd ed.) (pp. 327–341). Springfield, IL: Thomas.

Ginott, H. (1994). *Group psychotherapy with children: The theory and practice of play therapy.* Northvale, NJ: Jason Aronson.

Hillman, B., Penczar, J., & Barr, R. (1975). Activity group guidance: A developmental approach. *Personnel and Guidance Journal, 53*(10), 761–767.

Johnson, M. (1988). Use of play group therapy in promoting social skills. *Issues in Mental Health Nursing, 9*(1), 105–112.

Kazdin, A., Ayers, W., Bass, D., & Rodgers, A. (1990). Empirical and clinical focus of child and adolescent psychotherapy research. *Journal of Consulting and Clinical Psychology, 58,* 729–740.

Kot, S., Landreth, G. L., & Giordano, M. (1998). Intensive child-centered play therapy with child witnesses of domestic violence. *International Journal of Play Therapy, 7,* 17–36.

Kottman, T., Strother, J., & Deniger, M. (1987). Activity therapy: An alternative therapy for adolescents. *Journal of Humanistic Education and Development, 25*(4), 180–86.

Krall, V., & Irvin, F. (1973). Modalities in treatment in adolescence. *Psychotherapy: Theory, Research, and Practice, 10*(3), 248–250.

Landreth, G. L. (2002). *Play Therapy: The art of relationship* (2nd ed.). Muncie, IN: Accelerated Development.

Ormrod, J. E. (2009). *Essentials of educational psychology* (2nd ed.). Upper Saddle River, NJ: Merrill.

Packman, J., & Bratton, S. C. (2003). A school-based group play/activity therapy intervention with learning disabled preadolescents exhibiting behavior problems. *International Journal of Play Therapy, 12*(2), 7–29.

Paone, T. R., Packman, J., Maddux, C., & Rothman, T. (2008) A school-based group activity therapy intervention with at-risk high school students as it relates to their moral reasoning. *International Journal of Play Therapy, 17*(2), 122–137.

Piaget, J. (1977). *The development of thought: Equilibration of cognitive structures.* New York: Viking Press.

Reynolds, C. R., & Kamphaus, R. W. (1992). *Manual for the behavior assessment system for children.* Circle Pines, MN: American Guidance Service.

Schachter, R. (1974). Kinetic psychotherapy in the treatment of children. *American Journal of Psychotherapy, 28*(3), 430–437.

Schiffer, M. (1969). *The therapeutic play group.* New York: Grune & Stratton.

Task Force for the Development of Guidelines for the Provision of Humanistic Psychosocial Services (1997). Guidelines for the provision of humanistic psychosocial services. *The Humanistic Psychologist, 24,* 64–107.

Tyndall-Lind, A. (1999). *A comparative analysis of intensive individual play therapy and intensive sibling group play therapy with child witnesses of domestic violence.* Unpublished doctoral dissertation, University of North Texas, Denton, TX.

U.S. Public Health Service (2000). *Report of the Surgeon General's conference on children's mental health: A national action agenda.* Washington, DC Author.

Winston School Testing and Evaluation Center. (2003). http://www.winston-school.org/WW%20Summer%2003/Pages/Testing.htm.

Yasutake, D., & Bryan, T. (1995). The influence of affect on the achievement and behavior of students with learning disabilities. *Journal of Learning Disabilities, 28,* 329–334.

CHAPTER 10

School-Based Child-Centered Play Therapy with Hispanic Children

YVONNE GARZA

Un elefante se balanceba sobre la tela de una araña. Como veía que resistía fue a llamar a otro elefante.

One elephant balanced atop a cobweb. When he noticed it supported him, he called another elephant.

—Yolanda Nava (2000)

H OW MIGHT THIS children's saying give insight on Hispanic culture? Consider this: There are nuances of each culture that give us cues into its values and beliefs. Responsive application of these values in the helping professions may help this group, which historically underuses services, to seek out or adhere to services. There is an apparent consensus in the literature supporting cultural characteristics such as *familia*/family, interdependence, *personalismo*/personalism, and *respeto*/respect as characteristics commonly valued in Hispanic culture (Andres-Hyman, Ortiz, Anes, Paris, & Davidson, 2006; Garza & Watts, in press; Gil, 2005). First, take into account how each of these has an essence of relationship; and second, reflect on the overall implication as a play therapist.

The children's saying at the beginning of this chapter, for me, speaks to the heart of Hispanic culture regarding the importance of relationship in gaining the *confianza*, or trust, of the culture. In essence, if one feels supported (validated and valued) as the elephant did in the story, one is more likely to trust. Consequently, as play therapists, this equates to applying a strategy that is in agreement with the expectations and preferences of our clients. I believe that child-centered play therapy (CCPT) is a culturally responsive strategy for Hispanic children. To that end, I discuss in this chapter both the outcome of my study and the interplay between CCPT principles and Hispanic values.

RATIONALE: PUTTING AWARENESS INTO ACTION

I remember reading reviewer comments and feedback from a grant proposal for my study, stating that while they saw value in the cultural focus, the concern was that I would not acquire an adequate number of participants to proceed with my research. These reviewers held a collective concern, similar to statements in the literature, that people of Hispanic background historically underuse mental health services (Andres-Hyman et al., 2006; Foulks, 2004).

Researchers suggest that as a group, Hispanics are less likely to seek out or adhere to counseling services than people of other cultures. This may be truer for families in which English is not the language spoken in the home. Additional barriers include:

- If illegal immigrants, fear of being reported
- Unfamiliarity with the concept of mental health
- Cost
- Inaccessibility of services
- Mistrust of government systems (Foulks, 2004)

From a helping perspective, this issue is exacerbated as we bring to light that Hispanic children are at risk for academic failure, least likely to attend kindergarten, and are overrepresented in the population of school dropouts (Gudiño, Lau, & Hough, 2008; NAEYC, 2008; NCES, 2007). Yet in a study exploring reasons for dropping out of school among Hispanics, researchers found concerns that were appropriate for counseling and may have been prevented with an early intervention such as play therapy. Students reported that they don't fit in, they have problems with teachers, they have poor peer relations, and they don't feel safe as reasons for dropping out. Interestingly enough, all of these themes have a relationship factor (Texas Legislative Council, 2000).

Thinking back to the time of my research, the relationship factor was not a foreign concept to me. Being of Hispanic background myself, I lived it. I even noticed that after Catholic Mass at my church, both the priest and the elementary school's English language (ESL) teacher had equal amounts of Hispanic families waiting to speak with them. Again, reflecting on those reviewer comments and the need for participants, I wanted the type of relationship that existed between the ESL teacher and the Hispanic community. I needed to gain their trust because I would be asking them to sign consent forms whereby they agreed to allow their child to be in a study, be videotaped, and be tested. While the services were free, these concepts can be frightening for parents.

I began volunteering in the school in which I would conduct my study, helping at events planned around Mexican holiday celebrations and at school functions where Spanish-speaking parents would meet. I hoped this action would foster trust between me and the Spanish-speaking community. I moved from a place of cultural awareness to cultural responsiveness, thus setting a tone for my research (Bazron, Osher, & Fleischman, 2005). Subsequent application included speaking the language of the child, modifying the playroom toys and materials with cultural consideration (discussed later in the chapter), and tackling perceived common barriers to service. Because Hispanic families generally trust their child's school, a school-based play therapy study would minimize and even eliminate barriers to treatment, such as families dealing with fear of deportation, cost, inaccessibility, and mistrust.

A prevailing movement in the literature is addressing the mental health needs of children at a younger age, using school-based services (Flores et al., 2002; NHSA, 2006; United States Public Health Service, 2001). The curative factors of play therapy and its use as a viable modality is supported in literature (LeBlanc & Ritchie, 1999; Bratton, Ray, Rhine, & Jones, 2005). Unfortunately, there is little in the way of research regarding play therapy with diverse populations, particularly Hispanic children (Constantino, Malgady, & Rogler, 1986; Garza & Bratton, 2005). My study investigated the use of CCPT as a school-based modality for Hispanic children.

METHOD

One criticism of CCPT is that many studies are conducted using a control group rather than a comparison group design. Using a pre-test–post-test design, I wanted to address this concern by investigating the effects of play therapy compared to a well-researched school guidance curriculum on school-age Hispanic children's behaviors.

PARTICIPANTS

My study was conducted in a school district in the Southwest United States with a population of approximately 35 percent Hispanic students. The elementary schools selected for the study were Title 1 schools representative of the district ratio of Hispanic students. Participants (n = 30) were selected from Hispanic, Spanish-speaking kindergarten through fifth-grade students ranging in age from 5 to 11 years who were referred to school counseling services by their parents or teachers because of behavioral concerns. Using the behavior assessment scale for children (BASC), the child's parent and teacher rated the child on perceived behaviors. Children scoring in the at-risk or clinically significant range of the BASC were included in the study (Reynolds & Kamphaus, 1992). Participants were assigned by random drawing by grade level to either the CCPT treatment (n = 15) or curriculum-based small group counseling (n = 15). One student in the comparison treatment group moved out of the area, thus 29 participants completed the study.

Of interesting note, although school officials identified all subjects as Hispanic on child demographic sheets, parents were more explicit during parent interviews and clearly identified their child as Hispanic if born in the United States and Mexican if born in Mexico. All 30 parents who completed the data sheets indicated that they were born in Mexico, so they identified themselves as Mexican. Of the children, 16 were identified by their parents as Hispanic, and 13 children were identified as Mexican. The cultural breakdown is worthy of discussion since it may indicate that parents of children in my study were fairly traditional to the Mexican culture and that information gathered from this population may be unique to a more indigenous population of Hispanics. Because the majority of children were identified as Hispanic, for the purpose of my study, *Hispanic* was used throughout to refer to all participants.

INSTRUMENT

The Behavior Assessment System for Children-Parent Rating Scale (BASC-PRS) and teacher rating scale (BASC-TRS) by Reynolds and Kamphaus (1992) was designed to rate child behavior. This measure was chosen for its reliability and validity and because it is published in both English and Spanish. The Spanish version, BASC-PRS, was used with parents who were not fluent in English. The BASC has two scales: adaptive and clinical. For the purpose of my study, the two composite scores within the clinical scale, externalizing behaviors (aggression, conduct, and hyperactivity) and internalizing behaviors (anxiety, depression, and somatization) were used to assess problem behaviors. Reynolds and Kamphaus (1992), in a summarization of reliability and validity studies for the BASC-PRS and BASC-TRS, indicated that both composites have high internal consistency and test-retest reliability, with scores in the .80s to low .90s. At the time of the study, tests on reliability and validity had not been conducted for the Spanish version of the BASC-PRS.

TREATMENT

To accommodate the school schedule, children in both treatment groups received a 30-minute intervention once per week for 15 weeks (both treatments typically call for 45-minute interventions). Both treatment providers were bilingual Hispanic counselors with post-master's training and experience in person-centered counseling. The counselor for the play therapy treatment group had completed advanced training and supervision in the theory and application of CCPT. The counselor for the curriculum-based small group counseling was certified to teach the chosen curriculum and had received advanced training and supervision in person-centered group counseling. Both counselors introduced their respective intervention in both Spanish and English, informing the children that they could choose to speak either Spanish or English or both during sessions. Additionally, throughout treatment, counselors responded in-kind to the children's spontaneous use of language. When the child spoke Spanish, the therapist responded in Spanish, and when the child spoke English, the therapist responded in English.

Experimental Treatment The children in the experimental group received CCPT following the basic principles and methodology of CCPT proposed by Landreth (2002). Sessions were held in specially equipped playrooms in the school setting. The playrooms were stocked with toys and materials listed by Landreth (2002). Being an advocate of more responsive treatment, however, I included additional toys in attempt to accommodate the experiences of the Hispanic culture. The culturally specific toys were decided upon by a panel of five Hispanic Spanish-speaking registered play therapists who used CCPT in their work with Hispanic children (Garza, Hinojosa, Molina, Muzquiz, & Rinaldi, personal communication, July 18, 2003). Toys were selected on the basis of the perception that they would capture elements of Hispanic culture and environment and would be in line with Landreth's categories of real life, acting out, and creative expression. The intent of the toys was to demonstrate the counselor's openness to culture, facilitate choices of symbols that the child could readily identify with, and facilitate a familiar and safe space. An extensive toy list can be found in the article by Garza and Bratton (2005).

Comparison Treatment   The children in the comparison group received curriculum-based small group counseling. Kids Connection, a Rainbow Days product, was chosen on the basis of the following criteria:

- It was defined as a culturally competent program, with both English and Spanish handouts,
- Designated as a school-based counseling curriculum used in 33 states,
- Recognized as an "Exemplary" program,
- Noted as an empirically supported program (Rainbow Days, 2003).

The format for the group included a topic of focus and time for discussion, followed by a play-based activity. Topics included developing autonomy and self-esteem and improving peer relationships. Content and art activities were grade-level specific.

DATA COLLECTION

Home visits were conducted both at pre-testing and post-testing stages for both treatment groups in cases in which transportation was an issue so that testing could be conducted within a controlled time frame. A Spanish-speaking therapist was available for reading the testing instrument in cases in which the parent had difficulty reading Spanish. Also, in cases in which the family had very young or multiple children, a research assistant was available to care for those other children to allow the parent to focus attention on the questionnaire with limited distractions, thus ensuring consistency in data collection procedures across subjects. It was assumed that teachers could find a quiet time and place outside of class to complete the questionnaire as was provided for parents, so a controlled environment was not provided. This resulted in tests being returned late and teachers being observed hurriedly completing their instruments. The failure to provide a controlled testing environment resulted in inconsistent data collection procedures across subjects rated by teachers. It is important to note that because all children were receiving treatment, parents and teachers were blinded to which intervention children received.

A two (group) by two (time) repeated measures analysis of variance (ANOVA) was used to compare pre- and post-test scores of Hispanic children in the two treatment groups (CCPT and curriculum-based small group counseling). An alpha level of .05 was set so we could examine the significance of the change in scores across time. I also calculated the effect size or magnitude of the difference using Cohen's *d*. I followed Cohen's (1988) guidelines for interpretation, in which he proposed that .20 is considered a small treatment effect, .50 is a medium effect, and .80, is a large effect.

RESULTS AND DISCUSSION

EXTERNALIZING PROBLEMS

Regarding the externalizing problems composite scale of the BASC-PRS, results yielded statistically significant results ($p = .04$) in support of the CCPT treatment. The Cohen *d* test resulted in a large treatment effect ($d = .76$). These results indicated that according to parent reports, the CCPT treatment was indeed more effective than the comparison treatment and had a large treatment effect on the externalizing behaviors of participants. Regarding the externalizing problems composite scale of the BASC-TRS, results did not yield statistical or practical significance. I suspect that because of inconsistencies in the post-test collection of teacher data, previously discussed, I do not have confidence that the results are a true measure of the teachers' experience.

The results based on parent reports left me curious. Having completed the pre-test interviews with parents, I noted conduct problems as the most common referral complaint from parents, and I wanted to examine what role that played in the subscales. I asked two questions of the parent during pre-test interviews to solicit spontaneous feedback: "What concerns you most about your child?" and "What do you like most about your child?" What had an impact on me was how, in both cases, the consistent responses from parents was a focus on conduct. For example, "My concern is that he doesn't mind me" ("No me haga caso") or "I enjoy him when he minds me" ("Me gusta cuando me hasce caso").

Because of the parents' strong focus on their children's conduct, I conducted a post hoc analysis on the conduct problems subscale of the BASC-PRS. The externalizing composite scale of the BASC is composed of the subscales of hyperactivity, aggression, and conduct problems. The post hoc analysis yielded statistically significant results ($p = .02$) and a large effect size ($d = .86$). This finding supported my suspicion that parents who are Mexican immigrants, as a group, tend to place a high value on conduct in their parenting. I have used this data since in addressing families of similar backgrounds, particularly when recruiting parents for Child Parent Relationship Therapy (CPRT; Landreth & Bratton, 2006) or filial therapy. For example, I make it a point to list "strengthening good conduct as a result of CCPT" in flyers and recruiting materials when targeting this population. It is noteworthy to discuss that the list of behaviors identified under conduct problems are consistent with behaviors that have been identified with placing Hispanic children at a higher risk for academic struggles and delinquency (NCES, 2007). Thus, this treatment has the potential to prevent future problems often associated with this population.

INTERNALIZING PROBLEMS

Children receiving CCPT showed a reduction in internalizing behavior problems on the BASC-PRS over the children in the comparison group, but not at a statistically significant level ($p = .12$). A test for effect size produced a moderate effect size ($d = .58$). These results indicate that per parents' report, children in the CCPT group demonstrated moderate improvement in behavior as a result of the treatment. A larger participant group may have resulted in statistically significant scores. Results from the teachers' report on the internalizing problems scale did not reveal statistical or practical significance. As noted previously, irregularities in post-test collection of teacher data made it difficult to confidently interpret teacher results.

The moderate treatment effect on internalizing problems reported by parents is of particular clinical importance, since these types of behaviors are generally less disruptive and often go unnoticed by parents and teachers. If left untreated, these problems can lead to more serious and costly problems in adolescents (U.S. Public Health Service, 2001). Other controlled play therapy outcome studies, conducted with mostly Caucasian children, have shown moderate-to-large treatment effects on internalizing problems such as depression, somatization, and anxiety when compared to no treatment (Constantino et al., 1986; Jones et al., 2002; Packman & Bratton, 2003).

ANECDOTAL DATA

I collected anecdotal data throughout the study from school administrators and teachers as well as parents regarding how the treatment affected children's day-to-day functioning. These were spontaneous statements from sources close to the client who commented on the noticeable changes in the child's day-to-day life. Additionally, observations made by myself and the other clinician who conducted the curriculum-based group are discussed in this section.

SCHOOL PERSONNEL OBSERVATIONS

The playroom in one school was located in the back part of the administrative building. Along the back wall were several school desks in a row positioned to face the wall. The school desks were utilized as a consequence for children who were referred to the office because of conduct issues. It was around the third week of the study when office administrators mentioned that they had noticed a decrease in office referrals. By the end of the school year, they had removed all of the desks but one, stating that the need for the desks had substantially decreased.

In another example, a teacher described a five-year-old student she referred to the study as excessively withdrawn and anxious. This teacher was very familiar with the student since this was the second year that she would be assigned to be his teacher. By the third week of the study, she stopped me and said, "I don't know what you guys are doing in play therapy but keep it up; this week was the first time I've seen him smile in the two years he's been with me."

THE CASE OF THE BOY WHO COULDN'T WIN

PRESENTING PROBLEM

Aurelio, a seven-year-old boy, was referred by his teacher because of anxious behaviors. The teacher described Aurelio as a child who did not take academic risks and who struggled with building social relationships with peers. According to the teacher, Aurelio seemed to find comfort in standing next to her during recess and would become apparently nervous when encouraged to engage in free play with his classmates. During class activities, Aurelio needed prompting through each step and seldom completed a task without encouragement from the teacher.

PARENT MEETING

I met with Aurelio's mother in an effort to gain consent for treatment. She described Aurelio as a child with little motivation, noting that in the past he had joined both a baseball and a soccer team and had participated in karate, all with the end result of prematurely quitting the sport. Through further discussion, she mentioned that Aurelio had a brother one year older and that because of their closeness in age, they were enrolled in these events together. Apparently, the brother was developmentally more skilled at these sports than Aurelio, resulting in feelings of inadequacy and lack of enjoyment. So, because he couldn't compete, he gave up.

PLAY THERAPY

Aurelio was consistent in his play during our sessions together. A theme of mastery with feelings of defeat was typical of his play session. Aurelio would generally create games with the dart guns or wrestle the bop bag, creating fantasy characters as opponents. At times he gave his opponent his brother's name. In his play he would experiment with finding ways to give himself an edge, like manipulating the rules in his favor or giving himself a stronger weapon or magical powers. Regardless of the assistance, he almost always lost to his imaginary opponent and this resulted in feelings of disappointment and exhaustion.

I used basic child-centered play therapy responses to reflect Aurelio's experience in the playroom. I believe esteem-building statements that mirrored his experiences of determination and mastery—no matter how fleeting—were particularly helpful. For example, "You did that by yourself," "That was hard but you didn't give up," and "You weren't sure if it would work but you stuck with it." Also, esteem-building statements that captured elements of the person he wished he could be as he experienced them during fantasy play were used. These included, "You feel really strong," "You're showing me you can do that in several different ways," and "You used both your brains and your muscles that time."

While Aurelio's defeatist attitude was a prominent theme in most of his sessions, around Session 8 his teacher commented that he was beginning and completing assignments without encouragement from her and was raising his hand to answer questions during class discussions. By the end of the intervention, the teacher reported that Aurelio was "excelling in his grades" and had been named table captain of his work group. Subsequently, he was encouraging to others in his group and engaged in free play during recess. In Aurelio's next-to-last play therapy session, he won his first imaginary wrestling match against two brothers, labeled by Aurelio as the "powerful brothers, the most powerful of all the wrestlers."

CULTURALLY RELEVANT OBSERVATIONS

CCPT I made several observations during my study that caught my curiosity and, I believe, warrant consideration, especially since so little is known about play therapy with Hispanics—or any minority population of children. First, the very young children who spoke only Spanish at the beginning of treatment began inserting English words in their Spanish sentences in later weeks of treatment. The English words were emotional terms like "Cool," "Oh, man," or "Alright" and were used spontaneously. I wonder if these were terms learned on the playground during recess. The insertion of these types of words in English was common among Spanish speakers.

In a second observation regarding differences in ethnicity and gender, I experienced male participants to be more proficient with tools in the playroom than same-age children of other ethnicities. They knew the name of the tool and its purpose and seemed adept at using it. They also told stories of helping family members build and fix things with them. The female participants more frequently chose the Caucasian doll over the Hispanic one but Hispanic food items over American. Third, regarding overall toy selection, children noticeably used culturally specific toys during the first three play sessions, and their referencing seemed to be within the context of demonstrating familiarity or to engage me in relational conversation. The culturally specific toys did not seem to be crucial to play themes after the initial sessions, but rather to set the stages of safety and relationship.

Culturally Based Guidance Group The counselor who conducted the guidance group shared his observations specific to culture. First, the males in the groups frequently referenced one another as *compadres*, which translates to *godfather*. In a formal context, a compadre is a male relative or family friend selected to play the role of godfather in religious ceremonies such as baptism. Informally, the term is used loosely and connotations signify a life-long bond of friendship. I believe because the Hispanic culture values close and often dependent relationships with family and community, that these children found a way to mimic that within their group setting. It would be interesting to replicate my study substituting group play therapy for individuals to examine whether it is a more responsive fit for school-age Hispanic children.

A second example of significance is that the counselor noted the participants using their native Spanish language to discuss emotionally laden or taboo topics such as skipping school, experimenting with smoking, excessive drinking of parents, and, in one case, a mother's promiscuity.

In a third example, during the Thanksgiving holiday, the participants walked to their classrooms after group and pointed out their artwork posted on the hallway wall. Their class was given the assignment to decorate their turkeys and they were allowed to choose from a variety of art supplies including feathers, sequins, multicolored noodles, and such. The counselor was awestruck as each child in his group pointed to his or her turkey; they had utilized only rice and beans to design their turkey. While my observations do not provide definitive information, they are interesting to consider when providing counseling services to this population and offer direction for future research.

RECOMMENDATIONS

Although further research is warranted to corroborate these results, I believe my study shows strong support for CCPT as a viable treatment modality for Hispanic children. The results are noteworthy because this study compares CCPT to a research-supported intervention. There is a particularly strong indication that the behavioral outcome of children who receive CCPT interfaces with a behaviorally focused value (obedience) of Hispanic parents.

Current researchers encourage play therapy studies with minority groups; yet these types of studies are the least represented in play therapy literature (Ray, Bratton, Rhine, & Jones, 2001). While the present study addresses this need for research with culturally diverse groups and lays a foundation of empirical support for CCPT with Hispanic children, replication studies with a larger sample across multiple settings are needed to consider CCPT as an evidence-based treatment for this population. The present study leaves several questions unanswered that should be explored in further research. Would we receive different results if post-testing for teachers was conducted in the same careful manner as the post-testing for parents? How would the results have been different if a larger sample size was used? Would

Hispanic children from other areas receive the same treatment benefits as children in this study? Because the Hispanic culture values interdependence of family and community, would we achieve greater results from group CCPT?

Further research studying these and related factors will help those in the field of play therapy understand the effects of play therapy with Hispanic children. Conducting research in schools seems particularly important for this population. Children receiving school-based services are more likely to be identified early, more likely to receive services because of access to free services for all students, and less likely to drop out of treatment. These factors are significant for a population that generally underuses community mental health services (Andres-Hyman et al., 2006).

In closing, conducting this study confirmed an already held belief of mine that there is a significant need to recruit and train Hispanic Spanish-speaking counselors specifically trained in play therapy. We cannot ignore the increasing mental health needs of a rapidly growing Hispanic population in the United States. Perhaps a greater level of need, however, is for counselors of all ethnicities to be more culturally responsive in the services they provide, including consulting with colleagues regarding toys and materials that capture elements of culture and environment for clientele, consulting with community resources on the unique cultural needs of the group, and most importantly, applying cultural knowledge learned from clients and their families.

REFERENCES

Andres-Hyman, R., Ortiz, J., Anes, L., Paris, M., & Davidson, L. (2006). Culture and clinical practice: Recommendations for working with Puerto Ricans and other Latinas(os) in the United States. *Professional Psychology: Research and Practice, 37*(6), 694–701.

Bazron, B., Osher, D., & Fleischman, S. (2005). Creating culturally responsive schools. *Educational Leadership, 63*(1), 83–84.

Bratton, S. C., Ray, D. C., Rhine, T., & Jones, L. (2005). The efficacy of play therapy with children: A meta-analytic review of treatment outcomes. *Professional Psychology: Research and Practice, 36*(4), 367–390.

Cohen, J. (1988). *Statistical power analysis for the behavioral sciences* (2nd ed.). New York: Academic Press.

Constantino, G., Malgady, R., & Rogler, L. (1986). Cuento therapy: A culturally sensitive modality for Puerto Rican children. *Journal of Consulting and Clinical Psychology, 54*(5), 639–645.

Flores, G., Fuentes-Afflick, E., Barbot, O., Carter-Pokras, O., Claudio, L., Lara, M., et al. (2002). The health of Latino children: Urgent priorities, unanswered questions, and research agenda. *Journal of the American Medical Association, 288*, 82–90.

Foulks, E. F. (2004). Commentary: Racial bias in diagnosis and medication of mentally ill minorities in prisons and communities. *The Journal of the American Academy of Psychiatry and the Law, 32*(1), 46.

Garza, Y., & Bratton, S. C. (2005). School-based child-centered play therapy with Hispanic children: Outcomes and cultural considerations. *International Journal of Play Therapy, 14*, 51–71.

Garza, Y., & Watts, R. E. (in press). Filial therapy and Hispanic values: Common ground for culturally sensitive helping. *Journal of Counseling and Development.*

Gil, E. (2005). From sensitivity to competence in working across cultures. In E. Gil & A. Drewes (Eds.), *Cultural issues in play therapy* (pp. 3–25). New York: Guilford.

Gudiño, O., Lau, A., & Hough, R. (2008). Immigrant status, mental health need, and mental health service utilization among high-risk Hispanic and Asian Pacific Islander youth. *Child and Youth Care Forum, 37*, 139–152.

Jones, L., Rhine, T., & Bratton, S. C., (2002). High school students as therapeutic agents with young children experiencing school adjustment difficulties: The effectiveness of filial therapy training model. *International Journal for Play Therapy, 11*(2), 43–62.

Landreth, G. L. (2002). *Play therapy: The art of the relationship.* Bristol, PA: Accelerated Development.

Landreth, G. L., & Bratton, S. C. (2006). *Child parent relationship therapy (CPRT): A 10-session filial therapy model.* New York: Brunner-Routledge.

LeBlanc, M., & Ritchie, M. (1999). Predictors of play therapy outcomes. *International Journal of Play Therapy, 8*(2), 19–34.

National Association for the Education of Young Children (NAEYC). (2008). *Standard 8: NAEYC accreditation criteria for community relationship standard* (2008). Retrieved March 16, 2008, from http://www.naeyc.org/academy/standards/standard8/standard8A.asp.

National Center for Education Statistics (NCES). (2007). *Status and trends in the education of racial and ethnic minorities.* Washington, DC: Institute of Education Sciences, U.S. Department of Education.

National Head Start Association. (2006). *About the National Head Start Association.* Alexandria, VA: National Head Start Association.

Nava, Y. (2000). *It's all in the frijoles: 100 famous Latinos share real-life stories, time-tested dichos, favorite folktales, and inspiring words of wisdom.* New York: Fireside.

Packman, J., & Bratton, S. C., (2003). A school-based group play/activity therapy intervention with learning disabled preadolescents exhibiting behavior problems. *International Journal of Play Therapy, 12*(2), 7–29.

Rainbow Days, Inc. (2003). *Kids' connection: A support group curriculum for children, ages 4–12*. Dallas, TX: Rainbow Days, Inc.

Ray, D. C., Bratton, S. C., Rhine, T., & Jones, L. (2001). The effectiveness of play therapy: Responding to the critics. *International Journal of Play Therapy, 10*(1), 85–108.

Reynolds, C. R., & Kamphaus, R. W. (1992). *Behavior assessment scale for children*. Circle Pines, MN: American Guidance Service.

Robinson, J., Landreth, G. L., & Packman, J. (2007). Fifth-grade students as emotional helpers with kindergartners: Using play therapy procedures and skills. *International Journal of Play Therapy, 16*, 20–35.

Texas Legislative Council. (2000, April). *Facts at a glance: Youth violence in the United States and in Texas*. TLC Research Division. Retrieved October 15, 2004, from http://www.tlc.state.tx.us.tlc/reasearch/pubs.htm.

United States Public Health Service. (2001). *Report of the Surgeon General's conference on children's mental health: A national agenda*. Washington, DC: Author.

CHAPTER 11

Effectiveness of Child-Centered Play Therapy for Children Referred for Aggression

BRANDY SCHUMANN

USE OF PLAY THERAPY IN ELEMENTARY SCHOOLS

Two experiences during my graduate work served as the foundation for this study. I was involved in a pilot study educating teachers to become therapeutic agents for their most challenging students (see Ray, Muro, & Schumann, 2004). The study produced exciting data, including post-qualitative interviews I held with the participating teachers. Their stories of producing successful relationships with their students were inspiring. I particularly remember a teacher becoming tearful when describing the moment her selectively mute student began to speak. As recent literature suggests, I was witnessing first-hand the benefit of using play therapy in schools (Baker & Gerler, 2004; Newsome & Gladding, 2003; Schmidt, 2005; White & Flynt, 1999.) Around this time, I was also providing play therapy service to a second-grade African American boy at his school who was frequently described as highly aggressive and "exhaustingly oppositional." As we proceeded through the play therapy treatment, the frequency of problematic teacher reports and office referrals lessened. Both his teacher and I came to experience him as more cooperative and his behavior as more socially appropriate. His previously nonparticipative mother also experienced a change of such significance that she was willing to continue services during the summer at our clinic.

As I began to research the areas of school-based play therapy and play therapy in the treatment of aggression, I found that there remained gaps documenting effectiveness and that the research was often criticized for the use of control groups rather than comparison groups. This study was performed in an effort to address those gaps. The thought behind the study was to put play therapy to the test. I wanted to measure the effectiveness of play therapy in treating the most challenging of children within a school setting, those expressing aggression. I then wanted to compare the results against the widely accepted treatment modality for schools, group guidance.

The literature available justified my quest. The U.S. Public Health Service (2001) report indicated that a growing number of children's emotional, behavioral, and developmental needs are not being met effectively. The Surgeon General stressed a need for an increase in school-based counseling services, noting that greater access to services could facilitate a reduction in barriers to academic success and serve as prevention against the development of future mental health problems. With the increase in school referrals related to aggressive, acting-out behaviors, schools are in need of effective interventions to assist aggressive children with psychological problems.

Elementary school is one setting in which tolerance for aggression is low and usually met with punishment, such as expulsion, suspension, or alternative school placement. Following the American School Counselor Association national model (2005), school counselors are encouraged to offer prevention and intervention for schoolwide problems. As part of school counseling duties, school counselors provide guidance curriculum to help prevent problem behaviors and responsive services, such as counseling, to intervene with recurring problem behaviors. In response to the need for guidance curriculum needs to address aggression, schools strive to offer interventions that are preventative and will help children cope with aggressive compulsions through teaching coping skills. One such prevention program, which is affirmed by research and national award-granting agencies including the U.S. Departments of Education and Health and Human Services as well as the Collaborative for Academic, Social, and Emotional Learning (CASEL), is Second Step: A Violence Prevention Curriculum (Committee for Children, 2002a; Carey, Dimmitt, Hatch, Lapan, & Whitson, 2008). Second Step is a "universal prevention program that proactively teaches critical social and emotional skills to all children. The curriculum goals are focused on reducing aggressive and disruptive behavior while promoting social-emotional competence" (Committee for Children, 2002b, p. 4). The Second Step units are based primarily on cognitive-behavioral theory, and are designed to improve children's skills in three general areas: empathy, impulse control and problem solving, and anger management.

White and Flynt (1999) and Landreth (2002) emphasized that elementary school counselors should be aware of the developmental needs of their students and understand that play is a natural activity of children through which a child communicates, tests, incorporates, and masters his world. Children's language development lags behind their cognitive development. Thus, efforts to communicate with children solely on a verbal level will result in awkward and unnecessary miscommunications (Landreth, 2002). Berg (1971) stressed that school counselors should use play therapy skills equally with those of verbalization and behavior modification.

From their year-long pilot study, Ray, Muro, and Schumann (2004) indicated child-centered play therapy may be a valuable counseling intervention for school counselors when providing responsive services. They collected qualitative data from school administrators and teachers that suggested a decrease in office referrals, an increase in academic performance, and an improvement in classroom behavior. Ray et al. explained that play therapy fits the ASCA (2005) national model, serving the student population as a responsive service and appearing to be a valuable school intervention. More recently, Ray, Blanco, Sullivan, & Holliman (2009) found larger effect size gains for aggressive children who participated in play therapy when compared with control group children on the aggressive behavior subscale of the Child Behavior Checklist.

METHOD

DESIGN

This quantitative study used a matched pre-test–post-test comparison group quasi-experimental design (Vogt, 1999). Full details related to this study can be found in Schumann (2003). The population studied comprised volunteer children identified as aggressive in kindergarten through fourth grade, ages 5 to 12, who qualified for counseling services at a Title I public elementary school. A school is categorized as Title I if more than 50 percent of the school population receives reduced-cost or free lunch. The selected school had a population that was approximately 56 percent Hispanic, 28 percent Caucasian, and 15 percent African American, with the remaining percentage of the population represented by other ethnicities. The children were re-quired to meet the following criteria to be eligible for participation in this study:

- Had parental or guardian consent
- Agreed to participate in 15 weeks of individual play therapy or group guidance
- Spoke English
- Were referred for school counseling services through their school by their parents or teacher or from the student discipline board
- Were not currently receiving play therapy services or any other form of psychotherapy
- Were rated as at risk or clinically significantly aggressive as measured by the behavioral assessment system for children-parent report form or teacher report form by a parent, guardian, or teacher.

Children who were referred by teachers and parents and met the aforementioned criteria were then matched in pairs on grade level and assigned to one of the two interventions. One of each pair was assigned to either the play therapy treatment group, which received 12 to 15 individual child-centered play therapy sessions, or the curriculum-based small-group guidance group, which received 8 to 15 group guidance sessions, consisting of 12 to 19 lessons. Of the 56 children who volunteered to participate in the study, 19 were excluded from the analyses because 8 moved to a new campus, 1 was receiving weekly mental health services in a community setting, 8 were absent excessively, and 2 because their therapist did not meet the criteria to offer services for this study. Of the 37 children participating in this study, 20 (17 males and 3 females) were in the play therapy treatment group and 17 (15 males and 2 females) in the guidance comparison group. In regard to ethnicity, the play therapy group consisted of 10 Hispanic, 6 Caucasian, and 4 African American children. The group guidance group was composed of 4 Hispanic, 8 Caucasian, and 5 African American children. Further-more, the play therapy group was composed of 3 kindergartners, 3 first-graders, 4 second-graders, 4 third-graders, and 6 fourth-graders. The guidance group was composed of 3 kindergartners, 6 first-graders, 5 second-graders, and 3 third-graders. Because of un-controllable circumstances from the naturalistic setting of schools, the groups were not equally matched.

INSTRUMENTS

In an effort to enhance accuracy and consistency in measuring aggression, two types of behavioral instruments, with well-established reliability and validity, were used. Both the behavioral assessment system for children (BASC) (Reynolds & Kamphaus, 1992) and the Child Behavior Checklist/Caregiver-Teacher Report Form (CBCL/C-TRF), (Achenbach, 2002; Achenbach & Rescorla, 2000, 2001) were used as pre- and post-test measures of effectiveness for play therapy and the Second Step program. Each parent or guardian and teacher was asked to complete the BASC and CBCL/C-TRF for each participating child.

The BASC is a self-administered questionnaire that is recognized for its comprehensive measures of both adaptive and problem behaviors in the school, community, and home setting. The items are rated on a four-point scale of frequency, ranging from never to almost always. The BASC assesses both verbal and physical aggression in a combined score. Verbal aggression includes arguing, name-calling, criticizing, blaming, and verbally threatening others. Physical aggression includes breaking others' possessions, hitting others, and being cruel to animals. The BASC also calculates clinical problems in the broad composites of externalizing problems and internalizing problems. This study primarily focused on the aggressive subscale and the internalizing and externalizing problems composite scores of the behavior scales.

The CBCL/C-TRF are versions of a well-established and recognized family of instruments for the identification of behavior and emotional difficulties in children. The self-administered checklist provides a record of behavioral symptoms of children that parents, guardians, or teachers perceive as competencies or limitations. The 118-item instrument allowed the participant to rate behavioral symptoms and emotional descriptors on a three-point scale of frequency, ranging from not true to very true or often true. The items have been factor analyzed into the eight subscales, including aggressive behavior. Performing a second-order factor analysis of the behavior problem scale yields two primary composites termed *internalizing problems* and *externalizing problems*. This study focused primarily on the aggressive behaviors subscale and the internalizing and externalizing domains.

COLLECTION OF DATA

After ensuring informed consent, each parent or guardian was provided the pre-tests in a sealed envelope sent home with the child. Substitute teachers were provided for the participating teachers, allowing them to complete their instruments during the day without distractions. Post-test data were collected in the same manner. Information obtained from the instruments was recorded with a code number. Only I had a list of the participants' names. It should be noted that nine parents failed to complete post-testing in the time frame allotted. Thus, their scores were excluded from parent score analysis, but because post-testing scores were collected from the teachers for these same children, the children are still included in the teacher score analyses. Qualitative data in reference to children's behaviors were obtained from comments from the parents, teachers, and therapists to determine clinical implications of the study. To document significant verbalizations and happenings, the therapists completed a play therapy session summary form or a group guidance session summary form immediately following each session. Additional qualitative data were gathered from parents through face-to-face feedback sessions with their child's therapist held after the post-test instruments were completed.

TREATMENT

The 20 children who participated in the play therapy treatment group of this study received individual child-centered play therapy once a week for 30 minutes for a minimum of 12 sessions. The modified session length of 30 minutes was selected to match the typical length of counseling sessions in a school environment and to meet scheduling demands. All sessions were conducted in the play therapy room at the participants' school. The room was equipped with toys that conformed to Landreth's (2002) recommendations. The playroom was also equipped with culturally sensitive items such as multicultural toys that capture elements of the Hispanic culture, including Hispanic dolls, plastic food, and musical instruments. The play therapists responded to children by using basic and advanced nonverbal and verbal child-centered play therapy responsive skills at an appropriate rate with succinct and interactive responses (Landreth, 2002; Ray, 2004).

The 17 children who participated in the curriculum-based small-group guidance group of this study attended grade-level group guidance lessons based on the violence prevention curriculum of the Second Step program once a week for 30 minutes for a minimum of 12 lessons. The 30-minute session length was selected on a basis of recommendation from the Second Step program instruction and conveniently matched the length structure of the play therapy treatment group.

Second Step was designed to develop students' social and emotional skills while teaching them to change behaviors and attitudes that contribute to violence. The curriculum teaches students' skills central to healthy social and emotional development: empathy, impulse control, and problem solving. Although designed as a prevention program, the Second Step curriculum in this study was utilized as an intervention rather than a classroom guidance curriculum and was presented to children already identified as aggressive (see McMahon, Washburn, Felix, Yakin, & Childrey, 2000) in a small-group setting led by a counselor. Authors of the Second Step curriculum recommended that classroom teachers conduct the lessons in a universal classroom format, but they noted that it is not required (Committee for Children, 2002b). Thus, counselors were utilized as leaders of small groups to maintain a response service format typically provided by school counselors.

All therapists who participated were graduate-level counseling students who were experienced in play therapy. The eight therapists for the individual child-centered play therapy group had completed at least two play therapy courses and a counseling practicum with an emphasis on play therapy. The four therapists for the curriculum-based small-group guidance group received training in school guidance that consisted of attending a seminar taught by a university faculty member whose specialty was school counseling. They also attended training conducted by the investigator on the Second Step program.

RESULTS

QUANTITATIVE

Though I attempted random assignment, it was not purely conducted. Therefore, independent sample t-tests and Leven's tests for homogeneity of variances, $F = 67.1, p > .05$, were necessary to demonstrate that the two treatment groups were statistically equal prior to treatment. Because of my small sample size, another concern was the potential lack of power. Thus, a Cohen's d effect size was computed for each independent sample t-test in order to determine the practical significance of the t-test results (Thompson, 2002). All Cohen's d effect sizes were small, ranging from .004 to .353, indicating no to small practical significant difference between pre-test means (Cohen, 1988). These results demonstrated that the means of the treatment groups were equal before treatment and the differences thus documented on the post-test can tentatively be attributed to the treatment.

A two-factor mixed repeated measure analysis of variances (treatment group × time) was computed for each of the 12 variables to determine whether the play therapy treatment and curriculum-based small-group guidance groups behaved differently across time. An alpha level of .05 was established as the criterion for either retaining or rejecting the hypotheses. Eta squared (η^2) effect size was computed for each two-factor mixed repeated measures to determine the practical significance of the results (Thompson, 2002). Each calculation was interpreted using Cohen's (1988) suggested strength indexes.

The results for all 12 analyses, illustrated in Table 11.1, indicated significant main effects of time but no significant interaction effects (Thompson, 2002). These results document that the children of this study significantly improved their behavior over time, regardless of treatment group. These results suggest that both child-centered play therapy and curriculum-based small-group guidance in the school setting decreased the aggressive behaviors of children, decreased the internalizing problems of aggressive children, and decreased the externalizing problems of aggressive children. Moderate effect sizes were found for internalizing ratings scored by both parents and teachers and externalizing ratings scored by teachers. Thus, the data seem to indicate that school-based child-centered play therapy is as effective at improving the behaviors of aggressive children as the nationally recognized evidence-based guidance curriculum program Second Step: A Violence Prevention Curriculum. When statistically analyzing whether or not the play therapy treatment and curriculum-based small-group guidance groups behaved differently over the course of the study, no statistically significant difference and little practical significance was found. I would like to see further research, including the use of a control group, to determine conclusive results and to discern possible effects of maturation.

QUALITATIVE

Qualitatively, twice as many parents (10 to 5) and six times as many teachers (6 to 1) reported observable improvement of behavior among the children assigned to the play therapy group compared to children assigned to the curriculum-based small-group guidance group. For example, one parent who initially emphasized that her daughter "doesn't listen at school" could not identify any area of concern at the post-play therapy treatment interview. The parent instead reported that she "listens a whole lot better" and was now reading two times higher than her first-grade level. Another parent reported

Table 11-1

Main Effects of Time and Eta Squared for 12 Variables as Measured
by the BASC and CBCL

Variable	Main Effect of Time/ Eta Squared	Interaction Effect/ Eta Squared
BASC-TRS Aggression subscale	$[F(1, 37) = 8.448, p < .05]$ $\eta^2 = .041$	$[F(1, 37) = .133, p > .05]$. $\eta^2 = .001$
BASC-TRS Internalizing Problems	$[F(1, 37) = 13.712, p < .05]$ $\eta^2 = .073$	$[F(1, 37) = .979, p > .05]$ $\eta^2 = .005$
BASC-TRS Externalizing Problems	$[F(1, 37) = 11.072, p < .05]$ $\eta^2 = .054$	$[F(1, 37) = .776, p > .05]$ $\eta^2 = .004$
BASC-PRS Aggression subscale	$[F(1, 28) = 5.465, p < .05]$ $\eta^2 = .016$	$[F(1, 28) = .001, p > .05]$ $\eta^2 \leq .001$
BASC-PRS Internalizing Problems	$[F(1, 28) = 13.604, p < .05]$ $\eta^2 = .093$	$[F(1, 28) = .163, p > .05]$ $\eta^2 = .001$
BASC-PRS Externalizing Problems	$[F(1, 28) = 8.925, p < .05]$ $\eta^2 = .036$	$[F(1, 28) = .059, p > .05]$ $\eta^2 \leq .001$
CBCL-TRF Aggression subscale	$[F(1, 37) = 8.712, p < .05]$ $\eta^2 = .049$	$[F(1, 37) = 2.535, p > .05]$ $\eta^2 = .014$
CBCL-TRF Internalizing Problems	$[F(1, 37) = 8.791, p < .05]$ $\eta^2 = .056$	$[F(1, 37) = .226, p > .05]$ $\eta^2 = .001$
CBCL-TRF Externalizing Problems	$[F(1, 37) = 11.073, p < .05]$ $\eta^2 = .057$	$[F(1, 37) = 2.241, p > .05]$ $\eta^2 = .012$
CBCL-C Aggression subscale	$[F(1, 28) = 5.264, p < .05]$ $\eta^2 = .036$	$[F(1, 28) = .101, p > .05]$ $\eta^2 = .001$
CBCL-C Internalizing Problems	$[F(1, 28) = 4.239, p < .05]$ $\eta^2 = .036$	$[F(1, 28) = .200, p > .05]$ $\eta^2 = .002$
CBCL-C Externalizing Problems	$[F(1, 28) = 4.316, p < .05]$ $\eta^2 = .042$	$[F(1, 28) = .154, p > .05]$ $\eta^2 = .001$

increased independence and courage, improved confidence, and less-withdrawn behaviors in her son's post-play therapy interview. No parents reported an increase in behavioral problems from their children from the play therapy treatment group, whereas one parent noted an increase in problems from the group guidance group. I share this child's story later in this chapter. One teacher reported increases in behavioral problems from a member of the play therapy treatment group, and two teachers reported an increase among the group guidance group. These results demonstrate clinical support for the effectiveness of child-centered play therapy in improving the behaviors of aggressive children over that of curriculum-based group guidance.

Case Study: How to Help Justin

I present Justin's story for your consideration. Though his name has been changed for publication, I believe his story is helpful in illustrating the importance of this research. At the time of this study, Justin was a 5-year-old kindergartner recommended by his teacher for participation in this study because of his "defiant behavior" and "angry outbursts." She reported that he frequently threw tantrums and threatened to hurt others. He also used foul language and made alarming comments such as "I wish I were dead." Significant pre-measures from his teacher illustrated clear and significant concern for externalizing problems and aggression. His mother's pre-measures indicated no quantitative concerns, but she did go to extra effort to report "He has his father's temper. Once he decides he doesn't like something or someone, he will make himself miserable over it."

Just before the onset of services, Justin was transferred to a new class because of his continued behavior problems. Interestingly, his new teacher recommended him for the study within five days of knowing him. She wrote on the qualifying paperwork, "I'm concerned about the way he deals with connections—he yells, runs away, crawls around, and ignores teachers or hits or kicks them." Her pre-measures concurred with his former teacher's with significant ratings on the aggression subscales and externalizing problems composite scores.

Justin was assigned to the group guidance treatment group in which he attended all 15 sessions. He was described by his assigned therapist as *"very* aggressive." She specifically recalled a session in which she had to pick Justin up for a guidance session from the office rather than his classroom. He had been sent to the office as a disciplinary act and was eager to leave the office and join the therapist for group. In the guidance session, he became violent toward another member, requiring the therapist to become physically involved. As the therapist made an effort to protect the other member, Justin kicked her so hard he drew blood.

She further noted in other group guidance sessions he was "frequently distracted" and "out of control." He was destructive to the curriculum materials and repeatedly aggressive toward other members. He once turned the light off in an effort to make the room dark and then began to push other children. He would also run away when the group was over and it was time to return to class. The therapist recalled the groups as physically and emotionally exhausting and believed she was actually witnessing his aggression increase. Throughout the sessions, she experienced Justin's behaviors as predominantly seeking her attention. Therefore, at the conclusion of the study she recommended individual play therapy services so as to provide the individual attention he seemed to be seeking.

At the completion of the group guidance sessions, Justin's teacher's post-measures indicated continued significant concerns for aggression and externalizing problems. They also indicated an increase of concern for internalizing problems. Similarly, his mother's post-measures indicated significant concern for both aggression and externalizing problems. Her post-testing interview revealed comparable results. She experienced him as having an "increase in outbursts and behavior problems" and cited examples such as his suspension from school. It seemed, as a whole, Justin's aggression had increased through the course of the study.

Because of the high degree of concern reported from his teacher and therapist and now shared by herself, his mother agreed to have Justin attend individual child-centered play therapy session with the same therapist he had for the study. Though no quantitative data were collected as to the effects of the play therapy services, clinically significant reports were made by his teacher, mother, and therapist noting considerable improvements in his behavior. Moreover, the school counselor specifically sought out his therapist to share what a dramatic difference she had observed in Justin.

DISCUSSION

One of the major strengths of this study is that it was conducted at school, in a real-world setting. In addition, the use of 30-minute play therapy and guidance sessions conformed to typical school practice. Moreover, this study differed from previous play therapy research in several ways. First, data were collected across an average of 14.25 play therapy sessions, whereas previous studies investigating the effects of play therapy used typically 10 or fewer sessions. Second, this study compared play therapy to a nationally recognized and empirically supported guidance program, finding equality in their effectiveness. Third, this study was unique in that it utilized a violence prevention curriculum as an intervention or response service format with a population already identified as aggressive.

One possible explanation for the nonsignificant statistical results between the play therapy group and the group guidance group is the training of the therapists leading the guidance group. As with the play therapy treatment therapists, the curriculum-based small-group guidance group therapists were experienced in play therapy, having completed at least two play therapy courses and a practicum focused on play therapy. The therapists were instructed during their guidance training not to use their verbal and nonverbal child-centered play therapy communication skills during their group guidance sessions to isolate the modalities. It was not anticipated that the play therapists would have difficulty refraining from using their play therapy skills.

To determine whether or not this occurred, I interviewed each of the four group guidance therapists and surveyed a randomly selected single videotaped session from each of the four grade-level guidance groups. Results from the interviews indicated a wide use of play therapy communication skills, with three of the four group guidance therapists reporting they used their child-centered play therapy skills over half of the time they spent with their participants. The fourth therapist reported spending only 30 percent of the available group time on the group guidance curriculum because of the need to contain the children's behaviors. One therapist said during the interview, "I tried not to use them (play therapy skills), but I couldn't avoid using them." The therapist went on to say that she tried to use the rewards suggested by the Second Step group guidance curriculum, "but they (rewards used to promote curriculum) didn't matter when they (children) got aggressive, so I had to use limit setting." All four of the therapists reported that they responded with Landreth's (2002) ACT model of therapeutic limit setting when they felt it necessary to limit a behavior. One therapist humorously recalled, "I knew I had used my play skills in group when they started doing play therapy on each other . . . one (child) actually set an ACT limit on another (member)."

Remarks such as these suggest that the therapists may have had a tendency to switch to play therapy skills to subjectively improve the immediate result rather than continue with what appeared to be failing. It is not known how many of the Second Step suggestions for handling disruptive behavior (redirecting, transitional comments, reminding to use listening skills, introducing ways to calm down, taking a break, and ending the lesson) (Committee for Children, 2002c) were used by each of the therapists before attempting child-centered play therapy limit setting. It should be noted that the room used for the small-group guidance lessons met Second Step suggested criteria to encourage good listening and cooperative learning, including open space, no enticing toys within reach on open shelves, and visually blocked from "comings and goings in other parts of the school" (Committee for Children, 2002c, p. 40).

The therapists' struggle to avoid the use of their play therapy skills was also evident in the randomly selected videotaped sessions. In reviewing the tapes, I tallied timed uses of play therapy skills only if it led to a deviation from the group guidance curriculum. My reviews of the four sessions revealed that the leaders used their play therapy skills 22 to 58 times in their 30-minute sessions. This suggests that the guidance curriculum was not followed and may have significantly affected the results of this intervention.

Because the results of this study tentatively support the use of group guidance in schools to decrease the aggressive behaviors of children, it is important for future therapists to consider the characteristics of the group guidance provided. A high use of child-centered play therapy skills throughout the group guidance sessions became evident. They included reflection of feeling, the reflection of content, and limit setting. These skills are considered to be basic and essential in play therapy sessions (Axline, 1969; Landreth, 2002). Thus, to achieve similar results it is recommended that counselors who use small-group guidance or an intervention with aggressive children should, in a school setting, be adequately trained in play therapy skills.

I also postulate the potential contribution made by group versus individual therapies may have accounted for the nonsignificant results. Although play therapy was done on an individual basis, three to five children were assigned to each of the guidance groups. Landreth and Sweeney (1999) outlined multiple benefits the presence of another child or several children brings to the therapeutic relationship. They included facilitating child-therapist relationship, diminishing tension, stimulating activity and participation, and providing opportunity for vicarious learning.

RECOMMENDATIONS

Based on the results of this study, I have several recommendations for further research. It would be valuable to replicate this study using a larger sample size, including increasing the size of the group guidance groups to actual classroom proportions, thereby increasing the power of statistical measures. I recommended that a replication of this study be conducted using counselors who have not been trained in play therapy to lead the curriculum-based small-group guidance group or monitor or supervise guidance sessions throughout the duration of the study in an effort to improve the validity of the study, by isolating the variable of play therapy to the play therapy treatment group. I also recommended that a replication of this study be conducted with the addition of a control group. This addition will enhance the research design and permit additional conclusions to be drawn as to the effectiveness of play therapy on the aggressive behaviors of children. A well-controlled study that investigates the effectiveness of group play therapy with aggressive children is also recommended. Furthermore, a follow-up study should be conducted to determine the long-term effectiveness and generalizability of improved behavior.

REFERENCES

Achenbach, T. M. (2002). *Teacher's report form.* Retrieved January 6, 2004, from Achenbach system of empirically based assessments web site: http://www.aseba.org/PRODUCTS/trf.html.

Achenbach, T. M., & Rescorla, L. A. (2000). *Manual for the ASEBA preschool forms & profiles.* Burlington, VT: University of Vermont, Research Center for Children, Youth, & Families.

Achenbach, T. M., & Rescorla, L. A. (2001). *Manual for the ASEBA school-age forms & profiles.* Burlington, VT: University of Vermont, Research Center for Children, Youth, & Families.

American School Counselor Association. (2005). *The ASCA national model: A framework for school counseling programs* (2nd ed.). Alexandria, VA: Author.

Axline, V. M. (1969). *Play therapy.* New York: Ballantine.

Baker, S. B., & Gerler, E. R. (2004). *School counseling for the twenty-first century* (4th ed.). Upper Saddle River, NJ: Merrill/Prentice Hall.

Berg, C. (1971). Some thoughts on the need for a philosophical base in elementary counseling. *The School Counselor, 18*(4), 228–235.

Carey, J., Dimmitt, D., Hatch, T., Lapan, R., & Whiston, S. (2008). Report of the national panel for evidence-based school counseling: Outcome research coding protocol and evaluation of student success skills and second step. *Professional School Counseling, 11*, 197–206.

Cohen, J. (1988). *Statistical power analysis for the behavioral sciences* (2nd ed.). Hillsdale, NJ: Erlbaum.

Committee for Children. (2002a). *Second Step: A violence prevention curriculum.* Seattle: Author.

Committee for Children. (2002b). *Second Step: A violence prevention curriculum, Preschool/kindergarten-grade 5, administrator's guide.* Seattle: Author.

Committee for Children. (2002c). *Second Step: A violence prevention curriculum, Preschool/kindergarten, teacher's guide.* Seattle: Author.

Landreth, G. L. (2002). *Play therapy: The art of the relationship* (2nd ed.). New York: Brunner-Routledge.

Landreth, G. L., & Sweeney, D. (1999). The freedom to be. In D. S. Sweeney & L. E. Homeyer (Eds.), *Group play therapy: How to do it, how it works, whom it's best for* (pp. 39–64). San Francisco: Jossey-Bass.

McMahon, S. D., Washburn, J., Felix, E. D., Yakin, J., & Childrey, G. (2000). Violence prevention: Program effects on urban preschool and kindergarten children. *Applied and Preventive Psychology, 9*, 271–281.

Newsome, D., & Gladding, S. (2003). Counseling individual and groups in school. In B. Erford (Ed.), *Transforming the school counseling profession* (pp. 209–229). New York: Brunner-Routledge.

Ray, D. C. (2004). Supervision of basic and advanced skills in play therapy. *Journal of Professional Counseling: Practice, Theory, and Research, 32*(2), 28–41.

Ray, D. C., Blanco, P., Sullivan, J., & Holliman, R. (2009). An exploratory study of child-centered play therapy with aggressive children. *International Journal of Play Therapy, 18*(3), 162–175.

Ray, D. C., Muro, J., & Schumann, B. (2004). Implementing play therapy in the schools: Lessons learned. *International Journal of Play Therapy, 13*(1), 79–100.

Reynolds, C. R., & Kamphaus, R. W. (1992). *Behavior assessment system for children.* Circle Pines, MN: American Guidance Service.

Schmidt, J. (2003). *Counseling in schools: Essential services and comprehensive programs* (4th ed.). Boston: Allyn & Bacon.

Schumann, B. (2005). Effects of child-centered play therapy and curriculum-based small group guidance on the behaviors of children referred for aggression in an elementary school setting. Doctoral dissertation, University of North Texas, Denton, 2004. *Dissertation Abstracts International, 65/12*, 4476.

Thompson, B. (2002). "Statistical," "practical," and "clinical": How many kinds of significance do counselors need to consider? *Journal of Counseling Development, 80*, 64–71.

U.S. Public Health Service. (2001). *Report of the Surgeon General's conference on children's mental health: A national agenda*. Washington, DC: Author.

Vogt, W. P. (1999). *Dictionary of statistics and methodology: A nontechnical guide for the social sciences* (2nd ed). London: Sage.

White, J., & Flynt, M. (1999). Play groups in elementary school. In D. S. Sweeney & L. E. Homeyer (Eds.), *Group play therapy: How to do it, how it works, whom it's best for* (pp. 336–358). San Francisco: Jossey-Bass.

CHAPTER 12

Effectiveness of Child-Centered Play Therapy and Person-Centered Teacher Consultation on ADHD

A Single-Case Study Design

APRIL SCHOTTELKORB

A SINGLE-CASE PLAY THERAPY DESIGN FOR CHILDREN WITH ADHD

Carlos,* a fifth-grade Hispanic male, moved with his family from Mexico to the United States when he was a second-grader. In the second, third, and fourth grades, his teachers complained that he was hyperactive and had a difficult time focusing and paying attention in class. His teachers mentioned that he would often crawl around the classroom and talk too much with others. At the beginning of fifth grade, Carlos's teacher expressed concern to the school counselor about his inattentive, hyperactive, and impulsive behaviors. His teacher believed Carlos may have attention deficit hyperactivity disorder (ADHD).

---

*Name changed to protect client confidentiality.

RATIONALE

Attention deficit hyperactivity disorder (ADHD) is one of the most common mental health diagnoses in childhood, with approximately 3 to 7 percent of children meeting the criteria (American Psychiatric Association, 2000; Woodard, 2006). The behaviors of students with ADHD are stressful for teachers, and the long-term ramifications for the students are troubling. Researchers have found that children diagnosed with ADHD end up with less education, lower high school GPAs, lower job performance ratings, more symptoms of ADHD at work, and more arrests (Barkley, Fischer, Smallish, & Fletcher, 2002).

In my experience as a former elementary school counselor and a consultant in the schools, teachers often made referrals for students like Carlos, students with hyperactive, impulsive, and inattentive behaviors. Many of these students' behaviors would qualify them with ADHD. For children to receive this diagnosis, they must meet certain behavioral criteria listed in the American Psychiatric Association's *Diagnostic and Statistical Manual of Mental Disorders*, 4th edition, Text Revision (DSM-IV-TR: American Psychiatric Association, 2000). More specifically, children must exhibit inattentive behaviors or hyperactive or impulsive behaviors before the age of seven for at least six months, and these behaviors must cause impairment in two or more settings.

Many of the traditional methods of treating children with ADHD include stimulant medication, behavioral parent training, behavioral classroom interventions, social skills training, and summer treatment programs (American Psychological Association, 2007). These five interventions were identified by the American Psychological Association (APA) as "well-established" or "probably efficacious" treatments for children with ADHD. At this time, play therapy is not considered an evidence-based intervention for children with ADHD (DuPaul & Stoner, 2004; Pelham & Gnagy, 1999). Because play therapy is not considered an evidence-based intervention for children with ADHD and yet my personal experience working with this population has found it to be effective in reducing ADHD behaviors, I wanted to research the effectiveness of child-centered play therapy (CCPT) with these children.

PLAY THERAPY AND ADHD

The number of studies that have investigated the effectiveness of play therapy for children with ADHD is limited. Blinn (1999) conducted a case study examining the effectiveness of play therapy with a 6-year-old Caucasian boy diagnosed with ADHD. A psychiatrist diagnosed the child participant with ADHD, a phonetic disorder, stuttering difficulties, and mild mental retardation. Blinn used a licensed marriage and family counselor to provide 10 50-minute play therapy sessions over a period of seven months. Blinn assessed the child participant pre- and post-treatment for noncompliance, tantrums, and verbal and physical aggression through parent report, caregiver report, and direct observation. Based on the lack of significant change on the pre- and post-testing of the parents and the daycare provider, as well as the mixed results of the observational data, Blinn concluded that play therapy was not effective. Blinn's study contained many limitations, however, that reduced the meaningfulness of the findings. I believe that, at minimum, these limitations make the results questionable: the small number of play therapy sessions over a lengthy period of time, the lack of an operational definition for the type of play therapy used, the lack of information regarding the training and experience of the therapist, the use of different raters at pre- and post-testing, the lack of observational data, and the co-morbid diagnoses of the child.

A recent study investigating the effectiveness of CCPT for children with ADHD occurred concurrently with this study and was presented in an earlier chapter. Ray, Schottelkorb, and Tsai (2007) identified 60 elementary students with clinical levels of ADHD on the Conners Teacher Rating Scale-Revised: Short Form (CTRS-R:S). These students were randomly assigned to 16 30-minute sessions of either CCPT or reading mentoring. The researchers found that children in the CCPT group demonstrated statistically significant improvement in the reduction of anxiety or withdrawal symptoms and emotional lability in comparison to the children in the reading mentoring group. Both groups improved at statistically significant levels on the ADHD index of the CTRS-R:S.

With the mixed results in these studies, it is evident that further research examining the effectiveness of CCPT is needed for children with ADHD. Because of the push for evidence-based practice, I wanted to design a quality, rigorous research investigation. The APA (2007) has determined that only two types of research designs are sufficient for determining evidence-based interventions. These research designs must use experimental between-group or single-case methodology in which the researcher compares the intervention to another treatment, uses a treatment manual, and clearly specifies client characteristics (APA, 2007). Because of the emphasis on the need for controlled single-case designs and because of my interests, I decided to use a single-case design.

SINGLE-CASE DESIGN

Single-case research is considered the best type of research to use when trying to explain individual behavior changes (Morgan & Morgan, 2003). Experimental single-case research can demonstrate causal relationships and validity similar to group design research. In single-case research, however, each individual serves as his or her own control. To achieve this control, continuous assessment must occur before and during the intervention to allow the researcher to assess for change (Kazdin, 2003). Kazdin reported that these observations should occur multiple times each week at a minimum, but might take place on a daily basis. Besides continuous assessment, a second essential feature of single-case design is a baseline assessment phase (Kazdin, 2003). During the baseline phase, no intervention occurs. The researcher uses this phase to observe the participant and define a pre-intervention level of performance, which is used to compare with the treatment phase data. Without this baseline phase, the researcher would be unable to ascertain the effectiveness of a treatment.

A third essential feature of single-case research is the stability of performance. This concept refers to assessing the data variability and slope within a phase. When the data are more variable, it is difficult for a researcher to report conclusions (Kazdin, 2003). The researcher can also compare the slope of each phase (which is the data's trend) to determine the degree of change. Ideally, the data of the baseline phase should be relatively stable and invariable, thus providing a consistent baseline from which to compare any subsequent phase data. The final feature of a single-case experimental design is the use of different phases. Thus, at minimum, a baseline and a single treatment phase are needed. The researcher may choose, however, to include a baseline phase with several different treatment phases.

METHOD

For this study, I investigated the effectiveness of CCPT for children with ADHD behaviors. I used a single-case experimental design with five volunteer elementary students (Kindergarten through fifth grade). Because of space considerations, I have decided to focus on one of these five children, Carlos, the fifth-grade Hispanic child that I mentioned at the beginning of this chapter. For further information about all five children, please review my dissertation (Schottelkorb, 2007).

PARTICIPANTS

My study was part of a larger experimental research project examining CCPT with children labeled with ADHD symptoms (Ray, Schottelkorb, & Tsai, 2007). Participants were recruited from three low-income elementary schools. Each school's counselor solicited teacher referrals for students with ADHD behavioral difficulties in the classroom. Carlos was one of six children that qualified for participation because of his borderline or clinical scores on the ADHD subscale of the teacher rating form (TRF; Achenbach & Rescorla, 2001) and the borderline or clinical scores on the ADHD index score of the CTRS-R:S (Conners, 2001). Students with clinical scores in other areas on the TRF were not included in this study to reduce the likelihood that co-morbid factors contributed to their behaviors. Although six students began the study, one did not finish the study because he moved during the school year.

Carlos Carlos was a 10-year-old Hispanic male and in the fifth grade. His fifth-grade teacher identified Carlos for participation in this study because of his difficulty sitting still, focusing, and lack of attention in the classroom. Carlos's teacher was concerned that Carlos's inattention was significantly interfering with his ability to learn in the classroom.

INSTRUMENTS

In single-case design studies, it is necessary to measure change on a regular basis over time. Thus, the main instrument used in this study was the Direct Observation Form (DOF; Achenbach & Rescorla, 2001). Trained observers used the DOF three times per week to assess participant on-task behavior and to provide assessment of several areas related to ADHD behavioral problems. The DOF is a 10-minute observation in which a trained observer examines the behavior of an identified student within a group, classroom, or recess setting and rates the student at each minute interval for on- and off-task behavior. Achenbach and Rescorla (2001) recommended that three to six 10-minute observations be arranged together in order to obtain a more representative score of the child's on-task behaviors.

In this study, two observers were used for all observations of participants. The author and a counselor education faculty member performed all of the observations. Both observers trained and practiced together in the implementation of observations. Several observations were used to assess the inter-rater reliability between these two observers. All of the observations were averaged, and 97 percent agreement was found on the on- and off-task portion of the DOF. Kennedy (2005) stated that a minimum agreement of 80 percent is expected; thus for this study, the observers achieved a high level of consistency.

Additional data were collected to supplement the DOF data for this study. A doctoral-level research assistant collected teacher assessments and I collected all of the parent assessments in individual meetings with the parents at pre-, mid-, and post-intervention phases. I used these six instruments: the Teacher Report Form (TRF), the Conners Teacher Rating Scale-Revised: Short Form (CTRS-R:S), the Index of Teaching Stress (ITS), the Child Behavior Checklist (CBCL), the Conners Parent Rating Scale Revised-Short Form (CPRS-R:S), and the Parenting Stress Index (PSI). All instruments have adequate psychometric properties.

The Teacher Report Form (TRF; Achenbach & Rescorla, 2001) has 118 problem items and additional items that require teachers to rate a student's academic performance and behavior to classmates. The student's behavior is rated on the previous two months on a three-point scale. The TRF provides adaptive scores, problem scores, and DSM-oriented scores that fall into one of three ranges: normal, borderline, and clinical.

The Child Behavior Checklist (CBCL; Achenbach & Rescorla, 2001) is a 118-item parent-report measure that assesses a child's behavior and activities over the previous six months. The CBCL provides two broad scores of internalizing and externalizing behavior, as well as eleven scores in these areas: withdrawn, somatic complaints, anxious or depressed, social problems, thought problems, and attention problems. Like the TRF, normal, borderline, and clinical scores are provided.

The CTRS-R:S and CPRS-R:S are teacher and parent report instruments used to assess behaviors of children and adolescents most commonly associated with ADHD. Both scales consist of 28 questions that are scored on a 4-point frequency scale. The teacher and parent versions both provide four subscales: oppositional, cognitive problems or inattention, hyperactivity, and an ADHD index score (Conners, 2001). The ADHD index score is considered the best indicator of attention difficulties associated with the ADHD diagnosis (Conners, 2001).

The Index of Teaching Stress (ITS; Abidin, Greene, & Konold, 2004) is a 90-item teacher-report assessment that measures a teacher's level of stress in response to a specific student. Specific behaviors of an identified individual student are rated by the teacher on a scale of 1 (never stressful or frustrating) to 5 (very often stressful or frustrating). Three overall scores of attention deficit hyperactivity disorder, student characteristics, and teacher characteristics are provided. Within each scale, several subscale scores are also provided. Normal, elevated, and clinically significant scores are provided.

Finally, the Parenting Stress Index (PSI; Abidin, 1995) was used to measure the degree of stress a parent experiences in raising her child. The PSI has 120 items that produce a total stress score, a child domain score, and a parent domain score.

TREATMENT PROCEDURES

Five students were blindly assigned to participation in child-centered play therapy (CCPT) or reading mentoring at the start of the study. This blind assignment was done to prevent the observers from possible biased observational results. For this study, child participants received a different treatment depending on their particular needs over time. Kennedy (2005) reported that a strength of the single-case design is its ability to be flexible. Thus, as a pattern of behavior is revealed in the course of research, a shift in intervention may become necessary and, in single-case design, is allowed. In the present study, my original intention was for half of the participants to participate in CCPT and the other half to participate in reading mentoring only. However, because of individual participant needs, the students in the reading mentoring condition participated in CCPT to assist with a rapid increase in inappropriate student behaviors that were interfering with their learning. In particular, three students participated in 24 sessions of CCPT. Two students participated in 12 to 14 sessions of reading mentoring, followed by 14 sessions of CCPT.

For this study, all play sessions occurred in rooms within the school and with toys based on Landreth's (2002) recommendations. Two child-centered play therapists provided the play therapy for all participants. One play therapist had her PhD in counselor education with a specialty in play therapy. The second play therapist was an advanced doctoral student in counselor education earning her specialty in play therapy. Both play therapists had participated in and received supervision on their skills in a minimum of five child-centered play therapy courses and internships during their training. The two therapists incorporated nonverbal and verbal skills as identified by Ray (2004) in their sessions. For both play therapists, I observed 10-minute segments of two sessions that were chosen blindly of each participant and rated the therapists using the play therapy skills checklist (Ray, 2004). Results indicated that appropriate levels of nonverbal and verbal responses were used.

Reading mentors were undergraduate students who met twice weekly with the identified participants for 30 minutes at a time (the same amount of time as play therapy sessions). During these 30 minutes, reading mentors would read books of their choosing to the child participant, or the child would read to the mentor. These sessions occurred in the hallway outside the classroom.

Carlos After his teacher completed all teacher assessments (ITS, CTRS-R:S, TRF) and his mother completed the CBCL and the CPRS-R:S, baseline DOF observational data were collected for three weeks. Because Carlos's mother was Spanish-speaking, all parent assessment data were collected with a Spanish-speaking counseling doctoral student. This doctoral student interpreted the CPRS-R:S and read aloud the questions of the Spanish version of the CBCL at each of the three data collection points for this study. Because of the time required to translate and read the assessment instruments, I used the CBCL and CPRS-R:S, but not the PSI. After the baseline phase, Carlos participated in six weeks of 30-minute twice-weekly reading mentoring sessions (see Table 12.1). At the end of this reading mentoring phase, parent and teacher assessments were readministered, and the second treatment phase began. Although originally intended to continue with the reading mentoring, Carlos's teacher was very concerned with inattentive and disruptive behaviors in the classroom that were interfering with his learning. Therefore, Carlos participated in seven weeks of twice-weekly 30-minute play therapy sessions with an advanced doctoral student. After 14 CCPT sessions, the treatment phase ended, after which post-assessment and interviews with teachers and parents occurred. Three weeks of post-intervention observational data were collected through the DOF at this time.

RESULTS

I examined each participant's results separately using visual analysis of the DOF observational data. I graphed each participant's weekly mean of on-task behavior and examined changes between the phases: non-intervention baseline, intervention, and nonintervention maintenance.

Table 12-1
Carlos's Number of Treatment and Assessment Sessions

Week	Parent Assessments	Teacher Assessments	DOF	CCPT	Reading Mentoring
1	2	3	3		
2			3		
3			3		
4			3		2
5			3		2
6			3		2
7			3		2
8			3		2
9	2	3	3		2
10			3	2	
11			3	2	
12			3	2	
13			3	2	
14			3	2	
15			3	2	
16	2	3	3	2	
17			3		
18			3		
19			3		

Note: DOF = Direct Observation Form; CCPT = child-centered play therapy.

Specifically, I examined the level, trend, and variability of the data across the phases (Kennedy, 2005). Levels were quantified by comparing mean scores across each phase. The variability of the data was computed by comparing the data points of my results with the best-fit straight line. The trend was quantified by computing the least squares regression. This least squares regression calculation provides an effect size statistic of R^2. Cohen (1988) tells us that the R^2 effect size can be interpreted by examining the proportion of an individual's variance in score that is explained by differences between the phases. When examining the R^2 statistic, Cohen provided guidelines by which to describe the practical significance of the results. Cohen explained that an R^2 of .25 is demonstrating a large effect, an R^2 of .09 is demonstrating a medium effect, and an R^2 of .01 is a small effect.

In addition, parent and teacher data were graphed and examined through visual analysis comparing pre-, mid-, and post-means. Because inferential statistics are questionable with single-case data (Kennedy, 2005; Morgan & Morgan, 2003), I conducted a visual analysis of all data.

Because visual analysis can be a subjective method of analyzing results, which can increase Type I error, researchers recommend that individuals who use single-case design receive training in visual analysis (Kennedy, 2005). Additionally, researchers recommend that multiple individuals analyze one's results to determine whether a functional relationship exists. For this study, I received instruction and practice analyzing graphs with a professor and another doctoral student familiar with single-case analysis.

VISUAL ANALYSIS OF CARLOS'S DOF SCORES

Carlos's on-task behavior was assessed each week of the study through the use of the DOF. Figure 12.1 displays the data from all phases of Carlos's participation in this study. The graph makes evident that the

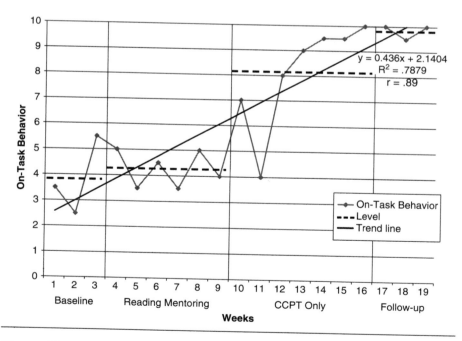

Figure 12.1   DOF Ratings of Carlos's On-Task Behavior (Increase indicates improved behaviors.)

level of each phase increases over time, particularly in Phase 3, the play therapy phase. More specifically, in Phase 1 (baseline phase), the level was 3.83; in Phase 2 (reading mentoring phase), the level was 4.25; in Phase 3 (play therapy phase), the level was 8.14; and in the final phase (nonintervention phase), the level was 9.83. The phase change from the baseline to the reading mentoring phase is minimal; a large shift in on-task behavior for Carlos occurred during the play therapy phase (Phase 3), however. I also examined the trend line of the data over all of the phases. The trend line indicated a high-magnitude, upward trend over time with a least squares regression of $R^2 = .79$ ($r = .89$). This trend line indicated a large effect over time. Thus, Carlos's behavior improved significantly over time. A third form of analysis of all four phases was to assess the data variability. In examining the trend line, it was evident that the variability across the phases differs, but overall there was a moderate amount of variability.

Individual Phase Analysis An examination of each individual phase provided additional assistance in determining the effectiveness of the interventions for Carlos's on-task behavior. In Phase 1, three weeks of no-intervention baseline data were gathered. The three data points indicated moderate variability; a high-magnitude, upward trend; and a mean of 3.83 (range of 2.5 to 5.5). The least squares regression line was $R^2 = .43$ ($r = .65$) (see Figure 12.1). Because the baseline indicated improvement in on-task behavior over time, it makes it more difficult to prove functional relations between the intervention and the on-task behavior. However, because the level differs drastically between the phases, the level may be a stronger indicator of change for Carlos. In Phase 2, the reading mentoring phase, the data revealed low variability, a mean of 4.25 (range 3.5 to 5.0), and a flat trend line with an R^2 of .01 ($r = .12$). The trend line for this phase had a small effect size (see Figure 12.1). The data from this reading mentoring phase indicated little change from the baseline no-intervention phase. In Phase 3, the CCPT phase, Carlos participated in 14 sessions of play therapy. In this phase, the data revealed moderate variability, a mean of 8.14 (range 4 to 10); a high-magnitude, upward trend; and a trend line with an R^2 of .63 ($r = .79$) (see Figure 12.1). The trend of this data indicated a large relationship between the intervention and Carlos's on-task behavior. In Phase 4, the follow-up phase, Carlos did not participate in an intervention. In this phase, the data revealed low variability, a mean of 9.83 (range 9.5 to 10.0), and a flat trend ($R^2 < .01$, $r < .01$) (see Figure 12.1). Carlos's on-task behavior at this level was nearly 100 percent on-task.

VISUAL ANALYSIS OF PARENT DATA

Child Behavior Checklist   Carlos's mother completed assessments of his behavior at three points (pre-, mid-, and post-intervention). On the CBCL, Carlos's mother reported no significant concerns with the internalizing, externalizing, and total problems categories. When examining each individual subscale, however, Carlos's mother reported concern with his ADHD problems (see Figure 12.2). This subscale was the only one within the clinical or borderline range, and thus was the only score reported here. As is evident in Figure 12.2, Carlos's mother reported clinically significant concerns with Carlos's ADHD behaviors at the pre-intervention period. At the mid-assessment period, after which Carlos had participated in reading mentoring, Carlos's mother continued to have borderline levels of concern with his ADHD behaviors. At the final testing period, after which Carlos participated in 14 CCPT sessions, Carlos's mother no longer reported concern with his ADHD behaviors. Thus, these data indicated a downward trend, meaning Carlos's ADHD behaviors decreased over time, with a notable change in behaviors evidenced at the final assessment period.

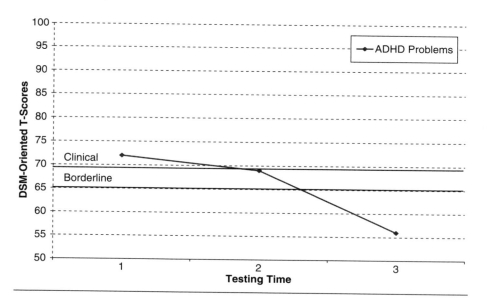

Figure 12.2   Ratings of Carlos's Mother on ADHD Problems Subscale of the CBCL (Increase indicates worsening of behaviors.)

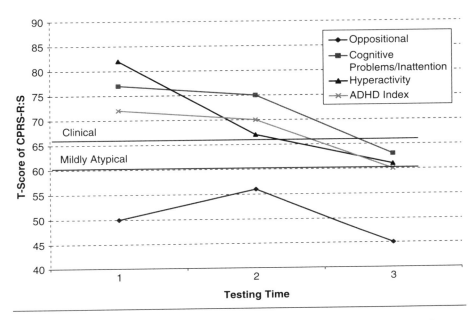

Figure 12.3 Ratings of Carlos's Mother on CPRS-R:S (Increase indicates worsening of behaviors.)

Conners Parent Rating Scale-Revised: Short Form Figure 12.3 displays the ratings of Carlos's mother on the CPRS-R:S. Carlos's mother rated Carlos as exhibiting clinical scores on the cognitive problems or inattention, hyperactivity, and ADHD index at the pre- and mid-assessment periods. All three areas were then rated within the mildly atypical range at the final assessment (after participation in CCPT). This decrease indicates a decrease in concern regarding Carlos's ADHD behaviors.

VISUAL ANALYSIS OF TEACHER DATA

Teacher Report Form Carlos's teacher completed three assessments at pre-, mid- (after reading mentoring), and post-intervention (after play therapy). Carlos's teacher rated Carlos's behavior to be at clinical levels on the externalizing and total problems domains at all phases of the study. The internalizing problems domain was rated by Carlos's teacher in the borderline range at pre-test and in the clinical range at the mid- and post-assessments. Figure 12.4 displays the ratings of Carlos's teacher on the ADHD problems subscale of the TRF. Similar to

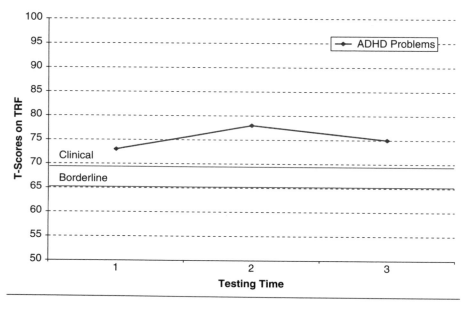

Figure 12.4 Ratings of Carlos's Teacher on the ADHD Problems Subscale of the TRF (Increase indicates worsening of behaviors.)

the results of the externalizing problems subscale, Carlos's teacher rated Carlos's ADHD behaviors to be in the clinical range at all three assessment periods. Thus, these results indicated that neither the reading mentoring nor the play therapy interventions made much impact on the perceptions of Carlos's teacher.

Index of Teaching Stress   The four domains of the ITS and the subscales for which an elevated or clinical score was reported by Carlos's teacher are included in Figure 12.5. The graph of the results indicates that ADHD, anxious, and aggressive behaviors became more severe after the reading mentoring phase (scores fell in the elevated range), but after participation in play therapy, Carlos's scores in these areas returned to the normal range. Additionally, while most of Carlos's behaviors on the subscales became worse after the reading mentoring phase, they improved after the play therapy phase. One exception to this finding is the score on the low ability or learning disability (LALD) subscale, which was in the normal range at the pre- and mid-assessment periods but changed to the elevated range at the final assessment. This LALD subscale represents the difficulty Carlos's teacher experienced when dealing with Carlos's special learning needs.

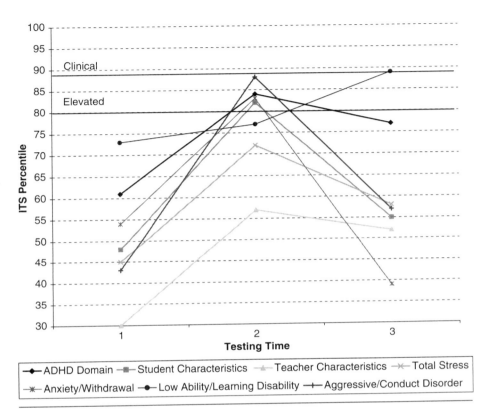

Figure 12.5 Ratings of Carlos's Teacher on the ITS (Increase indicates worsening of behaviors.)

Conners Teacher Rating Scale-Revised: Short Form Carlos's teacher rated Carlos's behavior on the CTRS-R:S at each testing period. Figure 12.6 displays the results graphically. The data indicated that Carlos's oppositional behavior demonstrated the most significant change over time. More specifically, Carlos's oppositional behavior was rated at a significant level of concern for Carlos's teacher at pre- and mid-assessment (after reading mentoring) but was rated in the normal range at the final assessment (after play therapy). The hyperactivity and ADHD index scores remained at the clinical level at each testing period, with slight variations (behaviors worsened after Phase 2 and improved slightly after Phase 3). The cognitive problems and inattention score remained the same at the pre- and mid-assessment periods but worsened at the final assessment. This score indicated that Carlos's

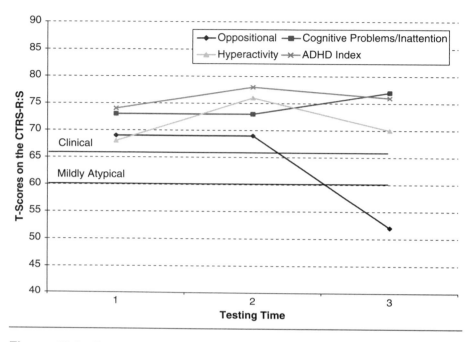

Figure 12.6 Ratings of Carlos's Teacher on the CTRS-R:S (Increase indicates worsening of behaviors.)

teacher rated Carlos to have more academic problems and inattentive behaviors than others his age.

PLAY THERAPIST OBSERVATIONS

The doctoral student who provided the play therapy sessions noticed that Carlos began the first few sessions in the playroom with exploratory play and uncertainty of the relationship. In Sessions 1 through 7, Carlos did not interact much with the therapist and instead focused on fighting play with the bobo, soldiers, and the animals. In these first sessions, Carlos displayed aggressive, chaotic, disorganized, intense play. In these sessions he displayed a flat affect and did not respond to the therapist with eye contact or with any significant verbalizations. The following is a segment from Session 5:

CARLOS: (In his play, he missed hitting a brick with a sword, so he fell to the ground and then starts hitting all of the dolls and furniture in the dollhouse with the sword.)

COUNSELOR: "You seem very frustrated."

CARLOS: (Continues hitting the dolls and furniture in the dollhouse and forcing them to fall out of the dollhouse.)

COUNSELOR: "You're hitting them over and over again."

CARLOS: (Continues with the same play and makes a little screaming noise, as if the dolls are yelling.)

COUNSELOR: "You really want them to get out of there."

CARLOS: (Continues to makes more yelling noises while forcing the dolls and furniture out.)

COUNSELOR: "Sounds like they are scared."

CARLOS: (Forces the last remaining items in the dollhouse out with the sword).

COUNSELOR: "You want to make sure that all of them get out of there."

CARLOS: (Once all items are out of the dollhouse, Carlos goes over to the animals and begins hitting each animal with the sword, one at a time).

In Sessions 8 and 10, the therapist reported that Carlos displayed only positive feelings and enjoyment of play. In Session 9, the therapist reported Carlos exhibited feelings of frustration when his goals could not be accomplished. In the final sessions, Carlos displayed more positive emotions of strength, power, and happiness. In addition, the therapist reported that Carlos engaged in a conversation with the therapist, which was unusual for him. The following is a segment from Session 13:

CARLOS: (Carlos lines up all of the animals in a particular order in about three minutes.)

COUNSELOR: "You're getting them just how you want them."

CARLOS: (Continues to finish lining up the animals, then begins shooting them one at at time.)

COUNSELOR: "You got that one!"

CARLOS: "Yay!" (and smiles triumphantly at counselor)

COUNSELOR: "You're proud of yourself!"

CARLOS: (Continues shooting each animal until he makes all of them fall down.)

As is evident here, Carlos is displaying more patience, self-control, organization, relaxation, and positive feelings. In the final sessions, Carlos also displayed feelings of sadness and disappointment that the sessions were ending. It appeared evident to the counselor that through his experience of safety and warmth in the relationship,

Carlos was able to express the many feelings he experienced in his life. The counselor reported that a dramatic shift occurred over the 14 sessions in regard to Carlos's expression of feelings and development of self-control.

DISCUSSION

Overall, when I reviewed the observational results for all of the children in the original study, it is clear that three children demonstrated a clear improvement in on-task behavior during participation in play therapy. However, two children did not show clear change during participation in play therapy. The parent and teacher assessments of each child's behaviors were inconsistent. Please see Schottelkorb (2007) for more specifics on these results.

CARLOS

The behavioral observations of Carlos's on-task behavior in the classroom indicated improvement during the play therapy phase of the study. Because little change occurred during the reading mentoring phase, it is inferred that the reading intervention was not helpful in improving his on-task behaviors. Inversely, the play therapy intervention seemed to assist in his ability to remain on-task in the classroom. The follow-up period, in which no intervention occurred, seemed to imply that the play therapy intervention had a lasting impact on his on-task behaviors. Thus, the results of Carlos's observations indicated that play therapy was helpful in improving his on-task behaviors.

The parent assessments completed by Carlos's mother indicated that she did not have as many initial concerns about Carlos in comparison with his teacher. However, in all of the assessments Carlos's mother completed, it is evident that she witnessed improvement in his ADHD behaviors over time. In the follow-up interview with the Spanish-speaking interpreter, Carlos's mother attributed positive changes with Carlos's behavior at school and at home to participation in play therapy. Specifically, Carlos's mother reported that Carlos demonstrated increased concentration and less hyperactive behavior at home and that he was trying harder in school, followed rules at home more often, and was able to initiate homework without her asking him to start working on it.

The teacher assessments completed regarding Carlos's behavior indicated that Carlos's teacher did not perceive much change in his

ADHD behaviors over the course of the study. Carlos's teacher's ratings in graphical analysis indicated that Carlos's behavior worsened after the reading mentoring phase and improved after the play therapy phase. One area of noteworthy improvement was Carlos's oppositional behavior after participation in play therapy (as rated on the CTRS-R:S). At the first and second testing periods (pre-intervention and post-reading mentoring), Carlos's teacher rated Carlos's oppositional behavior at clinical levels of functioning. However, after participation in play therapy, Carlos's teacher rated Carlos's oppositional behavior in the normal range on the CTRS-R:S. Thus, it appears that play therapy helped decrease Carlos's oppositional behaviors as rated by his teacher.

The one area that Carlos's teacher indicated as worsening over time was his academic abilities (as indicated by the cognitive problems and inattention subscale of the CTRS-R:S and the low ability or learning disability subscale of the ITS). This information taken together with a follow-up interview with Carlos's teacher indicated that he believed that Carlos had a learning disability that was undiagnosed. Carlos's teacher indicated that Carlos participated in a comprehensive assessment at the school at the end of the year but that he did not qualify for any additional assistance and was labeled with a 504 for other health impaired (for ADHD). Carlos's teacher reported dissatisfaction with this plan for Carlos as not providing him the assistance he needed in the classroom to be successful. When asked about changes in Carlos's behavior in the classroom in the follow-up interview, Carlos's teacher replied that Carlos seemed to have slightly matured in that he was not as apathetic about school. One example of change Carlos's teacher mentioned was that Carlos was now turning in some of his homework assignments. However, Carlos's teacher was not certain if this change was due to participation in play therapy or due to developmental growth over the school year.

RECOMMENDATIONS

The results of my study indicated that play therapy can be helpful for children with ADHD behaviors. For Carlos, objective ratings of his on-task behavior significantly improved while in play therapy according to behavioral data. Carlos's mother also witnessed an improvement in Carlos's ADHD behaviors; his teacher, however, did not see improvement. For Carlos, the teacher seemed to become more convinced of learning difficulties. Thus, it is unclear if Carlos was helped through play therapy for ADHD or for co-morbid difficulties that contributed to his off-task behaviors. Further research is needed with this population to achieve more clarity regarding the specific conditions that may be assisted by play therapy.

Also, the method I used to identify children for participation in this study was teacher assessment of ADHD behaviors. A stronger method of identifying students with ADHD behavioral problems would be to use an additional rater in determining that qualification, such as a parent, through the use of behavioral report assessments or through structured interviews.

Another recommendation is for play therapist researchers to re-consider how they assess change in play therapy. At this time, the majority of play therapy research has appeared to demonstrate behavioral change for children through the use of parent or teacher ratings. However, as was evident with Carlos, different raters (parent, teacher, objective rater) assessed Carlos's on- and off-task behaviors differently. I would argue that change should be assessed with multiple raters and through examining play behavior in session. Observers who are trained in play therapy and developmentally appropriate behaviors for children may assess the in-session behaviors. And because single-case methodology allows individual behavior change to be closely examined, I believe that these investigations would best be suited for single-case research.

For those planning to use single-case methodology, I recommend that a stable baseline be established first and foremost. The baseline is how the researcher provides control, so it is crucial that a stable baseline be achieved. In this study, a three-week baseline was established because of requests from teachers to begin the intervention. This study would have been stronger, though, if a clear, stable baseline had been established before starting the first treatment phase.

CONCLUSION

Carlos and four other children identified with clinical or borderline levels of ADHD behavioral problems participated in this single-case examination of the effectiveness of CCPT. At this time, play therapy is not considered an evidence-based intervention for ADHD, and this study intended to see if CCPT was, in fact, effective in reducing ADHD behaviors for these five students. The direct observations of on-task and off-task behaviors indicated CCPT was clearly effective in improving on-task behavior in the classroom for three students. For two students, clear improvement was not evident. Although Carlos clearly showed increased on-task behavior according to behavioral observations and his mother's report, his teacher did not see the same level of change. However, both mother and teacher reported notable decreases in other problematic behaviors during and following CCPT. These results indicate that further research is needed with this population.

REFERENCES

Abidin, R. R. (1995). *Parenting stress index: Professional manual* (3rd ed.) Odessa, FL: Psychological Assessment Resources.

Abidin, R. R., Greene, R. W., & Konold, T. R. (2004). *Index of teaching stress: Professional manual.* Lutz, FL: Psychological Assessment Resources.

Achenbach, T. M., & Rescorla, L. A. (2001). *Manual for the ASEBA School-Age Forms & Profiles.* Burlington, VT: University of Vermont, Research Center for Children, Youth, & Families.

American Psychiatric Association. (2000). *Diagnostic and statistical manual of mental disorders* (4th ed., text revision). Washington, DC: Author.

American Psychological Association. (n.d.). Evidence-based treatment for children and adolescents. Retrieved March 15, 2007, from http://www.wjh.harvard.edu/%7Enock/Div53/EST/index.htm.

Barkley, R. A., Fischer, M., Smallish, L., & Fletcher, K. (2002). The persistence of attention-deficit hyperactivity disorder into young adulthood as a function of reporting source and definition of disorder. *Journal of Abnormal Psychology, 111*(2), 279–289.

Blinn, E. L. (1999). *Efficacy of play therapy on problem behaviors of a child with attention deficit hyperactivity disorder.* Unpublished doctoral dissertation, California School of Professional Psychology, Fresno, CA.

Cohen, J. (1988). *Statistical power analysis for the behavior sciences* (2nd ed.). Hillsdale, NJ: Erlbaum.

Conners, C. K. (2001). *Conners Rating Scales-Revised: Technical manual.* North Tonawanda, NY: Multi-Health Systems.

DuPaul, G. J., & Stoner, G. (2004). *ADHD in the schools: Assessment and intervention strategies* (2nd ed.). New York: Guilford.

Kazdin, A. E. (2003). *Research design in clinical psychology.* Boston: Allyn & Bacon.

Kennedy, C. H. (2005). *Single-case designs for educational research.* Boston: Allyn & Bacon.

Landreth, G. L. (2002). *Play therapy: The art of the relationship* (2nd ed.). New York: Brunner-Routledge.

Morgan, D. L., & Morgan, R. K. (2003). Single-participant research design: Bringing science to managed care. In A. E. Kazdin (Ed.), *Methodological issues and strategies in clinical research* (3rd ed.) (pp. 635–654). Washington, DC: American Psychological Association.

Pelham, W. E., & Gnagy, E. M. (1999). Psychosocial and combined treatments for ADHD. *Mental Retardation and Developmental Disabilities Research Reviews, 5*, 225–236.

Ray, D. C. (2004). Supervision of basic and advanced skills in play therapy. *Journal of Professional Counseling: Practice, Theory, and Research, 32*(2), 28–41.

Ray, D. C., Schottelkorb, A., & Tsai, M. (2007). Play therapy with children exhibiting symptoms of attention deficit hyperactivity disorder. *International Journal of Play Therapy, 16*(2), 95–111.

Schottelkorb, A. (2007). Effectiveness of child-centered play therapy and person-centered teacher consultation on ADHD behavioral problems of elementary school children: A single-case design. *Dissertation Abstracts International, 69*(2), 208A. (UMI No. 3300972).

Woodard, R. (2006). The diagnosis and medical treatment of ADHD in children and adolescents in primary care: A practical guide. *Pediatric Nursing, 32*(4), 363–370.

CHAPTER 13

Child-Centered Play Therapy and Child Development: A Single-Case Analysis

APRIL GAROFANO-BROWN

RELATIONSHIP BETWEEN CHILD DEVELOPMENT AND PLAY THERAPY

Children with developmental delays, specifically intellectual disabilities, appear to be at an increased risk for developing emotional and behavioral problems. Emotional and behavioral difficulties may be related to a child's personality or characteristics of their age (Ilg, Ames, & Baker, 1981). Children develop through common stages of development, although each child goes through the developmental stages and expresses behavior according to their individuality (Ilg et al., 1981). Children with developmental delays often meet developmental milestones at a slower pace than their peers. This delay in development can be observed across the following areas: socioaffective, selective attention, sensorimotor development, language and symbol formation, pretend play, and attachment behaviors (Krakow & Kopp, 1983).

Temperament may directly or indirectly affect children's social behavior and emotionality (Spinrad et al., 2004). Children with even mild developmental delays experience considerable difficulty in peer interactions when compared to their nondelayed peers. This is important to counselors because many child clients are functioning at a developmental level lower than their chronological age, and this group does not often qualify or receive any additional school-related services to assist in social and academic progress. Specific areas of difficulty in children with mild developmental delays are social competence, sustaining play with peers both individually and in group play interactions, and the ability to problem solve when social conflicts arise. Guralnick, Hammond, Conner, and Neville (2006) found children with peer interaction problems tend to experience these difficulties over time, suggesting that the issue is chronic and stable in nature despite intervention. As a play therapist, this knowledge is imperative in assisting parents, families, and the child's teachers in looking at these issues through a different lens. After all, these issues typically are the catalysts for families seeking outside help.

I became interested in exploring this topic for several reasons. Children who do not move successfully through the stages or who exhibit delays as young as three years exhibit significantly more behavior problems than their same-age peers (Baker, Blacher, & Olsson, 2005). Schools often struggle with placement decisions for children who are not functioning on level when compared to their typically developing peers. Counselors are not exempt from this struggle and often find it difficult to provide developmentally appropriate recommendations for parents in regard to school placement and emotional and behavioral concerns. These findings further led me to contemplate whether the clients' presenting problem was related to a diagnostic issue or disruptions in mastering developmental stages. Pondering this, I began to wonder if there were, in fact, delays in our clients' development, how play therapy might help their presenting behavioral issues. These thoughts led to the rationale for my research and my beliefs that an increase in awareness and training in the area of child development and developmental appraisal is needed for play therapists, especially when children are operating slightly lower than their chronological ages. My hopes in pursuing this topic of research were to assist in meeting clients when they were functioning developmentally and to assist their therapists to best serve and provide developmentally appropriate recommendations for children and their parents.

Increasing awareness in these areas often involves the assessment and observation of children. In the early stages of formulating this study, I found many concerns related to the appropriate methods for assessing children's development. Despite society's emphasis on the importance of early childhood intervention for children with disabilities and developmental delays, difficulties persist in assessing for and identifying these difficulties. These difficulties are in part due to a lack of psychometrically sound assessment instruments for assessing young children (Voress & Maddox, 1998). Identifying valid and reliable instruments for assessing young children's development is difficult because of many factors. These factors include:

- Many tests assess only cognitive development.
- Most tests require only a single administration, thus limiting an accurate picture of children's rapid development.
- Individual administration is time consuming, yet group administration affects reliability.
- Many instruments are not standardized with cultural norms.
- Most instruments are not developmentally appropriate for young children and do not account for their unique developmental needs. (Wortham, 1999)

Casby (2003) studied the developmental status of children through their play. Play behaviors and interactions are often the only observable actions available for assessing young children suspected of having developmental delays. Casby also recommended the value of observation of the level and quality of solitary play as well as play with others when children play independently. Because there is variance in play behavior in children with developmental delays compared to typically developing children, Casby recommended repeated observation may be considered as an important component for the assessment of play-based early intervention. Repeated observation appeared to be a theme in research literature and in terms of conducting developmental assessment. This directed my research efforts toward a design that included repeated observation. From a practitioner's viewpoint, difficulties in assessing the quality and effectiveness of an intervention for practical use is often difficult with group experimental designs. Group experimental design does not meet the needs of counselors who need not only credible, but clinically feasible, methods of demonstrating the effectiveness and validity of counseling (Lundervold & Belwood, 2000). Counselors who are in private practice, schools, and agency settings are in need of quality research designs that allow them the ability to use such methods in their daily counseling practices.

METHODOLOGY

Searching for a research design that was both practical and included repeated observations of the participant, I decided the use of a single-case analysis would provide in-depth exploration of participants' performance and response to intervention. Single-case designs demonstrate causal relations between different conditions and their effects on performance over time. An n = 1 design essentially uses data from a single participant as the research design (Sharpley, 2007). The components of the single-case design are described as follows:

- Phase: a period of time during which a specific counselor action is taking place
- Baseline: phase (labeled *A*) established before implementing a systematic counseling intervention
- Treatment: Intervention or treatment phase (labeled *B*) is initiated

The researcher identifies the target of change for determining the effects of counselor actions (Lundervold & Belwood, 2000). The baseline phase occurs before an intervention takes place and provides information about the participant's performance before the intervention is introduced (Kazdin, 2003).

Participants in single-case designs serve as their own control group, and data are analyzed by visual methods to compare data from the participant's baseline and intervention phases (Sharpley, 2007). Graphs provide visual representations of change over time and are perceived as the most effective method for initial examinations of data. Visual inspection is used when there are continuous data for one or more participants available for observation (Kazdin, 2003). The tendency for performance to increase or decrease systematically or consistently over time is referred to as *slope* and is evaluated statistically to determine which line best illustrates the data (Kazdin, 2003). These terms and how they relate to actual client data are explored in detail later in the chapter.

Based on the research literature, I decided to use a single-case design to explore the impact of individual child-centered play therapy on children with developmental delays by examining its effectiveness in increasing measured developmental age, reducing problematic behaviors related to developmental delays, and increasing developmentally appropriate behaviors. My primary goals were to find out if child-centered play therapy improved a child's performance on developmental measures and improved behavior.

INSTRUMENTS

I chose the Gesell Developmental Observation (Ilg, 1965) to assess the participants' developmental age. The Gesell Developmental Observation consists of tests that are predominately perceptual-motor. The individual administration of this test takes approximately 20 minutes. Subtests are:

- Initial interview: Child is asked age, birthday, names of any siblings, and the nature of parents' occupations.
- Writing: Child is asked to write first and last names and the numbers 1 to 20.
- Copy forms: Child is asked to copy a circle, cross, square, equilateral triangle, diamond, and divided rectangle.
- Incomplete man: Child is asked to complete the facial and body parts of a partially drawn person.
- Animals: Child is asked to name as many animals as possible in one minute.

The child is assigned to a predetermined developmental age category for each section of the test on the basis of the child's responses to test items or specific tasks. Once the child completes all sections of the tests and the developmental ages are recorded on the scoring sheet, an overall developmental age is derived from an average of the child's performance on each individual section of the test.

Developmental Assessment of Young Children (DAYC)

The Developmental Assessment of Young Children (Voress & Maddox, 1998) is used to identify developmental delays or deficits in children from birth through 5 years 11 months who may benefit from early intervention. The DAYC is composed of five subtests that measure assessment areas of cognition, communication, social-emotional development, adaptive behavior, and physical development. Administration can be individual, separate, or as a comprehensive battery. The evaluator can collect information about a child's abilities through observation, caregiver interview, and direct assessment.

Child Behavior Checklist (CBCL)

The CBCL for children ages 1½ to 5 (Achenbach and Rescorla, 2000) was used for the purposes of this study because of the ages of the participants. The CBCL is designed for the parent of a child ranging in age from 1½ to 5 years old to identify problem behaviors (Achenbach & Rescorla, 2000).

Parenting Stress Index (PSI)

The Parenting Stress Index (Abidin, 1995) is a 120-item instrument to "identify parent-child systems that were under stress and at risk for the development of dysfunctional parenting behaviors or behavior problems in the child involved" (Abidin, 1995, p. 6). The PSI was standardized for use with parents of children between the ages of 1 month and 12 years.

Intervention

Participants who met specified criteria and were between the ages of 3 and 5 years and who were assessed with at least a six-month developmental age below their chronological age by the Gesell Developmental Observation and not currently receiving any concurrent psychological treatment were included in this research. The examiner and all play therapists were graduate students in a counseling program and completed at least three courses in play therapy, including an introduction to play therapy, an advanced play therapy course, and a clinical practicum. Each counselor received individual or triadic supervision on a weekly basis from an experienced play therapist and 1.5 hours of group supervision from a counselor education faculty member. All children selected for this study received treatment consisting of individual child-centered play therapy (CCPT) sessions.

I conducted three separate single-case designs with three children. Full results can be found in Garafano-Brown (2007). For the purpose of this chapter and the sake of brevity, I discuss the findings from just one case. Nate is a 3-year-and-3-month-old child who qualified for participation in this study because of an assessed Gesell Developmental Observation age of 2 and a half years, which is 9 months below his chronological age. He lived with his adoptive mother and father, his three adoptive siblings, and his biological younger brother. Nate and his younger brother were removed from their biological mother because of physical abuse and neglect and were adopted by their current parents. Early medical and developmental history was limited because of the adoption process. His parents reported strengths in areas of being affectionate, playful, and a loving child. Nate had a history of physical aggression, disruption in attachment, and excessive impulsivity. Nate often hit and kicked his siblings. There were times when his behavior was erratic and unpredictable. He had difficulty getting along with his siblings and peers and often did not follow directions. His parents reported a high degree of energy, distractibility, and in-attentiveness in Nate's behavior. He often refused to comply with directions and ran away from parents, regardless of the safety of the situation. Developmentally, Nate was reported to have delays in meeting developmental tasks such as toilet training, speech and language development, and self-control. He had not been treated for any medical or behavioral difficulties. His parents' biggest concerns were in the areas of aggression and impulsivity.

During the baseline phase, Nate was administered the Gesell Developmental Observation upon intake, while subtests from the DAYC were administered weekly for three weeks to obtain developmental-level data. His father completed pre-test assessments, including CBCL and PSI, and relevant background and developmental history was obtained. The treatment phase began after three weeks of baseline data collection. During first week of treatment (week 4), the play therapist met with the parent for consultation following an established protocol (see Garafano-Brown, 2007). The play therapist then facilitated a 30-minute play therapy session followed by an examiner administration of the DAYC cognitive, social-emotional, and communication subtests to collect developmental assessment data. During treatment weeks 5 and 6, the participant received a 30-minute CCPT session, and an examiner administered the DAYC subtests. During treatment week 7, the play therapist conducted a parent consultation following the established protocol, as well as a 30-minute child-centered play therapy session with the participant. His father completed mid-point assessments of CBCL and PSI. I met with Nate after the play therapy session to administer the DAYC subtests. Treatment weeks 8 to 10 included 30-minute child-centered play therapy sessions, followed by meeting with me to complete the DAYC subtests. The final week of the treatment phase (week 11) included a parent consultation and a 30-minute CCPT session followed by the administration of the DAYC. Nate's father completed post-test assessments of CBCL and PSI. During follow-up weeks 12 to 14, I met with the participant to administer the DAYC subtests to gain additional data without Nate receiving CCPT or parent consultation.

RESULTS AND DISCUSSION

Nate's results were examined separately using visual analyses. His weekly standard scores from the DAYC were graphed. Changes between the phases of nonintervention baseline, intervention, and nonintervention follow-up were examined. Specifically, the level, trend, and variability of the data across the phases were examined. Levels can be quantified by comparing mean scores across each phase. The level of data within a phase essentially demonstrates the mean of the data during the specified phase (Kennedy, 2005). The second dimension used to examine data is trend, which is quantitatively estimated by computing the least squares regression. This process fits a straight line to the slope of the participants' data by "minimizing the sum of squared deviations of the observed data from the line" (Kennedy, 2005, p. 198). The trend coefficient was interpreted by effect size of R^2 according to the guidelines established by Cohen (1988) of $R^2 = .01$ (small effect), $R^2 = .09$ (medium effect), and $R^2 = .25$ (large effect). The effect sizes explain the variance within the relationship between Nate's participation in child-centered play therapy and his performance over time.

Variability, the third examination of data, refers to the degree to which data points deviate from the overall trend, or the best-fit straight line. The variability of data is interpreted in terms of being high, medium, or low and is relatively qualitative in nature (Kennedy, 2005). It is important to note when visually inspecting the data points whether there are inconsistent patterns in the data points.

Kazdin (2003) defined visual analysis of data as a process of examining graphed data so as to reach judgments about the reliability and consistency of effects of the intervention. Researchers look for a series of patterns in the graphed data to draw conclusions about the intervention (Kennedy, 2005). Intervention effects are observed when a large and immediate change and level of target is noted after manipulation of the independent variable (Barlow & Hersen, 1984).

Visual analysis can be considered a subjective method for analyzing results that may increase Type 1 error, and thus researchers using single-case design are recommended to receive training in visual analysis (Kennedy, 2005). Researchers also recommend that multiple analyses of one's results are conducted by additional individuals trained in visual analysis to determine whether a functional relationship exists. For this study, I received instruction and practice analyzing graphs with an experienced associate professor and another doctoral student conducting single-case analyses. Visual analysis is an appropriate and preferred method for analyzing data in single-case design studies, and all data from this study are described and presented according to Kennedy's (2005) recommendations. Also, Nate's parent's data collected from behavior and parenting checklists were examined, comparing pre-, mid-, and post-test score means.

DAYC Subtests

Nate's averaged scores from the data across the three phases of baseline (before treatment), intervention (play therapy treatment), and follow-up (removal of treatment) on the DAYC cognitive, communication, and social emotional subtests were explored.

Figure 13.1 displays a graphical representation of the standard scores for Nate's performance on the cognitive subtest for the DAYC. The graph clearly demonstrates that the level (mean) of the intervention phase increased from the baseline phase. Also evident is the decrease in level during the follow-up phase. In phase one, the mean level is 76.66; in phase two, the mean level is 82.5; the mean level in phase three is 72.66. The increase in level during the intervention (play therapy) phase indicated that Nate's performance; on the cognitive subtest improved while receiving play therapy and his scores decreased when the play therapy intervention was removed. The analyses of level indicates improvement in Nate's performance and upon Kennedy's (2005) recommendations, additional calculations of trend were conducted. The trend line was calculated and is also displayed in Figure 13.1. The trend line for Nate was analyzed visually as flat with low variability. The least squares regression calculation was interpreted as a small relationship between the three phases and time indicated by $R^2 = .004$ ($r = .06$).

The data across the three phases of Nate's performance on the DAYC cognitive subtest indicated a low amount of variability, which Kennedy

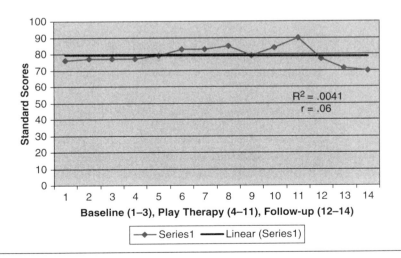

Figure 13.1   Nate's DAYC Cognitive Subtest Combined Phase Results

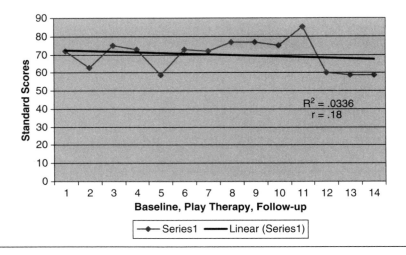

Figure 13.2   Nate's DAYC Communication Subtest Combined Phase
Results

(2005) described as the extent to which the individual data points vary
from the trend line. Graphical illustration indicates that most of Nate's
data fit cleanly to the trend line. To provide an even clearer picture of
the relationship between intervention and time, the trend and level are
useful indicators.

Next, Nate's averaged scores from the data across the three phases of
baseline, intervention (play therapy), and follow-up on the DAYC
communication subtest are presented in Figure 13.2.

The graph clearly demonstrates the level (mean) of the intervention
phase increased from the baseline phase. Also evident is the decrease in
level during the follow-up phase. In phase one, the mean level is 70; in
phase two, the mean level is 73.8; the mean level in phase three is 59.33.
The increase in level during the intervention (play therapy) phase
indicated that Nate's performance on the communication subtest
improved while receiving play therapy and his scores decreased
when the play therapy intervention was removed. The analysis of
level indicates improvement in Nate's performance. The trend line was
calculated and is displayed in Figure 13.2. The trend line for Nate
indicated a small downward trend through visual analysis. The least
squares regression calculation of $r = .18$ indicated a small relationship
between the three phases and time with an effect size of $R^2 = .03$. The
data across the three phases of Nate's performance on the communication subtest indicated a low amount of variability.

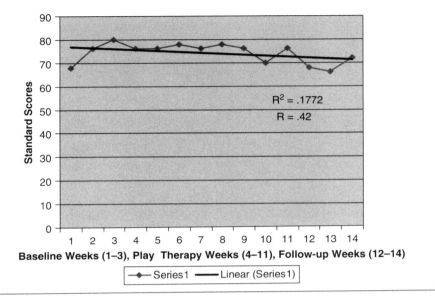

Figure 13.3   Nate's Performance on DAYC Social-Emotional Subtest

Figure 13.3 displays a graphical representation of the standard scores for Nate's performance on the social-emotional subtest for the DAYC. The graph clearly demonstrates the level (mean) of the intervention phase increased slightly from the baseline phase. Also evident is the decrease in level during the follow-up phase. In phase one, the mean level is 74.7; in phase two, the mean level is 75.75; the mean level in phase three is 68.67. The increase in level during the intervention (play therapy) phase indicated that Nate's performance on the social-emotional subtest improved while receiving play therapy and his performance decreased when the play therapy intervention was removed. The trend line for Nate indicated a moderate downward trend through visual analysis. The least squares regression calculation of $r = .42$ indicated a moderate relationship between the three phases and time with an effect size of $R^2 = .18$. The data across the three phases of Nate's performance on the social-emotional subtest indicated a low amount of variability. Graphical illustration indicates that most of Nate's data fit cleanly to the trend line.

GESELL DEVELOPMENTAL OBSERVATION

Nate was administered the Gesell Developmental Observation once during the first week of the baseline phase (pre-test) and once after the

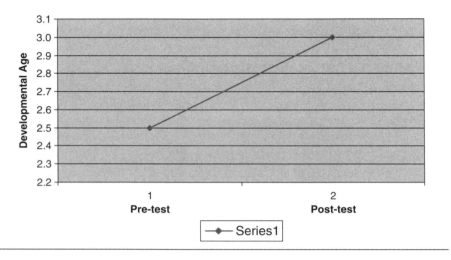

Figure 13.4 Nate's Results from Gesell Developmental Observation

eighth week of play therapy phase (post-test). The pre-test yielded a developmental quotient of two and a half years, which was close to one year below his chronological age. Nate's post-test results yielded a developmental quotient of three years. Results indicate a six-month improvement in Nate's developmental quotient after receiving eight weeks of the play therapy intervention phase.

CHILD BEHAVIOR CHECKLIST

Nate's father completed three CBCL assessments at three separate occurrences during the three phases: pre-test, mid-point, and post-test. Pre-test data were collected during the first week of the baseline phase; the results indicated that Nate's father rated Nate's internalizing behavior (t score $= 55$) in the average range, his externalizing behavior (t score $= 71$) in the clinical range, and the total problems scale (t score $= 63$) was rated in the borderline range. During the mid-point data collection, given during week 4 of the intervention phase, Nate's father rated his internalizing behavior (t score $= 56$) in the average range, his externalizing behavior (t score $= 67$) in the clinical range, and his total problem scale (t score $= 61$) was rated in the borderline range. Finally, the post-test administration, which occurred after the eighth week of the intervention phase, yielded results indicating average (t score $= 53$) internalizing behavior, externalizing problems (t score $= 66$)

in the clinical range, and total problem scale (*t* score = 59) in the average range. Improvement was noted in the post-test total problem scale from the previous two administrations. Although the externalizing scale remained in the clinical range, the *t* scores of each administration of this scale decreased each time data were collected.

PARENTING STRESS INDEX

Nate's father also rated his relationship with Nate using the PSI. Three administrations of the PSI occurred at the same intervals as the CBCL, including pre-test (during first week of baseline phase), mid-point (during the fourth week of the intervention phase), and finally, post-test (occurring after the eight play therapy sessions during the intervention phase). Pre-test results indicated Nate's father rated the child domain (*t* score = 137) and total stress (*t* score = 260) in the clinical range, and the parent domain (*t* score = 123) was rated in the non-clinical range. During the mid-point administration, Nate's father rated the child domain (*t* score = 145) and the total stress domain (*t* score = 261) in the clinical range, and the parent domain (*t* score = 116) in the nonclinical range. The post-test administration yielded clinical results in the child domain (*t* score = 130), and total stress (*t* score = 256), and nonclinical results for the parent domain (*t* score = 126). The post-test administration demonstrated clinical results in the child domain (*t* score = 130), and nonclinical results for the parent domain (*t* score = 126), and total stress (*t* score = 256). Improvement was noted in the post-test administration in the total stress domain, in which results were rated in the nonclinical range versus the previous two administration's ratings in the clinical range.

OVERALL RESULTS

Nate entered the study with a chronological age of three years and three months and a pre-test developmental quotient from the Gesell Developmental Observation of 2 and a half years. After completing eight weeks of intervention phase, his post-test developmental quotient was measured as 3 years, while his chronological age was 3 years and 6 months. He was assessed weekly throughout the entire three phases of the study of baseline, intervention, and follow-up, with the Developmental Assessment of Young Children Subtests of Cognitive, Communication, and Social-Emotional. Results of his mean level scores on all three phases are as follows: cognitive baseline, 76.66; cognitive intervention, 82.5; cognitive follow-up, 72.66; communication baseline, 70; communication intervention, 73.8; communication follow-up, 59.33; social-emotional baseline, 74.7; social-emotional intervention, 75.75; and social-emotional follow-up, 68.67. Results indicate overall improvement in his performance on all three subtests during the play therapy intervention phase, with decreases in his performance once the play therapy intervention was removed during the follow-up phase. Nate's parent data, including the Child Behavior Checklist and Parenting Stress Index, demonstrated high concern on the behavioral scales of externalizing and total problems of the CBCL. Nate's father rated his externalizing behavior decreasing across the mid-point and post-testing, yet still within the clinical range. He rated improvement in the total problems scale during the post-test administration as the scores moved from the borderline range to the nonclinical range. Nate's father rated improvement in the total stress domain on the PSI during the post-test administration when compared to the ratings from the previous two administrations.

These results suggest the need for an extension of the baseline phase to establish a stable pattern. It is problematic, however, to withhold treatment to those in need in the hopes of establishing a stable baseline. It is important to note the particularly strong relationship between the intervention and Nate's performance on the DAYC. Once the treatment was removed, his performance on the three subtests of the DAYC decreased considerably. These results demonstrate the robust causal relationship between the intervention and effect and strengthens the internal validity and generalizability of the single-case analysis (Sharpley, 2007). However, the inconsistent baseline results may limit this generalizability.

For Nate, the developmental measures of the Gesell Developmental Observation and DAYC yielded increases in performance and developmental age quotients, and the behavioral measures of the CBCL and the PSI showed mostly positive results of improvement. However, in the larger study, Garafano-Brown (2007) found behavioral measures demonstrated mixed results when compared to development measures, suggesting perhaps it is difficult to compare or measure these two constructs within one study. Considering that Baker et al. (2005) found that children who do not move successfully through the stages or who exhibit delays as young as 3 years exhibit more behavior problems than their same-age peers, it is possible that developmental changes precede behavioral changes. Perhaps developmental changes were easier to observe after some of the participants' emotional issues subsided to allow them to be more fully functioning or functioning closer to their chronological age.

Overall, results indicated improvement in Nate's standard scores on the DAYC while receiving child-centered play therapy sessions (intervention phase). Although, from a single-case design perspective, child-centered play therapy appeared to be an effective intervention, decrease in performance in standard scores during the follow-up phase suggests the need for continued child-centered play therapy intervention.

CLINICAL SIGNIFICANCE

Nate was reluctant to go with me to the evaluation room throughout the entire study. He often ran and hid and had to be redirected by his father, which was somewhat appropriate, given his young age. On other occasions, Nate grabbed his father's leg and would not let go for several minutes while the examiner offered encouragement to him to come to the assessment room. When Nate finally entered the assessment room, his behavior was erratic. Some days, he was more compliant than others. When presented with tasks he did not want to complete, he often spit at me or threw items from the table across the room and onto the floor. He often licked the toys and other materials along with the two-way observation mirror in the assessment room. Nate's speech was often difficult to understand, but toward the end of the intervention phase, his speech was much more articulate and coherent. He often drooled and soiled his diaper during the assessment or preceding play therapy session. Improvement was noted in Nate's compliance with directions and ability to change tasks and activities. I observed Nate playing more cooperatively in the waiting room with his siblings instead of the initial aggressive behavior noted at the beginning of the study. He appeared to exhibit more control of his body, or self-control, and less aggressive behavior toward me, siblings, and toys and materials.

Nate's play therapist reported observations similar to mine as the examiner, although Nate was typically very eager to go to the playroom. Nate tested limits with the therapist and often threw sand and objects at her during his play. Over time, she reported a noticeable difference in his ability to communicate with words and articulate his needs during his play session. Nate typically appeared happy and excited, even when playing aggressively and testing limits.

Nate's father reported ongoing stress related to his concerns for parenting Nate, as well as his other four children. He reported noticing an improvement in Nate's speech and communication skills. He reported noticing this, especially when Nate was with his extended family. Nate's father reported a decrease in separation issues and Nate showed improvement in his ability for self-control, following directions, and accepting limits.

Implications for Future Research

The purpose of using a single-case design for this study was to provide an in-depth look at the population and progress when assessed with several instruments and to develop a practical understanding for making recommendations for counseling intervention. It is important that the study be replicated so as to increase the reliability and validity of results. It is noteworthy, and especially important for practitioners to know, that Nate was angry and disappointed when he came to the clinic during the follow-up phase to be assessed and was not allowed to go into the playrooms. Future replication of this study may benefit from assessing children on different days or different locations from where they receive child-centered play therapy. It is possible that some of the emotional reactions that interfered with the developmental assessment were caused by his longing to go to the playroom and his anger toward the examiner for keeping him in the assessment room. This would be particularly apparent with children exhibiting willful behavior. It may be beneficial to increase the treatment phase to two times weekly when using an eight-week format or to extend treatment phase to 16 weeks to measure developmental and behavioral changes in young children. Results seem to support, however, the use of a CCPT intervention as a promising intervention for young children with developmental delays, even though the participants were not ready to terminate child-centered play therapy services.

Other factors to consider include the appropriateness of using single-case design. The design was beneficial in focusing on single participant's progress over time. This process allowed for the collection of multiple assessments lending a thorough and comprehensive approach of analyzing a participant's progress in terms of practical use for counseling interventions. Specifically, this research was affected by the need for an extended baseline, which is an ethical consideration for play therapy researchers who might continue to delay needed treatment for a child for the benefit of research design. Also, the qualitative nature of single-case design may increase the difficulty for other researchers to use the visual analysis over other designs' reliance on quantitative analysis, often perceived as more reliable.

Researchers are encouraged to report their findings from single-case designs in professional counseling journals to increase replication as well as increasing the potential for validation and generalizabilty for interventions (Sharpley, 2007). Counselors are also urged to consider the importance of using and reporting their results from single-case designs so they can "increase the scientist-practitioner reputation of counseling and the relative status as a therapeutic endeavor within the overall evidence-based mental health field" (Sharpley, 2007, p. 351). The presented study was an attempt to apply a practitioner-based research design to explore the effectiveness of play therapy. As a result, the play therapy intervention was explored in great detail, using multiple measures over multiple points of time, thereby resulting in an intricate look at the impact of play therapy on children with developmental delays.

REFERENCES

Abidin, R. R. (1995). *Parenting stress index* (3rd ed.) Odessa, FL: Psychological Assessment Resources.

Achenbach T. M., & Rescorla, L. A. (2000). *Manual for the ASEBA preschool forms and profiles.* Burlington, VT: University of Vermont, Department of Psychiatry.

Baker, B., Blacher, J., & Olsson, M. (2005). Preschool children with and without developmental delay: Behavior problems, parents' optimism, and well-being. *Journal of Intellectual Disability Research, 49*(8), 575–590.

Barlow, D., & Hersen, M. (1984). *Single-case experimental designs. Strategies for studying behavior change.* Elmsford, NY: Pergamon.

Casby, M. (2003). Developmental assessment of play: A model for early intervention. *Communication Disorders Quarterly, 24*(4), 175–183.

Cohen, J. (1988). *Statistical power analysis for the behavioral sciences* (2nd ed.). New York: Academic Press.

Garofano-Brown, A. (2007). Relationship between child-centered play therapy and developmental levels of young children: A single-case analysis. *Dissertation Abstracts International, 69*(2).

Guralnick, M., Hammond, M., Connor, R., & Neville, B. (2006). Stability, change, and correlates of the peer relationships of young children with mild developmental delays. *Child Development, 77*(2), 312–324.

Ilg, F. (1965). *Gesell developmental observation.* New Haven, CT: Gesell Institute of Human Development.

Ilg, F., Ames, L., & Baker, S. (1981). *Child behavior: The classic child care manual from the Gesell Institute of Human Development.* New York: Harper & Row.

Kazdin, A. (2003). *Research design in clinical psychology* (4th ed.). Boston: Allyn & Bacon.

Kennedy, C. (2005). *Single-case designs for educational research.* Boston: Allyn & Bacon.

Krakow, J., & Kopp, C. (1983). The effect of developmental delay on sustained attention in young children. *Child Development, 54,* 1143–1155.

Lundervold, D., & Belwood, M. (2000). The best-kept secret in counseling: Single-case (n = 1) experimental designs. *Journal of Counseling & Development, 78,* 92–102.

Sharpley, C. (2007). So why aren't counselors reporting n = 1 research designs? *Journal of Counseling and Development, 85,* 349–355.

Spinrad, T., Eisenberg, N., Harris, E., Hanish, L., Fabes, R., Kysanoff, K., et al. (2004). Academic socialization: Understanding parental influence on children's school-related development in the early years. *Review of General Psychology, 8*(37), 163–178.

Voress, J. K., & Maddox, T. (1988). *Developmental assessment of young children: Examiner's manual.* Austin, TX: PRO-ED.

Wortham, S. (1999). Assessing and reporting young children's progress: A review of the issues. In J. P. Isenberg & M. R. Jalongo (Eds.), *Major trends and issues in early childhood education* (pp. 104–122). New York: Teachers College Press.

CHAPTER 14

Children's Perceptions of Play Therapy*

ERIC J. GREEN**

RATIONALE

Children's perceptions of play therapy are something I wanted to explore throughout my doctoral program. I remember counseling children in my elementary school as a school counselor and thinking to myself, "I'm wondering what they think of this process?" I sought information about children's views of play therapy in schools but did not find much in the literature. Therefore, I, along with the invaluable guidance from Dr. Theresa Christensen, embarked on interviewing children about how they viewed play therapy. I found it fascinating to explore the mind of the child on such an important topic that we as child clinicians have been trained in primarily from the adult perspective.

According to Ray, Perkins, and Oden (2004), elementary-age school-children respond positively to creative interventions used by school counselors. By infusing play therapy interventions throughout a comprehensive school counseling program, school counselors may advance the school climate by providing more developmentally appropriate

*This chapter is adapted from the following journal article with the express permission of the Association for Play Therapy: Green, E., & Christensen, T. (2006). Children's perceptions of play therapy in school settings. *International Journal of Play Therapy, 15*(1), 65–85.

**Gratitude is expressed to Drs. Theresa Christensen, Dawn Ironside, and Peggy Ceballos for generously contributing to this research project.

and curative strategies to bolster academic and social success in students (Ray, Muro, & Schumann, 2004). Play therapy is an effective, creative counseling process that is sensitive to children's academic and social development (Bratton & Ray, 2000; Landreth, 2002).

Researchers studying the effectiveness of play therapy have derived some of their empirical knowledge quantitatively through surveys or questionnaires that are based on child developmental psychology (Del Po & Frick, 1988) and children's views of traditional psycho-therapy (Kranz, Kottman, & Lund, 1998). Because play therapy and child psychotherapies that mainly use talk therapy vary in approaches, methodologies, and outcomes (Landreth, Baggerly, & Tyndall-Lind, 1999), I found it necessary to qualitatively explore children's perceptions of the process of play therapy (Caroll, 2001).

PLAY THERAPY

The Association for Play Therapy (1997) defined *play therapy* as "the systematic use of a theoretical model to establish an interpersonal process wherein trained play therapists use the therapeutic powers of play to help clients prevent or resolve psychosocial difficulties and achieve optimal growth and development" (p. 4). Play therapists incorporate different play therapy media that are suited to the individual needs of children, while maintaining the therapeutic relationship as an important aspect of the counseling process (Christensen, 2003; Gil, 1991; Landreth, 2002).

According to Campbell (1993), the process of play therapy refers to the communication between counselors and children that builds a therapeutic relationship and facilitates emotional growth. The process of play therapy differs slightly, depending on the theoretical orienta-tion of the play therapist. Christensen (2003) described a generalized process of play therapy, which does not necessarily occur across all theoretical models, in five phases:

1. Relationship building and assessment
2. Exploration
3. Theme development and awareness
4. Independence and sense of autonomy
5. Termination

In these stages, children learn to integrate thoughts, feelings, and experiences in an effort to resolve psychosocial issues and develop a sense of mastery over their lives.

PLAY THERAPY IN ELEMENTARY SCHOOLS

Play therapy has been applied in elementary schools as part of responsive services to decrease behaviors associated with social, emotional, behavioral, and learning difficulties (Bratton & Ray, 2000; Packman & Bratton, 2003). According to Campbell (1993), when children engage in play, they are developing skills and knowledge that contribute to future school success. In a survey by Ray, Armstrong, Warren, and Balkin (2005), it was found that school counselors believed that play therapy was a developmentally appropriate counseling medium to use with young children, yet they desired both time and training in the use of play therapy techniques in their school settings.

LeBlanc and Ritchie (1999) conducted a meta-analysis of available studies that measured the effectiveness of play therapy with elementary-age schoolchildren and found significant variance between control and treatment studies, suggesting that play therapy may have been an effective intervention. Current literature supports school counselors' use of play therapy with children (Packman & Bratton, 2003); I was unable to locate, however, any studies in the literature in which researchers investigated children's perceptions of play therapy specifically in school settings.

METHOD

GROUNDED THEORY

I found two research studies in the literature (Axline, 1950; Caroll, 2001) on children's perceptions of the process of play therapy. Because the goal of this study was to illustrate children's perceptions of the counseling process that involved play therapy techniques, a relatively uninvestigated area, grounded theory procedures were used. Grounded theory is a procedure qualitative researchers use to systematically develop a theoretical framework from informed interpretations to build, synthesize, and integrate scientific knowledge (Strauss & Corbin, 1998).

The grand research question was, "What are elementary-age schoolchildren's perceptions of the process of counseling with school counselors who use play therapy techniques?" More specific questions included the following:

- What are elementary-age schoolchildren's perceptions of the process of individual change in counseling?
- What are elementary-age schoolchildren's favorite play therapy techniques and why?

- If given the freedom to choose, would elementary-age school-children prefer talking or playing in counseling? Why?
- What are elementary-age schoolchildren's perceptions regarding the purpose of counseling, in particular, why are they attending counseling?
- How might the therapeutic relationship and the process of play facilitate elementary-age schoolchildren's expression of difficult feelings and topics?

PARTICIPANTS

Participants were seven elementary-age schoolchildren currently engaged in a therapeutic relationship with a school counselor who used play therapy techniques. The school counselors received child-centered play therapy (CCPT) training in both graduate courses and workshops. They were both working toward their Registered Play Therapist credential. Also, they both identified with the CCPT modality. With warmth and empathic understanding, counselors who ascribe to child-centered play therapy focus on children's strengths, reflect their feelings, and facilitate children's journeys into self-exploration (Axline, 1950; Landreth, 2002; Landreth & Bratton, 2000). Unlike traditional CCPT, however, both play therapists occasionally asked open-ended questions and facilitated directed play based on the child's need. For this study, I selected children currently enrolled in play therapy because of their experiences and possible knowledge about the process of play therapy—the phenomenon investigated.

The participants were in therapy primarily because of stress from their parents' divorcing, anxiety related to peer relationships, and bereavement. Two school counselors at two different schools recruited the participants for this study based on whether the participants had experienced play therapy, if the legal guardians would be amenable to give consent for their children to participate in the study, and if the participants would be willing to and possessed the verbal abilities to answer questions about their experiences in counseling. Because the school counselors had pre-established relationships with the partic-ipants, they initially contacted the legal guardians about my study. I followed up by securing consent forms from the legal guardians before conducting the initial participant interviews. Henkelman and Everall (2001) recommended that researchers obtain children's assent to make them feel part of the process. Therefore, I obtained verbal assent from each of the participants when I first met the child.

For the purpose of this study, the participant pool was limited to the southern United States. Six participants were female, and one was male. Five of the participants were European American, and two were African American. Participants' ages ranged from 6 to 11. All participants were enrolled in elementary schools, with three in a public elementary school and four in a private school (K-12). Three of the participants were in fourth grade, two were in third grade, one was in second grade, and one participant was in first grade. The school counselors estimated that each participant had experienced at least five play therapy sessions in school settings, and they approximated that the total amount of sessions ranged from 5 to 35.

DATA COLLECTION

Aligned with the exploratory nature of qualitative research, data collected for this study included three rounds of in-person, semi-structured interviews, my personal observations of the participants' verbal and nonverbal behaviors and their environment, and document reviews.

Semi-structured interviews are a joint construction of meaning between the researcher and participant (Gay & Airasian, 2000). Because of time and logistical limitations associated with gaining access to the schools to interview the participants, three rounds of semi-structured interviews were the primary source of data collection. Interviews were face-to-face and were audiotaped and transcribed. Because I was unsure if the children in the study could answer all the questions posed, given their developmental levels, questions were restated in more developmentally appropriate and clear ways when the children were unable to provide an answer or explicitly stated, "I don't understand what you mean." As suggested by Caroll (2001), toys or props were used during the interviews of this research to encourage children's verbalization of the process of play therapy. Specifically, materials similar to those used by the school counselors during their counseling sessions with research participants were used. I employed the same probes for all children in all of the interviews so that the findings were not skewed because of the children's reactions to diverse toys or play materials. The props used in the interviews were similar to what the school counselors used when administering the play therapy interventions to the participants during this project to encourage recall and create a familiar environment.

Personal observations involve the researcher observing the participant to gain depth and breadth into the participant's insights and experiences (Gay & Airasian, 2000). Personal observations comprise the researcher's thoughts and feelings of participants' verbal and non-verbal communication (Creswell, 1998). I maintained a journal of my personal observations of the participant interviews, which comprised my thoughts regarding participants' verbal and nonverbal themes. Other observations involved in this study included:

- The physical environment at the school where the interviews occurred
- The participants' demeanor before, during, and after the interview
- Facial expressions and emotional reactions while the participants told their stories
- Changes in verbal expression, tone of voice, or body language while participants expressed thoughts and feelings

Document reviews are useful forms of data collection in qualitative research and provide additional information about the phenomenon under investigation (Merchant, 1997). I obtained one or more of the following documents from each of the school counselors involved with this study:

- School counselors' college transcripts
- School counselors' CEU certificates pertaining to play therapy training
- Accounts from school counselors of the participants' receptivity to play therapy techniques during counseling sessions
- Information school counselors maintained on play therapy techniques that they used with their clients

The document reviews helped answer some of the questions raised in this study by providing me with a context of understanding the school counselors' experiences and training in play therapy involved in this study, how they facilitated the therapeutic relationship with the participants, and how and why play therapy techniques were used.

DATA ANALYSIS

Miles and Huberman (1994) outlined three types of analytical tasks in qualitative data analysis: data reduction, data display, and conclusion drawing and verification. Data reduction in grounded theory comprises three procedures: open coding, axial coding, and selective coding (Strauss & Corbin, 1998), all of which were used in this investigation. The participants' interviews were recorded and transcribed for the purpose of data analysis. In the initial round of interviews, participants' responses were examined, and common themes were sought to reduce the data. Member checks were conducted at the beginning of each of the follow-up interviews to verify the accuracy of transcripts, clarify participants' responses, and assess the viability of themes. Once themes were identified from participants' responses, initial categories were developed and then new questions were formulated to narrow the focus of this investigation, confirm initial findings, and probe for new or additional information to answer the research question. Also, the process of data reduction and refinement of questions occurred after the second round of interviews. Open coding involved organizing the participants' responses into discrete parts, which were compared for similarities and differences. From these distinctions, central categories and subcategories were developed to assist in asking questions about the phenomena as reflected in the data. Axial coding was used by developing and interconnecting categories and subcategories across themes that emerged in the data. Finally, selective coding was used in the final steps of data reduction to build a story that connected the categories.

Data displays in this investigation consisted of conceptual matrixes in which participants' quotes were separated according to homogeneous characteristics, which allowed me to analyze participants' responses within and across categories. Conclusion drawing and verification were achieved through the use of triangulation procedures: a peer debriefer, a search for rival explanations, and expert consultation (Strauss & Corbin, 1998). A peer debriefer was used to review the preliminary findings during each round of data collection and analysis and to assist with minimizing any possible response bias. I sought rival explanations to the findings in this investigation by examining the literature related to the investigation's topic. Last, expert consultation consisted of sharing the findings of this investigation with other school counselors and experts in the field, such as those who have completed qualitative studies similar in scope, for reflection and further refinement. I also maintained a reflexive journal to record observations, assumptions, biases, reflections, and questions.

RESULTS AND DISCUSSION

Three overall themes emerged from the data. These themes were related to several components of the counseling process: therapeutic relationship, emotional expressiveness, and creative play.

THERAPEUTIC RELATIONSHIP

The counseling process was perceived across three themes, with the first theme being the therapeutic relationship. The therapeutic relationship referred to aspects of the process of counseling that involved an alliance formed between counselors and participants. Landreth and Bratton (2000) noted that by establishing a positive therapeutic relationship consisting of empathic understanding and acceptance, children and counselors create an entire therapeutic world in which children actively engage in appropriate expression of emotion and are able to focus on their strengths. Participants' responses indicated that specific similarities or properties existed in the therapeutic relationship: freedom to choose, empathy or acceptance, and collaborative problem solving.

Freedom to choose in the therapeutic relationship promoted creativity or self-expression and allowed for participants' preference of traditional verbal therapy, play techniques, or a combination of the two. Participants experienced the power of their unique potential through the freedom of choice inherent within the therapeutic relationship. This concept was supported by Landreth (2002), who stated that returning responsibility involves allowing children to make choices and to take responsibility for those choices. For example, Erika (names are pseudonyms) stated that children were given the freedom to choose in the playroom and express themselves: "Sometimes we get to pick the activity, sometimes she [the counselor] tells us. My favorite is when we get to pick, because we get to be more creative."

The freedom to choose in counseling also consisted of participants commenting on their preferences for traditional verbal interventions or playing. Erika stated the use of talking and playing in counseling depends on the magnitude of the problem: "If you're in a big fight . . . then you would like to talk it out. But if it's kind of minor . . . then I could play." Traditional verbal interventions helped the participants release difficult feelings, which made them feel better, while playing was viewed as fun. A mixture of both traditional verbal interventions and play during the counseling process appeared to be the optimal choice for participants:

DANICA: I think [I'd prefer] both talking and playing: [maybe] half talking, half playing. Sometimes talking makes me feel better. I like to play because it's fun to use the sand and that's mostly what we play.
JASMINE: [I like to] talk and play [in counseling]. When I talk, I get more stuff out. When I play, it's more active. I think playing is to show really what happened and how it happened.

Empathy and *acceptance* were important terms because the understanding shown by the counselor assisted participants with verbalizing difficult emotions and finding solutions to their concerns. Leroy commented on the benefit of therapeutic acceptance in terms of positive regard: "I like to draw a little, but I don't think I draw good. [My counselor] likes [my drawings]. . . . It makes me feel good." Jasmine commented on her counselor's empathy: "She [the counselor] understands us. She understands children. . . . You feel happy because you are being understood and not ignored." Participants' responses clarified empathy and acceptance as part of the therapeutic relationship and attributed such factors to the counselors' special training or education that assisted them with their understanding of problems, ability to maintain direct eye contact and be physically attentive, skill at offering meaningful insight, and the ability to remain nonjudgmental.

Collaborative problem solving was perceived by participants as working in partnership with an adult who accurately understood their problems and helped find practical solutions. Traditional verbal interventions, probing questions, and exploration of alternatives were three ways participants used to describe how they collaboratively solved problems within the therapeutic relationship that school counselors fostered. Traditional verbal interventions involved specific techniques through which participants felt comfortable expressing their worries because their counselors were attentive. Erika gave an example of why she preferred talking to her counselor: "I like to talk to [the counselor], because from the past, I've found that it's kind of hard to sort out problems with your parents." Counselors used probing questions with participants to elicit information and to gain a deeper understanding of problems. Once counselors gained such knowledge, they were better able to assist participants in clarifying solutions. For example, Greta described a situation in which her counselor used questioning probes during a collaborative problem-solving scenario: "I told her [the counselor] I didn't like when she [a friend] was mean to me. So [the counselor] asked me some questions like, 'Is she mean to you a lot, or just sometimes?' Then I felt better because I knew that she [the friend] probably didn't mean to hurt my feelings."

As participants described how counselors explored alternatives, they consistently described how counselors also offered participants choices regarding how they could develop ways to handle their stress. Ellen described why exploring alternatives with her counselor helped her with her worries: "If I'm sad on the weekend, I would think about what she [the counselor] would tell me: 'You can go talk to your dog, or you could just play the violin.'"

EMOTIONAL EXPRESSIVENESS

Participants perceived emotional expressiveness as part of the counseling process in the form of three sub-themes: safety, fun, and the process of change.

Participants indicated that throughout the process of counseling, they felt safe and participated in fun activities, which resulted in appropriate expressions of emotion. Participants also indicated that their feelings and behaviors changed positively while engaged in the therapeutic relationship.

Safety was perceived as feelings of comfort and relaxation, which resulted in participants making choices about trust regarding their counselors. Participants indicated that trust also enabled them to express emotions. One participant, Erika, offered the following definition of safety: "Being safe feels comfortable, like you can just relax. It feels like you can say anything you want." Participants perceived that their sense of safety involved relaxation, trust, and confidentiality as key components in the counseling relationship. Jana described how she trusted her counselor: "Whenever somebody yells at you, it makes you all upset, and [the counselor] doesn't yell and doesn't make you upset. So I can trust her." Jasmine gave an example of how she felt physically safe while attending counseling, "I feel safe. The children at school won't beat me up because they know I'm going to tell [my counselor]." Leroy demonstrated how confidentiality pertained to safety: "I know she [the counselor] won't go out and tell nobody else what is happening with me."

Fun referred to the sense of enjoyment and satisfaction that participants experienced in counseling, which facilitated emotional expressiveness in the playroom. For example, Leroy stated, "Sometimes I like to talk to her [the counselor] and . . . I like to come to counseling a lot 'cause it's fun. I like when we watch movies or read a book." This statement was supported by Campbell (1993) who noted that fun activities may be used by counselors to prevent children from an excessive focus on their specific problem, which possibly makes disclosure of emotional content easier.

The process of change, as defined by participants, was inextricably linked to their perceptions of how they made better choices while engaged in the counseling process. After being involved in counseling in which play therapy and traditional verbal techniques were used, participants indicated that they made better choices at home and at school, experienced less anxiety, were able to change negative thoughts, felt more confident with improved self-esteem, and were able to emotionally connect with someone else's feelings (for example, empathy).

Leroy described an improvement in the choices he made while attending counseling and explained how such choices had resulted in a positive climate at home: "My mom fusses at me when I'm in her way. . . . I try to stay out of her way like what [my counselor] told me to do. It kind of feels good because she [mom] doesn't fuss at me like she used to." Other participants also commented that they experienced decreased levels of anxiety and that this helped them to change unpleasant thoughts. For example, Ellen commented on the changes her mother noticed in her thought processes after attending counseling: "I haven't been worrying as much. I haven't been telling my mom all my silly thoughts and all that. I haven't been telling her all my worries. I think she has seen a change. I just feel better." Gil (1991) stated that in the playroom, children can create an entire therapeutic world in which they cognitively and emotionally overcome anxieties.

Participants described the process of change as being one in which they felt a sense of self-confidence that improved their social skills. Jasmine stated, "My momma noticed that I'm playing with the other students and not fighting with them anymore. Every day I would play with somebody, and then I wouldn't run in the house every day crying or anything 'cause they stopped picking on me." Enhanced empathy was yet another example of how participants changed as a result of the counseling process. In particular, participants described that the lessons they learned in counseling assisted them in acknowledging others' feelings and enhanced peer relationships. Erika described the process of change as developing empathy, which alleviated her shyness with peers: "I have more friends now. [Counseling] has taught me to understand people's feelings . . . to understand that they like to talk, and they have feelings, too."

CREATIVE PLAY

Participants depicted sand tray, role play or drama, and artwork or drawing as the three essential creative play activities that they enjoyed and experienced in counseling. As participants described the benefits of creative play in the process of counseling, they illustrated how play helped them express their feelings that may have been difficult to express verbally; facilitate a sense of enjoyment, pride, and independence from participating in creative, self-directed behaviors; and develop problem-solving strategies that created positive outcomes. When asked which would be their favorite creative play activity, participants chose sand tray and artwork or drawings.

Sand tray enabled participants to convey their issues creatively and find solutions to problems through the use of miniatures in a sandbox. For example, Erika described how sand tray promoted her creativity: "We took these [sand miniatures] and put them into the boxes, and anything could mean anything. I think it's for creativity, [which] means just letting your mind wander and do whatever you feel like doing." Ellen described how creative play had assisted her in "solving worries." When I asked Ellen how the sand tray activity specifically helped her with her concerns, she replied: "I made different choices [in sand tray], to know and to believe that my brain was telling me lies."

Role play or drama involved participants creating their own worlds and playing out scenarios and issues that represented their current home or school circumstances. Role plays or drama work took place in a dollhouse, with puppets, or dressing up in character costumes in front of the counselor. Jasmine commented on the usefulness of role play and drama in the counseling process: "Sometimes I show her [the counselor] about what happens in the [doll] house over there. Like some kind of things that go on in [my] house, and so she helps you with those problems." Leroy specified how drama work in counseling assisted him during his bereavement after his grandmother's death: "When my grandma died, I went over to the dollhouse and kind of did what I needed to do for my grandma."

Artwork or drawings in the counseling process provided participants with another medium to express their feelings and problems. Jana described how the process of artwork in counseling facilitated her expression of sadness: "If we're feeling sad and we can't tell [the counselor], then we express it whenever we're drawing." Jana described how her school counselor used questions to process art activities during a counseling session: "She [the counselor] would ask questions whenever we're done and stuff. She would be like, 'Who's that?' and we would tell her who she [the person in the drawing] is."

LIMITATIONS AND RECOMMENDATIONS

Inherent in this study are limitations, such as my biases and limited experience with qualitative research, which raises questions when considering the generalizability of findings. The qualitative nature of this study provided a rich examination of the counseling process. Although this qualitative investigation makes important contributions to the play therapy literature, the findings should not be generalized to other elementary-age schoolchildren without further inquiry.

Researcher bias was a limitation; therefore, multiple data collection procedures were used, and alternative explanations were searched for in the literature. Also, I shared findings with a peer debriefer to ensure that findings were indicative of participants' perspectives and not my personal convictions. I also used member checks at the beginning of each of the follow-up interviews as a means of verifying the accuracy of transcripts, clarifying participants' responses, and assessing initial perceptions and data analysis. Another limitation was the school counselors' training and level of experience in play therapy. While both counselors involved in this study had completed one year of graduate training in play therapy and practiced play therapy exclusively with their clients, neither counselor had extensive training in play therapy, a requirement to becoming a registered play therapist. However, I specifically chose school counselors who were not fully certified as registered play therapists so I could encapsulate the reality in schools in which counselors who are using play therapy techniques have limited play therapy training (Ray, Armstrong, Warren, & Balkin, 2005).

These findings offer new information grounded in the experiences of elementary-age schoolchildren. Play therapists and school counselors may use the findings of this study to further investigate the usefulness of incorporating traditional verbal interventions throughout their play therapy sessions. Because of children's perception of the problem-solving nature of the therapeutic relationship, play therapists and school counselors may want to develop new verbal skills to foster collaborations with children to solve concerns. Participants stated they preferred the freedom to choose activities. As these findings are congruent with nondirective play therapy (Landreth, 2002), play therapists and school counselors may want to revisit the nondirective play therapy literature. The findings from this study showed that participants chose sand tray and artwork as their favorite creative play media. When choosing play activities, play therapists and school counselors may want to take into consideration whether the activity will allow children to express their creativity and individuality.

The following research questions could be explored in future qualitative studies:

- What are the perceptions of school counselors who use play therapy techniques throughout the process of counseling with elementary-age schoolchildren?
- What are children's perceptions of the counseling process with school counselors who are also registered play therapists?
- What are children's perceptions of the process of counseling with school counselors who have no play therapy training?

Based on participants' responses, a theoretical framework emerged regarding the therapeutic relationship, emotional expressiveness, and creative play as dominant themes to describe the counseling process with school counselors who use play therapy techniques. The commonality among all themes was that children preferred the ability to choose exactly what goes on in the playroom. Along with the ability to make independent choices, children also valued a nonjudgmental, attentive adult who acknowledged their creativity and promoted individual, creative self-expression, as espoused by the tenets of non-directive play therapy (Axline, 1950). Furthermore, these participants articulated that attending counseling in a safe environment with a trusted adult directly affected their individual process of change and ability to solve their own problems at both home and school.

REFERENCES

Association for Play Therapy. (1997). Play therapy definition. *Association for Play Therapy Newsletter, 16*(2), 4.

Axline, V. M. (1950). Play therapy experiences as described by child participants. *Journal of Counseling Psychology, 14*, 53–63.

Bratton, S. C., & Ray, D. C. (2000). What the research shows about play therapy. *International Journal of Play Therapy, 9*, 47–88.

Campbell, C. A. (1993). Play: The fabric of elementary school counseling programs. *Elementary School Guidance and Counseling, 28*, 10–17.

Caroll, J. (2001). Play therapy: The children's views. *Child and Family Social Work, 7*, 177–187.

Christensen, T. M. (2003). *Introduction to play therapy.* [Handout]. New Orleans: Author.

Creswell, J. W. (1998). *Qualitative inquiry and research design: Choosing among five traditions.* Thousand Oaks, CA: Sage.

Del Po, E., & Frick, S. (1988). Directed and nondirected play as therapeutic modalities. *Children's Health Care, 16*, 261–267.

Gay, L. R., & Airasian, P. (2000). *Educational research: Competencies for analysis and application* (6th ed.). Upper Saddle River, NJ: Prentice-Hall.

Gil, E. (1991). *The healing power of play: Working with abused children*. New York: Guilford.

Henkelman, J. J., & Everall, R. D. (2001). Informed consent with children: Ethical and practical implications. *Canadian Journal of Counseling*, 6(1), 55–61.

Kranz, P. L., Kottman, T., & Lund, N. L. (1998). Play therapists' opinions concerning the education, training, and practice of play therapists. *International Journal of Play Therapy*, 7, 73–87.

Landreth, G. L. (2002). *Play therapy: The art of the relationship* (2nd ed.). New York: Brunner-Routledge.

Landreth, G. L., Baggerly, J., & Tyndall-Lind, A. (1999). Beyond adapting adult counseling skills for use with children: The paradigm shift to child-centered play therapy. *Journal of Individual Psychology*, 55, 272–288.

Landreth, G. L., & Bratton, S. C. (2000). Play therapy. *Journal of Counseling and Human Development*, 31(1), 1–12.

LeBlanc, M., & Ritchie, M. (1999). Predictors of play therapy outcomes. *International Journal of Play Therapy*, 8(2), 19–34.

Merchant, N. (1997). Qualitative research for counselors. *Counseling and Human Development*, 30, 1–19.

Miles, M., & Huberman, A. (1994). *Qualitative data analysis* (2nd ed.). Thousand Oaks, CA: Sage.

Packman, J., & Bratton, S. C. (2003). A school-based group play/activity therapy intervention with learning disabled preadolescents exhibiting behavior problems. *International Journal of Play Therapy*, 12, 7–29.

Ray, D. C., Armstrong, S. A., Warren, E. S., & Balkin, R. S. (2005). Play therapy practices among elementary school counselors. *Professional School Counseling*, 8, 360–365.

Ray, D. C., Muro, J., & Schumann, B. (2004). Implementing play therapy in the schools: Lessons learned. *International Journal of Play Therapy*, 13, 79–100.

Ray, D. C., Perkins, S. R., & Oden, K. (2004). Rosebush fantasy technique with elementary school students. *Professional School Counseling*, 7, 277–282.

Strauss, A., & Corbin, J. (1998). Grounded theory methodology: An overview. In N. K. Denzin & Y. S. Lincoln (Eds.), *Strategies of qualitative inquiry* (pp. 158–183). Thousand Oaks, CA: Sage.

RESEARCH IN FILIAL THERAPY

CHAPTER 15

Child Parent Relationship Therapy: A Review of Controlled-Outcome Research

SUE C. BRATTON and GARRY L. LANDRETH

Yung-Wei Dennis Lin, Doctoral Candidate

University of North Texas

C HILD PARENT RELATIONSHIP THERAPY (CPRT; Landreth & Bratton, 2006), a 10-session filial therapy model, is one of the more well-researched treatment protocols in the field of child psychotherapy with more than 40 studies investigating its effectiveness. CPRT is based on the filial therapy model developed by Bernard and Louise Guerney in the mid-1960s, in which caregivers are taught child-centered play therapy principles and skills to use with their own children. The Guerneys' approach was founded on their belief in the significance of the parent-child relationship and their confidence in parents' ability to learn the necessary skills to become therapeutic agents in their children's lives. Thus, they used the term *filial therapy* to describe their innovative approach (Guerney, 2001).

Based on my (second author) experiences conducting filial therapy in the late 1970s, I began to experiment with condensing the Guerneys' group format. Over the next two decades, I continued to develop and write about the 10-session model (Landreth, 1991/2002), based on my ongoing experiences with parents. My colleague (first author) and I further refined and formalized the 10-session training format in a text, *Child Parent Relationship Therapy (CPRT): A 10-Session Filial Therapy Model* (Landreth and Bratton, 2006), to distinguish the model from other filial therapy approaches. While CPRT's methods and structure of delivery vary from the Guerneys' original model, CPRT's underlying philosophy, including the benefits of a group training format, is essentially the same.

In the process of writing the CPRT text, we received feedback from practitioners and academicians on the need for a manualized protocol to allow for easier replication of the CPRT model and to provide researchers with a means of ensuring treatment fidelity. In response, we followed the text with the *CPRT Treatment Manual* and the accompanying CD-ROM (Bratton, Landreth, Kellam, & Blackard, 2006), which contains the 10-session protocol, therapist study guide, parent notebook, handouts, and resources.

For the purpose of this chapter we have limited our review to only those CPRT outcome studies that used a control or comparison group. The evidence for CPRT is impressive with 32 controlled-outcome research studies involving 916 participants. The positive findings demonstrate CPRT's effectiveness across presenting issues and diverse populations. This chapter provides a summary of findings from these studies in a convenient table format, along with a brief overview of meta-analytic research support for play therapy and filial therapy as a context for interpreting the individual research findings on the 10-session CPRT model. We also include a brief overview of the pioneering research efforts of Bernard and Louise Guerney.

HISTORY OF FILIAL THERAPY RESEARCH

The Guerneys' vision in developing filial therapy to meet the mental health needs of children, as well as their commitment to researching the effectiveness of their approach, laid the foundation for the development of CPRT. In the first study conducted on filial therapy, L. Stover and B. Guerney (1967) found that filial-trained mothers reported marked improvement in the parent-child relationship and in their children's behavior and general emotional adjustment. Building on their 1967 findings, B. Guerney and Stover (1971) conducted a more robust study of 51 mother-and-child pairs. Results indicated that mothers demonstrated statistically significant gains in empathic interactions with their children and reported improvement in their children's psychosocial adjustment and symptoms. Oxman (1972) studied a matched sample of mother-and-child pairs who received no treatment and found that the filial-trained mothers reported a statistically significant improvement in their children's behavior over the matched sample. A longitudinal investigation of the B. Guerney and Stover (1971) study was conducted by L. Guerney (1975), who found that 32 of the 42 respondents reported continued improvement one to three years after treatment. Following the Guerneys' lead, other researchers began to investigate the effects of this approach with success (Boll, 1972; Dematatis, 1981; Eardley, 1978; Kezur, 1980; Payton, 1980; Sensue, 1981; Sywulak, 1978; Wall, 1979). The largely statistically significant positive findings from the early research conducted by the Guerneys and their followers provided the impetus for Landreth and his protégés to join the Guerneys in researching the effectiveness of this innovative intervention in order to further its acceptance and use.

META-ANALYTIC RESEARCH SUPPORT

Historically, CPRT research, like most research in the field of psychotherapy, has been plagued by insufficient sample size. Meta-analytic reviews of research have made it possible to overcome individual study limitations resulting from small sample size by combining study findings to compute an overall treatment effect. Two meta-analyses on play therapy outcomes published over the last decade have demonstrated its utility and contributed to the acceptance of play therapy and filial therapy in the broader field of child psychotherapy (Bratton, Ray, Rhine, & Jones, 2005; LeBlanc & Ritchie, 2001). Due to space constraints we will focus only on the results from the more comprehensive 2005 meta-analysis by Bratton et al. Readers will find a more detailed summary of meta-analytic findings for play therapy, including results specific to studies coded filial therapy, in Chapter 1 of this text.

Bratton et al. (2005) conducted a meta-analysis of 93 controlled-outcome studies spanning five decades of play therapy research. The authors used Cohen's d (1988) guidelines (.20 = small; .50 = medium; .80 = large) to interpret treatment effect size (ES). They found that play therapy demonstrated an overall large treatment effect (ES = .80); meaning that, on average, children receiving play therapy improved by more than three-fourths of a standard deviation on specified outcome measures compared to children who did not receive play therapy. Of the 93 outcome studies, 26 measured the effects of play therapy conducted by paraprofessionals, defined as a parent, teacher, or peer mentor who was trained in play therapy procedures and supervised by a mental health professional. All studies coded to this group used CPRT or another filial therapy training methodology; thus all studies included were theoretically consistent in the use of child-centered play therapy principles and skills. Bratton et al. further analyzed this group of studies in order to explore the effect of filial therapy as a treatment modality apart from play therapy conducted by a mental health professional. The authors found that filial therapy showed stronger evidence of treatment effectiveness (ES = 1.05; a large effect) compared to traditional play therapy (ES = .72; a moderate effect), and in fewer sessions. Because all but four studies used parents to provide treatment, the authors included calculations for the effect size for the parent-only filial therapy studies, which revealed an even stronger treatment effect of 1.15.

During the process of writing the CPRT text and treatment manual, we (first and second author) decided to further analyze the meta-analytic data gathered by Bratton et al. (2005) to determine the overall treatment effect for filial therapy studies that employed CPRT methodology (generally referred to in early studies as the 10-session filial therapy model developed by Landreth). Statistical analysis yielded an overall ES of 1.25 for CPRT studies and an even stronger ES of 1.30 for parent-only CPRT studies (omitting teachers and student mentors). Only those CPRT studies in which the individual researchers were trained and supervised directly by one of us were included in the analysis to ensure adherence to the treatment protocol (which was unpublished at that time and therefore unavailable to researchers not trained by us).

RESEARCH SUPPORT FOR CHILD PARENT RELATIONSHIP THERAPY

CPRT is a well-researched modality with more than 40 studies investigating its effects on children and caregivers. The following review is limited to the 32 studies published 1995 to present that used a control group design. Statistically significant positive results were found on the vast majority of all measures. Studies were coded experimental or quasi-experimental, based on researchers' ability to employ random assignment of individual participants or intact groups (e.g., classrooms) to treatment. An impressive 13 studies were determined experimental in design, with the remainder judged quasi-experimental largely due to limitations in conducting research in real-world settings that interfered with random assignment. As an indicator of the high level of treatment fidelity in CPRT research, 28 studies were conducted by investigators that were directly trained and supervised in the CPRT protocol by the authors of the CPRT text (denoted by an asterisk [*] in Table 15.1). Unless otherwise specified, studies followed the standard CPRT protocol, which requires caregivers to attend 10 weekly 2-hour group training sessions and to conduct 7 weekly 30-minute play sessions with their child using child-centered play therapy principles and skills.

Child Parent Relationship Therapy (CPRT) Controlled Outcome Research 1995–2009

Authors	Participants/Methods	Findings
* Baggerly, J., & Landreth, G. L. (2001). Training children to help children: A new dimension in play therapy. *Companion study to Robinson & Landreth, 2007.*	N = 29 at-risk Kindergarteners; random drawing to treatment groups C = 14 no treatment wait-list E = 15 children received 10 weekly 20-minute play sessions from CPRT-trained 5th-grade mentors who were directly supervised by professionals trained in play therapy and CPRT protocol *Experimental design*	Compared to the control group, parents of experimental group children reported a statistically significant reduction in their Kindergarteners' internalizing behavior problems over time. Although not statistically significant, teachers and parents reported a greater reduction in overall behavior problems of children receiving CPRT and an increase in self-esteem following 10 supervised play mentoring sessions with their 5th-grade mentors, compared to control group.
* Beckloff, D. R. (1998). Filial therapy with children with spectrum pervasive development disorders.	N = 23 parents of 3- to 10-year-olds identified with Pervasive Developmental Disorder; assigned to treatment groups based on parents' schedules C = 11 no treatment wait-list E = 12 CPRT CPRT group received 10 sessions of CPRT training (1/wk, 2 hrs) and conducted 7 play sessions with their children (1/wk, 30 min) *Quasi-experimental design*	Compared to the control group, CPRT-trained parents made statistically significant gains from pre- to post-testing in their ability to recognize and accept their child's need for autonomy and independence. Although not statistically significant, parents reported a greater increase in their overall acceptance of their child, *compared to the control group.*

(*continued*)

Note: Treatment groups are denoted by E = Experimental, C = Control or Comparison.
* Indicates that researchers were directly trained and supervised in the CPRT protocol by Landreth or Bratton.

Table 15-1
(Continued)

Authors	Participants/Methods	Findings
* Bratton, S. C., & Landreth, G. L. (1995). Filial therapy with single parents: Effects on parental acceptance, empathy, and stress.	N = 43 single parents of 3- to 7-year-olds identified with behavioral concerns; random drawing to treatment groups C = 21 no treatment wait-list E = 22 CPRT CPRT group received 10 sessions of CPRT training (1/wk, 2 hrs) and conducted 7 play sessions with their children (1/wk, 30 min) *Experimental design*	Between-group differences over time revealed that parents in the CPRT group demonstrated a statistically significant increase in empathic interactions with their children as directly observed by independent raters. CPRT parents also reported a statistically significant gain in parental acceptance, as well as statistically significant reductions in parent-child relationship stress and in their children's behavior problems, compared to the control group over time.
* Brown C. (2003). Filial therapy training with undergraduate teacher trainees: Child-teacher relationship training.	N = 38 undergraduates enrolled in a required university course for preschool teachers; assigned to treatment groups based on schedules C = 20 STEP E = 18 adapted CPRT Both groups received 10 weeks of training (1.5 hr/wk) and conducted weekly 30-minute play sessions with a preschool-age child *Quasi-experimental design*	Compared to Systematic Training of Effective Parenting (STEP) group, CPRT-trained undergraduates demonstrated a statistically significant increase from pre to post in empathic interactions with children as directly observed in play sessions by independent raters. The experimental group also showed a statistically significant improvement in play therapy knowledge, attitudes, and skills.

* Ceballos, P., & Bratton, S. C. (in press). School-based child parent relationship therapy (CPRT) with low-income first-generation immigrant Latino parents: Effects on children's behaviors and parent-child relationship stress.	N = 48 immigrant Hispanic parents of Head Start children identified with behavioral problems; random drawing to treatment groups C = 24 no treatment wait-list E = 24 CPRT CPRT group received 11 sessions of culturally adapted CPRT training (1/wk, 2 hrs) and conducted 7 play sessions with their children (1/wk, 30 min); CPRT curriculum translated and sessions conducted in Spanish *Experimental design*	Compared to the control group over time, CPRT-trained parents reported statistically significant improvement in: a) their children's externalizing and internalizing behavior problems, and b) parent-child relationship stress. CPRT showed a large treatment effect on all dependent variables. Eighty-five percent of children in the CPRT group moved from clinical or borderline behavior problems to normal levels; 62 percent of parents reported a reduction from clinical levels of parenting stress to normative functioning. Findings were discussed in light of culturally relevant observations.
* Chau, I., & Landreth, G. L. (1997). Filial therapy with Chinese parents: Effects on parental empathic interactions, parental acceptance of child, and parental stress.	N = 34 immigrant Chinese parents of 2- to 10-year-olds; parents assigned to treatment groups based on random drawing and parents' schedules C = 16 no treatment wait-list E = 18 CPRT CPRT group received 10 sessions of CPRT training (1/wk, 2 hrs) and conducted 7 play sessions with their children (1/wk, 30 min) *Quasi-experimental design*	Compared to the control group over time, parents in the CPRT group demonstrated a statistically significant increase in empathic interactions with their children as directly observed in play sessions by independent raters. From pre to post, parents in the CPRT group also reported a statistically significant increase in parental acceptance and a statistically significant decrease in parent-child relationship stress, compared to the control group.

(continued)

Table 15-1
(Continued)

Authors	Participants/Methods	Findings
* Costas, M. B., & Landreth, G. L. (1999). Filial therapy with nonoffending parents of children who have been sexually abused.	N = 26 non-offending parents of sexually abused 5- to 9-year-olds; assigned to treatment groups based on random drawing and location C = 12 no treatment wait-list E = 14 CPRT CPRT group received 10 sessions of CPRT training (1/wk, 2 hrs) and conducted 7 play sessions with their children (1/wk, 30 min) *Quasi-experimental design*	Between-group differences over time revealed that parents receiving CPRT training 1) demonstrated statistically significant gains in their empathic interactions with their children as rated by independent raters, 2) reported a statistically significant increase in acceptance of their children, and 3) reported a statistically significant reduction in parent-child relationship stress. Although not statistically significant, CPRT-trained parents reported a marked improvement from pre- to post-testing in their children's behavior problems, anxiety, emotional adjustment, and self-concept.
* Crane , J. M., & Brown, C. J. (2003). Effectiveness of teaching play therapy attitudes and skills to undergraduate human service majors.	N = 20 undergraduate students enrolled in three human services courses C = 10 no treatment (volunteers from two human service courses received extra credit for participation in pre- and post-testing) E = 10 adapted CPRT (participants were students in one human service course on working with children)	Compared to the control group over time, undergraduate students in the CPRT group 1) demonstrated a statistically significant improvement in their empathic interactions with children as rated by independent raters, 2) reported a statistically significant reduction in inappropriate parenting expectations and views on corporal punishment, and

	CPRT group received training during weekly class meetings and conducted 7 or 8 weekly 30-minute play sessions with 3- to 9-year-olds *Quasi-experimental design*	3) reported a statistically significantly increase in play therapy knowledge and skill.
* Elling, E. R. (2003). A comparison of skill level of parents trained in the Landreth filial therapy model and graduate students trained in play therapy.	N = 34 participants; random assignment to treatment groups not possible because of composition of group members required by research design E1 = 13 graduate students enrolled in a graduate-level play therapy course E2 = 21 parents in traditional CPRT (from Bratton & Landreth, 1995). Parent demographics were similar for both groups. Children's age range was 3 to 7 years for both groups *Quasi-experimental design*	Data was obtained through direct observation of play sessions by raters blinded to study. Between group differences over time revealed that the play therapy–trained graduate students demonstrated a statistically significantly higher level of empathic interactions with children at post-test; however, the parent group's pre to post mean change score was greater. On measures of communication of acceptance and allowing child self-direction, no between group differences were found.
* Ferrell (2004). A comparison of an intensive 4-week format of the Landreth 10-week filial therapy training model with the traditional Landreth 10-week model of filial therapy.	N = 26 parents of 3- to 10-year-olds identified as having behavioral concerns; parents assigned to treatment groups based on parents' schedules and treatment location C = 13 - Traditional CPRT (1.5 hrs/wk for 10 weeks) E = 13 - Intensive CPRT (weekly 4-hour Saturday sessions for 4 weeks)	Results revealed no statistically significant difference between Intensive and Traditional CPRT groups over time. From pre to post, parents in both groups demonstrated statistically significant improvement in parental acceptance and in their empathic interactions with their children as rated by observers blinded to study. Both groups reported a decrease in child behavior problems and reduction

(continued)

Table 15-1
(Continued)

Authors	Participants/Methods	Findings
	Both groups received a total of 16 hours of training and conducted a total of seven 30-minute play sessions with their children *Quasi-experimental design*	in parent-child relationship stress, although not statistically significant.
* Glover, G., & Landreth, G. L. (2000). Filial therapy with Native Americans on the Flathead reservation.	N = 21 Native American parents of 3- to 10-year-olds, living on a reservation in western U.S.; parents assigned to treatment groups based on location they lived on the reservation C = 10 no treatment wait-list E = 11 CPRT CPRT group received 10 sessions of CPRT training (1/wk, 2 hrs) and conducted 7 play sessions with their children (1/wk, 30 min) *quasi- experimental design*	Compared to the control group over time, parents in CPRT group demonstrated a statistically significant increase in their empathic interactions with their children as directly observed in play sessions by independent raters, and their children also demonstrated a statistically significant increase in desirable play behaviors with their parents (independent raters). CPRT-trained parents also reported an increase in parental acceptance and a decrease in parent-child relationship stress, and their children reported increased self-concept, although these results were not statistically significant.
* Harris, Z. L., & Landreth, G. L. (1997). Filial therapy with incarcerated mothers: A five-week model.	N = 22 incarcerated mothers of 3- to 10-year-olds; assigned to treatment groups in cycles (based on number of mothers	Compared to the control group over time, mothers in the CPRT group demonstrated a statistically significant

276

	entering the county jail at a given point) through a combination of random drawing and selection of parents to groups to maintain equal number of subjects in each group C = 10 no treatment wait-list E = 12 CPRT CPRT group received 10 sessions of CPRT (2/wk, 2 hrs) and conducted 7 play sessions with their children at the jail during visitation (2/wk, 30 min) *Quasi-experimental design*	increase in their empathic interaction with their children as directly observed by independent raters, and reported statistically significant gains in their parental acceptance and a statistically significant decrease in their children's behavior problems.
*Helker, W. P., & Ray, D. (2009). The impact of child-teacher relationship training on teachers' and aides' use of relationship-building skills and the effect on student classroom behavior.	N = 24 Head Start teachers (12 teacher-aide pairs) of at-risk preschoolers identified with behavior problems; teachers assigned to treatment groups based on random drawing and teachers' schedules; children (n = 32) assigned to treatment group based on teachers' group assignment C = 12 (6 pairs) active control E = 12 (6 pairs) CTRT CTRT group received teacher-adapted 10-session CPRT protocol, followed by 8 weeks (3/wk, 15 min) in-class coaching *Quasi-experimental design*	Between-group differences over time revealed that CTRT-trained teachers and aides demonstrated a statistically significant greater use of relationship-building skills in the classroom. Results showed a statistically significant relationship between CTRT-trained teachers' and aides' higher use of relationship-building skills in the classroom and students' decrease in externalizing behaviors as compared to the active control group. Experimental group children demonstrated a statistically significant decrease in externalizing problems from pre to mid to

(continued)

Table 15-1
(Continued)

Authors	Participants/Methods	Findings
		post when compared to the children in the active control group.
Hess, B. A., Post, P., & Flowers, C. (2005). A follow-up study of kinder training for preschool teachers of children deemed at risk. *Follow-up to Post et al. (2004)*	N = 16 teachers of at-risk preschoolers with behavioral concerns; study logistics did not allow for random assignment of teachers or children to groups C = 8 no treatment wait-list E = 8 adapted CPRT *Quasi-experimental design*	At a one-year follow-up, blinded observers rated experimental and control group teachers in their classrooms and during one-on-one play sessions with students. Results revealed that experimental teachers demonstrated a statistically significant higher level of target skills and empathic responses in individual play sessions with students, but not in their classroom interactions, when compared to control teachers.
* Hilpl, K. A. (2002). Facilitating healthy attitudes and behaviors among adolescents using filial therapy in a high school curriculum. *Companion study to Jones, Rhine, & Bratton (2002).*	N = 31 junior and senior high school students enrolled in year-long peer mentoring courses; 1 class randomly drawn to receive CPRT protocol and the other class assigned to traditional PALS curriculum C = 15 Peer Assisted Leadership curriculum E = 16 adapted CPRT curriculum Both groups of mentors received training	Between-group differences on an overall measure of inappropriate parenting attitudes and expectations revealed no statistical difference between the two interventions; however, post hoc analysis revealed a statistically significant correlation between the CPRT group's reduction in inappropriate views on oppressing children's independence and their higher level of empathic responding, compared to the PALS group, found in a

278

	during their class time and conducted approximately 20 play sessions with their identified child (ages 4 to 6) over the course of the school year. Only the CPRT group's weekly 30-minute play sessions were directly supervised. *Experimental design*	companion study by Jones, Rhine, & Bratton (2002).
Jang, M. (2000). Effectiveness of filial therapy for Korean parents.	N = 30 Korean mothers of 3- to 9-year-olds C = 16 no treatment wait-list E = 14 adapted CPRT CPRT group received 8 sessions of CPRT (2/wk, 2 hrs) and conducted 7 play sessions with their children *Quasi-experimental design*	Compared to the control group, CPRT–trained parents demonstrated a statistically significant increase in empathic interactions with their children as directly observed in play sessions. CPRT–trained parents also reported a statistically significant decrease in their children's behavior problems compared to control group.
* Jones, L., Rhine, T., & Bratton, S. C. (2002). High school students as therapeutic agents with young children experiencing school adjustment difficulties: The effectiveness of filial therapy training model.	N = 31 junior and senior high school students enrolled in year-long peer mentoring courses; 1 class randomly drawn to receive CPRT protocol and the other class assigned to traditional PALS curriculum (children randomly drawn to treatment groups) C = 15 PALS curriculum E = 16 adapted CPRT (to fit year-long course structure)	Compared to high school mentors receiving the PALS curriculum, mentors trained in the adapted CPRT protocol demonstrated a statistically significant increase in empathic interactions with children, as directly observed by objective raters. According to parent report, children in the CPRT group demonstrated statistically significant reductions in internalizing and total behavior problems from pre- to

(continued)

Table 15-1
(Continued)

Authors	Participants/Methods	Findings
	Both groups of mentors received training during their class time and conducted approximately 20 play sessions with children (ages 4 to 6) identified as at risk for achieving academic success by teachers. CPRT mentors' weekly 20-min. play sessions were directly supervised by professionals trained in play therapy and CPRT protocol *Experimental design*	post-testing, compared to children in the PALS group. Parents of children in the CPRT group also reported marked improvement in their children's externalized behavior problems; however, between group differences were not statistically significant.
* Kale, A. L., & Landreth, G. L. (1999). Filial therapy with parents of children experiencing learning difficulties.	N = 22 Parents of 5- to 10-year-olds with learning difficulties; random drawing to treatment groups C = 11 no treatment wait-list E = 11 CPRT CPRT group received 10 sessions of CPRT training (1/wk, 2 hrs) and conducted 7 play sessions with their children (1/wk, 30 min) *Experimental design*	Results indicated statistically significant improvement in parental acceptance and reduction in parent-child relationship stress from pre- to post-testing for the CPRT-trained group compared to the no treatment control. While not statistically-significant, parents trained in CPRT reported greater improvement in child behavior problems compared to the control group.
Kellam, T. L. (2004). The effectiveness of modified filial therapy training in comparison to a parent education class	N = 37 parents referred by CPS; random drawing to treatment groups C = 17 parent education class	Results of this study showed no statistically significant between- or within-group differences over time for stress

Citation	Method	Results
on acceptance, stress, and child behavior.	E = 20 modified CPRT protocol Both groups attended 8 weekly sessions for 1.5 hrs/wk *Experimental design*	related to parenting and child behavior problems. CPRT-trained parents reported a greater increase in parental acceptance over the comparison group, although the finding was not statistically significant.
* Kidron, M. (2004). Filial therapy with Israeli parents.	N = 27 Israeli parents of 4- to 11-year-olds; assigned to treatment groups based on parents' schedules C = 13 no treatment wait-list E = 14 CPRT CPRT group received 10 sessions of CPRT training (1/wk, 2 hrs) and conducted 7 play sessions with their children (1/wk, 30 min) *Quasi-experimental design*	Compared to control parents, the CPRT group demonstrated a statistically significant increase pre to post in empathic interactions with their children as rated by observers blind to study, and reported a statistically significant reduction in parent-child relationship stress. Compared to the control group over time, CPRT parents also reported a statistically significant reduction in their children's externalized behavior problems.
* Landreth, G. L., & Lobaugh, A. (1998). Filial therapy with incarcerated fathers: Effects on parental acceptance of child, parental stress, and child adjustment.	N = 32 incarcerated fathers of 4- to 9-year-olds; random drawing to treatment groups C = 16 no treatment wait-list E = 16 CPRT CPRT group received 10 sessions of CPRT training (1/wk, 1.5 hrs) and conducted 8 to 10 play sessions with their children during weekly family visitation at the prison *Experimental design*	Compared to the control group over time, fathers in the CPRT group reported a statistically significant increase in their parental acceptance toward their children, and a statistically significant reduction in parent-child relationship stress. In addition, children whose fathers were in the CPRT group reported a statistically significant increase in their self-esteem from pre- to post-testing.

(*continued*)

Table 15-1
(Continued)

Authors	Participants/Methods	Findings
* Lee, M., & Landreth, G. L. (2003). Filial therapy with immigrant Korean parents in the United States.	N = 32 immigrant Korean parents of 2- to 10-year-olds; random drawing to treatment groups C = 15 no treatment wait-list E = 17 CPRT CPRT group received 10 sessions of CPRT training (1/wk, 2 hrs) and conducted 7 play sessions with their children (1/wk, 30 min) *Experimental design*	Between-group differences over time revealed that parents in the CPRT group 1) demonstrated a statistically significant increase in their empathic interactions with their children as directly observed by independent raters, and 2) reported a statistically significant increase in their parental acceptance toward their children as well as a statistically significant reduction in parent-child relationship stress.
* Morrison, M., & Bratton, S. (in review). An early mental health intervention for Head Start programs: The effectiveness of child-teacher relationship training (CTRT) on children's behavior problems.	N = 24 Head Start teachers (12 teacher-aide pairs) of at-risk preschoolers identified with significant behavior problems; teachers assigned to treatment groups based on random drawing and teachers' schedules; children (n = 52) were assigned to treatment group based on teachers' group assignment C = 12 (6 pairs) active control E = 12 (6 pairs) CTRT CTRT group received teacher-adapted 10-session CPRT protocol, followed by 8 weeks (3/wk, 15 min) in-class coaching *Quasi-experimental design*	According to teacher reports, children whose teachers received CTRT demonstrated statistically significant reductions in externalizing and total behavior problems, compared to the active control group across three points of measure. Treatment effects were determined to be large. CTRT also showed a moderate treatment effect on reducing children's internalizing problem behaviors, as compared to the active control group. Eighty-four percent of the children receiving CTRT moved from clinical or borderline behavior problems to normal levels of functioning.

Post, P., McAllister, M., Sheely, A., Hess, B., & Flowers, C. (2004). Child-centered kinder training for teachers of preschool children deemed at risk.	N = 17 teachers of at-risk preschoolers with behavioral concerns; study logistics did not allow for random assignment of teachers or children to treatment groups C = 8 no treatment E = 9 adapted CPRT CPRT teachers received a total of 23 weeks of intervention: 10 weeks of adapted CPRT group sessions (1/wk, 2 hrs) during which they also conducted 7 weekly 30-minute play sessions with an identified student and received 45 minutes. of individual supervision; the next 13 weeks of group intervention focused on helping teachers to generalize CPRT skills to classroom (1/wk, 2 hrs) *Quasi-experimental design*	According to teacher reports children in the experimental group, compared to the control group over time, demonstrated a statistically significant improvement in adaptive, internalized, and overall behavior. CPRT–trained teachers demonstrated a statistically significant increase in empathic interactions and use of target play therapy skills in one-on-one play sessions with children and in the classroom (assessed through direct observation by raters blinded to study).
Ray, D. E. (2003). The effect of filial therapy on parental acceptance and child adjustment.	N = 50 parents of 3- to 10-year-olds identified with attachment problems C = 25 no treatment wait-list E = 25 CPRT CPRT group followed 10 session outline for CPRT training (1/wk, 2 hrs) and conducted play sessions with their children. *Quasi-experimental design*	Compared to the control group, CPRT parents reported a statistically significant increase pre to post in parental acceptance. While not statistically significant, CPRT–trained parents reported a reduction in parent-child relationship stress as well as their children's behavioral problems, compared to control group parents.

(continued)

Table 15-1
(Continued)

Authors	Participants/Methods	Findings
* Robinson, J., Landreth, G. L., & Packman, J. (2007). Fifth-grade students as emotional helpers with kindergarten children. *Companion study to Baggerly & Landreth, 2001.*	N = 23 fifth-grade mentors to at-risk kindergarteners; mentors selected to treatment groups based on teacher recommendation C = 14 no treatment wait-list E = 15 adapted CPRT CPRT mentors received training (2/wk, 35 minutes) for 5 weeks, followed by 10 weekly 20-minute play sessions with kindergarteners *Quasi-experimental design*	Compared to the control group over time, CPRT-trained 5th grade mentors demonstrated a statistically significant increase in their empathic interactions with kindergarteners during one-on-one play sessions (direct observation by blinded raters).
* Sheely, A., & Bratton, S. (2010). A strengths-based parenting intervention with low-income African American families.	N = 23 low-income African American parents of Head Start children identified with behavioral problems; random drawing to treatment groups C = 10 no treatment wait-list E = 13 CPRT CPRT group received 10 sessions of CPRT training (1/wk, 2 hrs) and conducted 7 play sessions with their children (1/wk, 30 min) *Experimental design*	Findings indicated that when compared to the no treatment control group, the CPRT group demonstrated statistically significant improvements over time in children's overall behavior problems and parent-child relationship stress. Treatment effects were large. Cultural considerations were discussed in light of the findings.

Reference	Description	Results
* Smith, D. M., & Landreth, G. L. (2004). Filial therapy with teachers of deaf and hard of hearing preschool children.	N = 24 teachers of deaf and hard of hearing 2- to 6-year-olds; classrooms assigned to treatment groups based on stratified random drawing to ensure groups were equal regarding children's ages C = 12 no treatment wait-list E = 12 CPRT CPRT teachers received 10 training sessions (1/wk, 2 hrs) and conducted 7 play sessions with identified students (1/wk, 30 min) *Experimental design*	Between-group differences over time revealed that children in the CPRT group made statistically significant improvement in behavior problems and social-emotional functioning. Compared to control teachers, CPRT-trained teachers demonstrated statistically significant gains in their empathic interactions with students (direct observation by blinded raters) and also reported statistically significant increases in acceptance of their students.
* Smith, N., & Landreth, G. L. (2003). Intensive filial therapy with child witnesses of domestic violence: A comparison with individual and sibling group play therapy.	N = 44 4- to 10-year-olds who had witnessed domestic violence C = 11 children in no treatment comparison (from Kot et al., 1998) E1 = 11 children of mothers receiving CPRT E2 = 11 children in individual play therapy (from Kot et al., 1998) E3 = 11 children in sibling group play therapy (from Tyndall-Lind et al., 2001) CPRT group received 12 sessions (1.5 hrs) of CPRT training over 2 to 3 weeks and conducted an average of 7 play sessions (30 min) with their children *Quasi-experimental design*	Compared to no treatment control over time: 1) CPRT-trained parents reported statistically significant decreases in their children's behavior problems, and 2) children in CPRT group reported a statistically significant increase in self-esteem. Additionally, CPRT parents demonstrated a statistically significant increase from pre to post in their empathic interactions with their children (direct observation by blinded raters). Results across treatment groups revealed no statistically significant differences between interventions.

(continued)

Table 15-1
(*Continued*)

Authors	Participants/Methods	Findings
* Tew, K., Landreth, G. L., Joiner, K. D., & Solt, M. D. (2002). Filial therapy with parents of chronically ill children.	N = 23 parents of hospitalized, chronically ill 3- to 10-year-olds; parents assigned to treatment groups based on parents' schedule C = 11 no treatment wait-list E = 12 CPRT CPRT group received 10 sessions of CPRT training (1/wk, 2 hrs) and conducted 7 play sessions with their children (1/wk, 30 min) *Quasi-experimental design*	Compared to control group, CPRT-trained parents reported a statistically significant reduction in parent-child relationship stress and in their children's behavior problems. CPRT parents also reported a statistically significant increase in parental acceptance, compared to control parents over time.
Villarreal, C. E. (2008). School-based child parent relationship therapy (CPRT) with Hispanic parents.	N = 13 Hispanic parents of 4- to 10-year-olds; random drawing to treatment groups C = 7 no treatment wait-list E = 6 CPRT CPRT group received 10 sessions of CPRT training (1/wk, 1.5 hrs) and conducted 7 play sessions with their children (1/wk, 30 min) *Experimental design*	CPRT-trained parents reported a statistically significant decrease in their children's internalizing problems from pre- to post-testing as compared to parents in control group. While not statistically significant, CPRT-trained parents also reported a greater decrease in their children's externalizing problems over the control group.

* Yuen, T. C., Landreth, G. L., & Baggerly, J. (2002). Filial therapy with immigrant Chinese parents in Canada.	N = 35 immigrant Chinese parents of 3- to 10-year-olds; random drawing to treatment groups C = 17 no treatment wait-list E = 18 CPRT CPRT group received 10 sessions of CPRT training (1/wk, 2 hrs) and conducted 7 play sessions with their children (1/wk, 30 min) *Experimental design*	Between-group differences over time revealed that parents in the CPRT group demonstrated a statistically significant increase in empathic interactions with their children as directly observed in play sessions by independent raters. Statistically significant between-group results in favor of CPRT were also found for increased parental acceptance, a reduction in parent-child relationship stress, and reduced child behavior problems.

287

Of the 32 outcome studies summarized in Table 15.1, 23 focused on the impact of training parents as therapeutic agents for their children exhibiting social-emotional or behavioral concern, 5 studies investigated the effectiveness of training teachers as agents of change, and 4 studies focused on the effects of training student mentors in CCPT skills to use with children identified as at risk for school success. CPRT studies have examined its effect with a variety of issues and populations, including sexually abused children, children living in domestic violence shelters, children whose mothers or fathers were incarcerated, and children diagnosed with learning differences, pervasive developmental disorders, chronic illness, and a broad range of internalized and externalized behavior problems. Children experiencing adjustment difficulties to changes at home and school have also been the subject of CPRT studies. Children receiving the CPRT intervention ranged in age from 3 to 10, with an average age of 5½. CPRT has been conducted in a variety of settings, including hospitals, churches, shelters, a Native American reservation, prison, county jail, Head Start programs, public and private schools, and community agencies. The effects of CPRT have also been investigated with diverse populations of parents, including Hispanic, immigrant Latino, African American, Native American, Israeli, immigrant Chinese, Korean, and immigrant Korean. Table 15.1 is presented to provide a concise summary of research results of the 32 controlled-outcome studies conducted on CPRT.

SUMMARY

The large number of controlled studies demonstrating the effectiveness of CPRT provides evidence that training parents in child-centered play therapy principles and skills is a viable intervention for children exhibiting a variety of emotional and behavioral difficulties. These findings do not merely suggest the value of involving parents in their child's therapy. Rather, we believe that the overwhelmingly positive outcomes from these studies are the result of:

- *Fully* involving parents as the therapeutic change agents in their child's treatment
- Parents receiving child-centered play therapy training and close supervision from a specially trained mental health professional
- Providing video-recorded and supervised experiences for parents to practice CPRT skills with their child and receive feedback

- Perhaps most importantly, therapists' training in and adherence to the CPRT protocol

The use of a treatment manual and the treatment integrity established in all but four of the studies speak to the overall rigor of CPRT research. Almost half the studies employed experimental designs regarded as the "gold standard with regards to questions of treatment efficacy" (Nezu & Nezu, 2008, p. vii), with the other half judged quasi-experimental, typically due to an inability to fully randomize participants to treatment groups due to challenges of conducting research in real-world settings. While play therapy research with diverse populations is scarce, this is an area of strength for CPRT research. Eight CPRT studies have researched its effectiveness across diverse cultural groups with positive results. CPRT's focus on the family and the uniqueness of each person seems to make it especially responsive cross-culturally.

The evidence base for CPRT has implications for practitioners and managed care providers who are ethically bound to use interventions known to be most effective and efficient. CPRT is a child therapy model that not only can be delivered effectively in a group format in a relatively short amount of time, but also provides the additional benefit of providing parents with skills that equip them to cope with future problems. The positive findings for both parent and child outcomes in the majority of studies provide further proof of the robustness of this approach. Further, meta-analytic results suggest that play therapy–trained parents can be more effective with their own children than a trained professional can be. While these results are compelling and clearly support the need for play therapists to strongly consider using CPRT with their clientele, we urge readers to use caution in interpreting these results. There are cases when the presenting issue or parent or child characteristics would indicate play therapy treatment directly from a professional rather than CPRT or as an adjunct to CPRT (Landreth & Bratton, 2006) and instances when parents lack the motivation or personal resources to commit to the significant investment required in this approach. Landreth and Bratton provide a more detailed discussion of this topic and maintain that the question is not whether to involve parents, but rather, how and when.

CPRT research has increased in rigor over its relatively short history by investigating clearly defined populations and target behaviors and by the use of randomized controlled trials with larger sample sizes. CPRT's use of a manualized protocol (Bratton et al., 2006) adds to its methodological strength, allowing for treatment replication and assurance of treatment fidelity by researchers. According to standards adopted by the American Psychological Association, CPRT currently meets the criteria for a "promising" or "probably efficacious treatment" (Baggerly & Bratton, 2010; Chambless et al., 1998). A continued focus on strengthening CPRT's research rigor along with replication of well-designed studies by independent researchers are needed to move CPRT toward recognition as an evidence-based or "well-established" treatment for specific childhood disorders (Silverman & Hinshaw, 2008). Current research support for CPRT indicates that if a child and a parent are both suitable candidates, child therapists should consider CPRT as the intervention of choice for their clientele.

REFERENCES

Baggerly, J., & Bratton, S. C. (2010). Building a firm foundation in play therapy research: Response to Phillips (2010). *International Journal of Play Therapy, 19*(1), 26–38.

Baggerly, J., & Landreth, G. L. (2001). Training children to help children: A new dimension in play therapy. *Peer Facilitator Quarterly, 18*(1), 6–14.

Beckloff, D. R. (1998). CPRT with children with spectrum-pervasive development disorders (Doctoral dissertation, University of North Texas, 1997). *Dissertation Abstracts International, B, 58*(11), 6224.

Boll, L. A. (1973). Effects of filial therapy on maternal perceptions of their mentally retarded children's social behavior (Doctoral dissertation, University of Oklahoma, 1972). *Dissertation Abstracts International, A, 33*(12), 6661.

Bratton, S. C., & Landreth, G. L. (1995). Filial therapy with single parents: Effects on parental acceptance, empathy, and stress. *International Journal of Play Therapy, 4*(1), 61–80.

Bratton, S. C., Landreth, G. L., Kellam, T. L. T., & Blackard, S. (2006). *Child parent relationship therapy (CPRT) treatment manual: A 10-session filial therapy model for training parents* (includes CD-ROM). New York: Brunner-Routledge.

Bratton, S. C., Ray, D. C., Rhine, T., & Jones, L. (2005). The efficacy of play therapy with children: A meta-analytic review of treatment outcomes. *Professional Psychology: Research and Practice, 36*(4).

Brown, C. J. (2003). Filial therapy with undergraduate teacher trainees; Child-teacher relationship training (Doctoral dissertation, University of North Texas, Denton, 2000). *Dissertation Abstracts International, A, 63*(09), 3112.

Ceballos, P., & Bratton, S. C. (2010). Empowering Latino families: A culturally responsive, school-based intervention with low-income immigrant Latino parents and their children identified with academic and behavioral concerns. *Psychology in the Schools.*

Chambless, D. L., Baker, M., Baucom, D. H., Beutler, L. E., Calhoun, K. S., et al. (1998). Update on empirically validated therapies, II. *Clinical Psychologist* 51(1), 3–16.
Chau, I., & Landreth, G. L. (1997). Filial therapy with Chinese parents: Effects on parental empathic interactions, parental acceptance of child and parental stress. *International Journal of Play Therapy, 6*(2), 75–92.
Cohen, J. (1988). *Statistical power analysis for the behavioral sciences* (2nd ed.). Hillside, NJ: Erlbaum.
Costas, M. B., & Landreth, G. L. (1999). Filial therapy with nonoffending parents of children who have been sexually abused. *International Journal of Play Therapy, 8*(1), 43–66.
Crane, J. M., & Brown, C. J. (2003). Effectiveness of teaching play therapy attitudes and skills to undergraduate human service majors. *International Journal for Play Therapy, 12*(2), 49–65.
Dematatis, C. (1982). A comparison of the traditional filal therapy program to an integrated Filial-IPR program (Doctoral dissertation, Michigan State University, 1981). *Dissertation Abstracts International, B, 42*(10) 4187.
Eardley, D. A. (1978). *An initial investigation of a didactic version of filial therapy dealing with self-concept increase and problematic behavior decrease.* Unpublished doctoral dissertation, Pennsylvania State University, University Park.
Elling, E. R. P. (2003). A comparison of skill level of parents trained in the Landreth Filial Therapy Model and graduate students trained in play therapy (Doctoral dissertation, University of North Texas, 2003). *Dissertation Abstracts International, 64*(06), 1983.
Ferrell, L. G. (2004). A comparison of an intensive 4-week format of the Landreth 10-week filial therapy training model with the traditional Landreth 10-week model of filial therapy (Doctoral dissertation, University of North Texas, Denton, 2003). *Dissertation Abstract International, A, 64*(12), 4369.
Glover, G., & Landreth, G. L. (2000). Filial therapy with Native Americans on the Flathead reservation. *International Journal of Play Therapy, 9*(2), 57–80.
Guerney, B. G., Jr. (1964). Filial therapy: Description and rationale. *Journal of Consulting Psychology, 28*(4), 303–310.
Guerney, B. G., Jr., & Stover, L. (1971). *Filial therapy: Final report on MH 18264-01.* Unpublished manuscript, Pennsylvania State University, University Park.
Guerney, L. (1975). *Follow-up study on filial therapy.* Paper presented at the annual convention of the Eastern Psychological Association, New York.
Guerney, L. (2001). Child-centered play therapy. *International Journal of Play Therapy, 10*(2), 13–31.
Harris, Z. L., & Landreth, G. L. (1997). Filial therapy with incarcerated mothers: A five-week model. *International Journal of Play Therapy, 6*(2), 53–73.
Helker, W. P., & Ray, D. C. (2009). Impact of child-teacher relationship training on teachers' and aides' use of relationship-building skills and the effects on student classroom behavior. *International Journal of Play Therapy, 18*(2), 70–83.

Hess, B. A., Post, P., & Flowers, C. (2005). A follow-up study of kinder training for preschool teachers of children deemed at risk. *International Journal of Play Therapy, 14*, 103–115.

Hilpl, K. A. (2002). Facilitating healthy attitudes and behaviors among adolescents using filial therapy in a high school curriculum (Doctoral dissertation, University of North Texas, Denton, 2001). *Dissertation Abstracts International, 63*(02), 550A.

Jang, M. (2000). Effectiveness of filial therapy for Korean parents. *International Journal of Play Therapy, 9*(2), 39–56.

Jones, L., Rhine, T., & Bratton, S. C., (2002). High school students as therapeutic agents with young children experiencing school adjustment difficulties: The effectiveness of filial therapy training model. *International Journal for Play Therapy, 11*(2), 43–62.

Kale, A. L., & Landreth, G. L. (1999). Filial therapy with parents of children experiencing learning difficulties. *International Journal of Play Therapy, 8*(2), 35–56.

Kellam, T. L. T. (2004). The effectiveness of modified filial therapy training in comparison to a parent education class on acceptance, stress, and child behavior (Doctoral dissertation, Texas Woman's University, 2004). *Dissertation Abstracts International, 64*(08), 4043B.

Kezur, B. A. (1981). Mother-child communication patterns based on therapeutic principles (Doctoral dissertation, Humanistic Psychology Institute, 1980). *Dissertation Abstracts International, B, 41*(12), 4671.

Kidron, M. (2004). Filial therapy with Israeli parents (Doctoral dissertation, University of North Texas, Denton, 2003). *Dissertation Abstracts International, A, 64*(12).

Landreth, G. L. (2002). *Play therapy: The art of the relationship* (2nd ed.). New York: Brunner-Routledge.

Landreth, G. L., & Bratton, S. C. (2006). *Child parent relationship therapy (CPRT): A 10-session filial therapy model.* New York: Brunner-Routledge.

Landreth, G. L., & Lobaugh, A. (1998). Filial therapy with incarcerated fathers: Effects on parental acceptance of child, parental stress, and child adjustment. *Journal of Counseling & Development, 76*, 157–165.

LeBlanc, M., & Ritchie, M. (2001). A meta-analysis of play therapy outcomes. *Counseling Psychology Quarterly, 14*(2), 149–163.

Lee, M., & Landreth, G. L. (2003). Filial therapy with immigrant Korean parents in the United States. *International Journal of Play Therapy, 12*(2), 67–85.

Morrison, M., & Bratton, S. C. (in review). *An early mental health intervention for disadvantaged preschool children with behavior problems: The effectiveness of training Head Start teachers in child-teacher relationship training (CTRT).* Manuscript submitted for publications.

Nezu, A. M., & Nezu, C. M. (2008). *Evidence-based outcome research.* New York: Oxford Press.

Oxman, L. (1972). The effectiveness of filial therapy: A controlled study (Doctoral dissertation, Rutgers, The State University of New Jersey, 1972). *Dissertation Abstracts International, B, 32*(11), 6656.

Payton, I. (1981). Filial therapy as a potential primary preventative process with children between the ages of four and ten (Doctoral dissertation, University of Northern Colorado, 1980). *Dissertation Abstracts International, B, 41*(07), 2942.

Post, P., McAllister, M., Sheely, A., Hess, B., & Flowers, C. (2004). Child-centered kinder training for teachers of pre-school children deemed at risk. *International Journal of Play Therapy, 13*(2), 53–74.

Ray, D. E. (2003). *The effect of filial therapy on parental acceptance and child adjustment.* Unpublished master's thesis, Emporia State University, Emporia, KS.

Robinson, J., Landreth, G. L., & Packman, J. (2007). Fifth-grade students as emotional helpers with kindergartners: Using play therapy procedures and skills. *International Journal of Play Therapy, 16*(1), 20–35.

Sensue, M. E. (1981). Filial therapy follow-up study: Effects on parental acceptance and child adjustment (Doctoral dissertation, Pennsylvania State University, 1981). *Dissertation Abstracts International, A, 42*(01) 148.

Sheely, A., & Bratton, S. C. (2010). A strengths-based parenting intervention with low-income African American families. *Professional School Counseling, 13*(3), 175–183.

Silverman, W. K., & Hinshaw, S. P. (2008). The second special issue on evidence-based psychosocial treatments for children and adolescents: A 10-year update. *Journal of Clinical Child & Adolescent Psychology, 37*(1), 1–7.

Smith, D. M., & Landreth, G. L. (2004). Filial therapy with teachers of deaf and hard of hearing preschool children. *International Journal of Play Therapy, 13*(1), 13–33.

Smith, N., & Landreth, G. L. (2003). Filial therapy with child witnesses of domestic violence: A comparison with individual and sibling group play therapy. *International Journal for Play Therapy, 12*(1), 67–88.

Stover, L., & Guerney, B. G., Jr. (1967). The efficacy of training procedures for mothers in filial therapy. *Psychotherapy: Theory, Research, and Practice, 4*(3), 110–115.

Sywulak, A. (1978). The effect of filial therapy on parental acceptance and child adjustment (Doctoral dissertation, Pennsylvania State University, 1977). *Dissertation Abstracts International, B, 38*(12), 6180.

Tew, K., Landreth, G. L., Joiner, K. D., & Solt, M. D. (2002). Filial therapy with parents of chronically ill children. *International Journal of Play Therapy, 11*(1), 79–100.

Wall, L. (1979). Parents as play therapists: A comparison of three interventions into children's play (Doctoral dissertation, University of Northern Colorado, 1979). *Dissertation Abstracts International, B, 39*(11), 5597.

Villarreal, C. E. (2008). School-based child parent relationship therapy (CPRT) with Hispanic parents (Doctoral dissertation, Regent University, 2008). *Dissertation Abstracts International, A, 69*(2).

Yuen, T., Landreth, G. L., & Baggerly, J., (2002). Filial therapy with immigrant Chinese families. *International Journal of Play Therapy, 11*(2), 63–90.

CHAPTER 16

Filial Therapy with Parents of Chronically Ill Children*

KRISTI TEW

M Y INTEREST IN working with chronically ill children and selecting this research topic for my dissertation were completed before having children. I did not focus on this topic for any particular reason except that I have always had compassion and sensitivity for families that had ill children. After being a researcher and gaining academic knowledge regarding chronically ill children, I subsequently learned much more about this subject through the lives of two of my five daughters. In 1999, my third daughter, Caroline, was diagnosed with a brain disease with seizures, and she lived for only two and a half years. Then in 2004 we were blessed with twin girls and one of the twins was also affected with the same condition until she died in 2008. While my two daughters' medical conditions ended in a terminal way, our family experienced the difficulties and battles that many families typically face with a chronically ill child. My husband and I and our three other daughters survived six years while our precious children battled chronic illnesses before we experienced the devastating losses. I feel very fortunate and blessed that I have the research knowledge regarding chronically ill children and families and have the skills of filial therapy to have helped my own children. Our family has remained intact and psychologically healthy as we stay connected to

*Author's Note: Sections of this chapter were reprinted with the express permission of the *International Journal of Play Therapy* from Tew, K., Landreth, G. L., Joiner, K., & Solt, M. (2002). Filial therapy with parents of chronically ill children. *International Journal of Play Therapy*, 11(1), 79–100.

our community. Our daughters are sweet, compassionate, healthy, vibrant, and well-adjusted young ladies. Their lives are a testament that children can experience such deep difficulties and yet emerge from the problems without being negatively affected. Instead of becoming bitter, our family has become better through our difficulties and tragedies that we have faced. Because of our experience, I am keenly aware of the issues faced by families with a chronically ill child and am passionate in discovering supportive ways to assist these families.

The study I describe in this chapter investigated the effects of filial therapy with chronically ill children. In the study, I was hoping to alleviate some parenting stress, increase parental acceptance, and help reduce negative behaviors as well as anxiety and depression common to many chronically ill children, and also help diminish negative behaviors of the siblings of the chronically ill child.

CHILDHOOD CHRONIC ILLNESSES

Medical science has dramatically decreased infant mortality and increased the ability to sustain life, which has resulted in an increase in the prevalence of chronic illnesses in many children (Van der Lee, Mokkink, Grootenhuis, Heymans, & Offringa, 2007). Many children who would have been considered terminal a few years ago are now learning to live with illnesses of a chronic nature. With the dramatic rise of childhood chronic illnesses, these children comprise a large and growing population that are experiencing a childhood with various issues and complex struggles along with the normal difficulties of development. Van der Lee et al. (2007) estimated that as much as 15 percent of the pediatric population had a chronic illness back in the 1990s. Yet, current estimates are 22 percent to 44 percent (depending on the parameters set as the definition of a chronic illness) of the childhood population has a chronic illness (Van der Lee et al., 2007).

There are many chronic illnesses, but there seems to be some adjustment issues common to all chronic illnesses. Even though the medical disorders vary in their physical consequences, they seem to produce the same type of psychological concerns and can have similar maladaptive behaviors (Cohen, 1999). This suggests that the general challenges faced by children with a chronic illness are quite similar and can be studied and treated as a group (Van der Lee et al., 2007). While there is a greater risk for behavioral and social problems compared to healthy peers, only a small proportion of chronically ill children would be considered clinically maladjusted (Barlow & Ellard, 2006).

Chronically ill children are increasingly being diagnosed and treated medically, but far less research has been conducted to help the families deal with the sociopsychological issues surrounding the diagnosis and treatment of a chronic illness (Cohen, 1999). These children with a chronic illness, as well as their siblings, appear to be at greater risk for developing some psychosocial problems (Barlow & Ellard, 2006; Sayger, Bowersox, & Steinberg, 1996). The maladjustment can be represented in a wide variety of ways, including lowered self-esteem, dependency, hyperactivity, depression, and concern with body image (Barlow & Ellard, 2006).

EFFECTS OF A CHRONIC ILLNESS ON A CHILD

For a child with a chronic illness, the effects can include pain, discomfort, loss of energy, physical restrictions, changes in outward appearance, and mood variations, depending on the medical condition (Nabors & Lehmkuhl, 2004). In addition to the illness, these children must also endure the management of their disease, in which the treatments are often painful, invasive, and frightening and can have unpleasant side effects. Fears, persistent nightmares, changes in appetite, sleep disturbances, and regressive behaviors are common (Nabors & Lehmkuhl, 2004). Some aspects of the normal developmental process may also be more difficult because emotional needs such as independence, autonomy, self-respect, security, acceptance as an individual, and achievement may not be met because of the disruption the illness causes the child and the family (Cohen, 1999; Nabors & Lehmkuhl, 2004).

EFFECTS ON SIBLINGS

Chronic illness is a psychosocial stressor not only for ill children, but also for their siblings. Frequently, the siblings of a sick child feel anxiety, jealousy, embarrassment, neglect, resentment, and guilt (Barlow & Ellard, 2006; Meyer & Vadasy, 2008). Siblings may feel a loss of attention with overburdened parents, yet feel guilty for being jealous of the parental attention given to their sick sibling (Barlow & Ellard, 2006; Meyer & Vadasy, 2008). They may also fear contracting the illness and have anger toward the disease. Feeling guilty for being healthy is also common. With all of these various emotions, it is not surprising that maladjustment, underachievement, and socialization problems are common among siblings of chronically ill children (Meyer & Vadasy, 2008).

When my first daughter was diagnosed with seizures caused from a brain disease, the two older sisters (ages three and four) were worried that something was wrong with them or would become wrong with them and played out dying for a brief period of time with their dolls. If they caught a cold, they would seriously ask, "Am I going to die?" Later, when Alexandria was diagnosed, her twin sister, Katherine, was very jealous of the time that I spent with Alexandria and the extra attention she received. Since Katherine was too young to try to cover up her jealousy, it was very blatant in her words and actions. Yet, we resolved the siblings' concerns, fears, jealousy, and anger through talking and playing.

EFFECTS ON FAMILIES

There is a chronic level of strain inherent in the care of a child with a chronic illness. Families progress through several stages: initial shock, denial, sadness, anger, equilibrium, and reorganization (Sayger et al., 1996). A qualitative study by Martin, Brady, and Kotarba (1992) obtained the perspectives of families with a chronically ill child and found the illness affected the families' daily lives to a tremendous extent. Areas affected include financial, medical, social, career, and family relationships. The burden of a chronic illness can tax the financial resources of families. For most families, the expense of caring for their chronically ill child can prove to be an additional source of pressure and anxiety. Doctor and hospital bills, medications, and needed equipment may necessitate having to seek another source of income. Although additional income may be needed, the demands of caring for a chronically ill child often constrain employment of one of the parents because of the caregiving that must be done.

There are some family characteristics that are good indicators to predict better coping strategies for a chronically ill child and his or her family: good problem-solving abilities, an expressive family environment, lower parental depression, religious beliefs, strong marital relationship, satisfaction with medical care, and lower family conflicts (Eiser, 1990). These variables have been found to produce greater self-esteem and more adaptive means of acceptance of an illness and treatment.

PARENTS OF CHRONICALLY ILL CHILDREN

The parents are also affected, as many of them experience intense stress, marital difficulties, and other problems that can have detrimental effects on the parent-child relationship (Barlow & Ellard, 2006; Cohen, 1999). Parents of chronically ill children are faced with many decisions and concerns. Two basic issues for parents are learning to deal with their child's health care and coping with the inherent emotional stress (Cohen, 1999). It is clear that the existence of an ill child places extra responsibilities and stress on parents. Parents of chronically ill children spend significantly more time in caregiving activities, and they also report less intimacy, more parenting stress, less social support, more maternal depression, and increased strain on the role of parenting because of the additional duties (Cappelli, 1990). There is also evidence that mothers experience more stress than do fathers with regard to chronically ill children, which could be related to being the primary caregiver. Anxiety and depression are well documented among mothers of chronically ill children (Cohen, 1999).

Since it is clear that parents of chronically ill children significantly affect these children's ability to cope with their own illnesses, it seems best to include parents in the training and treatment with their children. One model that includes parents in the psychological treatment of their children is filial therapy (Landreth & Bratton, 2006). The filial therapist trains parents to use child-centered play therapy skills in special play sessions with their children and educates them on parenting skills, which facilitate more effective communication between parents and their children (Landreth & Bratton, 2006).

PLAY AND THE CHRONICALLY ILL CHILD

For children, play is universal and necessary and can be therapeutic (Landreth, 2002). As with all children, the use of play can be an important tool in the life of a chronically ill child. Play helps children with chronic illness express their fears, questions, misunderstandings, and frustrations (May, 1999). Play also helps children develop coping mechanisms for challenges such as doctor visits, treatments, physical limitations, changes in outward appearance, and possible painful or scary procedures (Boyd-Webb, 2009).

RESEARCH QUESTIONS

Since filial therapy combines the healing power of play with parents' therapeutic interaction with their own children (Landreth & Bratton, 2006), it appeared to be a viable intervention for parents of chronically ill children. However, research was needed to determine the impact on parents and their chronically ill children. Therefore, I designed my research study to determine the effectiveness of filial therapy in increasing parental acceptance of chronically ill children, reducing the stress level of parents with chronically ill children, and decreasing the emotional and behavioral problems exhibited by chronically ill children.

METHOD

PARTICIPANTS

Approval was obtained to conduct this research from the institutional review board at a children's medical center in a large urban area. Participants were required to meet the following criteria to be included in this study:

- The parent must have a chronically ill child, such as, but not limited to, arthritis, cerebral palsy, chronic renal failure, cleft lip or palate, congenital heart disease, cystic fibrosis, diabetes mellitus, hemophilia, muscular dystrophy, severe asthma, sickle cell disease, spina bifida, or seizure disorders.
- The chronically ill child must be between the ages of 3 and 10.
- The parent must be able to read, speak, and write in the English language.

Parents involved in the experimental group were also required to attend 10 filial therapy training, which took place at the children's medical center, and agree to participate in weekly 30-minute home play sessions with their chronically ill child and any siblings between the ages of 3 and 10 years old.

Child life specialists at the children's medical center helped obtain the 28 parents who volunteered for this study. Initially, 13 parents were in the treatment group and 15 parents in the control group. Assignment to the treatment or control group was based on which parents were able and willing to attend all 10 sessions. Twelve of the 13 parents in the treatment group completed the course; 11 of the parents in the control group completed both the pre- and post-battery of test instruments. This study did not exclude any person on the basis of race, religion, age, or gender. Each of the treatment and control groups had three divorced individuals, with all other persons being married. There were nine females and two males in the control group, which consisted of nine Caucasians and two Hispanics. The treatment group included nine females and three males; the racial make-up of this group was one Hispanic and eleven Caucasians. Volunteers for this study signed an informed consent form.

ASSESSMENT INSTRUMENTS

The pre- and post-assessment instruments used for this study and completed by the parents were the Child Behavior Checklist (CBCL-PR) (Achenbach & Edelbrock, 1983); the Parenting Stress Index (PSI) (Abidin, 1983); and the Porter Parental Acceptance Scale (PPAS) (Porter, 1954). The PSI was used because parental stress was found to be prevalent in literature regarding the parents of chronically ill children. In addition, one of the subscales relates to the parents' ability to accept their child, which is part of the filial training and is found to be vital in the literature review for the positive development of the chronically ill child. The PPAS was included in this study for the value it can add to assess the changes in the parent-child relationship and because of the similarity between the dimensions of this instrument and the tenets of filial therapy. The CBCL-PR was used in the study to assess the parents' reports of the competencies and problems of the children in the study. Specifically examined in this study were the total behavior problem scale and the subscale of anxiety and depression, because it is a main concern in the literature regarding chronically ill children. All instruments have solid reliability and validity as described in other chapters of this book. Parents in the treatment and control groups completed these assessment instruments at the beginning and the end of the same 10-week training period.

FILIAL THERAPY TREATMENT

The 13 parents in the experimental group were divided into three filial therapy training groups to facilitate the small-group arrangement as recommended by Landreth (2002). The parents were assigned to their training groups according to their work schedules. One group of seven parents and one group of three parents was led by a doctoral candidate, who was a licensed professional counselor. The other group of three parents was co-led by two master's degree–level child life specialists. The three leaders had completed an introduction to play therapy course, a filial therapy course, and a supervised play therapy practicum. The three leaders met weekly for consultation purposes. Each group met weekly for two-hour training sessions for 10 consecutive weeks in a conference room at the children's medical center.

Each group followed the Landreth (2002) 10-week filial therapy training model, which uses both didactic and dynamic components to teach basic child-centered play therapy skills. The training is designed to enhance and strengthen the parent-child relationship by helping parents learn how to create an accepting environment in which their children feel safe enough to express and explore thoughts and feelings. In the training sessions, the facilitators focused on increasing the parents' sensitivity to their children, acceptance of thoughts and feelings, understanding of their child's emotional needs, reflective listening, empathic responding, identification of feelings, and therapeutic limit setting. The basic principles of child-centered play therapy were discussed, modeled through role-playing demonstrations, shown on videotapes, and practiced by the parents through role-playing within the training sessions. The parents were required to practice these skills with their child of focus in weekly 30-minute special play sessions in their home and to share their experiences with the training group.

Special toy kits recommended by Landreth (2002) were provided for each parent. Each parent also videotaped one of their play sessions for reviewing purposes by the training group. This provided an opportunity for the parent to receive feedback, support, and encouragement. This also provided parents with an opportunity to observe other parents' special play times, which facilitated additional learning vicariously. Child care was provided at the facility.

RESULTS

For purposes of statistical analysis, data from the three filial therapy training groups were pooled to form the experimental group. An analysis of covariance (ANCOVA) was computed to test the significance of the difference between the experimental group and the control group on the adjusted post-test means for each hypothesis. In each case, the post-test specified in each hypothesis was used as the dependent variable and the pre-test as the covariant. ANCOVA was used to adjust the group means on the post-test on the basis of the pre-test, thus statistically equating the control and experimental groups. Significance of difference between means was tested at the .05 level.

Pre-test and post-test means and standard deviations for each instrument are as follows: Parents in the filial therapy experimental group scored significantly higher than parents in the control group on the PPAS total score, $F(1, 22) = 8.30$, $p = .009$; respect for the child's feelings and right to express them subscale, $F(1, 22) = 8.50$, $p = .009$; and recognition for the child's need for autonomy and independence subscale, $F(1, 22) = 14.05$, $p = .001$. Filial therapy parents' scores on the appreciation of the child's unique makeup subscale, $F(1, 22) = .18$, $p = .680$, and unconditional love subscale, $F(1, 22) = 1.28$, $p = .272$ of the PPAS were not significantly higher than the control group parents' scores. Parents in the filial therapy experimental group scored significantly lower than parents in the control group on the PSI total score, $F(1, 22) = 6.64$, $p = .018$, and child domain subscale, $F(1, 22) = 10.15$, $p = .005$. Their score on the parent domain subscale of the PSI was not significantly lower than the control group parents' score, $F(1, 22) = 3.18$, $p = .090$. Children in the filial therapy experimental group scored significantly lower than children in the control group on the CBCL total score, $F(1, 22) = 12.5$, $p = .002$, and the anxiety and depression subscale, $F(1, 22) = 6.75$, $p = .017$.

DISCUSSION

The results of this study combined with the parents' report and my observations support filial therapy training as an effective intervention with chronically ill children and their families. The parents reported an increase of accepting attitudes toward their children, a decrease in stress related to parenting, and a reduction in their children's behavior problems as well as their anxiety and depression. Each area is discussed next.

PARENTAL ACCEPTANCE

The PPAS measured four areas, including respect for the child's right and need to express feelings, value of the unique makeup of the child and fostering that uniqueness within the limits of healthy personal and social adjustment, recognition of the child's need to differentiate and separate from parents and become an autonomous individual, and loving the child unconditionally (Porter, 1954). After the completion of filial therapy training, parents in the experimental group scored significantly higher than parents in the control group on perceived acceptance of their children as measured by the PPAS and on subscales of their children's feelings and their children's rights to express those feelings and on recognition of their children's needs for autonomy and independence. These are significant dimensions for chronically ill children who have experienced being in hospital environments that typically exercise considerable control over children and where many experiences provoke strong feelings of anger, bewilderment, frustration, and fright. Positive growth by parents in the filial therapy group in accepting their children's feelings may be attributed to the fact that this is a specific area of emphasis in the training. An additional factor contributing to growth in this dimension may be the notion that children experienced the freedom to express their feelings in the special play times, and parents experienced the emotional impact of understanding and accepting their children's feelings. In the special play times, children could construct their experiences to be the way they wanted them to be and in that process experience being in control. The significantly higher scores obtained by parents in the filial therapy training group on recognition for the child's need for autonomy and independence provides evidence that parents who received training gained awareness and respect for their child's individuality and the benefits of their children developing more self-control.

Positive gains, although not statistically significant, were reported by parents in the filial training group in appreciation for their child's unique makeup and in unconditional love for their children. These parents seemed to develop insight into the individual uniqueness of their children and a deeper appreciation for that uniqueness. The results on the PPAS suggest filial therapy training is effective in helping parents become more accepting of chronically ill children. Although the parents of chronically ill children may not have scored significantly higher in all areas of the PPAS, the results support earlier studies of filial therapy that determined filial therapy to be effective with parents in increasing their acceptance of their children (Bratton & Landreth, 1995; Chau & Landreth, 1997; Dematatis, 1981; Glass, 1987; Glazer-Waldman, Zimmerman, Landreth, & Norton, 1992; Guerney & Gavigan, 1981; Harris & Landreth, 1997; Landreth & Lobaugh, 1998).

PARENTAL STRESS

After completion of the filial therapy training, parents in the experimental group scored significantly lower than parents in the control group did on the overall level of stress related to parenting as measured by the total score on the PSI. The mean level of parental stress of parents in the control group remained essentially unchanged over the period of 10 weeks. Parents in the filial therapy group scored significantly lower than parents in the control group on the level of stress related to their children's behavior. At the end of 10 weeks, parents in the filial therapy group appeared to be more accepting of their children and were feeling less stress about their children.

There was not a significant decrease in the filial therapy group parents' level of stress related to their perceptions of themselves as parents on the parent domain subscale of the PSI, perhaps because the questions on the parent domain subscale of the PSI may need to be revised and normed specifically for parents of chronically ill children. Parents of chronically ill children may respond differently from parents without an ill child to items such as "I often feel that my child's needs control my life," "When my child came home from the hospital, I had doubtful feelings about my ability to handle being a parent," or "I feel capable and on top of things when I am caring for my child." A typical parent might read one idea of caring into these questions, while a parent of a chronically ill child might have a different view of what is included in the term *caring* for her child. Another possibility for the lack of significant change in the Parent domain might be explained by the idea that several questions in the PSI deal with the relationship with the spouse, such as "Since having my child, my spouse or significant other has not given me as much help and support as I expected." All of the parents involved in the study would be considered the primary caregivers to their sick children; most of the parents expressed some level of frustration that their spouses did not take a more prominent role in the care of their sick children. Tasks and certain dynamics of the parental relationship may not be changed with filial therapy training, but some of the overall parental stress certainly was decreased with the training.

The results of the PSI suggest that filial therapy training is effective in decreasing overall parental stress and stress related to certain characteristics demonstrated in the child. The findings in the present study are similar to those of other studies on the effectiveness of filial therapy in reducing parental stress (Bratton & Landreth, 1995; Chau & Landreth, 1997; Guerney & Gavigan, 1981; Harris & Landreth, 1997; Lebovitz, 1983; Landreth & Lobaugh, 1998).

Problematic Behaviors of Chronically Ill Children

Children in the experimental group scored significantly lower on the Child Behavior Checklist (CBCL) after the filial therapy training versus children in the control group. The total mean scores for the children in the experimental group dropped an average of 13 points on the post-test following the filial training, while the children in the control group reported an average gain of 1 point on the post-test. Parents reported fewer problematic behaviors in their children following the training as well as less anxious or depressed behaviors. The anxiety and depression subscales are linked together because these feelings are closely related in many children. Overly anxious children have a tendency to continuously seek approval and require excessive reassurance because their self-esteem is often low. The depressed symptoms that are rated on the Child Behavior Checklist (CBCL) on this subscale are low energy, low self-esteem, poor concentration, poor appetite, and irritability. Children who are anxious or depressed have a tendency to do poorly in school and lack decision-making skills. Parents in the experimental group described their role as a parent as being more manageable and more fun because of the 30-minute play sessions. These sessions allowed the parents to provide an opportunity for their children to be in control and to make their own decisions. As the parents began to trust their children, their children gained trust in themselves. The findings in the present study are similar to those of other studies on the effectiveness of filial therapy in reducing children's behavior problems (Bratton & Landreth, 1995; Chau & Landreth, 1997; Guerney, 1991; Guerney & Stover, 1971; Harris & Landreth, 1997; Landreth & Lobaugh, 1998; Sywulak, 1977).

CONCLUSIONS

The significant results of this study support the Landreth (2002) 10-week filial therapy training model as an effective intervention for parents of chronically ill children. The filial therapy trainers reported that the parents learned the basic skills taught during the 10-week course and that they were able to demonstrate these skills on an effective level. The parents and children in the filial therapy training found value in the experience as the parents reported a decrease in stress related to parenting, an increase of accepting attitudes toward their children, and a reduction in their children's behavior problems, anxiety, and depression. The results of this study suggest that the parents of chronically ill children were able to adopt a more therapeutic role with their children during the special play times. Follow-up studies are needed to determine the long-term effects of these behavioral changes. Additional research is needed to clarify the generalized effect of filial therapy training on family relationships of families with chronically ill children.

The significant results of this study provide several implications for parent training programs for families with hospitalized or sick children:

- The importance of the small support group format allowing for interaction between parents with similar experiences
- The use of both didactic and dynamic training
- The benefit of using professionals trained in play therapy skills to provide emotional support and to model the skills taught in the sessions
- The advantage of having practice play sessions at home based on the learning taking place in the group sessions
- The therapeutic value of play sessions based on child-centered play therapy procedures

REFERENCES

Abidin, R. R. (1983). *Parenting stress index*. Charlottesville, VA: Pediatric Psychology Press.

Achenbach, T. M., & Edelbrock, C. S. (1983). *Manual for the Child Behavior Checklist and Revised Behavior Profile*. Burlington: University of Vermont.

Barlow, J. H., & Ellard, D. R. (2006). The psychosocial well-being of children with chronic disease, their parents and siblings: An overview of the research evidence base. *Child Care, Health and Development, 32*(1), 19–31.

Boyd-Webb, N. (2009). Play and expressive therapies with medically challenged children and adolescents. In N. Boyd-Webb (Ed.), *Helping youth and families cope with acute and chronic health conditions: A collaborative strengths-based guide to practice*. Hoboken, NJ: John Wiley & Sons.

Bratton, S. C., & Landreth, G. L. (1995). Filial therapy with single parents: Effects on parental acceptance, empathy and stress. *International Journal of Play Therapy, 41*(1), 61–80.

Cappelli, M. (1990). Marital interaction of couples with children with spina bifida: A case-control study. *Dissertation Abstracts International*. Carleton University, Canada.

Chau, I., & Landreth, G. L. (1997). Filial therapy with Chinese parents: Effects on parental empathic reactions, parental acceptance and parental stress. *International Journal of Play Therapy, 6*(2), 75–92.

Cohen, M. S. (1999). Families coping with childhood chronic illness: A research review. *Families, Systems & Health, 17*(2), 149–164.

Dematatis, C. (1981). A comparison of the traditional filial therapy program to an integrated filial-IPR program. (Doctoral dissertation, Michigan State University, 1980). *Dissertation Abstracts International, 42* 10B.

Eiser, C. (1990). *Chronic childhood disease: an introduction to psychological theory and research.* Cambridge, England: Cambridge University Press.

Glass, N. (1987). Parents as therapeutic agents: A study of the effect of filial therapy. (Doctoral dissertation, University of North Texas, 1986). *Dissertation Abstracts International, 47*(07), A2457.

Glazer-Waldman, H., Zimmerman, J., Landreth, G. L., & Norton, D. (1992). Filial therapy: An intervention for parents of children with chronic illness. *International Journal of Play Therapy, 2*(1), 31–42.

Guerney, B., & Stover, L. (1971). *Filial therapy: Final report on MH 18354-01,* Unpublished manuscript: The Pennsylvania State University, University Park.

Guerney, L., & Gavigan, M. (1981). Parental acceptance and foster parents. *Journal of Clinical Child Psychology, 10*(1), 27–32.

Guerney, L. F. (1991). Parents as partners in treating behavior problems in early childhood settings. *Topics in Early Childhood Special Education, 11*(2), 74–90.

Harris, Z., & Landreth, G. L. (1997). Filial therapy with incarcerated mothers: A five-week model. *International Journal of Play Therapy, 6*(2), 53–73.

Landreth, G. L. (2002). *Play therapy: The art of the relationship.* New York: Brunner-Routledge.

Landreth, G. L., & Bratton, S. C. (2006). *Child parent relationship therapy (CPRT): A 10-session filial therapy model.* New York: Taylor & Francis Group.

Landreth, G. L., & Lobaugh, A. (1998). Filial therapy with incarcerated fathers: Effects of parental acceptance, parental stress, and child adjustment. *Journal of Counseling and Development, 76*(2), 157–165.

Lebovitz, C. (1983). Filial therapy: Outcome and process (Doctoral dissertation, Texas Tech University, 1982). *Dissertation Abstracts International, 43*(12), B4152.

Martin, S. S., Brady, M. P., & Kotarba, J. A. (1992). Families with chronically ill young children: The unsinkable family. *Remedial and Special Education, 13*(2), 6–15.

May, L. (1999). I've got a tummy-ache in my head: Communicating with sick children. *Pediatric Nursing, 11*(2), 21–23.

Meyer, D., & Vadasy, P. (2008). *Sibshops: Workshops for siblings of children with special needs* (rev. ed.). Baltimore, MD: Brookes Publishing.

Nabors, L. A., & Lehmkuhl, H. D. (2004). Children with chronic medical conditions: Recommendations for school mental health clinicians. *Journal of Developmental and Physical Disabilities, 16*(1), 1–15.

Porter, B. R. (1954). Measurement of parental acceptance of children. *Journal of Home Economics, 46*(3), 176–182.

Sayger, T. V., Bowersox, M. P., & Steinberg, E. B. (1996). Family therapy and the treatment of chronic illness in a multidisciplinary world. *The Family Journal: Counseling and Therapy for Couples and Families*, 4(1), 12–21.

Sywulak, A. (1977). *The effect of filial therapy on parental acceptance and child adjustment.* Unpublished doctoral dissertation, The Pennsylvania State University, University Park.

Van der Lee, J. H., Mokkink, L. B., Grootenhuis, M. A., Heymans, H. S., & Offringa, M. (2007). Definitions and measurement of chronic health conditions in childhood: A systematic review. *JAMA: The Journal of the American Medical Association*, 297(24), 2741–2751.

CHAPTER 17

Filial Therapy with Native Americans on the Flathead Reservation*

GERI GLOVER

INTRODUCTION

There are an estimated 4.1 million people who consider themselves to be American Indian and Alaska Native (AI/AN) alone or in combination with one or more other races (U.S. Census, 2000). The Native American population continues to increase, growing in the last decade from less than 1 percent of the total United States population to just over 1.5 percent. Still, this small segment of the population is troubled by a number of social problems. The poverty rate for individuals is 22 percent, compared to the national average of 12.4 percent, and 24 percent of those age five and over have disability status, as compared to the national average of 17.7 percent (U.S. Census, 2000). Also, the Native American family and their family systems were significantly damaged through geographical relocations, boarding schools, and other mechanisms of ethnocide (Kelly, 2003). Children who spent much of their childhood in boarding schools never really experienced family life. They reached adulthood without a clear concept of parenting behavior and family functioning. Boarding schools effectively

---

*Portions of this manuscript were taken with permission from Glover, G. J., & Landreth, G. L. (2000). Filial therapy with Native Americans. *International Journal of Play Therapy, 9*(2), 57–58.

destroyed the intergenerational transmission of family and parenting knowledge. Boarding schools also introduced new and dysfunctional behaviors, such as the use of severe corporal punishment and sexual abuse.

This disruption of the Native American family is what motivated me to conduct this study. I chose to do the study on the Flathead Reservation of northern Montana because that is where my father was born and raised. My paternal grandparents, my father, and his four brothers turned away from traditional Native values and struggled in their roles as parents. Through my training and research in filial therapy, I discovered a compatibility with several Native American values, including involvement of the extended family, a deep respect for individuals, a liberal child-rearing ideology, and independence. I wanted to see if filial therapy training, with some modifications to meet the specific needs of Native Americans, could be an effective way to reintroduce traditional parenting skills and support traditional values.

The extended family has been an integral part of child-rearing practices among Native Americans for centuries. Native Americans draw strength from the extended family. Through its focus on the parent-child relationship, filial therapy can positively affect and reinforce the extended family concept. Respect for others is a prominent traditional Native American value. Parents are urged to teach by example, to treat all people politely and nicely, to accept and appreciate differences in people, to show concern for others' feelings, to help others express their feelings, and to show confidence in each—all of which are compatible with the goals of filial therapy. Filial therapy allows the child to communicate thoughts, needs, and feelings to the parent and brings the child a greater feeling of self-respect, self-worth, and confidence (Landreth & Bratton, 2006).

Gfellner (1990) found that Native American parents demonstrated a more liberal child-rearing ideology in comparison with white parents. The dominant culture often perceives this attitude as a lack of parental concern about the child's behavior. Filial therapy principles support Native American parents in providing a nonjudgmental, understanding, and accepting environment to foster the positive development of their children. Another traditional Native American value is independence. Children are given abundant opportunities to make choices without coercion with the understanding that to make a decision for a child is to make the child weak. Filial therapy recognizes children's need to differentiate and separate from their parents so they can mature in a healthy manner.

METHOD

RESEARCH DESIGN

This study employed a pre-test–post-test control group design, using an untreated control group to reduce threats to validity. It was a quasi-experimental design using convenience sampling by location. Leaving all other factors random, parents from three identified communities were assigned to the experimental group. All others were assigned to the wait-list control group and were offered training upon completion of the first series.

PARTICIPANTS

Participants of this study were Native American parents who lived on the Flatwood Reservation in northwestern Montana. All but two were enrolled members of the Confederated Salish and Kootenai Indian Tribes. One participant was an enrolled member of the Blackfeet Nation, also of Montana, and one participant was an enrolled member of the Papago Nation of Arizona. Twenty-five adult participants and 25 children were included in the study. One of the children had been diagnosed with depression. All other children displayed typical, age-appropriate behavior and emotions. Twenty-five percent of parents were living below the poverty level. Of the 25, 14 were assigned to the experimental group and 11 to the control group. The control group parents were offered training upon completion of the first series. Twenty-one participants completed the study, with 11 in the experimental group and 10 in the control group.

INSTRUMENTATION

Several instruments were used to collect data from different perspectives. Parents completed the Porter Parental Acceptance Scale (PPAS), developed by Porter (1954), and the Parenting Stress Index (PSI), developed by Abidin (1983). These self-report inventories are designed to measure parental acceptance as revealed in behavior and feelings toward, about, or with their child and the level of stress in the parent-child system.

The Measurement of Empathy in Adult-Child Interaction (MEACI), created by Bratton (1994) from a scale developed by Stover, Guerney, and O'Connell (1971), and the Children's Play Behavior with Parent Rating Form (CPBWPRF), created by Bratton (1995), are direct observational scale measures. The first operationally defines empathy as related to parent-child interactions through three specific parental behaviors, including communication of acceptance, allowing the child self-direction, and involvement. The second operationally defines children's play behavior as related to parent-child interactions during play sessions by measuring three specific child behaviors, including the child's sustained play, self-directiveness, and parent-child connectedness.

The Joseph Pre-School and Primary Self-Concept Screening Test (JPPSST) was originally developed by Joseph (1979) and is designed to measure the self-concept of a child by using pictures to stimulate responses from the child.

INTERVENTION PROTOCOL

This study tested the hypothesis that the 10-session filial therapy training model (Landreth, 2002), now called Child Parent Relationship Therapy (CPRT; Landreth & Bratton, 2006), would be an attractive and effective parent training program for a Native American population because the skills promoted in filial therapy support traditional Native American parenting values. The experimental group parents participated in the 10-session model of CPRT and filial therapy, meeting for two hours each week. This model uses both didactic and dynamic components designed to enhance the parent-child relationship by helping parents learn how to create an accepting environment in which their children feel safe enough to express and explore thoughts and feelings (Landreth & Bratton, 2006). Furthermore, the supportive group environment seemed particularly valuable for parents to share their experiences and perceptions and, as a result, helped create a more culturally relevant experience for parents.

PROCEDURE

Pre-training sessions were scheduled for parents and children during the two weeks before the first series of filial therapy training classes for the purpose of collecting data. Parents were individually scheduled for the pre-training, during which time they completed the demographics form, the Porter Parental Acceptance Scale, and the Parenting Stress Index. Child participants were interviewed for the purpose of completing the Joseph Self-Concept Screening. Both parent and child participants were asked to participate together in a 20-minute video-taped play session before and after the training. A space was specially equipped with toys similar to those used in the filial kits for the actual parent training.

The experimental group parents participated in a 10-week model of filial therapy training (Landreth & Bratton, 2006) two hours each week. The parents were taught skills through demonstration and role-play and were then required to practice with their child of focus in weekly 30-minute special play sessions and share their experiences with the group. The parents were supplied with a special toy kit, which included the typical set of filial toys (creative, aggressive, nurturing, and competence). Particular attention was paid to being sure to include a Native American baby doll and Native American dollhouse family. Each participant was videotaped once during the 10-week training. This tape was reviewed during a group so that the participants could receive feedback as well as the opportunity to observe other parents during their special playtimes.

During the two weeks following the filial therapy training sessions, the post-test battery of instruments was administered to both the experimental and control groups. The post-training sessions followed the same procedures outlined in the pre-training sessions.

RESULTS AND DISCUSSION

PORTER PARENTAL ACCEPTANCE SCALE (PPAS)

Parents in the experimental group demonstrated positive gains in their perceived acceptance of their children in all four subscales measured by the PPAS, as well as the total score; those gains, however, were not significant at the .05 level. For the experimental group, the subscale "respect for the child's feelings and right to express them" showed the largest increase. The three remaining subscales showed minimal positive change.

PARENT STRESS INDEX (PSI)

The experimental group participants showed only a minimal decrease in overall parental stress as measured by the PSI. Although positive change occurred in the experimental group, such change cannot be inferred to have been a result of the filial therapy training since the control group experienced a similar reduction in stress scores.

MEASUREMENT OF EMPATHY IN ADULT-CHILD INTERACTION (MEACI)

Significant increases for the experimental group participants ($p < .001$) in empathic behavior during observed play sessions with their children were measured by the three subscales of the MEACI. The experimental group demonstrated increased skill in communicating acceptance, allowing the child self-direction, and being involved with the child during a special play session. The greatest improvement was noted in the area of allowing the child self-direction.

CHILDREN'S PLAY BEHAVIOR WITH PARENT RATING FORM (CPBWPRF)

Significant increases for the experimental group children ($p < .01$) in desirable play behavior during observed play sessions with their parents were measured by the total score of the CPBWPRF. The experimental group children demonstrated significantly greater self-directiveness and connectedness with their parents. The experimental group children showed a positive increase in sustained play, although not at the .05 level of significance. The children's overall mood score also increased by 1.2 between the pre-test and post-test; this, however, was not significant at the .05 level.

JOSEPH PRE-SCHOOL AND PRIMARY SELF-CONCEPT SCREENING TEST (JOSEPH)

Although there was a positive increase in self-esteem of the children whose parents participated in filial therapy training as measured by the Joseph, the results were not significant at the .05 level.

DISCUSSION

It is important to note that the results of this study, when compared with results from studies with other populations, are not as effective in increasing parental acceptance as measured by the PPAS. One factor contributing to the lack of significant change in the parental acceptance scores could be the sporadic participation in the group meetings. For five of the sessions, only half of the participants attended the group meetings. During the other five sessions, approximately 75 percent of the participants attended the group meetings. According to Horejsi (1987), a Native American individual's first priority is to family and friends. This takes precedence over all other obligations, including appointments, work, or school. Although participants received individual make-up sessions, they missed the impact of the group context for sharing parenting strategies, as well as the opportunity to support one another in the role of parent.

This research, when compared with other populations studied, was not as effective in decreasing parental stress as measured by the PSI. For example, in both Bratton (1994) and Harris (1995), single parents and incarcerated mothers showed significantly higher levels of stress before their training. With scores farther from the mean, the likelihood of more significant change is possible. Scores that begin in the normal range tend to remain in the normal range. Also, lower levels of stress may be appropriate for a Native American population. Harmonious living is valued. Stress often occurs as a result of conflict with the environment. The Native American perspective advocates living as much as possible in the present and adapting to rather than resisting change.

Although the parental acceptance scores and stress scores did not improve as was predicted, the significant positive changes indicated by the MEACI do suggest that filial therapy parent training is effective in increasing empathy in parent-child interactions. A high level of empathic behavior in parents has been found to be a critical component in the filial therapy training process (Stover et al., 1971).

The results of this research indicate that filial therapy training is an effective method for enhancing empathic responsiveness in parents and increasing desirable play behaviors in children. Participants did learn the specific basic skills taught during the training sequence. All participants were able to demonstrate these skills on at least a minimally effective level by the end of training as measured by the MEACI. All of the children displayed behavior, which indicated a higher level of comfort and feeling of safety in the play session with their parents as measured by the CPBWPRF.

During weekly meetings with parents, there were many opportunities to talk with parents about their experiences. Parents reported that their children were all very excited about the play sessions and immediately understood the special nature of the playtime. One 6-year-old boy reminded his mother not to be late getting home from work. Another 8-year-old boy commented during his first play session, "If this was the real world, you wouldn't let me do this."

One parent described the process her son went through during his play session as especially revealing to her. Her son had come home from a difficult day at school and had immediately gone into his play session angrily attacking the punching bag. Within a few minutes, the anger had dissipated, and her son's behavior for the rest of the session was more playful. The mother reported that her son never verbalized what had been bothering him, but that his mood was noticeably calmer after the play session.

At the ninth training session, some parents commented that they had begun to use some of the reflective listening and limit-setting skills outside of the play sessions and with their other children. The last session was spent with parents sharing their evaluation of the experience and how and if they and their children had changed. One parent, whose son was eight, commented that the training reminded her of working with a very small child who is just developing. At that early stage, you are more likely to get on the floor and play. This parent stated that she took more notice of her child. Most parents commented that as the play sessions progressed their children seemed more confident in the play sessions and chose what they wanted to do more quickly and specifically. Most parents reported feeling more comfortable in their role.

Several parents commented on how the training had already generalized to life outside of the play session. They had learned to reflect feelings and behaviors. One parent in particular noted that she thought she wasn't learning anything and then realized that she had begun to use choices successfully in her interactions with her children. Several parents stated that their limit-setting skills had gotten better. The special playtimes were particularly enjoyable for one grandmother and her granddaughter. This parent explained that she enjoyed letting her guard down during the half hour of allowing her child to do what she chose. After the half an hour of this change in roles, the child was satisfied and ready to give back that responsibility. One parent noticed that rather than saying "Good job" all the time, she now focused more on encouraging her child's efforts by describing what her child had done well. Another parent especially enjoyed the activity of writing her children special notes. She was touched by the response she received from her children when they read her notes to them.

A Closer Look at Self-Esteem

The most interesting part of this project was the discovery that the instrument chosen to measure self-concept in the children was so inaccurate. The Joseph revealed a markedly low self-concept for both the experimental and control groups of children. However, the children who participated in the study had not been identified as at risk by their parents, nor did I observe behaviors that would support such low scores.

Five questions in particular seemed to be consistently answered in the negative. Question 1 asks children to decide whether they are more like the clean child or the dirty child. Cleanliness may not be as significant an issue for Native American children, whose parents are not as concerned with a child's appearance and instead promote exploration of the natural environment. Question 4 asks a child to identify the child his or her parent likes best. Competition is discouraged in traditional Native American homes. Children may not understand the concept of being better liked than a sibling. Question 9 asks whether the child would like to be called by a different name. Traditionally raised children often have several nicknames over the various stages of their lives. They also often have a specially given Indian name in addition to their non-Native name. The idea of choosing only one name may be unusual. Question 11 speaks to winning or losing a game. Once again, the concept of competition may not be fully accepted. Finally, Question 15 asks whether the child would like to live in a different place. Many Native American children enjoy camping with their families and say they would like to live in the woods. Also, Native American children who are accustomed to the extended family concept may feel they have more choices, but not that they necessarily dislike where they currently live.

Using instruments that incorrectly measure an aspect of a person's being such as self-concept can negatively affect one's impression of an individual or even of a group. Native Americans are continually fighting stereotypes and when a respected research tool identifies their children as lacking in some way that does not appear to be legitimate, a more culturally sensitive and accurate tool is required. Native parents (as cited in Dawson, 1988) state simply the importance of self-esteem in their children: "If my children are proud, if my children have an identity, if my children know who they are and if they are proud to be who they are, they'll be able to encounter anything in life" (p. 48).

RECOMMENDATIONS

Any type of parenting program for Native American families will more likely be successful if a number of things are kept in mind. Native Americans prefer to include the whole family in any experience. Flexibility in regard to both time and structure is essential. And incorporation of traditional teaching methods such as storytelling can greatly enhance participation.

A format more conducive to positive results with a Native American population might include longer training segments with fewer sessions and providing for practice play sessions onsite. Creating an atmosphere of a social event by providing food for all participants, babysitting and entertainment for the children, and transportation might make the training more attractive. Family groups could be encouraged to attend and include all children in the practice sessions. For example, if a single parent has three young children, a partner, sister or brother, or grandparent could be encouraged to also participate.

Suggestions for making the training process more attractive were made by participants in the study. Open-ended groups might be more appealing for people who were unable to commit to the entire 10-week period. Also, because of word of mouth, many people hear about trainings after they have started, and they would like to join. Conducting the training with the children available during the group time for practice would alleviate some of the difficulties of doing the play sessions at home. Most of the parents would like for their children's fathers to learn these same techniques for giving children positive attention.

The attrition rate for participants in both the experimental and the control groups was high, with approximately 30 percent of those beginning the process eventually dropping out. Future researchers working with a Native American population need to be aware that initial enthusiasm for a project may subside. Current family matters often take priority over previous commitments. A larger sample size than previously estimated may be required to meet the needs of a particular study.

The inconsistency in the self-concept screening for the children points to a possible area of cultural difference, requiring greater sensitivity in selecting measurement instruments for research with a Native American population. It would be critical to investigate the self-concept of Native American children from an internal vantage point using measurement instruments designed for this population.

CONCLUSION

Working with Native American families is challenging and rewarding, and doing research with this group is especially so. All of the necessary constraints that are put into place to limit the variables become limiting in themselves. This study was done with a group of average Native Americans living on a reservation in northern Montana. It was not a clinical population. The purpose of the study was primarily to test whether filial therapy would be a comfortable fit for this population and secondarily to examine the outcomes from the study. The comments made by participants, the enthusiasm of those who attended the groups, and the joy expressed by both parents and children regarding the special play sessions support the hypotheses even though statistical significance was not found on all measures.

REFERENCES

Abidin, R. R. (1983). *Parenting stress index*. Charlottesville, VA: Pediatric Psychology Press.

Bratton, S. C. (1994). Filial therapy with single parents (Doctoral dissertation, University of North Texas, 1993). *Dissertation Abstracts International, 54*, (08), A2890.

Bratton, S. C. (1995). *Children's play behavior with parent rating form*. Unpublished manuscript, University of North Texas at Denton.

Dawson, J. (1988). "If my children are proud": Native education and the problem of self-esteem. *Canadian Journal of Native American Education, 15*(1), 43–50.

Gfellner, B. M. (1990). Culture and consistency in ideal and actual child-rearing practices: A study of Canadian Indian and white parents. *Journal of Comparative Family Studies, 21*(3), 413–423.

Harris, Z. L. (1995). *Filial therapy with incarcerated mothers*. Unpublished doctoral dissertation, University of North Texas, Denton.

Horejsi, C. (1987). *Child welfare practice and the Native American family in Montana: A handbook for social workers*. Missoula, MT: University of Montana.

Joseph, J. (1979). *Joseph pre-school and primary self-concept screening test: Instruction manual*. Chicago: Stoelting.

Kelly, C. (2003). *Nursing implications of intergenerational concerns among Native American clients*. Unpublished master's thesis, University of Arizona, Tucson.

Landreth, G. L. (2002). *Play therapy: The art of the relationship* (2nd ed.). New York: Brunner-Routledge.

Landreth, G. L., & Bratton, S. C. (2006). *Child parent relationship therapy (CPRT): A 10-session filial therapy model*. New York: Brunner-Routledge.

Porter, B. (1954). Measurement of parental acceptance of children. *Journal of Home Economics, 46*(3), 176–182.

Stover, L., Guerney, B., & O'Connell, M. (1971). Measurements of acceptance, allowing self-direction, involvement, and empathy in adult-child interaction. *Journal of Psychology, 77*, 261–269.

U.S. Census Bureau. (2000). *American factfinder: Maps*. Retrieved April 1, 2009, from http://factfinder.census.gov/jsp/saff/SAFFInfo.jsp?_pageId=gn7_maps.

CHAPTER 18

Filial Therapy with Chinese Parents

TOM YUEN

T HE 2006 CENSUS indicated that there were about 1,029,000 Chinese, mostly foreign born, residing in Canada. When Chinese immigrants move into Canada, they are exposed to a different culture and different ways of living. The acculturation of the new immigrants is a complex process involving individual, family, and cultural factors. According to Chao (1994), the principles of Confucius appear to have a great influence on Chinese child-rearing practices. Parental control, obedience, strict discipline, filial piety, respect for elders, family obligations, maintenance of harmony, and negation of conflict are emphasized in Chinese parent-child relationships (Lam, 2005; Lin & Fu, 1990; Sung, 1985). These factors not only affect the structure of the family, but also significantly increase the level of stress in family members as they adapt to changing roles. High levels of stress in parents can negatively affect their ability to make positive contributions to their children's development (Chiu, 1987; Kelley & Tseng, 1992; Lam, 2005; Lin & Fu, 1990; Sayegh & Lasry, 1993; Shek & Chan, 1999; Winkelman, 1994; Yao, 1985; Zheng & Berry, 1991).

According to Sue and Sue (2007), most Chinese are reluctant to go to mental health services because they attach a marked stigma to mental illness. Chinese are discouraged by their family from disclosing personal problems to a stranger. If one's failure is exposed to somebody outside the family, it is a shame not just to the individual but also to the entire family. Thus, discussions with close friends, self-discipline, and physical cures are more accepted than going to seek help from a professional

(Jung, 1984; Zheng & Berry, 1991). Because of the different cultural perspectives in seeking professional help, the Chinese populations consequently are not adequately served by the traditional network of social agencies (Jung, 1984; Nann, 1982; Statistics Canada, 2006).

FILIAL THERAPY

Filial therapy is a helpful approach for culturally diverse immigrant parents and their children for a number of reasons. First, filial therapy teaches parents to create a nonjudgmental, understanding, and accepting environment, which decreases parent-child relationship stress created within a new culture (Landreth, 2002; Watts & Broaddus, 2002). Second, during play therapy the child learns to accommodate a different set of standards and types of communication, which is similar to adjusting to a new culture (Fidler, Guerney, Andronico, & Guerney, 1969). The parent and child cooperate in accommodating new and old behavioral practices. This process helps minimize the stress and confusion involved in applying a new cultural framework within the old one (Guerney & Guerney, 1989; Watts & Broaddus, 2002). Third, as parents create and maintain a family atmosphere of open communication and commitment to each other, they are able to resolve intergenerational conflicts due to changes in role, cultural conflicts, and differences in acculturation levels. Fourth, other research has shown that filial therapy benefits culturally diverse populations such as Native Americans (Glover & Landreth, 2000). Finally, the group format of filial therapy can address the social isolation, emotional disturbance, and psychological conflicts that many Chinese immigrants experience (Esquivel & Keitel, 1990; Jung, 1984; Nann, 1982; Yao, 1985; Zheng & Berry, 1991). Because of these unique needs of Chinese immigrants and the benefits of filial therapy, I conducted a study with Chinese parents in Canada to determine the impact of filial therapy on their parenting stress, empathic and accepting relationship with their children, and their children's self-concept. As a Chinese immigrant and father, this study had personal meaning for me as well. I was eager to see if other Chinese parents would experience the same positive impact of filial therapy that I had experienced.

METHOD

PARTICIPANTS

Announcements stating the beginning of "parent-child relationship enhancement classes for immigrant Chinese parents in Canada" were made, and flyers were posted at various Chinese churches and at various Chinese community agencies that provide child and family services in the Vancouver metropolitan area. Parents who met the following criteria were selected to participate in the study:

- Chinese immigrant
- Able to speak and read Cantonese, Mandarin, or English
- Have a child between the ages of 3 and 10 years who has not received therapy and is not currently in therapy
- Not have taken a parenting class in the last two years
- Able to attend the 10 weeks of filial therapy at the scheduled times
- Able to attend a pre- and post-training session to complete test instruments and to be videotaped playing with their child
- Agree to conduct a weekly 30-minute home play session for 10 weeks with their child
- Willing to sign the consent-to-participate form

A total of 35 parents who volunteered for the filial therapy training met the selection criteria. Eighteen of these parents were randomly selected for the experimental group and divided into two groups with 9 parents in each group. The other 17 parents were placed in the control group and received no treatment. The experimental group was composed of 14 mothers and 4 fathers. The control group was composed of 11 mothers and 6 fathers. The children of focus of the experimental group parents consisted of 9 boys and 9 girls, with an age range of 3 to 10 years of age and a mean age of 5.9 years. The children of focus of the control group parents consisted of 10 boys and 7 girls with an age range of 4 to 10 years and a mean age of 6.8 years.

INSTRUMENTS

Parent-Child Empathic Interaction The Measurement of Empathy in Adult-Child Interaction (MEACI) is an observational scale (Stover, Guerney, & O'Connell, 1971) used to rate videotapes of parent-child empathic interaction within play therapy sessions. An MEACI total score is derived as well as subscales for communication of acceptance, allowing the child self-direction, and involvement.

Parental Acceptance of Child The Porter Parental Acceptance Scale (PPAS; Porter, 1954) is a 40-item self-report inventory designed to measure parental acceptance of children as revealed in the behavior and feelings parents express toward, with, or about their child. The scale measures four variables:

1. Respect for the child's feelings and right to express them
2. Appreciation of the child's uniqueness
3. Recognition of the child's need for autonomy and independence
4. Unconditional love

Reliability was established by a split-half reliability correlation of .76, and validity was established by agreement of a minimum of three of five expert judges on all of the items (Porter, 1954).

Parenting Stress   The Parenting Stress Index (PSI; Abidin, 1983), a 101-item self-report index, was used to measure the level of stress in the parent-child relationship. The items are separated into two domains, child and parent. The child domain measures parental stress related to the child's levels of adaptability, acceptability, demandingness, mood, distractibility, and reinforcing behavior for parents. The parent domain measures the parent's perceptions of their level of depression, attachment, role restrictions, competence, social isolation, spouse relations, and health. Reliability was established by a test-retest method that produced coefficients of .69 for the parent domain, .77 for the child domain, and .88 for the total index (Zakreski, 1983). The PSI is also purported to have strong validity (Abidin, 1983).

Child Problem Behaviors   The Filial Problem Checklist (FPC; Horner, 1974) is a self-report instrument consisting of 108 potentially problematic situations related to parenting. Normative statistics concerning validity or reliability are not available on this instrument. The FPC has been used extensively in filial therapy research and was used as a means to compare results obtained in this study with other studies of filial therapy.

Child Self-Concept   The Self-Perception Profile for Children (SPPC) is a revision of the perceived competence scale for children (Harter, 1982), which measures six areas of competence: scholastic, social, athletic, physical, behavioral conduct, and global self-worth of children in grades three to six. Reliabilities for all subscales based on Cronbach's alpha have ranged from .71 to .86 on four samples tested (Harter, 1985). The translation used in this study was completed by Chinese doctoral students in the United States. The reliabilities for this translation among those samples were similar to the reliabilities reported by Harter (1985) and Stigler, Smith, and Mao (1985). The Pictorial Scale of Perceived Competence and Social Acceptance for Young Children (PSPCSAYC) was developed by Harter and Pike (1984) and is an extension of the perceived competence scale for children (Harter, 1982). It measures four domains: cognitive competence, physical competence, peer acceptance, and maternal acceptance.

PROCEDURES

Before the treatment, parents and children in the experimental and control groups completed all the assessments listed earlier and participated in a 20-minute videotaped play session together. The two treatment groups of nine parents each met weekly for a two-hour training session for 10 consecutive weeks in a church. The training sessions followed the methodology outlined by Landreth (2002) for a 10-week filial therapy training group. The groups were conducted in Cantonese. Materials used in the training were translated into Chinese. Parents used English, Mandarin, or Cantonese to conduct their play sessions. Following completion of the 10 weekly filial therapy training sessions or after 10 weeks for the control group, the post-test battery of instruments and videotaping of play sessions were administered to both the experimental and control group parents and children in the same way as the pre-training sessions. An analysis of covariance (ANCOVA) was computed to test the significance of the difference between the experimental group and the control group on the adjusted post-test means. The pre- and post-testing videotapes of parent-child play sessions were blind-rated to prevent rater bias by two Chinese counselors who understood Cantonese, Mandarin, and English. Inter-rater reliability for the two raters was established during training sessions.

RESULTS

Results for all measures are presented in Table 18.1. For videotaped parent-child empathic interactions, parents in the experimental group scored significantly higher than parents in the control group on MEACI total score, $F(1, 35) = 6.580$, $p = .015$; communication of acceptance subscale, $F(1, 35) = 21.466$, $p < .001$; allowing the child self-direction subscale, $F(1, 35) = 15.084$, $p < .001$; and involvement subscale, $F(1, 35) = 10.496$, $p = .003$.

Table 18-1
Pre-Test and Post-Test Means (M) and Standard Deviations (SD) for the
Dependent Variables by Each Condition

	Pre-Test		Post-Test	
	M	SD	M	SD
Measure				
MEACI*				
E	47.972	5.326	38.806	8.028
C	46.559	4.531	46.029	5.995
Communication of Acceptance**				
E	17.972	1.556	15.417	2.277
C	17.500	1.118	15.618	2.043
Allowing Child's Self-Direction**				
E	17.222	3.353	12.667	3.726
C	16.412	2.181	17.177	2.963
Involvement**				
E	12.778	2.625	10.722	2.396
C	13.000	3.163	13.177	2.899
PPAS**				
E	127.167	12.720	154.389	12.939
C	125.353	15.264	124.353	13.205
Respects Child's Feelings**				
E	28.444	4.841	42.667	5.181
C	28.588	5.316	28.412	5.149
Appreciates Child's Uniqueness**				
E	29.944	4.304	34.833	4.218
C	28.941	5.539	29.353	6.284
Recognizes Autonomy Needs**				
E	37.167	3.485	42.889	3.740
C	36.471	4.862	37.294	4.427
Unconditional Love**				
E	31.611	8.396	37.278	6.115
C	31.353	6.782	29.294	6.890
PSI**				
E	269.444	28.471	238.667	26.615
C	261.823	40.168	266.941	39.851
Parent Domain**				
E	148.778	22.265	131.889	18.000
C	148.706	21.359	153.235	20.840

Child Domain**				
E	120.667	12.471	106.778	11.254
C	113.118	23.484	113.882	23.241
FPC*				
E	53.222	31.116	30.611	24.900
C	46.706	38.286	50.235	33.861
SPPC				
E	2.901	0.293	2.939	0.221
C	2.806	0.390	2.788	0.430
PSPCSAYC**				
E	3.020	0.467	3.562	2.886
C	2.853	0.322	2.886	0.446

Note: MEACI = Measurement of Empathy in Adult-Child Interaction Scales; E = Experimental Group; C = Control Group; PPAS = Porter Parental Acceptance Scale; PSI = Parenting Stress Index; FPC = Filial Problem Checklist; SPPC = Self-Perception Profile for Children; PSPCSAYC = Pictorial Scale of Perceived Competence and Social Acceptance for Young Children; * = $p < .05$; ** = $p < .01$

Parents in the experimental group scored significantly higher than parents in the control group on all measures of perceived acceptance of their children: PPAS total score, $F(1, 35) = 67.418, p < .001$; respect for child's feelings subscale, $F(1, 35) = 70.912, p < .001$; appreciation of the child's uniqueness subscale, $F(1, 35) = 14.210, p < .001$; recognition of the child's need for autonomy subscale, $F(1, 35) = 24.702, p < .001$; and unconditional love subscale, $F(1, 35) = 18.210, p < .001$.

Parents in the experimental group scored significantly lower than parents in the control group in perceived level of stress related to parenting as measured by the PSI total score, $F(1, 35) = 18.561, p < .001$; parent domain, $F(1, 35) = 14.971, p < .001$; and child domain, $F(1, 35) = 26.935, p < .001$.

Parents in the experimental group scored significantly lower than parents in the control group in perceived number of problems related to their children's behavior as measured by the FPC, $F(1, 35) = 13.920, p < .001$.

Regarding self-concept, children ages 3 through 7 of parents in the experimental group scored significantly higher than children in the control group in self-perception as measured by the PSPCSAYC, $F(1, 23) = 20.219, p < .001$. However, children ages 8 through 10 in the experimental group did not score significantly higher than children in the control group in self-perception as measured by the SPPC, $F(1, 12) = .287, p = .605$.

DISCUSSION

The results of this study supported the effectiveness of the Landreth (2002) 10-week filial therapy training with immigrant Chinese parents in Canada. A discussion of the meaning of these results follows.

Empathy in Parent-Child Interactions

Under the assumptions of Confucianism, Chinese culture is moralistically rather than psychologically oriented. Unlike Western culture, in which expressions of empathy and affection are outwardly effusive and commonly exhibited, traditional Chinese perceive physical intimacy and love as private matters. It is also not appropriate to praise one's children in public (Ekblad, 1986). After completion of the filial therapy training, parents in the experimental group showed significantly higher empathic behavior during observed play sessions with their children than the control group. One father shared:

> I have been emotionally distant from my children. I am not used to show much of my affection because I think my deeds can reveal how much I love them. But now, I learn that each one of us needs to receive verbal expression of love and encouragement. . . .

The findings of this study on the communication of acceptance subscale confirmed that Chinese parents were able to accept the skills that were taught in a filial therapy group and also were able to apply those skills in the parent-child relationship. It is important to note that the changes in the parents' behavior were verified with direct observations rather than by self-report data.

Chinese parents tend to be highly lenient, warm, and affectionate toward infants and very young children until they reach the age of reasoning, which is around three to four years old. Then, Chinese parents tend to use external punishments and scolding as a means to maintain compliance in the family. Hence, they are not apt to listen to their children's complaints but tend to give strict directions. Yet, a filial therapy training group father of a nine-year-old girl said:

> One night I was sitting on my daughter's bed, and she told me that she was feeling lonely and isolated at school. It was hard for me to just sit there and listen, to let her express frustration. But I did a great job just listening to her and accepting her feelings.

The findings of this study suggest that immigrant Chinese parents can learn to communicate understanding and acceptance of their children's behavior and feelings, including anger, loneliness, and frustration.

Generally, Chinese parents use a high degree of physical control over their children (Lin & Fu, 1990). Sometimes Chinese parents may seem to smother their children and restrict their freedom of action. The findings of this study on the MEACI child self-direction subscale indicate that immigrant Chinese parents can learn to allow their children self-direction in 10 weeks of filial therapy training, even though the concept of individualism is different from their cultural upbringing. A parent in the filial therapy training group said:

> I have learned to keep communication open with my child. She has brought her ideas to me more. And I have a chance to learn about her thinking and her problems. My husband and I are able to keep track of her development.

Parents in the experimental group also scored significantly higher than parents in the control group on the MEACI involvement in the child's play subscale. This kind of change was described by a parent in the filial therapy training group:

> I have started the "alone dates" with my older child. I realize he needs to feel special too. . . . Maybe we would go to dinner, maybe we would take a walk, but always it would be something during which we would not get interrupted, when we would have a chance to talk and I would get to really listen. It was time that was really valued on both sides.

Chinese parents typically think that playing is wasting time and only working is meaningful. The findings of this study demonstrate that immigrant Chinese parents can learn to be more involved in their children's play.

PARENTAL ACCEPTANCE

After completion of the filial therapy training, parents in the experimental group showed significantly higher than those in the control group on perceived acceptance of their children on all four subscales and the total score of the Porter Parental Acceptance Scale. The parents in the experimental group demonstrated a significant increase on the respect for the child's feelings and right to express them subscale. The increases in this subscale may be a result of the parents' attitudes and behaviors as measured by the PPAS and are closely related to specific play therapy skills that were taught during the training course. One parent shared:

> My daughter has been talking back to me. While there are more arguments at home, it helps me understand more about what she thinks. I feel she has become more secure to express herself to me. More important, I do not feel my role of a mother being challenged.

The parents in the experimental group demonstrated a significant increase on the appreciation of the child's unique makeup subscale. Chinese culture is collective-oriented, and conformity is highly emphasized in the family and society. Each person is assumed to play certain roles. It is not uncommon to see adult Chinese hand over their entire paychecks to their parents for financial support or for Chinese children to pursue a course of study chosen for them by their parents rather than one of their own choice. The 10 weeks of filial therapy training had a profound effect on the parents' perception of their children. One parent commented:

> I have become less critical of my children and try to refrain from molding them into a certain type of children I would like to see. I do not need to choose a career path for them, nor do I make comparisons among my children.

The parents in the experimental group demonstrated a significant increase on the recognition of the child's need for autonomy subscale. This may be because the parents felt empowered in the skill of parenting and were then able to be more accepting of their children. Traditional Chinese parents have a high degree of physical control over their children (Bond, 1986). They may seem to be controlling, restrictive, and overprotective. However, the Chinese culture assumes that parents take complete responsibility for their child's development, and parents are therefore very much involved in their children's decision-making processes. Filial therapy training helped these parents value their children's growth, development, autonomy, and maturity. One parent shared her insight about letting go of her control:

I am an overprotective mother. I thought the way to show I am a good parent is to do things for my child, but I overdo it. . . . I offer help that is not necessary. I decide when he is warm and when he is cold. Now, I remind myself not to be so imposing.

Parents in the experimental group scored significantly higher than parents in the control group on the PPAS unconditional love subscale. One parent commented:

Although it is still natural for me to have negative feelings when my son is fussy, I am more able to accept the fact that he also has a low mood. I am learning to accept what he is, not just the one who can meet my expectations.

Filial therapy training is a growth model that focuses on strengths rather than on weaknesses. It is a didactic and educative approach that attempts to build on the parents' accomplishments rather on their failures. The filial therapy training group provided an accepting atmosphere in which parents were not threatened and therefore did not need to be defensive. As the parents experienced unconditional acceptance in the training group, they were able to extend this acceptance to relationships with their children.

PARENTAL STRESS

After completion of the filial therapy training, parents in the experimental group showed significantly lower parenting stress as measured by the PSI than parents in the control group. The significant decrease in parental stress may be due to the enhancement of parent-child communication, the development of self-control by children, and the therapeutic limit setting and choice giving provided by the parents. The impact of decreased stress is illustrated by a parent who was struggling with a decision about her family moving back to Hong Kong:

My daughter reminded me that I have a choice between going or not going back to Hong Kong. I guess she has picked up what I always say to her during the special playtime. She sounds more autonomous and independent.

Another factor that may have contributed to the decrease of parenting stress was the emotional support and encouragement among the parents in the group. Chinese typically keep their difficulties within the family and feel inferior when they are not able to resolve their problems. The filial therapy training group provided the parents with a safe atmosphere in which they could share their struggles. In this setting, the parents seemed to readily identify with each other's feelings of being an immigrant in Canada.

Children's Problematic Behavior

Parents in the experimental group scored significantly lower after completing filial therapy training than did parents in the control group on a number of child problem behaviors identified on the FRC. Improved parenting skills and increased self-confidence of the parents apparently enabled them to handle many situations that were previously listed as problems. Moreover, parents reported that they felt an emotional closeness to their children. The intimacy helped them see things from their children's perspectives. As parents were more understanding to the underlying messages of the children's problem behaviors, they became more competent to deal with the situation.

Children's Self-Concept

Children aged 3 to 7 of the parents in the experimental parent group scored significantly higher than same-age children in the control group on self-concept as measured by PSPCSAYC. These children also demonstrated improvement in the social acceptance domain, which includes the maternal acceptance and peer acceptance subscales. The 30-minute special play sessions each week in which the parents communicated acceptance, understanding, support, and unconditional love may account for the improvement in self-concept. Children aged 8 to 10 of the parents in the experimental parent group demonstrated a slightly positive, although not statistically significant, improvement in self-concept on the SPPC. Same-age children in the control group achieved a slightly lower score on the SPPC.

SUMMARY

Chinese immigrants are confronted by a new culture and are overwhelmed with the necessary assimilation processes. The most significant loss in this process for Chinese immigrants is the loss of social support in the form of family ties and close interpersonal relationships.

In many cases Chinese parents have little or no preparation for the challenge to their traditional values and ways of life that they encounter in the local society. Aside from their personal adjustment, immigrant Chinese parents encounter the challenge of helping their children adjust to the local society while maintaining their own cultural traditions. The emphasis of Western culture on individualism, the rights of children, the democratic attitudes toward parenting, and more open interpersonal relationships are antithetical and threatening to traditional Chinese values (Jung, 1984; Nann, 1982; Yao, 1985).

The results of this study demonstrate that these immigrant Chinese parents were able to incorporate new relationship skills in their interactions with their children during special play sessions. They were able to learn to label their children's emotions just as quickly as other parents of other cultural backgrounds (Glover, 2001; Jang, 2000; Shen, 2002). Parents in the experimental group reported significantly more accepting attitudes toward their children. They also reported a decrease in stress related to parenting and noted a marked reduction in their children's behavior problems. Their children's self-concepts were also enhanced.

Filial therapy is a unique approach to equip parents with basic child-centered play therapy skills to become therapeutic agents in their children's lives. The accepting and respectful relationship makes child-centered play therapy an ideal intervention for children who are of a different culture from the therapist (Glover, 2001). Parents are free to continue the traditional parenting style of their family's countries of origin because parents are required to use the child-centered play therapy skills only during the once-a-week 30-minute special session. The accepting parent-child relationship emphasized in the filial therapy approach allows the parents and the child to maintain traditional cultural values, beliefs, and traditions, thus creating a healthy blend of Eastern and Western-style approaches to parenting.

The findings showed that Landreth's (2002) 10-week filial therapy training model is compatible with traditional Chinese parenting values. The training equips parents with better communication skills to change dysfunctional family interactions. This emphasis is important because family relationship, not an individual, is the basic unit in Chinese culture. Also, filial therapy's focus on structure, an essence in Chinese learning orientation, provides a concrete direction for the participants to follow. Counselors who have a background in play therapy are in a unique position to provide parents with the training needed to positively affect the lives of their children.

REFERENCES

Abidin, R. R. (1983). *Parenting stress index*. Charlottesville, VA: Pediatric Psychology Press.

Bond, M. (1986). *The psychology of the Chinese people*. Hong Kong: Oxford University.

Chao, R. (1994). Beyond parental control and authoritarian parenting style: Understanding Chinese parenting through the cultural notion of training. *Child Development, 65*, 1111–1119.

Chiu, L. (1987). Child-rearing attitudes of Chinese, Chinese-American, and Anglo-American mothers. *International Journal of Psychology, 22*, 409–419.

Ekblad, S. (1986). Relationships between child-rearing practices and primary school children's functional adjustment in the People's Republic of China. *Scandinavian Journal of Psychology, 27*, 220–230.

Esquivel, G. B., & Keitel, M. A. (1990). Counseling immigrant children in the schools. *Elementary School Guidance & Counseling, 24*, 213–221.

Fidler, J., Guerney, B., Andronico, M., & Guerney, L. (1969). In B. Guerney (Ed.), *Psychotherapeutic agents: New roles for nonprofessional, parents, and teachers* (pp. 47–55). New York: Holt, Rinehart, & Winston.

Glover, G. J. (2001). Cultural considerations in play therapy. In G. L. Landreth (Ed.), *Innovations in play therapy* (pp. 31–41). New York: Brunner-Routledge.

Glover, G. J., & Landreth, G. L. (2000). Play therapy with Native Americans on the Flathead reservation. *International Journal of Play Therapy, 9*, 57–80.

Guerney, L., & Guerney, B. (1989). Child relationship enhancement: Family therapy and parent education. Special issue: Person-centered approaches with families. *Person-Centered Review, 4*, 344–357.

Harter, S. (1982). The perceived competence scale for children. *Child Development, 53*, 87–97.

Harter, S. (1985). *Manual for the self-perception profile for children*. Denver, CO: University of Denver.

Harter, S., & Pike, R. (1984). The pictorial scale of perceived competence and social acceptance for young children. *Child Development, 55*, 1969–1982.

Horner, P. (1974). *Dimensions of child behavior as described by parents: A monotonicity analysis*. Unpublished doctoral dissertation, The Pennsylvania State University, University Park, PA.

Jang, M. (2000). Effectiveness of filial therapy for Korean parents. *International Journal of Play Therapy, 9*(2), 39–56.

Jung, M. (1984). Structural family therapy: Its application to Chinese families. *Family Process, 23*, 365–374.

Kelley, M., & Tseng, H. (1992). Cultural differences in child-rearing: A comparison of immigrant Chinese and Caucasian American mothers. *Journal of Cross-Cultural Psychology, 23*(4), 444–455.

Lam, C. (2005). Chinese construction of adolescent development outcome: Themes discerned in a qualitative study. *Child and Adolescent Social Work Journal, 22*(2), 111–131.

Landreth, G. L. (2002). *Play therapy: The art of the relationship.* Muncie, IN: Accelerated Development.

Lin, C., & Fu, V. (1990). A comparison of child-rearing practices among Chinese, immigrant Chinese, and Caucasian-American parents. *Child Development, 61,* 429–433.

Nann, B. (1982). Settlement programs for immigrant women and families. In R. Nann (Ed.), *Uprooting and surviving: Adaptation and resettlement of migrant families and children* (pp. 85–94). Dordrecht, the Netherlands: D. Reidel.

Porter, B. (1954). Measurement of parental acceptance of children. *Journal of Home Economics, 46,* 176–182.

Sayegh, L., & Lasry, J. (1993). Immigrants' adaptation in Canada: Assimilation, acculturation, and orthogonal cultural identification. *Canadian Psychology, 34*(1), 98–109.

Shek, D., & Chan, L. (1999). Hong Kong Chinese parents' perceptions of the ideal child. *The Journal of Psychology, 133*(3), 291–302.

Shen, Y. (2002). Short-term group play therapy with Chinese earthquake victims: Effects on anxiety, depression, and adjustment. *International Journal of Play Therapy, 11*(1), 43–63.

Statistics Canada (2006). *Immigrants in Canada.* Ottawa, ON, Canada: Supply and Services.

Stigler, J. W., Smith, S., & Mao, L. (1985). The self-perception of competence by Chinese children. *Child Development, 56,* 1259–1270.

Stover, L., Guerney, B., & O'Connell, M. (1971). Measurement of acceptance, allowing self-direction, involvement, and empathy in adult-child interaction. *Journal of Psychology, 77,* 261–269.

Sue, D. W., & Sue, D. (2007). *Counseling the culturally different: Theory and practice* (5th ed.). Hoboken, NJ: John Wiley & Sons.

Sung, B. L. (1985). Bicultural conflicts in Chinese immigrant children. *Journal of Comparative Studies, 16,* 255–269.

Watts, R., & Broaddus, J. (2002). Improving parent-child relationships through filial therapy: An interview with Garry Landreth. *Journal of Counseling & Development, 80,* 372–379.

Winkelman, M. (1994). Cultural shock and adaptation. *Journal of Counseling and Development, 73,* 121–126.

Yao, E. (1985). Adjustment needs of Asian immigrant children. *Elementary School Guidance & Counseling, 20,* 222–227.

Zakreski, J. (1983). *Prematurity and the single parent: Effects of cumulative stress on child development.* Unpublished doctoral dissertation, University of Virginia, Institute of Clinical Psychology.

Zheng, X., & Berry, J. (1991). Psychological adaptation of Chinese sojourners in Canada. *International Journal of Psychology, 26*(4), 451–470.

CHAPTER 19

Child Parent Relationship Therapy with African American Parents

ANGELA I. SHEELY-MOORE

My cell phone vibrated in my purse, indicating an incoming phone call. Not recognizing the number, I assumed it was another parent responding to the Child Parent Relationship Therapy promotional flyer. I pressed the okay button on my phone and greeted the caller with a warm "Hello." Responding in a clipped manner, Kim* briefly expressed her interest in the filial therapy group and began to challenge my rationale for selecting African Americans as my focus of study. I recalled Kim's tone of voice as being tense and suspicious, as if my purpose served a hidden agenda. I began to provide my typical explanation when Kim immediately interrupted to forth-rightly ask about my ethnic background. After disclosing that I was of African American and Asian descent, I heard a huge sigh of relief and a chuckle as Kim stated that she thought I was Caucasian. The tone of the conversation changed as Kim's voice seemed more casual and more relaxed as she began to disclose her struggles of being geographically displaced as a result of Hurricane Katrina and her behavioral concerns for her five-year-old son.

Historically, African Americans have underused mental health services in community settings and a review of the literature indicates

---

*The name of the parent has been changed to ensure confidentiality.

a slow response within the mental health profession in addressing the unique needs of this population, particularly the needs of young African American children and their families (Baggerly & Parker, 2005; Glover, 2001; Bratton, Ray, Rhine, & Jones, 2005; Ray, Bratton, Rhine, & Jones, 2001; Solis, Meyers, & Varjas, 2004). Reasons for African Americans being underrepresented and underserved in mental health services include distrust of Caucasian service providers, misdiagnosis and overdiagnosis of mental disorders, and discrepancy of expectations between therapist and client (Boyd-Franklin, 2003; Parham & Parham, 2002; Parham White, & Ajamu, 1999; Solis et al., 2004; Sue, 1977). The notion of distrust toward Caucasian mental health service providers appeared to apply in my phone conversation with Kim, as she seemed guarded with personal information until she became aware of my ethnic background. With the tendency of African Americans to use mental health services as a last resort (Parham et al., 1999) and the tendency for people of color terminating therapy after one session twice as much compared to their Caucasian counterparts (Sue, 1977), a strengths-based approach to counseling services is proposed to empower African American parents and children. The need to highlight positive characteristics within the African American family system was exemplified in the case of Kim when she reflected upon her fear of attending an African American filial therapy group that her parenting approach would be deemed "wrong" by treatment providers.

As the second-largest racial minority in the United States, African Americans represented 13 percent of our nation's population, with almost a quarter of this population living in poverty (McKinnon, 2003). Social and environmental forces, such as racial discrimination, serve as threats to the physical, social, and psychological well-being of African American families. Racial oppression and injustice correlate to a disparity in health status between African American and Caucasian adults that includes higher incidents of substance abuse and inconsistent parental discipline within the family (Gibbons et al., 2001; Pinderhughes et al., 2001). Furthermore, African Americans are more likely than any other race to have been incarcerated (Harrison & Beck, 2005). African American children, in particular, appear to be at higher risk for low academic and personal success because of their disproportionate rate of school discipline problems compared to their peers (National Center for Educational Statistics [NCES], 2003). According to NCES, African American students have higher retention, suspension, and expulsion rates compared to Caucasian and Latino students.

With the increased risk factors of African American children, parents can serve to mitigate such factors because of their strong influences on children's socio-emotional development and academic success (Jackson, Gyamfi, Brooks-Gunn, & Blake, 1998; Slater & Power, 1987). In fact, Baggerly and Parker (2005) specifically addressed the need to conduct filial training with African American parents to promote optimal child development. In response to the challenge, Child Parent Relationship Therapy seems to provide a culturally sensitive approach to mitigate possible stigma related to mental health services. With an emphasis on enhancing the parent-child relationship, CPRT provides a pro-active, preventative approach, rather than a problem-solving approach. Instead of the therapist serving as the expert, in CPRT the parents are empowered through learning child-centered play therapy skills and procedures to better understand their children's needs (Landreth & Bratton, 2006). Thus, the power shifts from the mental health professional to the parent, which can lead to increased trust within the therapeutic process in addition to increased parental confidence and capability. This pro-active approach to working with African American parents can serve to alleviate feelings of being viewed by those in power or privileged status as inferior (Kerl, 2001).

In addition to the CPRT training model's emphasis on the family, the value of extended family with African Americans complements the group format approach to CPRT. Parham et al. (1999) proposed the historical significance of family loyalty and interdependence within African Americans today as a continuation of values derived from African slaves. In efforts to maintain a form of psychological control and safety, slaves developed family interactions based on a community-based approach, where cooperation and responsibility for others were paramount to psychological and physical survival. In the case of Kim, her family members were geographically dispersed throughout the 48 contiguous states because of the evacuation of New Orleans in response to Hurricane Katrina. Lacking an extended network of support in her current residence, Kim reported that participating in the parenting group served as her only hope to improve her child's behavior. The value of interdependence within many African American communities is demonstrated in the CPRT format because parents provide encouragement and support for one another as they learn new parenting behaviors.

METHOD

With possible socio-cultural barriers African Americans face, such as a lack of trust toward mental health providers and early termination of therapy services (Boyd-Franklin, 2003; Parham & Parham, 2002; Parham et al., 1999; Solis et al., 2004; Sue, 1977), I decided to provide the filial therapy training in a more accessible and less stigmatized setting—school. Soliciting parents through the schools in which their children were enrolled served as an opportunity for me to meet the parents in a more familiar environment.

Using a quasi-experimental control group design, I examined the effectiveness of CPRT with low-income, African American parents of children exhibiting behavioral problems. Specifically, I wanted to know whether parents who reported problematic behaviors with their children noticed improvement after participating in CPRT compared to parents who did not participate in the training. I was also interested to see whether parents who reported parent-child relationship stress noticed any changes after completing the CPRT treatment, compared to those parents who did not participate in the training.

INSTRUMENTATION

To determine the effectiveness of the treatment, I selected one instrument to measure parents' view of problematic child behaviors and another instrument to measure parents' report of parent-child relationship stress: the Child Behavior Checklist-Parent Form (CBCL; Achenbach & Rescorla, 2000) and the Parent Stress Index (PSI; Abidin, 1995), respectively. The 1½-to-5-year-olds version of the CBCL provides scores for seven syndrome and five DSM-oriented scales in addition to three domain scores: internalizing problems, externalizing problems, and total problems. The CBCL yields t-scores with a mean of 50 and a standard deviation of 10. Borderline scores range from 65 to 69, while scores at or above 70 are considered clinically significant. A decrease in syndrome scores indicates improvement in the targeted behavior (Achenbach & Rescorla, 2000). The mean score of the test-retest reliability for the CBCL 1½-to-5-year-olds version was established at .85 over 8- to 16-day intervals. Test-retest reliability for domain scores of the CBCL for 1½-to 5-year-olds is as follows: internalizing problems ($r = .90$), externalizing problems ($r = .87$), and total problems ($r = .90$). Strong content validity evidence for CBCL problem scales has been supported by research (Achenbach & Rescorla, 2000).

Used for children aged 1 month to 12 years, the PSI is composed of three domain scores: child domain, parent domain, and life stress. The parent domain and child domain are combined to present an overall total stress score. Life stress is an optional component of the PSI, indicating situational life stress that occurred within the previous 12 months. Reported scores above the 85th percentile indicate high stress. Strong validity research evidence for PSI scores has been well-established through multiple research studies (Abidin, 1995). Test-retest reliability was reported at .63 for child domain, .91 for parent domain, and .96 for total stress scores over one to three months (Abidin, 1995).

PARTICIPANT SELECTION

Parents of children from two Head Start/pre-kindergarten schools and one Title I elementary school were recruited for this study. I recruited potential participants during school events such as registration, open house, and "Meet the Teacher" night. Knowing many parents were unable to attend the aforementioned school events, I also recruited parents during morning drop-off and afternoon pick-up times at participating schools through the distribution of flyers highlighting the potential benefits of CPRT. In the case of Kim, she became aware of the training opportunity through a CPRT promotion flyer, which included a visual representation of an African American family, that was distributed through her son's classroom teacher.

To qualify for the study, parents had to report either borderline or clinical range scores (Achenbach & Rescorla, 2000) on at least one of the seven syndrome scales of the CBCL. As a result, a total of 31 parents qualified and consented to participate in the study. All participants identified themselves and their children as Black American or African American with reported household income falling within the U.S. Department of Health and Human Services (2007) poverty guidelines.

Parents were randomly assigned to the experimental or control group (16 and 15, respectively). During treatment group assignment, it came to my attention that four participants were unable to attend the scheduled CPRT time because of their work schedules. Rather than omit these parents from the study because of their work priorities, I wanted to provide these parents another opportunity to participate in the training by placing them in the control group. The remaining parents were randomly drawn to participate in the experimental or control group. Of the 31 total participants, 4 parents did not complete the study (4 control) because of geographic relocation or for reasons unknown because of disconnected phone numbers (Sheely-Moore & Bratton, in press). Although 27 parents completed the study (16 experimental, 11 control), 4 parents were identified as outliers (3 experimental, 1 control) and were removed from data analysis due to reported extreme life events. Hence, 23 parents (13 experimental, 10 control) were utilized for data analysis.

Males represented a smaller portion of the sample than women for both groups (1 experimental, 1 control). Parents assigned to the experimental group ranged in ages from 25 to 38, with a mean of 29.5 years. The children of the parents assigned to the experimental group ranged in ages from 3 to 5, with a mean of 4.4 years. Parents assigned to the control group ranged in ages from 24 to 50, with a mean of 32.2 years. The children of the parents assigned to the control group ranged in ages from 3 to 6, with a mean of 4.0 years.

TREATMENT

Experimental Treatment Group   Parents assigned to the experimental group participated in CPRT training and supervision over 11 weeks. Based on Guerney's (1969) previous work, Landreth (2002) created a time-limited model of filial therapy in response to parent attrition rates for filial trainings that exceeded 10 sessions. Landreth and Bratton (2006) formalized the 10-session filial therapy model within their textbook and termed the model *Child Parent Relationship Therapy* (CPRT). Grounded in person-centered therapy, CPRT reflects a strengths-based approach by using play to facilitate parents' understanding of their child's world (Landreth & Bratton, 2006). Training and supervision followed the CPRT 10-session manualized protocol (Bratton, Landreth, Kellam, & Blackard, 2006) with minor adaptations to address the tendency of African Americans underusing mental health services (Boyd-Franklin, 2003; Parham & Parham, 2002; Parham et al., 1999; Solis et al., 2004; Sue, 1977). Specifically, to decrease the likelihood of stigma related to mental health services and the possibility of early termination of counseling services, I extended the 10-week CPRT program into 11 weeks.

With the additional training session, an extra hour was allotted for parent questions during the initial meeting in order to facilitate trust and openness with the group facilitators. The additional hour within the first meeting also provided the opportunity for group members to hear results of the CPRT training from an African American parent who had completed the training. The seasoned parent shared her initial speculations regarding the CPRT model and shared examples of positive changes as a result of the training. The remaining hour from the extended 11-week session also provided an extra check-in time at the beginning of the remaining meetings to provide an opportunity for parents to connect and provide social support related to reported stressors (Sheely-Moore & Bratton, in press).

The training format included 11 weekly two-hour meetings. The first three meetings of CPRT focused on teaching parents the foundations of child-centered play therapy. Through didactic instruction and role-play, parents learned skills such as tracking and reflective listening to communicate genuine interest, empathy, and understanding to their child. Furthermore, parents learned alternative discipline approaches that included limit setting and choice giving. After the third meeting, parents conducted 30-minute play sessions with their child at home for seven sessions. These play sessions were videotaped so parents could receive specific feedback through the completion of a skills checklist during the remaining group meetings, as well as to ensure treatment integrity (Sheely-Moore & Bratton, in press).

In light of the myriad of challenges faced by families living in poverty, several accommodations were made on the basis of efforts to increase the likelihood for parents to complete the training. For example, to accommodate parents' work schedules, I scheduled all group meeting in the evening with free child care and complimentary dinner provided during the meeting times. A typical group session would begin with parents dropping off their children in the adjacent room where they were monitored during the two-hour training session. Parents would arrange dinner plates for their children and deliver to the adjacent room and immediately return to the group room to set their own dinner plate before the start of the group meeting. Furthermore, to reduce the financial burden on these families, toy kits and video equipment were lent to parents so they could complete their play sessions at home.

I served as one of the treatment providers. At the time of the study, I was an advanced doctoral counseling student. CPRT training and supervision were also provided by an African American female, master's-level counselor. Together, we both had extensive training and supervised experience in play therapy, filial therapy, and CPRT methodology. All training meetings were videotaped for supervisory purposes. To ensure treatment integrity, supervision was provided by Sue Bratton, co-author of the CPRT textbook and treatment manual (Bratton, Landreth et al., 2006; Landreth & Bratton, 2006).

No-Treatment Control Group Parents assigned to the control group received no treatment during the study. Parents assigned to the control group were provided an opportunity to receive treatment after completion of the study.

DATA COLLECTION

Parental consent was obtained before data collection. Serving as data collector, I administered the CBCL and PSI before treatment and again upon completion of treatment. I was present during all data collection to answer questions and ensure consistency in data collection. To ensure integrity of data collection, all parents completed documents in a monitored environment, free from distractions. Free child care services were provided while parents completed the instruments.

DATA ANALYSIS

I wanted to know if there would be a difference in pre-test and post-test scores on the CBCL and PSI for parents who participated in CPRT compared to those parents who did not receive the treatment. Hence, a two-group repeated measures multivariate analysis of covariance (MANCOVA) was selected to analyze the effectiveness of CPRT on children's behavior and parent-child relationship stress after controlling for pre-treatment differences in family structure. To examine possible changes, my dependent measures included pre- and post-test CBCL ratings from the externalizing, internalizing, and total problems scales and the pre- and post-test PSI ratings from the overall total stress scores (Sheely-Moore & Bratton, in press). All assumptions for a two-group repeated measures MANCOVA were met for the CBLC and PSI. Four cases were removed as outliers (three experimental, one control) on the CBCL pre-test and PSI pre-test, respectfully, because of reported extreme life events that could confound results (Sheely-Moore & Bratton, in press). Partial η^2 were calculated to assess how much of a difference the treatment had on the parents who participated in CPRT (Kazdin, 1999). The following guidelines proposed by Cohen (1988) were used to interpret partial η^2: .01 = small, .06 = medium, and .14 = large.

RESULTS

The results of the two-group repeated measures MANCOVA indicate a statistically significant difference between the treatment group and the control group on the combined dependent variables, $F(2, 19) =$ 8.257, $p = .003$, partial $\eta^2 = .47$ (Sheely-Moore & Bratton, in press). After controlling for pretreatment differences in single-parent and two-parent family structures, univariate analyses of covariance (ANCOVAs) were performed to examine differences between the groups on each dependent variable. The ANCOVA results for total problems indicated statistically significant results, $F(1, 22) = 5.075$, $p < .036$ (Sheely-Moore & Bratton); that is, parents who participated in CPRT, regardless of family structure, were more likely to report decreases in total problems than those who did not participate in the treatment. Findings further indicated that the effects of the CPRT intervention on the dependent variable, total problems, were large (partial $\eta^2 = .20$). Results of the ANCOVA of the dependent variables, externalizing problem and internalizing problems, were not found to be statistically significant from pre- to post-treatment when compared to the no-treatment control group (Sheely-Moore & Bratton).

Statistically significant ANCOVA results were found for the dependent variable, total stress of the PSI (Sheely-Moore & Bratton, in press). The results indicate that after controlling for family structure, the parents in the CPRT group reported a statistically significant decrease in total stress from pre- to post-treatment when compared to the control group, $F(1, 22) = 17.121$, $p < .001$ (Sheely-Moore & Bratton). The strength of the association between CPRT and dependent variable, total stress, was large, with a partial $\eta^2 = .46$.

DISCUSSION

Results from this study provide support for the CPRT model as a viable treatment modality to reduce parent-child relationship stress and to ameliorate child behavior problems for low-income African American families. The following is a discussion of implications when working with this population.

CPRT Effects on Behavioral Problems

Child Behavior Outcomes for Total Problems   *Total problems* consists of a combination of externalizing and internalizing problems that children express. The majority of children in this study demonstrated elevated scores in both externalizing and internalizing domains. *Externalizing behavior problems* are difficulties that children express outwardly toward others (Achenbach & Rescorla, 2000). In the case of Kim, she reported externalizing problems such as demandingness and defiancy for her 5-year-old son. Using child-centered play therapy skills during the 30-minute play session might attribute to the statistical and practical significance of findings for total problems, which includes externalizing problems. Specifically, engaging in the weekly 30-minute play session might have resulted in parents' increased ability to respond to their child's needs in a positive manner. Further, parents' heightened degree of sensitivity and understanding of their child's world could result in increased ability for children to express themselves fully and reduce the need to act out in order to satisfy their needs. Because of the stability of parenting behavior across one's life span, Collins, Gyamfi, Brooks-Gunn, and Blake (2000) postulated an accumulating effect of parenting practices that continue through adolescent years. The CPRT model serves as a promising treatment to mitigate externalizing behavior problems for young children and, if left untreated, potential long-term consequences, such as depression, drug abuse, juvenile delinquency, and violence (Webster-Stratton & Reid, 2003).

Internalizing behavior problems are difficulties that children express within themselves, rather than physically acting them out toward others. These behaviors include somatic complaints, anxiety, and depression (Achenbach & Rescorla, 2000). In the case of Kim, despite the lack of statistical significance for findings on the CBCL's internalizing problems scale from pre-test to post-test, the results may in part be explained by the parents increased or decreased level of sensitivity related by accurate identification of internalizing problems.

The statistical and practical significance of findings for CPRT's effects on total behavior problems are particularly noteworthy because the majority of qualifying children displayed clinical-to-borderline levels of concern on multiple subscales of the CBCL (Sheely-Moore & Bratton, in press). With the reported difficulty in making a single diagnosis for young children (Achenbach & Rescorla, 2000), this study supports the idea that young children present with a multiple range of behavioral concerns. Hence, treatments such as the CPRT model, which are responsive to young children's overall behavior problems, serves to mitigate potential long-term behavioral consequences (Sheely-Moore & Bratton).

CPRT EFFECTS ON PARENT-CHILD RELATIONSHIP STRESS

As a result of participation in CPRT, African American parents reported a statistically significant decrease on the total stress of the

PSI, which is combined score of the child domain and parent domain. In the case of Kim, her reported child domain score reduced from clinical status at pre-test to nonclinical status at post-test. It can be speculated that the CPRT curriculum emphasis on increasing parental empathy and normalizing parent concerns regarding their child's developmental level could have positively affected parents' ability to accept their child, thus, resulting in the significant decrease on the total stress score. Furthermore, through the acquisition of child-centered play therapy skills and an increased level of parental competence, it can be postulated that engaging in parent-child play sessions positively affected the child's behavior in addition to improving parent-child relationship stress related to the child's behavior.

The statistical and practical significance of the findings for CPRT's effects on the total stress score of the PSI is noteworthy in light of research indicating a positive correlation between stress and negative parenting styles for those families living in poverty (Bluestone & Tamis-LeMonda, 1999; Deater-Deckard & Dodge, 1997). More emphasis on the supportive group format may have served as a factor in the reported improvement in reported stress within the total stress score of the PSI.

African Americans tend to seek support from their nuclear and extended family in times of struggle (Boyd-Franklin, 2003; Drewes, 2005; Glover, 2001; Kerl, 2001; Hines & Boyd-Franklin, 2005; Parham & Parham, 2002; Parham et al., 1999). The importance of the supportive group setting appeared to be particularly meaningful in the delivery of CPRT for African American parents. In the case of Kim, lacking an extended family for support, she reported a strong connection with group members. Additional parents reported strong connections and an increased level of comfort with other group members because of their shared experiences as low-income African Americans, as indicated by one parent:

> Our families may have issues that could be considered like a hardship that we may not feel so comfortable sharing with other people that aren't in our ethnicity, but since we all have them, we're all poor . . . that's one thing that's irrelevant. It's not an issue that we have to address or explain; it's just understood.

These similarities appeared to have facilitated an extended sense of family, in which parents seemed particularly open to share their struggles as parents. This level of personal disclosure within the CPRT training served to increase the level of acceptance and cohesion within the group. It can be postulated that as the level of acceptance between the group members increased, the more accepting they were of themselves (Sheely, 2008). Hence, it is plausible that as a result of feeling supported and accepted, levels of reported parent-child stress were reduced.

RECOMMENDATIONS

One of the major contributions of the present study is that it appears to be the first to empirically examine the effects of CPRT with low-income African American families (Landreth & Bratton, 2006). In fact, an exhaustive review of the literature in the broader field of play therapy revealed no outcome studies with this targeted population. However, more work remains to be done when examining the effectiveness of CPRT with African American families.

One of the main limitations to my study was the small sample size, which limits the generalizability of the results. I anticipate reading replications of this study using the same CPRT protocol with a larger sample size. In addition to a larger sample size, I would also recommend future research to target African Americans across the socioeconomic strata, with more male representation within the sample group.

Based upon the results of this study, recommendations for future research should entail conducting follow-up studies to determine long-term effects of CPRT for participating parents and their children. For example, I wonder if the reported results for the CBCL and PSI at post-testing remained consistent for Kim and her son after six months or even a year. Another setback to the study involves the use of parents as the source of data collection, which may have introduced a degree of bias. Using multiple sources of measurement of children's behavior change, such as teacher reports and direct observations by trained professionals, to measure the impact of CPRT would add to the confidence of findings (Sheely-Moore & Bratton, in press).

In closing, my final recommendation to future research reflects back to my initial phone conversation with Kim. As one of the treatment providers and also a person of color, I observed the benefit of ethnic match of treatment providers and parent participants serving as a factor in parents' decision to participate in CPRT. Additional studies examining intracultural sensitivity through the use of treatment providers of similar ethnic background to lessen the stigma of mental health care services for African Americans are warranted. As mental health professionals trained in filial therapy such as the CPRT model, we need to reassure parents such as Kim that we will not focus on what is wrong; we will focus instead on what is effective and will empower parents through sharing additional strategies in efforts to create a closer bond with their child.

REFERENCES

Abidin, R. R. (1995). *Parenting stress index: Professional manual.* Lutz, FL: Psychological Assessment Resources.

Achenbach, T. M., & Rescorla, L. A. (2000). Manual for the ASEBA preschool forms & profiles. Burlington, VT: University of Vermont, Research Center for Children, Youth, & Families.

Baggerly, J., & Parker, M. (2005). Child-centered group play therapy with African American boys at the elementary school level. *Journal of Counseling and Development, 83,* 387–396.

Bluestone, C., & Tamis-LeMonda, C. S. (1999). Correlates of parenting style in predominantly working- and middle-class African American mothers. *Journal of Marriage and the Family, 61,* 881–893.

Boyd-Franklin, N. (2003). *Black families in therapy: Understanding the African American experience* (2nd ed.). New York: Guilford.

Bratton, S. C., Landreth, G. L., Kellam, T., & Blackard, S. (2006). *Child parent relationship therapy (CPRT) treatment manual: A 10-session filial therapy model for training parents.* New York: Routledge.

Bratton, S. C., Ray, D. C., Rhine, T., & Jones, L. (2005). The efficacy of play therapy with children: A meta-analytic review of treatment outcomes. *Professional Psychology: Research and Practice, 36*(4), 376–390.

Cohen, J. (1988). *Statistical power analysis for the behavioral sciences* (2nd ed.). New York: Academic Press.

Collins, W. A., Gyamfi, P., Brooks-Gunn, J., & Blake, M. (2000). Contemporary research on parenting: The case for nature and nurture. *American Psychologist, 55*(2), 218–232.

Deater-Deckard, K., & Dodge, K. A. (1997). Externalizing behavior problems and discipline revisited: Nonlinear effects and variation by culture, context, and gender. *Psychological Inquiry, 8*(3), 161–175.

Drewes, A. A. (2005). Suggestions and research on multicultural play therapy. In E. Gil & A. A. Drewes (Eds.), *Cultural issues in play therapy* (pp. 72–95). New York: Guilford.

Gibbons, F., Yeh, H., Gerrard, M., Cleveland, M., Cutrona, C., Simons, R., et al. (2007). Early experience with racial discrimination and conduct disorder as predictors of subsequent drug use: A critical period hypothesis. *Drug and Alcohol Dependence, 88,* 27–37.

Glover, G. J. (2001). Cultural considerations in play therapy. In G. L. Landreth (Ed.), *Innovations in play therapy* (pp. 31–41). Philadelphia: Taylor & Francis.

Guerney, B. (1969). *Psychotherapeutic agents: New roles for nonprofessionals, parents, and teachers*. New York: Holt, Rinehart, & Winston.

Harrison, P. M., & Beck, A. J. (2005). *Bureau of Justice statistics bulletin: Prison and jail inmates at midyear 2004*. Retrieved March 12, 2007, from http://www.ojp.usdoj.gov/bjs/pub/pdf/pjim04.pdf

Hines, P. M., & Boyd-Franklin, N. (2005). African American families. In M. McGoldrick, J. Giordano, & N. Garcia-Preto (Eds.), *Ethnicity and family therapy* (pp. 87–100). New York: Guilford.

Jackson, A. P., Gyamfi, P., Brooks-Gunn, J., & Blake, M. (1998). Employment status, psychological well-being, social support, and physical discipline practice of single African mothers. *Journal of Marriage and the Family, 60*, 894–902.

Kazdin, A. E. (1999). The meanings and measurement of clinical significance. *Journal of Counseling and Clinical Psychology, 67*, 332–339.

Kerl, S. (2001). Working with African American children. *Association for Play Therapy Newsletter, 20*(1), 25.

Landreth, G. L., (2002). *Play therapy: The art of the relationship* (2nd ed.). New York: Brunner-Routledge.

Landreth, G. L., & Bratton, S. C. (2006). *Child parent relationship therapy: A 10-session filial therapy model*. New York: Routledge.

McKinnon, J. (2003). *The African population in the United States: March 2002*. U.S. Census Bureau, Current Population Reports, Series P20-541. Washington, DC. Retrieved March 12, 2007, from http://www.census.gov/prod/2003pubs/p20-541.pdf

National Center for Education Statistics. (2003, April). Status and trends in the education of Blacks. Retrieved January 10, 2009, from http://nces.ed.gov/pubs2003/2003034.pdf

Parham, T. A., & Parham, W. D. (2002). Understanding African American mental health: The necessity of new conceptual paradigms. In T. A. Parham (Ed.), *Counseling persons of African descent: Raising the bar of practitioner competence* (pp. 25–37). Thousands Oaks, CA: Sage.

Parham, T. A., White, J. L., & Ajamu, A. (1999). *The psychology of Africans: An African-centered perspective*. Upper Saddle River, NJ: Prentice-Hall.

Pinderhughes, E., Nix, R., Foster, E., Jones, D., Bierman, K., Coie, J., et al. (2001). Parenting in context: Impact of neighborhood poverty, residential stability, public services, social networks, and danger on parental behaviors. *Journal of Marriage and Family, 63*(4), 941–954.

Ray, D. C., Bratton, S. C., Rhine, T., & Jones, L. (2001). The effectiveness of play therapy: Responding to the critics. *International Journal of Play Therapy, 10*(1), 85–108.

Sheely, A. (2008). *School-based child parent relationship therapy (CPRT) with low-income Black American parents: Effects on children's behaviors and parent-child relationship stress, a pilot study* (Doctoral dissertation). Retrieved from http://digital.library.unt.edu/data/etd/2008_1/open/meta-dc-6053.tkl

Sheely-Moore, A., & Bratton, S. C. (in press). A strengths-based parenting intervention with low-income African American families. *Professional School Counseling.*

Slater, M. A., & Power, T. (1987). Multidimensional assessment of parenting in single-parent families. *Advances in Family Intervention, Assessment, and Theory, 4*, 197–228.

Solis, C., Meyers, J., & Varjas, K. M. (2004). A qualitative case study on the process and impact of filial therapy with an African American parent. *International Journal of Play Therapy, 13*, 99–118.

Sue, S. (1977). Community mental health services to minority groups: Some optimism, some pessimism. *American Psychologist, 32*(8), 616–624.

U.S. Department of Health and Human Services. (2007). *Federal Register, 72* (15), 3147–3148.

Webster-Stratton, C., & Reid, M. J. (2003). The incredible years parents, teachers, and children training services: A multifaceted treatment approach for young children with conduct problems. In A. E. Kazdin & J. R. Weisz (Eds.), *Evidence-based psychotherapies for children and adolescents* (pp. 224–240). New York: Guilford.

CHAPTER 20

Child Parent Relationship Therapy with Hispanic Parents

PEGGY CEBALLOS

I didn't tell you before because I was too embarrassed, but before we started the training I was feeling so overwhelmed and frustrated that I had gotten to the point to where I looked at my child's eyes and told him I hated him; and eleven weeks later, last night, we were hugging each other and I was telling him how much I love him. . . . This training changed our lives. (Rebeca, 33-year-old Latina mother)

In my work with immigrant Latino families, I have come face-to-face with many parents like Rebeca, who are experiencing a high level of stress from trying to cope with adverse social factors in their life—stress that is negatively affecting their relationship with their child.

Parenting is recognized as a powerful influence on children's emotional, social, and cognitive development (Ryan & Bratton, 2008; Thompson, 2002). The lack of a secure attachment between parent and child has been linked to long-term negative effects for children's academic success and to behavioral and mental health problems (Knitzer, 2000). Yet, risk factors faced by many minority groups have a negative effect on the parent-child relationship (Bamara, Umana-Taylor, Shin, & Alfaro, 2005; Burton, & Jarrett, 2000; Knitzer, 2000).

Latinos represent the largest and the fastest-growing minority group in the United States, and this ethnic group is projected to represent 30 percent of the U.S. population by the year 2050 (U.S. Census, 2008). More important, the National Center for Education Statistics (NCES;

2003) reported that the number of Latino children is increasing faster than any other ethnic group and estimated that by the year 2020 one in every five children under the age of 18 will be of Latino origin. Statistics show that Latino children face numerous at-risk factors, such as poverty (U.S. Census, 2005), low parental educational level (National Center for Children in Poverty, 2002), exposure to violence (U.S. Department of Health and Human Services, 2004), and English as a second language (NCES).

Rebeca, a single mother in my study on the effects of Child Parent Relationship Therapy (CPRT; Landreth & Bratton, 2006) with Latino parents, was struggling with many of the adverse factors named here. She presented with concerns about her child's behavior and reported very high levels of stress in the parent-child relationship. She had recently immigrated to the United States, had a third-grade educational level, and struggled with speaking English. Her only income came from cleaning houses. She struggled on a daily basis to survive economically. The stress caused by her living situation had become so overwhelming that she was emotionally unavailable to her son, Antonio. Rebeca reported that she started to use harsh discipline once Antonio started having behavioral problems at school. The school counselor referred Rebeca to participate in the CPRT group as a last attempt to help her and her child. The school counselor described Rebeca as being defensive toward school personnel and as lacking a sense of responsibility for her child's behavioral problems. It was reported that Antonio was hitting others, cursing, and constantly engaging in power struggles with his teacher. According to the school counselor, Rebeca refused to seek mental health services outside of the school, even though an affordable referral had been given to her.

My experience of Rebeca and the impact her level of stress was having on Antonio mirrored what I had learned from the literature. Parental stress has been associated with negative dynamics in the parent-child dyad and with an increase in child problem behaviors (Deater-Deckard, 1998; Kazdin & Whitley, 2003). Hughes and Barad (1983) explained that mothers under stress become more easily frustrated with their children's problem behaviors. Like Rebeca, all of the parents who participated in my study were immigrants who struggled with English as a second language, dealt with the acculturation process, lived at or below the poverty level, and experienced discrimination. The effects of these at-risk factors on these families were noticeable in children's display of externalized and internalized behavioral problems and in the high degree of parental stress that these parents reported before starting CPRT.

Reaching out to the Latino population to offer mental health services is challenging. This population tends to underuse counseling services because of such factors as:

- Lack of transportation
- Lack of culturally responsive interventions
- Latinos' preference to use folk medicine and close family members as a source to solve emotional problems
- Lack of trust in institutions and people from outside their culture because of experiences of being discriminated against
- Language barriers (Andres-Hyman, Ortiz, Anes, Paris, & Davidson, 2006; Altbach, 1991; La Roche, 1999; Padilla, Ruiz, & Alvarez, 1975; Santiago-Rivera, 1995).

Mental health providers and school systems often fail to acknowledge these intervening variables, and the end result can be a negative relationship with Latino parents characterized by defensiveness, as was the case with Rebeca. For example, in her case, it was not that she refused to seek mental health services outside of the school; it was her economic situation, mistrust of institutions, and lack of transportation that made it difficult for her to follow through with the referrals.

To respond to the underuse of services by Latino families and to prevent Latino children from continuing a cycle of negative outcomes, mental health providers must actively look for ways to reach out to this population through proven strategies. Because many Latino families face at-risk factors in society that leave them feeling helpless, it is imperative to find strength-based treatments that focus on empowering parents. CPRT is a strengths-based treatment that empowers parents to become therapeutic agents in their children's lives. In addition, CPRT focuses on creating a nonjudgmental, understanding, and accepting environment that enhances the parent-child relationship, which can help mitigate risk factors faced by Latino children.

CPRT is a 10-session format of filial therapy in which a play therapist trains parents in a didactic and supportive group format to use child-centered principles with their children during weekly structured 30-minute play sessions (Landreth & Bratton, 2006). Bratton, Landreth, Kellum, & Blackard (2006) published a manual that outlines the 10-session CPRT treatment protocol. Literature on Latino values in relation to mental health services supports the use of CPRT with this population. Researchers have stressed the need to render services that are family oriented when working with Latinos because of their value of *familismo* (Vlach, 2002); thus CPRT, which works with the family unit instead of working only with the child, is well suited for Latinos. CPRT, based on child-centered theory, works from a humanistic approach, which has been recognized as culturally responsive to various cultural groups because it provides clients with a nonjudgmental, accepting attitude (Bailey & Bradbury-Bailey, 2007; Cochran, 1996; Constantine, 2001). For these reasons and because of my previous success using a person-centered and child-centered approach with Latino families, I chose to conduct an outcome research study to investigate the effectiveness of CPRT on reducing problem behaviors of Latino children identified as at risk for not achieving academic success. My study also sought to investigate the effectiveness of CPRT on reducing parental stress.

METHODOLOGY AND PROCEDURES

To study the effectiveness of CPRT with low-income Latino immigrant parents whose children were experiencing behavioral problems, this study used a two group by two repeated measures, control group design (Ceballos & Bratton, in press). The study was conducted in two school districts with similar demographics of Latino children and families. After obtaining permission from the principals at each of the participating schools, I recruited participants by attending Spanish-speaking parenting meetings at the beginning of the school year as they registered for preschool programs and attended open house meetings for elementary schools and Head Start programs. During these meetings, I explained the purpose of the study and qualifying criteria to the parents. I also collaborated with school personnel such as school counselors and teachers to recruit additional participants for the study. Because Latinos tend to underuse mental health services (La Roche, 1999; Andres-Hyman et al., 2006), it was important to reach out to participants through school personnel who had already established relationships with them. This helped me to overcome the barrier of mistrust that Latinos have toward mental health services.

I met with parents who consented to participate during school days to collect data. I arranged to have a private room at each of the sites and for child care services to be offered to ensure that parents were free from distractions while completing assessments. To encourage participation of parents with low reading skills, parents were given the choice of completing the surveys themselves or having me read to them and mark their answers. The following criteria had to be met to qualify for the study (Ceballos & Bratton, in press):

- Parents were Latino immigrants living at or below poverty level as qualified by the U.S. Department of Health and Human Services (2007) guidelines.
- Parents reported Spanish as the primary language used at home.
- Children scored at borderline or clinical level on internalizing, externalizing, and total problem scale of the Spanish version of the parent Child Behavior Checklist (CBCL).

Parents who met the criteria were contacted to fill out the Spanish version of the PSI.

PARTICIPANTS

Of the 200 parents who responded and were assessed, 62 parents qualified and were randomly assigned by school site to the treatment or the control group. Forty-eight parents completed the study, with 24 participants in the CPRT treatment group and 24 in the control group. Demographics for both, the experimental and the control groups, were similar for participating children and parents (Ceballos & Bratton, in press). In the experimental group, 13 male and 11 female children, with an average age of 4.12 participated whereas for the control group, 14 males and 10 females with a mean age of 4.42 participated. All of the participating parents were females except for one male in the experimental group. Parents in the experimental group had an average age of 30, while the mean age of parents in the control group was 29. The sample for both groups was largely representative of parents born in Mexico with eight participants from South America and Central America.

MEASUREMENTS

For this study, using assessments that were available in Spanish and that had an established reliability and validity with a Latino population was imperative. Thus, the Spanish version of the 1½-to-5-year-old Parent-Child Behavior Checklist (CBCL; Achenbach & Rescorla, 2000) and the Spanish version of the Parenting Stress Index (PSI; Abidin, 1995) were selected (Ceballos & Bratton, in press). The CBCL has an established reliability ($r = .85$) and a strong content validity. Furthermore, a study conducted by Gross, Fogg, and Young (2006) found that the Spanish version of the CBCL was reliable and valid with Latino populations. The PSI has established reliability coefficients for each of the subscales: Parent domain ranges from .69 and .91, child domain ranges from .55 and .82, and total stress ranges from .65 to .96. The Spanish version of the PSI was validated in one study carried by Solis and Abidin in 1991. For the purpose of this study, data were analyzed for the three main scales in the CBCL: internalizing problems, externalizing problems, and total problems. Similarly, the three main scales of the PSI were analyzed: parent domain, child domain, and total stress. None of the subscales in either one of the assessments was used for statistical analysis.

CPRT TREATMENT GROUP

Parents who were randomly assigned to the treatment group participated in CPRT groups. All procedures were followed as stated in the CPRT treatment manual (Bratton et al., 2006). To make the treatment culturally responsive for Latino populations, an additional session was added; thus, as recommended by Powell, Zambrana, and Silva-Palacios (1990), the first session was designed for parents to socialize with each other (Ceballos & Bratton, in press). Importantly, to address the language barrier, all materials and training were offered in Spanish. To this end, the parent handbook found in the CPRT manual was translated to Spanish. To encourage consistent participation and to decrease the likelihood of dropping out, I offered the groups the times and days that the parents reported worked best for them. Additionally, parents attended groups at the schools where their children attended. Both strategies seemed to minimize absences due to conflicts in schedule or transportation problems. Similarly, child care was offered for free, as many parents indicated that without such service they could not attend the groups. All parents were offered the opportunity to check out filial kits and video cameras to conduct and record their seven play sessions at home, or they could choose to do it at the school in designated play rooms (Ceballos & Bratton, in press). As the only Spanish speaker on the research team trained in CPRT, I led a total of five groups with an average of five to seven parents once a week for two hours. Parents' play sessions were supervised during group meetings as explained in the treatment manual to ensure parents' skills attainment.

CONTROL GROUP

The no-treatment control group was offered the opportunity to partici-pate in CPRT at the end of the study (Ceballos & Bratton, in press). Thus, I led five CPRT groups after completion of the study to provide treatment to parents in the control group and any parents who did not originally qualify for the study but wanted to participate. For these groups, I followed the same procedures and curriculum that I did for the experimental group.

RESULTS

After examining data to ensure they met all assumptions, a two group by two repeated measures, split plot ANOVA was conducted for all dependent variables. Dependent variables included the CBCL ratings for externalizing problems, internalizing problems, and total problems scales and the PSI ratings for child domain, parent domain, and total stress. Results for all dependent variables were interpreted using Pillai's trace analysis. To avoid a Type I error resulting from the testing of multiple hypotheses, a .025 alpha level was established to either reject or accept hypotheses. The CBCL and PSI were administered before treatment and at the end of treatment. A reduction in scores on the CBCL and PSI scales indicated improvement in the targeted behavior. Partial eta squared effect sizes were calculated to assess the magnitude of difference between the two groups and to better understand the practi-cal significance of the study (Kazdin, 1999). The following guidelines proposed by Cohen (1988) were used to interpret effect size: $.01 = $ small, $.06 = $ medium, and $.14 = $ large.

Results indicated that from pre-test to post-test all dependent var-iables on the CBCL revealed a statistically significant interaction effect of time (pre-test, post-test) by group membership (experimental, con-trol). Results were reported as follows (Ceballos & Bratton, in press): internalizing problems scale, Pillai's trace $= .56$, $F(1, 46) = 58.75$, $p < .001$ with a large treatment effect ($\varepsilon_p^2 = .56$); externalizing problem scale, Pillai's trace $= .59$, $F(1, 46) = 66.42$, $p < .001$ with a large treatment effect ($\varepsilon_p^2 = .59$); and total problem scale, Pillai's trace $= .67$, $F(1, 46) = 95.43$, $p < .001$ with a large treatment effect ($\varepsilon_p^2 = .68$). These results indicated that from pre-test to post-test, parents who participated in CPRT reported a statistically significant decrease in their children's internalized, externalized, and total problem behaviors.

Results for the dependent variables on the PSI indicated a statisti-cally significant interaction effect of time (pre-test, post-test) by group membership (experimental, control). Results were as follows: for the child domain, Pillai's trace = .39, $F(1, 46) = 29.95$, $p < .001$ with a large treatment effect ($\varepsilon_p^2 = .39$); for the parent domain, Pillai's trace = .52, F $(1, 46) = 49.10$, $p < .001$ with a large treatment effect ($\varepsilon_p^2 = .52$); and for the total stress (Ceballos & Bratton, in press), Pillai's trace = .42, $F(1, 46) = 33.12$, $p < .001$ with a large treatment effect ($\varepsilon_p^2 = .42$). These results indicated that from pre-test to post-test, parents who participated in CPRT reported a statistically significant decrease in their stress in the child domain, parent domain, and total stress of the PSI.

In summary, a statistically significant reduction ($p < .001$) from pre-test to post-test was found for all dependent variables as reported by parents in the CBCL and PSI. In addition, clinical significance was assessed by determining the number of experimental children (n = 24) and parents (n = 24) who moved from clinical or borderline levels of concern at pre-testing into the normal range of functioning following treatment. The analysis of the clinical significance for each scale as well as a discussion of the statistical results is provided next.

DISCUSSION

INTERNALIZED PROBLEM BEHAVIORS

Analysis of the clinical significance revealed that of the 20 children demonstrating clinical or borderline levels of internalizing problems before treatment, 17 (85 percent) moved into the normal range of functioning after their parents participated in CPRT (Ceballos & Bratton, in press). Achenbach and Rescorla (2000) defined the internalizing problems scale on the CBCL form as consisting of children's behavioral problems measured through the emotionally reactive, anxious or depressed, somatic complaints, and withdrawn scales.

In the case of Rebeca's son, Antonio, the pre-test CBCL revealed that he scored at the clinical level of concern on internalizing problems, with somatic complaints and withdrawn as being the highest scales. At the end of treatment, Rebeca reported a dramatic decrease on these symptoms, and the post-test scores revealed that her son scored at the normal range on internalizing problems. Rebeca explained that before the training she rarely spent time playing with her son, and she did not pay close attention to how her son was feeling. She said that as she started practicing reflection of feelings, she noticed an increase in her sensitivity to recognize her child's frustration and anger. This, in turn, helped her to become less frustrated; instead of reacting, she was able to respond more empathically to her son's needs. She believed that this decreased his anxiety and increased his ability to verbalize his own feelings. Other parents in the groups reported similar changes in their relationships with their children.

Research and statistics show a high level of depression for Latino youth compared to youth from other ethnic groups (Multicultural and International Outreach Center, 2002; Twenge & Nolen-Hoeksema, 2002). Crean (2008) found that parental support is negatively correlated to internalizing problems for Latino youth. The author reported that high levels of parental support appeared to be a protective force toward the development of internalized problems for this population. CPRT focuses on strengthening the parent-child relationship, thus increasing parental support, which could explain the reasons for the results on this study. Additionally, CPRT teaches parents to be sensitive and to respond to children's feelings through the use of skills such as reflection of feelings and through enhancing parents' understanding of children's development (Ceballos & Bratton, in press).

EXTERNALIZED PROBLEM BEHAVIORS

The externalizing problem scale on the CBCL assesses children's behaviors such as attention deficit and aggression (Achenbach & Rescorla, 2000). Clinical significance showed that 15 of the 17 children (88 percent) whose parents reported pre-treatment externalizing behavior problems in the clinical to borderline range improved to normal levels of concern following CPRT (Ceballos & Bratton, in press).

Rebeca's son scored above the 97th percentile on the externalized scale of the CBCL before treatment, indicating he was at the clinical range, particularly on the aggressive behavior scale. During the exit interview, Rebeca said that learning the skills for limit setting and choice giving were essential in helping her to decrease power struggles with her son. She also said that as she practiced these skills, she noticed her son increased his ability to express anger in more appropriate ways. For example, toward the end of the training, episodes during which he threw objects around when he got angry in the house and at school had significantly decreased. She said she worked on giving him better choices to express anger such as tearing paper or drawing his anger. She recognized that an important factor for this change was her ability to be consistent in the way she applied limit setting and choice giving with him. According to Rebeca, prior to CPRT, she typically reacted to her son's anger by screaming and spanking him. She reported that her punishments were inconsistent and mostly depended on her level of stress at the time, which was generally high. Through CPRT, she learned the importance of being in control and being consistent in her response when her son became aggressive.

Across all five CPRT groups, parents reported the impact of applying limit setting and choice giving on their ability to better deal with children's misbehaviors. They all recognized that being able to empathize with their children's feelings while being firm on the limits helped reduce externalized behaviors. The findings that CPRT can help reduce externalized behaviors in young at-risk Latino children are encouraging because of literature suggesting that externalizing behavior problems are particularly resistant to treatment (Hinshaw, 1992). Furthermore, aggression in young children has been associated with the development of more serious problems during adolescence such as juvenile delinquency (Webster-Stratton & Reid, 2003). Because Latino youth are over-represented in the juvenile system (Multicultural and International Outreach Center, 2002), finding treatments that can prevent the development of more significant problems is imperative (Ceballos & Bratton, in press).

Total Problem Behaviors

Clinical significance revealed that 90 percent of the children moved from the clinical or borderline levels of concern to the normal range of functioning following CPRT (Ceballos & Bratton, in press). These findings are important given the co-morbidity of behavioral symptoms for young children (Achenbach & Rescorla, 2000). Consistent with this view, the majority of parents in the study reported their children exhibited behavioral problems in both the internalizing and the externalizing scales. Interventions that are responsive to multiple symptomology in young children offer promise as an answer to addressing the child's holistic needs (Ceballos & Bratton, in press). Rebeca reported a decrease of 15 points from pre-test to post-test in her son's total problem scale on the CBCL. This decrease moved Antonio from the clinical range to the normal range after treatment. Rebecca reported that following CPRT she experienced a change in her son's overall demeanor, and she noted changes in her child's anxiety and aggressive behaviors. Similarly, the school counselor who had referred Rebeca to treatment reported that the number of referrals to the principal's office had decreased from an average of four times per week to one or two times per week. Antonio's behavioral changes were evident at school as well as at home.

PARENT-CHILD RELATIONSHIP STRESS: CHILD CHARACTERISTICS

Abidin (1995) explained that high scores in the PSI child domain reflect children's qualities that contribute to difficulties in the parent-child relationship; thus the total score is measured through subscales such as demandingness, mood, and hyperactivity. Thus, when scores for child domain are high, it is advised to focus on treatments that can positively affect children's behaviors. Clinical significance showed that roughly 75 percent of parents who reported clinical levels of concern at pre-test moved to normal functioning levels following treatment.

In Rebeca's case, she showed a decrease of 24 points in stress related to child characteristics (PSI child domain). A closer look at the subscales under this domain of the PSI revealed that Rebeca reported a notable decrease on the acceptability subscale. She reported that participating in CPRT helped her develop more realistic expectations of Antonio as she better understood his developmental stage and behaviors associated with his age. As a result, Rebeca reported having more patience with her son. During the exit interviews, most parents reported having a more in-depth understanding and acceptance of their children's developmental stage and, consequently, increased patience. CPRT focuses on increasing parental empathy and helping parents normalize their concerns in light of their children's developmental level. These factors could have positively affected parents' ability to accept their child, resulting in the significant decrease on this subscale.

Most parents in the study reported a marked decrease on the demandingness subscale score from pre-test to post-test. I observed that a common characteristic among parents in the CPRT groups was the tendency to do things for their children that their children could do for themselves. Moreover, when skills on returning responsibility were taught, parents across all groups showed a great need to process feeling like bad parents when they returned responsibility to their children. At the end of training, one mother stated, "I have learned that he is an independent person and even though I will always be with him, he needs to be autonomous." This change in perception reported by most parents appeared to have affected the overall scores for the demandingness subscale.

Also, Hastings (2002) suggested that children's problem behaviors and parental stress influence one another, creating a reciprocal cycle. The present study found a statistically significant decrease in children's problem behaviors (internalizing, externalizing, and total) as reported by parents on the CBCL. It is possible that the statistically significant decrease on the scores of the child domain is a reflection of parents' perception of a decrease in their children's behavioral problems.

PARENT-CHILD RELATIONSHIP STRESS: PARENT CHARACTERISTICS

The finding that 66 percent of parents who reported clinical levels of concern at pre-test moved to normal functioning following treatment shows strong support for the clinical significance of the CPRT intervention on reducing parent-child relationship stress related to parent characteristics.

High scores in the parent domain indicate parents feeling "overwhelmed and inadequate to the task of parenting" (Abidin, 1995, p. 10). This domain measures parental depression, competence, and isolation among others. Most of the parents in this study reported high scores on the parent domain, indicating a level of stress in the areas measured in this domain. Such high stress may be due to the many stressors that Latino immigrants experience, such as living in poverty, dealing with the acculturation process, and experiencing language barriers (Santiago-Rivera, 1995; Klebanov, Brooks-Gunn, & Duncan, 1994; La Roche, 1999; Gibbs, 2003). Thus, finding treatments that can potentially decrease these stressors can help minimize the onset of mental health problems such as depression. Rebeca experienced many of these stressors and often talked during the CPRT group meetings about her feelings of isolation, depression, frustration with her lack of English skills, and stress associated with the acculturation process. These stressors were commonly shared by participants as they pertained to how they diminished their emotional ability to their children. Similarly, I noticed that these stressors caused these parents to constantly feel overwhelmed, which diminished their capacity to have patience and to be empathic to their children.

The CPRT format provides both didactic and supportive group experiences in a safe environment. This environment provided parents with the opportunity to offer support for each other (Ceballos & Bratton, in press). Rebeca reported that such a supportive environment was crucial for her to feel less depressed and less isolated. The parents in the group formed close relationships with one another and reported that being in the group helped them realize they were not alone in their struggles as immigrants. I noticed that the parents not only provided one another support during group time, but they helped one another outside of group. Examples of outside-of-group activities included sharing information regarding community resources, providing child care for one another, and holding social gatherings outside of the group—all of which seemed to reduce their feelings of isolation. Additionally, CPRT provides parenting skills that can positively influence feelings of parental competence. In fact, Rebeca and other parents reported feeling better equipped to deal with their children's misbehaviors as a result of the skills they learned in CPRT, creating a sense of empowerment for these parents. Moreover, CPRT focuses on strengthening the child-parent relationship; so it would be expected that as parents experienced a closer relationship with their children, they experienced higher levels of attachment, which is one of the factors examined in the parent domain.

PARENT-CHILD RELATIONSHIP STRESS: TOTAL STRESS

Clinical significance showed that 62 percent of parents who reported clinical levels of concern at pre-test moved to normal functioning levels following treatment, showing a strong support for the CPRT intervention on reducing total parenting stress (Ceballos & Bratton, in press). Rebeca reported a decrease of 30 points on her overall parental stress from pre-test to post-test. Such a decrease is important considering that mothers under stress have a tendency to become easily frustrated with their children's behaviors (Hughes & Barad, 1983). Furthermore, Kazdin and Whitley (2003) explained that parental stress increases "parent irritability and attention to deviant behavior and the likelihood that parents initiate or maintain aversive interchanges with their children" (p. 504), resulting in the perpetuation of a negative parent-child relationship and problematic behaviors in children (Deater-Deckard, 2005).

In Rebeca's case, she started CPRT being extremely frustrated with her child's behavior and with very little tolerance toward her child. Her frustration and lack of acceptance led her to tell her child that she hated him, which in turned caused her to feel less competent as a mother and guilty about Antonio's behavioral problems in school. These types of interactions between Rebeca and her son had damaged the mother-child attachment. Through CPRT, Rebeca was able to lower her overall stress level, which led her to become more emotionally available to Antonio. As she experienced the support from other parents in the group, Rebeca was able to be less defensive to treatment. I noticed that throughout the 11 weeks, she was able to allocate more energy and time to Antonio, instead of focusing on her feelings of depression and isolation. Similar changes were reported by most parents, with all parents in the CPRT group reporting feelings of less isolation and increased competence during exit interviews.

CONCLUSION

The need for evidence-based treatments that are responsive to the needs of young Latino children is well documented (Multicultural and International Outreach Center, 2003; National Task Force on Early Childhood Education for Hispanics, 2007). Latino children are the fastest-growing population in the United States, with significant mental health needs attributed to factors such as poverty, speaking English as a second language, and low parental education (National Center for Children in Poverty, 2002; NCES, 2003; U.S. Census, 2005; U.S. Department of Health and Human Services, 2004). The statistical, practical, and clinical significance of the findings are promising and support the effectiveness of CPRT on reducing young Latino children's problem behaviors and immigrant Latino parents' child-parent relationship stress. Additionally, because CPRT is delivered in group format, it offers a solution to the shortage of Spanish-speaking mental health professionals trained to work with young children and their parents (Ceballos & Bratton, in press). CPRT group format also provides parents who are isolated, as it is often the case with Latino immigrants, social contacts that can help them reduce stress.

While the present study is a good starting point to investigate the effectiveness of play therapy interventions for young Latino children and immigrant Latino parents, it has limitations that should be addressed in future research. To offer additional support for CPRT as an evidence-based treatment for Latino children and their parents, future research should concentrate on studying the long-term effects of CPRT. Thus, a six-month or one-year follow-up study when conducting CPRT with this population is recommended. A major limitation of the present study is that the only source of measurement was parents who were also the recipients of the intervention. Although anecdotal data from school personnel supported parents' report, collecting formal assessments from teachers would provide validity to the findings. Future research should include a larger sample size to increase the power of statistical analysis and involve multiple sites to increase generalizability. Out of the 48 participants in this study, only 8 participants were from South and Central American countries; the rest of the participants were from Mexico. Also, only one participant was male. Thus, increasing the diversity of the sample by including more males and more participants from South and Central America in future research can further add to the generalizability of findings (Ceballos & Bratton, in press).

Like Rebeca, many parents experienced positive changes in the relationship with their children as a result of CPRT. During the exit interview, one of the participants said:

> About the training, what I liked the most is that I learned . . . to value more the time I spent with my daughter . . . that does not come about by giving her food, a bath, taking care of her. Instead, as a mom, I have to have special times with her, demonstrate that I am listening to her, that I am with her, that I can notice what she feels.

This quote reflects the impact that CPRT can have on the quality of the parent-child attachment for Latino immigrant parents who face numerous at-risk factors on a daily basis. The results of this study suggest that CPRT has a large beneficial effect on the performance of Latino children who are identified as at risk for not achieving school success because of behavioral problems. Furthermore, findings show a dramatic decrease in parents' report of stress in the parent-child relationship—a factor that has been shown to negatively affect children's overall mental health. Intervening early in the family system not only offers the possibility of ameliorating current difficulties, but also provides the family with a protective factor that can help prevent the onset of more severe long-term effects that can develop when early mental health needs and warning signs are ignored. CPRT offers promise as a culturally responsive, strengths-based, early intervention for Latino parents and their children identified as at risk—one that can easily be implemented in Head Start programs nationwide.

REFERENCES

Abidin, R. R. (1995). *Parenting stress index: Professional manual.* Lutz, FL: Psychological Assessment Resources.

Achenbach, T. M., & Rescorla, L. A. (2000). *Manual for the ASEBA preschool forms & profiles.* Burlington, VT: University of Vermont, Research Center for Children, Youth, & Families.

Altbach, P. (1991). Impact and adjustment: Foreign students in comparative perspectives. *Higher Education, 21*(3), 305–323.

Andres-Hyman, R., Ortiz, J., Anes, L., Paris, M., & Davidson, L. (2006). Culture and clinical practice: Recommendations for working with Puerto Ricans and other Latinas(os) in the United States. *Professional Psychology: Research and Practice, 37*(6), 694–701.

Bailey, D. F., & Bradbury-Bailey, M. E. (2007). Promoting achievement for African American males through group work. *Journal for Specialists in Group Work, 32*, 83–96.

Bamara, M., Umana-Taylor, A., Shin, N., & Alfaro, E. (2005). Latino adolescents' perceptions of parenting behaviors and self-esteem: Examining the role of neighborhood risks. *Family Relations, 54*(5), 621–632.

Bratton, S. C., Landreth, G. L., Kellum, T., & Blackard, S. (2006). *Child parent relationship therapy (CPRT) treatment manual: A 10-session filial therapy model for training parents.* New York: Routledge.

Burton, L. M., & Jarrett, R. L. (2000). In the mix, yet on the margins: The place of families in urban neighborhood and child development research. *Journal of Marriage and Family, 62*, 1114–1135.

Ceballos, P., & Bratton, S. C. (in press). Empowering Latino families: A culturally responsive intervention for low-income immigrant Latino parents and their children identified with academic and behavioral concerns. *Psychology in the Schools.*

Cochran, J. L. (1996). Using play and art therapy to help culturally diverse students overcome barriers to school success. *School Counselor, 43*, 287–299.

Cohen, J. (1988). *Statistical power analysis for the behavioral sciences* (2nd ed.) New York: Academic Press.

Constantine, M. G. (2001). Multicultural training, theoretical orientation, empathy, and multicultural case conceptualization ability in counselors. *Journal of Mental Health Counseling, 23*, 357–374.

Crean, H. (2008). Conflict in the Latino parent-youth dyad: The role of emotional support from the opposite parent. *Journal of Family Psychology, 22*(3), 484–493.

Deater-Deckard, K. (1998). Parenting stress and child adjustment: Some old hypotheses and new questions. *American Psychological Association, 5*(3), 314–332.

Deater-Deckerd, K. (2005). Parenting stress and children's development: Introduction to the special issue. *Infant and Child Development, 14*(2), 111–115.

Gibbs, J. T. (2003). *Children of color: Psychological interventions with culturally diverse groups.* San Francisco, CA: Jossey-Bass.

Gross, D., Fogg, L., & Young, M. (2006). The equivalence of the child behavior checklist 1½–5 across parent race/ethnicity, income level, and language. *Psychological Assessment, 18*(3), 313–323.

Hastings, R. P. (2002). Parental stress and behaviour problems of children with developmental disability. *Journal of Intellectual and Developmental Disability, 27*(3), 149–60.

Hinshaw, S. P. (1992). Academic underachievement, attention deficits, and aggression: Co-morbidity and implications for intervention. *Journal of Consulting and Clinical Psychology, 60*(6), 893–903.

Hughes, H. M., & Barad, S. J. (1983). Psychological functioning of children in a battered women's shelter: A preliminary investigation. *American Journal of Orthopsychiatry, 53*, 525–531.

Kazdin, A. E. (1999). The meanings and measurement of clinical significance. *Journal of Counseling and Clinical Psychology, 67*, 332–339.

Kazdin, A. E., & Whitley, M. K. (2003). Treatment of parental stress to enhance therapeutic change among children referred for aggressive and antisocial behavior. *Journal of Consulting and Clinical Psychology, 71*, 504–515.

Klebanov, P., Brooks-Gunn, J., & Duncan, G. (1994). Does neighborhood and family poverty affect mothers' parenting, mental health, and social support? *Journal of Marriage and the Family, 56*(2), 441–455.

Knitzer, J. (2000, February). Promoting resilience: Helping young children and parents affected by substance abuse, domestic violence, and depression in the context of welfare reform. Retrieved April 20, 2007, from http://www.nccp.org./pub_cwr00h.html.

Landreth, G. L., & Bratton, S. C. (2006). *Child parent relationship therapy: A 10-session filial therapy model.* New York: Routledge.

La Roche, M. (1999). Culture, transference, and countertransference among Latinos. *Psychotherapy, 36*(4), 389–397.

Multicultural and International Outreach Center. (2003, June). Improving access to treatment for all people with mental illness. Retrieved February 20, 2007, from http://www.cdc.gov/od/oc/media/mmwrnews/n040611.htm.

National Center for Children in Poverty. (2002). Children of immigrants: A statistical profile. Retrieved January 8, 2008, from http://www.nccp.org/publications/pub_475.html.

National Center for Education Statistics. (2003, April). Status and trends in the education of Hispanics. Retrieved April 13, 2007, from http://nces.ed.gov/pubs2003/2003008.pdf.

National Task Force on Early Childhood Education for Hispanics. (2007). Para nuestros niños: Expanding and improving early education for Hispanics. Retrieved March 4, 2007, from http://www.ecehispanic.org/.

Padilla, A., Ruiz, R., & Alvarez, R. (1975). Community mental health services for the Spanish-speaking/surnamed population. *American Psychologist, 30*(9), 892–905.

Powell, D. R., Zambrana, R., & Silva-Palacios, V. (1990). Designing culturally responsive parent programs: A comparison of low-income, Mexican and Mexican-American mothers' preferences. *Family Relations, 39*, 298–304.

Ryan, V., & Bratton, S. C. (2008). Child-centered/non-directive play therapy with very young children. In C. Schaefer, P. Kelly-Zion, & J. McCormick (Eds.), *Play therapy with very young children.* New York: Rowman & Littlefield.

Santiago-Rivera, A. (1995). Developing a culturally sensitive treatment modality for bilingual Spanish-speaking clients: Incorporating language and culture in counseling. *Journal of Counseling & Development, 74*(1), 12–17.

Solis, M., & Abidin, R. (1991). The Spanish version parenting stress index: A psychometric study. *Journal of of Clinical Child Psychology, 20*(4), 372–378.

Thompson, R. (2002). *The roots of school readiness in social and emotional development (Rep. No. 1)*. Kansas City, MO: The Ewing Marion Kauffman Foundation.

Twenge, J. M., & Nolen-Hoeksema, S. (2002). Age, gender, race, socioeconomic status, and birth cohort differences on the children's depression inventory: A meta-analysis. *Journal of Abnormal Psychology, 111*, 578–588.

United States Census Bureau. (2005). Facts for future. Retrieved January 5, 2009, from http://www.census.gov/Press-release/www/releases/archives/cb05 ff-14-3.pdf.

United States Census Bureau. (2008). An older and more diverse nation by midcentury. Retrieved December 18, 2008, from http://www.census.gov/Press-release/www/releases/archives/population/012496.html.

U.S. Department of Health and Human Services. (2004). Youth violence prevention in Latino communities: A resource guide for MCH professionals. Retrieved April 05, 2009, from http://www.promoteprevent.org.

Vlach, N. (2002). Central American children and adolescents. In J. T. Gibbs, L. N. Huang, & Associates (Eds.), *Children of color: Psychological interventions with culturally diverse youth* (pp. 301–343). San Francisco: Wiley Imprints.

Webster-Stratton, C., & Reid, M. J. (2003). The incredible years parents, teachers, and children training services: A multifaceted treatment approach for young children with conduct problems. In A. E. Kazdin & J. R. Weisz (Eds.), *Evidence-based psychotherapies for children and adolescents* (pp. 224–240). New York: Guilford.

CHAPTER 21

High School Students as Therapeutic Agents with Young Children

LESLIE JONES

FILIAL THERAPY WITH HIGH SCHOOL STUDENTS

In 2001, after reading the U.S. Surgeon General's report titled "A National Action Agenda for Children's Mental Health" (U.S. Public Health Service, 2001), which described the shortage of appropriate mental health services for children and adolescents as a major health crisis in the United States, I began to explore the possibility of paraprofessionals as change agents for younger children. Although 1 in 10 children and adolescents suffer from mental illness severe enough to cause some level of impairment, it is estimated that less than 1 in 5 of these children receives the help they need (U.S. Surgeon General, 2001). One of the main reasons children and adolescents were not receiving the help they needed was the lack of trained professionals, which again led me to explore the use of paraprofessionals as change agents.

Based on the research, the critical need for mental health services for children and the lack of sufficient numbers of professionals to perform these services had been documented for several decades (Guerney, 1964; Albee, 1969; Troester & Darby, 1976; Felner & Abner, 1983; Hankerson, 1983; Kazden, 1993; Landreth, 1993). Even when there are well-trained professionals, there are too many children to serve, or families do not have the financial resources to seek help. This is particularly true in the school setting where the student-to-counselor ratio is high and makes it difficult for counselors to meet all the needs of their students (Guerney & Flumen, 1970; White, Flynt, & Draper, 1997; Alexander, 1964). Therefore, the American School Counselor Association (ASCA) recommended that peer counseling programs be implemented as part of school guidance services (Myrick, Highland, & Sabella, 1995). One solution to the growing needs of school children experiencing adjustment difficulties and insufficient resources is student peer facilitator programs. Teens have been shown to be effective in reaching their peers and young children because they can be effective role models (Tindall, 1995). Young children also perceive teens as more fun and less threatening. Peer helper programs have been shown to have a positive impact on the students who receive help as well as the students who are trained to provide the help (Bowman & Myrick, 1987; Brake & Gerler, 1994; Foster-Harrison, 1995; Huey & Rank, 1984; Myrick, Highland, & Sabella, 1995; Tindall, 1995; Draper et al., 2001). All of these factors led to training high school students to be the therapeutic change agents for children.

The Peer Assistance and Leadership program, called PALs, is one such program that focuses on training students to be effective listeners and communicators with at-risk students in kindergarten through twelfth grade. PALs began in Austin, Texas, in 1980 and has expanded to several other states. The PALs program has served more than 1,100 schools in 500 districts throughout Texas. The PALs program uses a structured program to train students enrolled in a for-credit course in a basic set of communication and helping skills so they can work one-on-one with at-risk elementary, middle, and high school students. Although the program focuses on teaching effective communication skills, the program does not specifically train students in developmentally sensitive skills for working with younger children.

The question then became how to train the high school students to achieve maximum results and focus on training peer helpers to work with younger children in a developmentally appropriate manner. With the knowledge that play therapy has been shown to be an effective intervention for children exhibiting a variety of concerns in a meta-analysis of six decades of outcome play therapy research (Bratton, Ray, Rhines, & Jones, 2005), I decided to train the high school students in the basic skills of play therapy. Training peer helpers in basic play therapy skills and procedures is a viable alternative for school counselors to better meet the needs of young children and enhance the effectiveness of the PALs program.

I drew on my training in filial therapy, a developmentally appropriate and proven method of training paraprofessionals as therapeutic change agents for working with young children, to train the high school students in the basic skills of play therapy. Bernard and Louise Guerney developed filial therapy in the 1960s to help children overcome pre-existing problems and help prevent future problems through continued healthy parent-child interactions (Guerney, 1976; Guerney & Guerney, 1989). Although filial therapy was originally developed by the Guerneys as a 6-to-12-month training model, Landreth (1991) proposed a 10-session training model to address the needs of parents with financial or time constraints and emphasized the preventative nature of filial therapy for children. Landreth and Bratton (2006) formalized the 10-session model in a text, calling it *Child Parent Relationship Therapy* (CPRT; Landreth & Bratton, 2006). Several experimental outcome studies using the 10-session CPRT and filial therapy model have shown this approach to be effective with a variety of presenting issues (Ray et al., 2001; Bratton & Ray, 2002; Landreth & Bratton, 2006). Both the Landreth and the Guerney models have been extended to use with pre-service teachers as well as parents (Brown, 2000; Foley, 1970; Guerney & Flumen, 1970; Guerney & Stover, 1971; Ginsberg, 1976). Although filial therapy had been proven effective in training adult paraprofessionals, it had not been used to train adolescents as paraprofessionals. I believed that the use of a filial therapy model adapted to train high school students in a peer assistance program in developmentally appropriate methods could enhance their skills when working with children.

METHODS AND PROCEDURES

A pre-test–post-test control group design was used to measure the adjustment of pre-kindergarten and kindergarten children identified as at risk. The experimental group children received 20-minute structured play sessions for an average of 20 weeks over seven months. Play sessions were facilitated by high school juniors and seniors in a Peer Assistance and Leadership (PALs) class trained in child-centered play therapy skills and procedures. Comparison group high school students were trained in traditional PALs curriculum during their class time. The students were assigned to treatment group by their classroom assignment. There were two regularly scheduled PALS classes in the participating school. One class was randomly drawn to participate in the experimental treatment, and the other class was drawn to participate in the control treatment.

PARTICIPANTS

Participants were selected from a rural school district located near an urban area in North Texas. The ethnic percentages of the student population in the school district were European American 85 percent, African American 3 percent, Hispanic American 10 percent, Asian American 1 percent, Native American 1 percent.

HIGH SCHOOL STUDENTS

The 32 volunteer high school participants were from a naturally occurring cluster sample (classroom assignment) of juniors and seniors enrolled in the two Peer Assistance and Leadership classes (PALs) offered at their high school. Students in the PALs program undergo a rigorous screening and selection process, which involves teacher referral, application submission, and an interview with a PALs instructor. The high schools students had a mean age of 16.8; 12 males and 19 females; 28 European Americans and 3 Hispanic Americans. For comparison purposes, one PALs class was randomly assigned to receive the filial training, and the other PALs class was designated as the comparison group. The comparison group received training in the traditional PALs curriculum for peer helpers.

CHILDREN

Thirty children and their parents who met the following criteria were included in the study:

- The family met the study's criteria for school adjustment problems.
- The parent or legal guardian must either be able to speak, read, and write in English or must have someone who can help fill out all information.
- The family must be planning to keep the child in the primary school through May of 2000.
- The child must not currently be in counseling.
- The child must be able to speak English.
- The parent or legal guardian must agree to complete all pre-testing and post-testing.
- The parent or legal guardian and the child must agree to the child's participation in a weekly 20-minute play session with a trained high school student for the remainder of the school year.

The children in the study had a mean age of 5.4; 15 males and 11 females; 25 European Americans and 1 Hispanic American. The pre-kindergarten and kindergarten students were randomly assigned to either the experimental group receiving the PALs–conducted play therapy intervention or the control group.

INSTRUMENTATION

The Measurement of Empathy in Adult-Child Interactions (MEACI) by Stover, Guerney, and O'Connell (1971) and modified by Bratton and Landreth (1995) was used to operationally define empathy in relation to adult-child interactions. The MEACI is a direct observational scale that provides a total empathy score, as well as measures three behaviors that identify major aspects of empathy in adult-child interactions: communication of acceptance, allowing self-direction, and involvement.

The Child Behavior Checklist (CBCL) by Achenbach and Edelbrock (1986) and Achenbach (1991) consists of parent, teacher, and self-report versions. The CBCL reports a total problem scale, an internalizing scale, and an externalizing scale, which are further categorized into eight problem scales.

The Early Childhood Behavior Scale (ECBS) by McCarney (1994) was developed for use by teachers to identify early childhood behaviors in children ages 2 through 6 that are often associated with behaviorally disordered and emotionally disturbed children. The total score is subcategorized into academic progress, social relationships, and personal adjustment.

TREATMENT PROCEDURES

The group of PALs students who received training in basic child-centered play therapy skills followed the methodology of Landreth's (1991) filial therapy training model (Bratton, Landreth, Kellam, & Blackard, 2006; Landreth & Bratton, 2006). Although Landreth (1991) proposed 10 weekly, two-hour training sessions for parents, the format was adapted and lengthened to meet the developmental level and learning needs of adolescents, as well as to conform to the class format and course requirements for PALs. Jones (2002) provided a detailed outline of the adapted filial training model. Training included didactic lecture, discussion groups, experiential activities such as role-playing, and direct supervision through observation and viewing videos of the PALs' play sessions. Following the basic concepts of Landreth's (1991) filial model, the training focused on basic child-centered play therapy principles of creating a safe and accepting atmosphere, following the child's lead, reflecting feelings and behaviors, enhancing self-esteem, facilitating decision making, and setting therapeutic limits. Three advanced doctoral students with advanced coursework in play and filial therapy provided the training during the PALs regularly scheduled class time. Filial training was divided into four phases: Phase One: training in basic filial concepts, skills, and procedures; Phase Two: filial training and supervision of play sessions; Phase Three: supervised play sessions; Phase Four: supervision and integration.

PHASE ONE: TRAINING IN BASIC FILIAL CONCEPTS, SKILLS, AND PROCEDURES

During Phase One of training, reflective listening was discussed and taught through the use of worksheets and demonstration. The four basic feelings—happy, sad, mad, and scared—were reviewed and incorporated into role-plays. Next, the importance of play, play as the language of children, and the basics of tracking behavior were taught. The basic principles of special playtimes according to Landreth's (1991) filial therapy model were also explored and limit setting was taught following Landreth's (1991) ACT model.

PHASE TWO: FILIAL TRAINING AND SUPERVISION OF PLAY SESSIONS

During Phase Two, didactic training continued, and the PALs students began to conduct 20-minute playtimes with an assigned young child at the local primary school. A specific set of toys was provided for the playtimes (Jones, 2002). Half of the PALs students conducted their play session, while the other half of the PALs students met for supervision with two of the doctoral students. Sessions were videotaped and monitored live by one of the filial trainers for supervision purposes.

PHASE THREE: SUPERVISED PLAY SESSIONS

During Phase Three, high school students discussed and received peer and supervisor feedback on that week's playtime with the child.

PHASE FOUR: INTEGRATION

PALs students continued to conduct their supervised special playtimes with their assigned child, and two additional training sessions were held to help the PALs students reinforce and integrate their play therapy knowledge and skills. One method researchers utilized to facilitate integration was by assigning the high school students to read *Dibs in Search of Self* (Axline, 1964) in order to see the similarities in what they were doing with their pre-kindergarten/kindergarten student and how trained professionals work with children. The high school students were assigned several chapters to read each week and completed worksheets on the chapters.

RESULTS AND DISCUSSION
BEHAVIORAL OUTCOMES FOR YOUNG CHILDREN

Following the completion of the study, all scores obtained from the Child Behavior Checklist-Parent Report Form (CBCL-PRF) and Early Childhood Behavior Scale (ECBS) pre-tests from the experimental and control groups were analyzed and compared to the CBCL-PRF and ECBS post-tests from the experimental and control groups to determine whether child-centered play sessions conducted by filial-trained juniors and seniors were an effective intervention to reduce problematic behaviors in pre-kindergarten and kindergarten children (Jones, Rhine, & Bratton, 2002). A multivariate analysis of variance (MANOVA) was computed to test the significance of the differences between the control and the experimental groups on the hypotheses based on the CBCL-PRF and the ECBS. Significance of the difference between means was tested at the .05 level. The .10 level was used as the threshold to note any trends in the differences between the change scores. The hypotheses were either retained or rejected on the basis of the results of the MANOVA.

The experimental group children demonstrated a statistically significant ($p = .025$) reduction in their total behavior problems as reported by parents on the CBCL-PRF, while the control group experienced a slight increase in their total behavior problems. Results on the internalizing behavior problems scale of the CBCL-PRF indicated a statistically significant ($p = .025$) reduction in the experimental group children's internalizing behaviors such as withdrawal, depression, and anxiety, while the control group children experienced a slight increase in their internalizing behaviors. The children in the experimental group also showed a positive trend ($p = .07$) in the decrease of external behavior problems such as aggressive and delinquent behavior as indicated by the externalizing behavior scale of the CBCL-PRF, while the children in the control group experienced a slight increase in their externalizing behavior problems.

Also, the experimental group children also demonstrated a marked reduction in behavior problems as measured by the ECBS ($p = .056$), while the control group showed a slight increase in their total behavior problems as reported by teachers.

BEHAVIORAL OUTCOMES FOR HIGH SCHOOL STUDENTS

Following the completion of the study, all pre-test and post-test video-tapes of the high school students' play sessions with an assigned child were rated using the Measurement of Empathy in Adult-Child Inter-action (MEACI). Before the videotapes were rated, inter-rater reliability was established ($r = .9171$) over three training sessions. An analysis of covariance (ANCOVA) was computed to test the significance of the difference between the experimental group and the comparison group on the adjusted post-test means for each hypothesis in order to deter-mine whether a filial therapy model is more effective than a traditional PALs curriculum in increasing empathic play behaviors and interac-tions with children. Significance of the difference between the means was tested at the .05 level. On the basis of the results of the ANCOVA, the hypotheses were retained or rejected.

The experimental group of filial-trained PALs students demon-strated a statistically significant ($p = .001$) increase in empathic play behaviors and interactions during playtimes with children, while the comparison group of high school students remained relatively consist-ent. The experimental group of PALs students also demonstrated statistically significant increases in communication of acceptance ($p = .001$), in allowing self-direction in children ($p = .001$), and in attention to and participation in children's play ($p = .005$) as measured by the corresponding subscales on the MEACI.

The results of this study prove that using a filial therapy model to train high school students as therapeutic agents is effective with pre-kindergarten and kindergarten children experiencing school adjust-ment difficulties and suggest the use of a filial therapy training model as an effective method of training peer helpers. The developmentally responsive play therapy skills taught in the filial training model allowed the peer helpers to form meaningful relationships with the children as a basis for helping the children develop more self-enhancing and appropriate behaviors.

The high school PALs students trained in filial therapy demonstrated statistically significant increases in empathic interactions with young children, including the ability to convey acceptance, facilitate children's self-directedness, and engage in appropriate levels of involvement with children. These results are noteworthy because they are based on direct observations of specific skills by trained play therapy professionals rather than self-report measures. Training the PALs students in reflective listening allowed them to communicate with the young children more effectively by focusing on the importance of using feeling words and paraphrasing what they heard in conversations.

While further research is needed to validate these results, findings indicate that high school students are capable of integrating and implementing play therapy skills with young children. The results are particularly significant because they are consistent with the findings from studies that focused on filial training with adults, including parents, teachers, and college students (Brown, 2000; Rhine, 2002; Bratton & Landreth, 1995; Costas & Landreth, 1999; Foley, 1997; White, Flynt, & Draper, 1997; Guerney & Flumen, 1970; Lindan & Stollak, 1969). By using this model of training and supervision in a peer helper curriculum, school counselors can ensure that more children get the mental health services they need. By implementing this training in peer helper programs, the number of children that receive services through the school would greatly increase and provide one way to address the shortage of professionals trained to meet the mental health care needs of children (Satcher, 2001). Over a 24-week period, the PALs students received a total of nine training sessions, approximately 1½ hours in length. In addition, the PALs students participated in a total of twenty 20-minute supervised playtimes with their assigned pre-kindergarten and kindergarten student immediately followed by 20 minutes of supervision.

Additional benefits for the experimental group of high school students were observed during the course of training. In overall interactions with the researchers, PALs students in the filial group were increasingly more open, genuine, spontaneous, and playful. The experimental group of PALs students was able to communicate openly and discuss other situations in which they were able to apply the skills learned in the training to other relationships with children, co-workers, friends, and family. One student commented how she implemented many of the skills while babysitting. Another student stated she was able to use the skills in her position as a lifeguard at the city pool, and an additional student stated she was able to communicate more effectively with her friends and her boyfriend. These are but a few examples of the many comments that the filial-trained students made regarding their generalizing the skills to their everyday life. I also observed the experimental group of PALs students as more confident in themselves by the end of the training. Further, the PALs students were able to relate what they had learned to how their new skills would affect their future roles as parents.

Training of the PALs students using the modified Landreth 10-week filial model appeared to contribute to these positive comments and the results from data analysis. Modifications that proved significant included allowing the PALs students to participate in two pre-training sessions designed to develop rapport with the trainers, stronger group connections, and self-awareness before introducing filial therapy concepts. The activities used in the pre-training sessions helped the high school students become more open to participating in experiential activities. This strategy allowed the experimental group students to be more open to the filial and play therapy training, which uses experiential components throughout the training process. Also, since none of the students had children of their own or interacted with young children on a daily basis, the students appeared to benefit from a longer time to learn and apply basic play therapy skills while receiving supervision.

The supervision provided to the students was also crucial to the significance of the results. During supervision, PALs students discussed difficulties they encountered during their playtimes with the children and generated more effective plans to deal with these difficulties. Facilitators discussed and demonstrated techniques the PALs students could use, such as the whisper technique (Bratton et al., 2006). Although watching themselves on videotape was new for the PALs students, it allowed them to receive feedback on their strengths and areas for growth in conducting the play sessions with the pre-kindergarten and kindergarten students. Viewing themselves on tape and using the skills they learned in training allowed them to receive suggestions, encouragement, and instructions from the filial trainers. This type of feedback along with group interactions facilitated the learning of skills in a supportive atmosphere. The filial trainers helped the PALs students see they were not alone in their struggles to learn the skills by commenting on experiences shared by several students. High school students were also given the opportunity to ask questions and address concerns regarding the play times they were conducting. Students were also allowed to observe other students conducting play sessions and gave one another feedback on the play sessions.

Through this process, the PALs students seemed to become more comfortable and confident in themselves. In the beginning, the high school students were very timid about being videotaped and then watching those tapes with peers. However, by the end of training, the PALs students were comfortable and relaxed not only with being videotaped but also in receiving supervision and giving feedback to others.

PALs students also completed self-evaluation forms focusing on the use of specific skills, strengths, and areas for growth each week at the end of their special play times. This was beneficial in helping the high school students evaluate their own skills and not rely completely on trainer feedback. Initially, when the high school students completed the playtime review forms, they focused on themselves. One student stated, "I wanted to play more." Other responses focused on how they felt about their ability to perform the skills from the training sessions. As training progressed and the students were more comfortable conducting playtimes, students focused on improving in specific skill areas, such as increasing their rate of tracking, not asking questions, and being less repetitive. By the end of the project, the students were more focused on how their behavior affected the child they were working with in the playtime. One student wrote, "Pay more attention," while another student wrote, "Encourage him more. " Additional responses from the high school students that indicated an increase in empathic behavior included "Track more feeling," "Respond to feelings more," and " Be more involved."

This project also resulted in significant results and positive trends in decreasing behavior problems of young children. Children with behavioral, emotional, and social problems need appropriate intervention for school success. The findings from this study as well as the observations from the researchers, parents, and teachers support the value of play sessions between children who have adjustment problems and high schools students who have been trained in child-centered play therapy skills and procedures. The belief that children who receive child-centered play therapy will move toward becoming more capable, creative, self-directed, and self-responsible is supported by the results on the internalizing behavior scale on the Child Behavior Checklist-Parent Report Form (CBCL-PRF). Because internalizing behavior problems are more difficult to detect and are oftentimes overlooked by parents, the significance of the parents' report of a reduction in internalizing behavior problems is particularly profound.

Another benefit of this study was that it used a model that can be easily incorporated into school districts and that can maximize school counselors' resources and time. School counselors can be trained to use filial therapy techniques to incorporate into peer mentoring programs, thereby increasing the number of students they can serve. Requirements for implementation of this program in a school district include

- The counselor trained in filial and play therapy techniques and willing to participate
- A for-credit high school peer mentoring program
- Filial play therapy toy kits
- Arrangements for high school students to travel to primary schools to conduct play sessions

Counselors may face challenges and may need to adapt this program to fit into their own school, yet this model shows much potential as a viable intervention as well as preventative measure for addressing the underserved mental health needs for children.

RECOMMENDATIONS

The positive results of this study suggest further research and implementation of filial and play therapy training model in peer assistance programs. The training equipped the PALs students with developmentally appropriate ways to relate with young children. There are many children who need mental health services, and peer helper programs are one way to meet those needs. By implementing this training in peer helper programs, the number of children that receive services through the school would greatly increase and allow peer helpers to meet the needs of children that school counselors are unable to serve due to time constraints and number of children in need.

The following recommendations are offered to add to the further success of the training model used:

- Adapt the filial and play therapy model by providing intensive training for the first three weeks to allow the high school students to begin their playtimes with younger children earlier in the school year. Immediate application could help the young children adjust to attending school. The extended initial training would also serve to generate a stronger base as the high school students begin playtimes.

- Allow high school students time to play with and become used to working with play materials. Many of the students reported a desire to play with the toys as training began and a desire to play with the toys more during the playtimes.
- To help high school students to increase their understanding of play therapy, require the reading of *Dibs: In Search of Self* early in the training process. This would reinforce and integrate their play therapy knowledge and skills by allowing the high school students to see the similarities in what they were doing with their young child and how trained professionals work with children.
- Implement filial and play therapy training in peer assistance classes and child development classes. This would provide a developmentally appropriate method supported by research to work with young children and meet their mental health needs.
- Incorporate peer supervision as a standard practice in training high school students in filial therapy to help students gain a better understanding of their knowledge of play therapy.

REFERENCES

Achenbach, T. M. (1991). *Manual for the child behavior checklist and 1991 profile.* Burlington, VT: University Associates in Psychiatry.

Achenbach, T. M., & Edelbrock, C. S. (1986). *Manual for the child behavior checklist and revised behavioral profile.* Burlington, VT: University of Vermont.

Albee, G. (1969). Conceptual and manpower requirements in psychology. *American Psychologist, 23,* 317–320.

Alexander, E. D. (1964). School-centered play therapy program. *Personnel and Guidance Journal, 43,* 256–261.

Axline, V. M. (1964). *Dibs in search of self.* New York: Ballantine.

Bowman, R. P., & Myrick, R. D. (1987). Effects on elementary school peer facilitator program on children with behavior problems. *School Counselor, 34,* 369–378.

Brake, K. J., & Gerler, E. R. (1994). Discovery: A program for fourth and fifth graders identified as discipline problems. *Elementary School Guidance & Counseling, 28,* 170–181.

Bratton, S. C., & Landreth, G. L. (1995). Filial therapy with single parents: Effects on parental acceptance, empathy, and stress. *International Journal of Play Therapy, 4*(1), 61–80.

Bratton, S., Landreth, G. L., Kellam, T. L. T., & Blackard, S. (2006). *Child parent relationship therapy (CPRT) treatment manual: A 10-session filial therapy model for training parents.* New York: Brunner-Routledge.

Bratton, S. C., & Ray, D. C. (2000). What the research shows about play therapy. *International Journal of Play Therapy, 9*(1), 47–88.

Bratton, S. C., Ray, D., Rhine, T., & Jones, L. (2005). The efficacy of play therapy with children: A meta-analytic review of treatment outcomes. *Professional Psychology: Research and Practice, 36*(4), 376–390.

Brown, C. J. (2000). *Filial therapy with undergraduate teacher trainees: Child-teacher relationship training.* Unpublished doctoral dissertation, University of North Texas, Denton.

Costas, M., & Landreth, G. (1999). Filial therapy with non-offending parents of children who have been sexually abused. *International Journal of Play Therapy 8*(1), 43–66.

Draper, K., White, J., O'Shaughnessy, T. E., Flynt, M., & Jones, N. (2001). Kinder training: Play-based consultation to improve the school adjustment of discouraged kindergarten and first grade students. *International Journal of Play Therapy, 10*(1), 1–30.

Felner, R., & Abner, M. (1983). Primary prevention for children: A framework for the assessment of need. *Prevention in Human Services, 2,* 109–121.

Foley, J. M. (1970). *Training future teachers as play therapists: An investigation of therapeutic outcome and orientation toward pupils.* Unpublished doctoral dissertation, Loyola University of Chicago.

Foster-Harrison, E. S. (1995). Peer helping in the elementary and middle grades: A developmental perspective. *Elementary School Guidance and Counseling, 30,* 94–104.

Ginsberg, B. G. (1976). Parents as therapeutic agents: The usefulness of filial therapy in a community mental health center. *American Journal of Community Psychology, 4*(1), 47–54.

Guerney, B. (1964). Filial therapy: Description and rationale. *Journal of Consulting Psychology, 28,* 304–310.

Guerney, B. (1976). Filial therapy as a treatment method for disturbed children. *Evaluation, 3,* 34–35.

Guerney, B., & Flumen, A. B., (1970). Teachers as psychotherapeutic agents for withdrawn children. *Journal of School Psychology, 8*(2), 107–113.

Guerney, L., & Guerney, B. (1989). Child relationship enhancement: Family therapy and parent education. Special issue: Person-centered approaches with families. *Person Centered Review, 4,* 344–357.

Hankerson, H. (1983). Utilizing parents for paraprofessional intervention. *Urban Review, 15,* 75–87.

Huey, W. C., & Rank, R. C. (1984). Effects of counselor and peer-led group assertive training on Black adolescent aggression. *Journal of Counseling Psychology, 31,* 95–98.

Jones, L., Rhine, T., & Bratton, S. (2002). High school students as therapeutic agents with young children experiencing school adjustment difficulties: The effectiveness of a filial therapy training model. *International Journal of Play Therapy, 11*(2), 43–62.

Jones, L. D. (2002). *Effectiveness of filial therapy training on high school students' empathic behavior with young children.* (Doctoral dissertation, University of North Texas, Denton, 2001). Dissertation Abstracts International, A63(02), 508.

Kazdin, A. (1993). Psychotherapy for children and adolescents. *American Psychologist, 48*(6), 644–657.

Landreth, G. L. (1991). *Play therapy: The art of the relationship.* Bristol, PA: Accelerated Development.

Landreth, G. L. (1993). Child-centered play therapy. *Elementary School Guidance & Counseling, 28,* 17–29.

Landreth, G. L., & Bratton, S. C. (2006). *Child parent relationship therapy (CPRT): A 10-session filial therapy model.* New York: Brunner-Routledge.

Linden, J. I., & Stollak, G. E. (1969). The training of undergraduates in play techniques. *Journal of Clinical Psychology, 25,* 213–218.

McCarney, S. (1994). *Early childhood behavior scale.* Columbia: Hawthorne Educational Services.

Myrick, R. D., Highland, W. H., & Sabella, R. A. (1995). Peer helpers and perceived effectiveness. *Elementary School Guidance and Counseling, 29,* 278–288.

Ray, D. C., Bratton, S. C., Rhine, T., & Jones, L. (2001). The effectiveness of play therapy: Responding to the critics. *International Journal of Play Therapy, 10*(1), 85–108.

Rhine, T. J. (2002). *The effects of a play therapy intervention conducted by trained high school students on the behavior of maladjusted young children: Implications for school counselors.* (Doctoral dissertation, University of North Texas, Denton, 2001.) Dissertation Abstracts International, A62(10), 3304.

Satcher, D. (2001). A national action agenda for children's mental health. Available: http://www.surgeongeneral.gov/cmh/childreport.htm.

Stover, L., Guerney, B., & O'Connell, M. (1971). Measurements of acceptance, allowing self-direction, involvement, and empathy in adult-child interaction. *Journal of Psychology, 77,* 261–269.

Tindall, J. A. (1995). *Peer programs: An in-depth look at peer helping.* Bristol, PA: Accelerated Development.

Troester, J. D., & Darby, J. A. (1976). The role of the mini-meal in therapeutic play groups. *Social Casework, 57,* 97–103.

United States Surgeon General. (2001) A national action agenda for children's mental health. Retrieved September 15, 2001, from http://www.surgeon general.gov/cmh/childreport.htm.

White, J., Flynt, M., & Draper, K. (1997). Kindertherapy: Teachers as therapeutic agents. *International Journal of Play Therapy, 6*(2), 33–49.

CHAPTER 22

Filial Therapy with Teachers of Deaf and Hard of Hearing Preschool Children*

D. MICHAEL SMITH

INTRODUCTION

Approximately 15 years before entering the PhD program in counselor education at the University of North Texas (UNT), I was privileged to work professionally with Dr. Garry Landreth, Regents Professor, founder of the Center for Play Therapy at UNT, and a prime mover in the fields of play and filial therapy. At that point in his career, Dr. Landreth was looking to move beyond the academic setting to teach his 10-week model of Bernard Guerney's filial therapy (1964) to parents in a real-world setting. Thus he began to teach a series of filial therapy classes to parent-clients at the nonprofit counseling center in Dallas that I co-founded and at which I then served as clinical director. After being trained in play and filial therapy by Dr. Landreth, I regularly taught the 10-week Landreth (2002) model of filial therapy classes to parents for approximately 10 years before beginning my doctoral work. Also during this time, I became a registered play therapist-supervisor

*Acknowledgments: Sections from Smith and Landreth (2004). Copyright 2004 by the Association for Play Therapy. Reprinted by permission of the Association for Play Therapy.

and provided play and filial therapy training and supervision to other therapists and professionals and presented on play and filial therapy at various regional and national play therapy conferences.

All of this is to say that when the time came for me to do my doctoral dissertation, I had many times seen the positive effects of teaching filial therapy to groups of parents.

I decided I wanted to investigate whether filial therapy could also be effective with other caretakers beyond the child's parents and immediate family system. I wanted to see if teachers could be taught to be effective therapeutic agents with their students, especially teachers who worked with very challenging students with difficulties beyond those found in most classrooms.

Reason for the Study

Cursory research revealed that deaf and hard of hearing children were among the most challenging student populations because of their combination of physical and emotional difficulties (DeSelle & Pearlmutter, 1997; Ita, 1999; Schum, 2004). This led to the idea of working with teachers of deaf and hard of hearing preschool students in a respected service provider and research facility in Dallas. In this study, I was interested to see whether instructing a group of teachers in the basic skills of child-centered play therapy, using an adaptation of the Landreth 10-week filial therapy model, could be shown to reduce the number and extent of negative behaviors among their students. If this proved possible, then it could be shown that these teachers could in fact be taught to function as effective therapeutic agents with their students (White, Draper, & Flynt, 1999), which would positively benefit the students, their families, the teachers, and, we hoped, society at large.

Special Challenges of Deaf and Hard of Hearing Children

Deafness and limited hearing in adults and children has been part of the human experience since before recorded history. Since the origin of the public education system in the United States, teachers, counselors, social workers, hearing specialists, physicians, and other helping professionals have sought to discover workable methods of educating and meeting the emotional and social needs of children who are deaf and hard of hearing (Harris, Van Zandt, & Rees, 1997). Children who are born deaf or develop a hearing loss in their early childhood years have significant challenges acquiring language and the ability to communicate with others (Marshark & Clark, 1993; Schum, 2004). Research has shown as well that difficulties acquiring the ability to communicate and express oneself can greatly affect a child's cognitive, social, and emotional development (DeSelle & Pearlmutter, 1997; Ita, 1999; Schum, 2004). Despite the efforts of educators and other helping professionals, many deaf and hard of hearing children struggle to form satisfactory social relationships with individuals in their world, and to develop the emotional health and maturity commensurate with their hearing counterparts (Cates, 1991; Luterman, 1999, 2004; Murdock & Lybarger, 1997; Smith & Landreth, 2004).

Research has also demonstrated that deaf and hard of hearing students, whether in mainstream public education classes, special education classes, or schools designed for deaf and hard of hearing students only, experience higher incidences of emotional and behavioral difficulties within the school environment (Mantanini-Manfredi, 1993; Luterman, 1999; Schum, 2004). Perhaps because hard of hearing and deaf children initially experience greater difficulty expressing their needs, wants, thoughts, and feelings than do their hearing peers, they tend to exhibit lower self-esteem and less ability to show empathy for others (Cates, 1991; Lederberg, 1991; Ita, 1999). Furthermore, they experience higher incidences of anger, aggression, depression, frustration, estrangement, and isolation (Ita, 1999; Luterman, 1999; Schum, 2004).

Most often, preschools and special elementary schools for deaf and hard of hearing children use specially trained school counselors to respond to students' increased emotional needs (Harris, Van Zandt, & Rees, 1997). It is common for teachers and paraprofessionals to refer students with special emotional needs to the school counselor or psychologist for consultation. However, school counselors are often unable to conduct enough therapy sessions to effect lasting change in students referred for treatment (Jeannie Allen, personal communication, March 30, 2001). Taking all of this into account, it seemed to me that a more comprehensive approach was needed to assist deaf and hard of hearing preschool teachers in their efforts to help deaf and hard of hearing preschool students not only in acquiring language and the ability to express themselves, but also to assist in the healthy development of their social and emotional needs (Smith, 2002).

PLAY THERAPY

Widely documented research has demonstrated that the use of play therapy can be a viable intervention in assisting children with self-expression when facilitated by a trained play therapist (Axline, 1947; Bratton & Ray, 2000; Landreth, 2002). To date, however, there have been very few research studies using play therapy with deaf and hard of hearing children. In one study, Oualline (1975) found that short-term, individual child–centered, nondirective play therapy with deaf and hard of hearing children facilitated an increase in mature behavior patterns. Expected improvements in manifest behavior and personality adjustments were not supported by the data analysis, however.

Research has also shown that filial therapy and play therapy can be clinically helpful in training school counselors to work therapeutically with students in preschool, elementary, middle, and high school settings (Guerney, 1964; Guerney, 2000; Landreth, 2002; White, Draper, & Flynt, 1997). Building on the pioneering work of Axline (1947), Landreth (2002) expanded the concept that play is the child's most natural means of communication, regardless of their developmental or special needs. Play is an innate and universal means for children to express themselves. Through play, children learn about reality and their world; experiment with pretend roles; and come to know themselves, their specific abilities, and their strengths (Smith, 2002).

Play also allows children the opportunity to explore their difficulties and challenges. With the assistance of a trained play therapist, play therapy makes it possible for children to work through and resolve troubling wounds, traumas, and experiences that they likely would be unable to resolve in talk therapy alone (Yoshinga-Itano, Snyder, & Day, 1998).

Furthermore, it is increasingly apparent that school counselors are often expected to provide interventions to meet behavioral and emotional needs of preschool and elementary school children (ASCA, 2003). It appears that for many children, if their required therapeutic needs are met at all, they are most likely to be met in the school setting, through the work of the school counselor. However, it is also apparent that despite their concerted efforts, because of the increasing demands for their services and the fact that more deeply disturbed children are being seen at younger ages, school counselors are having difficulty managing all they are asked to do (Ray, Armstrong, Warren, & Balkin, 2005). Thus it seems that a new model is especially necessary to make further training available to preschool teachers so that they also can help meet the burgeoning emotional and behavioral needs of ever-growing numbers of children, especially those with special needs, including deaf and hard of hearing students.

FILIAL THERAPY

For this purpose, it appeared that filial therapy was a logical choice for teaching preschool classroom teachers to meet the increased behavior and emotional needs of their students, including deaf and hard of hearing children. The primary aims of filial therapy are to assist parents in acquiring basic play therapy skills, to strengthen and enhance the parent-child relationship, and to help children reduce their problem behaviors and internal emotional distress (Guerney, 1997; Smith, 2002). Within a small-group psychoeducational format, parents are taught by a combination of didactic instruction, hands-on practical learning experiences, and emotional support from other parent group members and the leader. A goal is for parents to practice and learn new relational skills in special playtime sessions with their child of focus to increase acceptance, empathy, and nurturance. Clinical trials in a wide variety of settings have shown that filial therapy is an effective means for parents to free their children to be self-enhancing and self-limiting in age-appropriate ways, within the scope of the individual child's particular abilities and talents, and special needs and limitations (Bratton & Landreth, 1995; Chau & Landreth, 1997; Smith & Landreth, 2003).

In 1967, Andronico and Guerney recognized that, in the classroom setting, teachers also had the ability to generalize to students the relationship skills that could be gleaned from filial therapy training. Stover, Guerney, and O'Connell (1971) trained teachers in the use of basic play therapy skills for use with their own students. Although the research data from this project were anecdotal, the results appeared promising.

To meet the deaf or hard of hearing child's unique needs for assistance with the acquisition of language, it seemed to me vitally important that a group of preschool and early childhood teachers learn to relate with their deaf and hard of hearing students using the child's innate and most natural form of communication, play. Also, the literature review revealed a notable scarcity of research on the usefulness of play therapy with deaf and hard of hearing students and filial therapy training with their teachers. Most curricula for training teachers of deaf and hard of hearing preschoolers do not necessarily include instruction in play or play therapy as taught in filial therapy training (Jones, Ross, & Kendall, 2001).

Purpose of the Study

The purpose of my study was to determine the effectiveness of an adaptation of Landreth's (2002) 10-week filial therapy model in increasing the empathic responsiveness and communication of acceptance of teachers of deaf and hard of hearing students, and to allow their students greater self-direction. A second purpose of the study was to determine the effectiveness of this same model as a method of intervention for deaf and hard of hearing preschool students in reducing the students' overall behavior problems; internalizing behaviors, including depression, anxiety, and withdrawal; and externalizing behavior problems, including aggressive, acting-out behaviors.

METHOD

Participants

Participants in the study were volunteers composed of preschool students and their teachers recruited from a child development preschool and research facility that included deaf and hard of hearing students. The preschool is designated as a regional day school for the deaf, serving deaf and hard of hearing children from ages 2 to 6, as well as hearing children the same age. Integrated into the regular preschool setting, the deaf and hard of hearing children also receive special deaf education services.

Teacher participants were recruited for the study based on the following criteria of eligibility:

- Must be an early childhood, deaf education, or paraprofessional teacher in the preschool, assigned to either a 2- and 3-year-old class, a 3- and 4-year-old class, a 4- and 5-year-old class, or a 5- and 6-year-old kindergarten class.
- After receiving written permission, must select from his own classroom at least one of his students as a student of focus, the student being between the ages of 2.0 and 6 years 11 months.
- Must be able to speak, read, and write the English language and, if teaching in a class using a combination of sign language and oral speech (called total communication), proficient in sign language.

- Must agree to complete 25 hours of filial therapy training within the designated time frame for the study, which I would lead.
- Must be willing to attend pre- and post-testing videotape sessions, complete two testing instruments for pre- and post-testing purposes, and conduct videotaped teacher-student play sessions at prescribed intervals between instructional sessions.
- Must be willing to participate in 10 teacher-student play sessions, averaging 30 minutes in length, once a week, and commit to videotaping at least three or four sessions for review in the teacher instructional classes.
- Must be willing to sign the teacher consent form.

There were 27 teachers in the preschool; 24 agreed to participate in the study. I met with each teacher participant who met the specified criteria to clarify the purpose and requirements of the filial therapy training, provide information about confidentiality, and answer questions.

EXPERIMENTAL AND CONTROL GROUPS

The ideal composition of the experimental group would include two auditory (oral speech only, no sign language) and two total communication (sign language plus oral speech) classes. This combination was not possible, however, for a variety of reasons beyond my control. To provide a comparable range of ages of students participating in the study, the experimental group was composed of teachers of one auditory communication class (composed of children between the ages of 2 and 3 years with three teachers) and three total communication classes (children ages 3 and 4 with four teachers; 4- and 5-year-olds with three teachers; and 5- and 6-year-olds with two teachers) ($n = 12$). The auditory communication classes were made up of the other class of 3- and 4-year-olds with four teachers, 4- and 5-year-olds with three teachers, and kindergartners with two teachers ($n = 12$).

The eligibility criteria for the participating students were these:

- Must be a child diagnosed as deaf or hard of hearing by the special education placement process.
- Must be a student of a participating teacher.
- Must be between the ages of 2 years to 6 years 11 months.
- Must be able to communicate through sign language or verbally at a minimal level determined by the student's teacher or the director/associate director of education of the center.

- Must have received written permission from a parent or legal guardian to participate.
- Must be able to participate in pre- and post-testing and videotaped teacher-student play sessions.
- Must be able to participate in 10 teacher-student play sessions, with an average length of 30 minutes each.

Participating teachers were assigned to either the experimental (n = 12) or the nontreatment comparison (control group) (n = 12), after which each teacher chose a student of focus from among the hard of hearing or deaf students in the class. Hence, a total of 24 students were chosen.

The students of focus whose teachers were in the control (nontreatment comparison) group participated only in the pre- and post-testing videotaped sessions. The students of focus whose teachers were in the experimental group participated in the pre- and post-testing videotaped sessions; their teachers also received the experimental treatment, in this case, the filial therapy skills training. Furthermore, while their teachers were in the process of attending the filial therapy training, the experimental group students and their teachers were videotaped at intervals in the playroom set up for the purpose. As part of their learning experience, these between-instructional-session videotapes were used for in-class supervision of the teachers with their students of focus.

Of the 12 teachers composing the experimental group, 10 were females and 2 were males, of whom 58 percent were Caucasian, 34 percent were African American, and 8 percent were Hispanic. One of the males was African American; the other was Hispanic. The nontreatment comparison group of teachers also contained 10 females and 2 males, of whom 80 percent were Caucasian, 10 percent were African American, and 10 percent were Hispanic. Both of the males were Caucasian.

The students in the experimental group included 6 males and 6 females, of whom 25 percent were Caucasian, 33 percent were African American, and 42 percent were Hispanic. The mean age of these students was 49.7 months. Students in the nontreatment comparison group included 7 males and 5 females, of whom 42 percent were Caucasian, 16 percent were African American, and 42 percent were Hispanic. The mean age of these students was 48.7 months.

TESTING INSTRUMENTS

Three testing instruments were used to evaluate and measure the teachers' and students' behaviors. The teachers' empathic behaviors were measured by the Measurement of Empathy in Adult-Child Interaction

(MEACI), a direct observational rating scale developed by Stover, Guerney, and O'Connell (1971). Its purpose is to measure communication of acceptance, allowing the child self-direction, and involvement with the child. On the subscales and total scores, lower scores indicate higher levels of positive behavior. The average reliability correlation coefficient for the communication of acceptance scale was .92. The medial correlation was .89 for the allowing the child self-direction subscale, and .89 for the parental involvement subscale (Stover et al., 1971). A study group of 51 mothers was used to demonstrate construct validity for each subscale and the total empathy score (Guerney, Stover, & DeMerit, 1968).

The students' behavior problems were measured using the Child Behavior Checklist/Caregiver-Teacher Report Form (CBC/TR; Achenbach & Edelbrock, 2000), which records the behavioral competencies and symptoms of children as perceived and judged by their teachers or primary caregivers. Chronbach's alpha was used to demonstrate internal consistency. Chronbach's alpha was .90 for internalizing behavior problems for girls between the ages of 4 and 11 and .93 for externalizing behavior problems. Chronbach's alpha for boys in the same age range was .89 for internalizing and .93 for externalizing behavior problems. A high level of reliability between raters was shown by intra-class correlations from three matched samples of children, indicating that scores obtained from each item are relative to scores from each other item. Content validity for the CBC/TR was established, as was test-retest reliability, at .89 for internalizing and .93 for externalizing behavior problems.

The Meadow-Kendall Social-Emotional Assessment Inventory for deaf and hearing-impaired students (SEAI) is a specialized instrument designed to be completed by teachers and other educational personnel who are in close contact with deaf and hearing-impaired students (Meadow, 1983). Using Chronbach's alpha, an inter-item reliability score of .92 was received for the sociable and communicative behaviors scale, .91 for the impulsive/dominating behaviors scale, .80 for the developmental lags/tasks scale, and .75 for the anxious/compulsive behaviors scale. On the Meadow-Kendall, high scores reflect the absence of negative behaviors. Derived from combining the correlation coefficients from four programs involving 159 children, Pearson's r was used to establish test-retest reliability scores.

Method

The filial therapy training curriculum of the Landreth (2002) 10-week training model was presented to the experimental group of 12 teachers.

To fit the needs of these particular preschool teachers and their students of focus, I modified the material as necessary. Two different groups of teachers together attended five 2-hour training sessions, during which I presented a total of 25 hours of instruction. After the first week of training, each teacher began 30-minute play sessions with her student of focus in a playroom I prepared for the purpose.

One major challenge was to modify typical filial therapy language to fit American sign language, in which not every word is signed because there is not a sign for every word. To take one example, instead of trying to reflect the more complicated "You feel happy playing with that dinosaur," or as the teachers were initially inclined to ask the question: "Are you happy playing with that dinosaur?" they decided to respond "You look happy . . . the dinosaur is fun . . . you like playing with it." Similar issues arose when the teachers were faced with using *choose* and *decide*, language central to the key filial therapy concepts of giving choices and setting limits. The teachers believed that the usual language, "If you choose to (or continue to) choose to) throw sand outside the sandbox, you choose to give up playing with it for the rest of our time today," was incomprehensible to their students because they lacked the fundamental language ability to understand this abstract hypothetical kind of logic or language. During the training sessions, by our talking together, they evolved a more concrete, simpler translation: "You pick. Keep sand in the box. Or throw outside. Throw outside, no more play with sand. Keep inside, play with sand."

PROCEDURE

I used a pre-test–post-test, nonequivalent control group design to carry out the objectives of this study. Before we began the training for the experimental group of teachers, we held the pre-testing sessions for the experimental and nontreatment comparison groups at the preschool during the school day. Immediately after I completed filial training with the experimental group of teachers, I did post-testing for both groups. For pre- and post-testing, teachers from both groups completed the three testing instruments noted earlier: the CBC/TR, the SEAI, and the MEACI. Pre- and post-testing for both groups also included videotaping in a prepared play area, a 20-minute teacher-student play session for the MEACI, using toys and materials recommended by Landreth (2002). The pre- and post-testing video-tapes of teacher-student play sessions were rated by trained raters at the University of North Texas. Inter-rater reliability was established prior to and at the completion of the ratings.

RESULTS

Despite the relatively small sizes of the two groups, a common statistical method was used for analysis and comparison of test results. To test the significance of the difference between the experimental group, the control group, and the variance within groups, an analysis of covariance (ANCOVA) was computed. The post-test scores were used as the dependent variable and the pre-test scores as the covariant on the adjusted post-test means for each hypothesis of scores, as measured by the CBC/TR and the SEAI. To adjust the group means on the pre- and post-test on the basis of the pre-test, ANCOVA was used, thereby statistically equating the experimental and control groups. To test the significance of difference between the means of the two groups, the level of significance for rejection was set at the .05 level. Table 22.1 shows the pre- and post-test means and standard deviations for the experimental and nontreatment comparison groups on the CBC/TR and SEAI.

The experimental group of teachers who received filial therapy training significantly increased their ability (scored significantly lower) on all scales as shown by the mean post-test scores on the following subscales of the MEACI: total empathy, $F(1, 21) = 69.084$, $p = .001$, $\eta^2 = .638$ (large effect size); communication of acceptance, $F(1, 21) = 34.103$, $p = .001$, $\eta^2 = .607$ (large effect size); allowing the child self-direction, $F(1, 21) = 57.298$, $p = .001$, $\eta^2 = .506$ (large effect size); involvement $F(1, 21) = 42.125$, $p = .001$, $\eta^2 = .662$ (large effect size), as compared to the control group.

Preschool students of the experimental group of teachers scored significantly lower than students of teachers in the comparison group on the following measures: the CBC/TR total behavior problems subscale, $F(1, 21) = 9.042$, $p = .007$, $\eta^2 = .601$ (large effect size); internalizing behavior subscale, $F(1, 21) = 12.114$, $p = .002$, $\eta^2 = .167$ (large effect size); withdrawn behavior subscale, $F(1, 21) = 14.884$, $p = .001$, $\eta^2 = .222$ (large effect size). On the following measures, students of experimental group teachers did not score significantly lower than students of control group teachers: the CBC/TR externalizing behavior subscale, $F(1, 21) = 4.016$, $p = .05$, $\eta^2 = .022$; the anxious or depressed subscale, $F(1, 21) = 3.187$, $p = .05$, $\eta^2 = .041$; aggressive behavior subscale, $F(1, 21) = .135$, $p = .05$, $\eta^2 = .001$.

Table 22-1
Mean (M) and Standard Deviation (SD) Scores of the Experimental and Nontreatment Comparison Groups for the Child Behavior Checklist–Caregiver-Teacher Report Form and the Meadow-Kendall Social-Emotional Inventory for Deaf and Hearing-Impaired Students

	Experimental Test Group N = 12				Control Group N = 12			
	Pre-test		Post-test		Pre-test		Post-test	
	M	SD	M	SD	M	SD	M	SD
TBP	29.33	25.20	15.70	17.45	34.75	16.42	29.17	17.21
ITB	6.92	5.45	2.33	2.46	8.17	6.32	6.92	5.54
EBP	14.50	14.99	8.67	11.07	18.50	10.01	14.50	8.43
ADP	1.75	1.77	.833	1.19	2.08	2.19	1.75	2.05
WD	3.42	3.12	.917	1.31	3.58	3.66	3.08	2.54
AGG	9.42	11.72	6.67	10.09	11.83	7.74	9.17	7.37
SCB	2.84	.984	3.35	.440	3.32	.305	3.39	.311
IDB	2.27	1.19	2.95	1.10	2.96	.514	2.88	.632
ACB	3.46	.492	3.61	.447	3.57	.592	3.63	.381

Note:
TBP: Total Behavior Problems subscale of CBC/TR
ITB: Internalizing Behaviors subscale of CBC/TR
EBP: Externalizing Behaviors subscale of CBC/TR
ADP: Anxious/Depressed Behaviors subscale of CBC/TR
WD: Withdrawn Behaviors subscale of CBC/TR
AGG: Aggressive Behaviors subscale of CBC/TR
SCB: Sociable/Communicative Behaviors subscale of SEAI
IDB: Impulsive/Dominating Behaviors subscale of SEAI
ACB: Anxious/Compulsive Behaviors subscale of SEAI
A decrease in mean scores on the CBC/TR and SEAI indicates a decrease in specific problem behaviors.

On the following SEAI subscale scores, there were no significant differences between students whose teachers were in the experimental group and those in the control group: sociable, communicative behaviors, $F(1, 21) = .170, p = .05, \eta^2 = .007$; impulsive, dominating behaviors, $F(1, 21), p = .05, \eta^2 = .043$; anxious, compulsive behaviors, $F(1, 21) = .007, p = .05, \eta^2 = .0003$.

DISCUSSION

The findings of the study indicate that the experimental group of teachers significantly improved their therapeutic relational skills with their students as measured by the different domains of the MEACI compared to the control group. Likewise, the students significantly improved their behavior as a result of their teachers' changed responses compared to the control group. The students' improvements were also reflected on several domains of the CBC/TR.

EMPATHIC BEHAVIOR

As measured by the MEACI, by participating in the filial therapy training, the teachers in the experimental group were able to significantly improve their ability to convey empathy to their students ($p = .001$) with a large effect size (.638), on the basis of ratings of videotaped play sessions with their students (a decrease on the subscales of the MEACI indicates a positive change in the desired behavior); communicate acceptance to their students ($p = .001$) with a large effect size (.607); allow their students to be self-directive, which entailed following the student's lead rather than controlling or directing the child ($p = .001$), again with a large effect size (.506); and increase their level of involvement with the students ($p = .001$) with a large effect size (.662).

Common knowledge suggests that all children require approval and acceptance from adults, especially parents and teachers, and especially deaf and hard of hearing children. However, the research of Stover et al. (1971) indicated that verbal expressions of acceptance did not usually occur during spontaneous interactions between parents and children.

This study confirmed similar findings. A review of the pre-test videotapes of both groups indicated that a substantial majority of the teachers exhibited an initial tendency to view the student play sessions as a continuation of in-class teaching time. Because teachers of deaf and hard of hearing preschoolers view teaching their students how to interact and communicate as a primary responsibility, this tendency was understandable. Therefore, pre-test videotapes were full of teachers' responses such as: "Can you say 'car'? Try and sign 'car' with me. You know what cars do, don't you?" (when a child picked up a toy car) or, "What can you do with it? Here, let me show you how you can play with it. Look here; try it this way. I'll help you. Ooohh, isn't this fun?"

Among the pre-test videotapes of both groups, there were almost no reflections of feeling responses, the chief behavioral indicator of acceptance in the MEACI. While the post-test videotapes of the non-treatment comparison group continued these responses, the experimental group did not.

The potential ramifications of these significant changes for teachers of deaf and hard of hearing children seem noteworthy. If, as research suggests, these children experience higher incidences of aggression, depression, impulsivity, anxiety estrangement, and isolation than their hearing peers (Luterman, 1999, 2004), it would seem important that their teachers be able to genuinely reflect empathy and acceptance for the student's struggles, while at the same time know how to be meaningfully involved and allow the students appropriate self-direction.

BEHAVIOR PROBLEMS

As measured by the CBC/TR, students of teachers who received filial therapy training showed a decrease ($p = .007$) in total behavior problems with a large effect size (.601). In light of the high incidence of behavior problems prevalent in this group of students, such a reduction in overall behavior problems is noteworthy. Experimental group students also demonstrated a significant decrease in internalizing behaviors ($p = .002$), though with a small effect size (.167). According to Marshark and Clark (1993), hard of hearing and deaf children are more likely to live from an internal frame of reference, which is believed to foster internalizing behavior problems. Also, internalizing behaviors are generally regarded as precursors to the development of anxiety, depression, and emotional withdrawal, all common in hard of hearing and deaf children (Hindley, 1997). Since a reduction in the students' internalizing behaviors suggests a reduction in their tendency to develop more serious emotional difficulties, this reduction seems worthy to note. It appears that the dual combination of the accepting, empathic presence of the teacher and child-directed play furnished the children with an avenue of relief for some of the ongoing frustration of not hearing, allowing them to be more trusting, thereby reducing their need to internalize distress (Smith, 2004).

When the two groups were compared, the results of the CBC/TR externalizing behavior scale did not attain statistical significance as expected. In comparison to the nontreatment comparison group, students whose teachers received filial therapy training did not show a significant decrease ($p < .05$) on the CBC/TR anxious or depressed subscale. Because significant decreases were demonstrated on the withdrawn and internalizing scale overall, this lack of expected decrease was initially puzzling. However, a closer evaluation of the anxious or depressed pre- and post-test scores revealed a notably low level of anxious and depressed behaviors among experimental group students, as perceived by their teachers. On the pre-test, none of the scores of individual students approached clinical levels of significance. Thus, among this group of students as judged by their teachers, there did not appear to be enough anxious or depressed behaviors to constitute a difficulty. Therefore, the comparison scores did not attain significance.

Compared to the no-treatment control, the filial therapy intervention demonstrated a large treatment effect ($\eta^2 = .222$) on children's withdrawn behavior. Further, the between-group difference over time was statistically significant ($p = .001$). This suggests that children whose teachers did receive filial therapy training increased behaviors associated with age-appropriate interactions with peers and adults, decreased behaviors associated with isolation and withdrawal and decreased physical and emotional distancing of self from others.

Looking again at the CBC/TR, when comparing the two groups' aggressive behavior scores, experimental group students did not show a significant decrease ($p < .05$) as expected. Furthermore, experimental group students did not demonstrate a significant increase ($p > .05$) in sociable or communicative behaviors as measured by the Meadow-Kendall Social-Emotional Assessment Inventory for deaf and hearing-impaired students.

VIGNETTES AND EXAMPLES

At our last meeting, teachers in the experimental group were excited to share anecdotal examples of children who had significantly improved their behaviors in the playroom and classroom and on the playground. Speaking of her student of focus, a kindergarten child who, because of his deafness, had almost no understandable spoken language, one teacher put it this way: "Since Timothy did not have his hearing loss identified until he was four years old, he has only been in our school for six months. I did not have the opportunity to bond with him the way I have with the other children in the class. If things did not go his way, he would jump up in the air and land on his bottom, screaming and crying. The crying would often last 45 minutes. The training has been most successful in helping me bond with Timothy. Today, he hugged me this morning, sat in my lap during music time, and ran up and hugged me on the playground. He would never have done this before. He has not had a temper tantrum in a month. He now works through his feelings without jumping and crying. Other teachers have noticed and commented to me on his improved behavior and attitude. He loves special playtime. Often, he asks me if it's time to 'go get the key' (to the playroom)."

Another teacher said this: "I chose Demarcus for my student of focus because he had little eye contact and few signs (little ability or interest in using sign language to communicate) and was not well-bonded with me or the other children. At 18 months, he had meningitis, which took his hearing. He was on a normal developmental track until then. After a few sessions in the playroom, he started to smile, in and outside the playroom. Then he began to laugh appropriately at silly activities. He started to play 'peek-a-boo' in the playroom. This was his way of starting to make eye contact. Now he makes eye contact for longer periods of time. He now seeks me out when he has a problem. He is now working to talk and sign."

Reflecting on her 4-year-old deaf student of focus, still another teacher said: "Jennifer has a real temper. Last year, if things did not go exactly as she wanted, she would explode. She was very aggressive, hitting, kicking, biting, scratching, and throwing things, including chairs. Many times I had to restrain her, and it took forever for her to calm down. *There was absolutely no reasoning with her* (author's italics). Now that we've had the play sessions and I've had the classes, I have noticed a deep bonding that is emerging between us. She has begun to seek me out for hugs instead of my having to approach her. She now regulates and modifies her anger and is less reactive in situations that would have set her off last year. I am excited about this new, self-checking behavior. She is now very helpful and often considerate to everyone. Sometimes she even acts like a mediator when other students are in conflict. This never would have happened last year. I think the filial therapy training is responsible for both of our changes" (Smith, 2002).

What seems especially noteworthy to me in this context is that the teacher's prior attempts to reason with Jennifer had been totally ineffective. Talking to or attempting to reason with an out-of-control deaf or hard of hearing preschool child is not likely to be successful because of the inherent difficulty in communicating with a deaf, acting-out child. In other words, the delayed ability to communicate effectively was likely a big factor contributing to Jennifer's ongoing feelings of frustration and anger, as well as her tendency to act out aggressively. Further, it appears that before her teacher's filial therapy training, applying physical restraints had not been successful in diminishing Jennifer's aggressive behaviors. It appears that in the course of regular student-teacher play sessions, a different quality of emotional relationship emerged between Jennifer and her teacher, one that was more positive both in and outside the playroom. This example suggests the effectiveness of filial therapy in fostering positive relationship changes and a reduction in aggressive, acting out behavior problems as verified in both quantitative and qualitative research studies.

CONCLUSION

My research study demonstrated that preschool teachers of hard of hearing and deaf children may become effective agents for change in assisting their students by learning and applying the basic skills of filial therapy training in one-to-one, special play sessions. The study suggests that both the teacher and the student develop a different, more helpful quality of emotional relationship. This developing relationship has been shown to positively affect the students' difficult behaviors in both the playroom and classroom and on the playground. This study also suggests that classroom teachers of deaf and hard of hearing children are capable of learning and applying filial therapy skills in a helpful manner and integrating them into their broader regimen of helping skills that they use daily. Finally, the study suggests that play may well be the universal language of children, even for children whose primary difficulty in life is acquiring and learning to communicate and master a language they cannot hear, without the use of play.

REFERENCES

Achenbach, T. M., & Edelbrock, C. S. (2000). *Child behavior checklist/Caregiver-teacher report form*. Burlington, VT: University Associates in Psychiatry.

American School Counseling Association. (2003). The ASCA National Model: A framework for school counseling programs: Executive summary. *Professional School Counseling, 6*(3), 165–168.

Andronico, M., & Guerney, B. (1967). The potential application of filial therapy to the school situation. *Journal of School Psychology, 6*(1), 2–7.

Axline, V. M. (1947). *Play therapy: The inner dynamics of childhood*. Boston: Houghton Mifflin.

Bratton, S. C., & Landreth, G. L. (1995). Filial therapy with single parents: Effects on parental acceptance, empathy and stress. *International Journal of Play Therapy, 41*(1), 61–80.

Bratton, S. C., & Ray, D. C. (2000). What the research shows about play therapy. *International Journal of Play Therapy, 9*(1), 47–88, 101–117.

Cates, J. (1991). Self-concept in hearing and prelingual, profoundly deaf students. *American Annals of the Deaf, 136*, 354–359.

Chau, I., & Landreth, G. (1997). Filial therapy with Chinese parents: Effects on parental empathic reactions, parental acceptance and parental stress. *International Journal of Play Therapy, 6*(2), 75–92.

Deselle, D., & Pearlmutter, L. (1997). Navigating two cultures: Deaf children, self-esteem and parents' communication patterns. *Social Work in Education, 19*, 23–30.

Guerney, B. (1964). Filial therapy: Description and rationale. *Journal of Counseling and Psychology, 28*(4), 304–310.

Guerney, B., Stover, L., & DeMerit, S. (1968). A measurement of empathy for parent-child interaction. *Journal of Genetic Psychology, 12*, 49–55.

Guerney, L. (1997). Filial therapy. In K. O'Connor & I. Braverman (Eds.), *Play therapy theory and practice: A comparative presentation* (pp. 131–157). New York: John Wiley & Sons.

Guerney, L. (2000). Filial therapy into the 21st century. *International Journal of Play Therapy, 1*(1), 31–42.

Guerney, L., & Stover, L. (1971). *Filial therapy: Final report on MH 18254–01.* Unpublished manuscript, The Pennsylvania State University, University Park, PA.

Harris, L., Van Zandt, C., & Rees, T. (1997). Counseling needs of students who are deaf and hard of hearing. *The School Counselor, 44*, 271–279.

Hindley, P. (1997). Psychiatric aspects of hearing impairment. *Journal of Child Psychology, Psychiatry and Allied Disciplines, 38*, 101–117.

Ita, C. (1999). The psychological development of children who are deaf or hard of hearing: A critical review. *Volta Review, 101*(3), 165–182.

Jones, T., Ross, P., & Kendall, J. (2001). Inclusion strategies for deaf students with special needs. Retrieved April 30, 2004 from http://www.deafchildren.org/home/html/endart_ende05.html.

Landreth, G. L. (2002). *Play therapy: The art of the relationship* (2nd ed). New York: Brunner-Routledge.

Lederberg, A. (1991). *Antecedents of language competence and social emotional adjustment of young deaf children: Final report.* Atlanta: Georgia State University.

Luterman, D. (1999). Emotional aspects of hearing loss. *Volta Review, 99*(5), 75–84.

Luterman, D. (2004). Counseling families of children with hearing loss and special needs. *Volta Review, 104*(4), 215–220.

Mantanini-Manfredi, M. (1993). The emotional development of deaf children. In M. Marshark & M. Clark (Eds.), *Psychological perspectives on deafness* (pp. 46–93). Hillsdale, NJ: Erlbaum.

Marshark, M., & Clark, M. (Eds.). (1993). *Psychological perspectives on deafness.* Hillsdale, NJ: Erlbaum.

Meadow, K. (1983). An instrument for assessment of social emotional adjustment in hearing impaired preschoolers. *American Annals of the Deaf, 128,* 826–834.

Murdock, T., & Lybarger, R. (1997). An attributional analysis of aggression among children who are deaf. *Journal of American Deafness and Rehabilitation Association, 31*(23), 10–22.

Oualline, J. (1975). *Behavioral outcomes of short-term nondirective play therapy with preschool deaf children.* Unpublished doctoral dissertation, University of North Texas, Denton.

Ray, D. C., Armstrong, S. A., Warren, E. S., & Balkin, R. S. (2005). Play therapy practices among elementary school counselors. *Professional School Counseling, 8*(4), 360–365.

Schum, R. (2004). Psychological assessment of children with multiple handicaps who have hearing loss. *Volta Review, 104*(4), 237–255.

Smith, M. (2002). *Filial therapy with teachers of deaf and hard of hearing preschool children.* Unpublished doctoral dissertation, University of North Texas, Denton.

Smith, M., & Landreth, G. L. (2004). Filial therapy with teachers of deaf and hard of hearing preschool children. *International Journal of Play Therapy, 13*(1), 13–33.

Smith, N., & Landreth, G. L. (2003). Intensive filial therapy with child witnesses of domestic violence: A comparison with individual and sibling group play therapy. *International Journal of Play Therapy, 12*(1), 67–88.

Stover, L., Guerney, B., & O'Connell, M. (1971). Measurements of acceptance, allowing self-direction, involvement and empathy in adult-child interaction. *Journal of Psychology, 77,* 261–269.

White, J., Draper, K., & Flynt, M. (1997). Kindertherapy: Teachers as therapeutic agents. *International Journal of Play Therapy, 6*(2), 33–49.

Yoshinga-Itano, C., Snyder, L., & Day, D. (1998). The relationship of language and symbolic play in children with hearing loss. *Volta Review, 100*(3), 135–185.

CHAPTER 23

Child-Centered Kinder Training for Teachers of Preschool Children Deemed at Risk

PHYLLIS POST

Rosa is a preschool teacher. She teaches twelve 4-year-old children in her bright, well-furnished classroom in a limited-income area of a Southern city. Ten of the children are African American, and most of their families have low socioeconomic status. Almost weekly, Rosa learns that one of the children has moved from where he or she lives. One child has cycled through the homeless shelter twice this year—once because the girl and her mom were evicted from their home in the middle of the night after her mom had a fistfight with her aunt. Rosa hears when the electricity has been turned off in children's homes. One child sometimes comes to school hungry. Several of the parents seem so overwhelmed surviving day-to-day that they cannot attend to their children. Rosa is committed to her work. She loves children, is well educated, and wants to teach children with great needs. She tries to help them in the best ways she knows. Her goals are to keep them safe, to help them learn essential skills, and to maintain an engaging and consistent classroom. She disciplines freely using a clear authoritarian style, and the children know what to expect. But often it seems like the chaos of their home life spills into the classroom, and the children become aggressive and inattentive. Rosa struggles to maintain control in her classroom and often feels disconnected from the children. She leaves school exhausted many days, and after only three years in the classroom she is considering other careers.

Rosa's experience is echoed in the literature. Children who live in poverty begin school with fewer cognitive, social, and emotional school-readiness skills than children not at risk (Edlefsen & Baird, 1994). These children often exhibit lack of impulse control, short attention spans, poor academic performance (Frick-Helms, 1997), depression, and poor social skills (Post, 1999). Numerous scholars have linked poverty to at-risk behaviors that include academic failure, socio-emotional problems, and future incarceration (Gibbs, 2003; Harrison & Beck, 2005; La Roche, 1991; Nievar & Luster, 2006). Research also indicates that the cycle of poverty and mental disorders is self-perpetuating and lifelong (Myers & Gill, 2004). For many at-risk children, the constant uncertainty and sense of impending crisis in their lives can make learning and behaving difficult. Because children of all cultural and ethnic groups communicate their concerns and their needs through their play (Cochran, 1996; Landreth, 2006; Sweeney & Skurja, 2001), communicating with children using the relationship-building skills of play therapy is one promising way to help these children.

BENEFITS OF PLAY THERAPY

Research over the last 60 years has demonstrated the effectiveness of play therapy in reducing children's behavioral, emotional, and mental health problems (Ray, 2006). In their meta-analysis, Bratton, Ray, Rhine, and Jones (2005) found a large treatment effect for play therapy interventions with children ($p < .001$). With regard to children deemed at risk, research indicates that when play therapy is included in a program of services, the children feel happier at school, show improved concentration at school, handle fears more effectively (Albaum, 1990), exhibit greater self-control and self-acceptance (Trostle, 1988), and are absent from school less (Baecher, Cicchelli, & Baratta, 1989). Because teachers interact with at-risk children every day in their classrooms, focusing on the teacher-child relationship can not only provide support for the children (Baker, 2006) but also help increase teachers' competence and confidence that they can help children with such enormous needs.

CHILD TEACHER RELATIONSHIP TRAINING

Working effectively with at-risk children in a classroom with many children needing extra attention is a tremendous challenge for teachers like Rosa. One hopeful approach, however, is training teachers to use play therapy skills in the classroom, for it addresses the needs of both the children and the teachers. For the children, it can help interrupt the cycle of stress in their lives and help them gain a sense of control over their own lives. For the teachers, it can provide effective communication skills that can help them have a greater sense of acceptance of the children, sense of control about their ways of relating to the children, and competence when interacting with all children in the classroom (White, Flynt, & Jones, 1999).

Over 30 years ago, Guerney and Flumen (1970) proposed that teachers, like parents in filial therapy (Guerney, 1964; Landreth, 2006), could be effective therapeutic change agents for children. Their focus was on changing the teacher to help children. White, Flynt, and Draper (1997) conceptualized kinder therapy, a consultation model for training teachers, based on Guerney's model of filial therapy and Adler's (1983) theory of individual psychology (Draper, White, O'Shaughnessy, Flynt, & Jones, 2001). Research indicates that kinder training not only improved classroom interactions between teachers and students, but also improved student behaviors and academic skills (Draper et al., 2001; White et al., 1999).

Using the filial model developed by Landreth (2002), several studies explored the impact of training teachers. Brown (2000) and Smith and Landreth (2004) both found that teacher trainees who were instructed in child-teacher relationship training demonstrated increased empathy, more self-direction, and greater acceptance and involvement with children compared to untrained teacher trainees. Subsequent to the research presented in this chapter, Landreth and Bratton (1999) published the principles of Child Parent Relationship Therapy (CPRT), which described a 10-session filial therapy model based on Landreth's (2002) model of filial therapy. The training materials were published in the *Child Parent Relationship Therapy (CPRT) Treatment Manual* (Bratton, Landreth, Kellam, & Blackard, 2006). The training model, adapted for teachers, is now known as Child-Teacher Relationship Training (CTRT). In two recent studies examining the impact of CTRT on children, Helker and Ray (2009) and Morrison (2006) found that the children in the classrooms of trained teachers demonstrated a decrease in externalizing behaviors, such as aggression and inattentiveness. This body of work indicates the effectiveness of working training teachers as therapeutic agents for children.

RESEARCH GOALS

The goal of this project, originally published in 2004 (Post, McAllister, Sheely, Hess, & Flowers, 2004), was to use Landreth's filial therapy

(Landreth 2002) model with preschool teachers of children deemed at risk. The term CTRT is used in this chapter because it is an accurate representation of the process used. This project had three separate phases, each with a different goal. In the first phase, the goal was to determine the impact of CTRT on the children's externalizing, internalizing, and adaptive behaviors both in the classroom and at home. The goal of the second phase was to examine the impact of the CTRT training on teachers' behaviors as a part of the CTRT process both with individual children and with all children in their classrooms after extending CTRT with 13 weekly group sessions that focused on generalizing the skills. The third phase of the project extended into the next academic year, and the goal was to determine whether teachers who participated in the CTRT training could demonstrate the skills learned one year later both in individual play sessions with children and in the classroom setting to a greater extent than nonparticipating teachers. To this end, the research questions were:

- Is there a difference in children's internalizing and externalizing behaviors, as perceived by teachers and parents, between teachers who were trained and not trained in CTRT?
- Is there a difference in demonstration of play therapy skills and empathy in individual play sessions between teachers who were trained and not trained in CTRT?
- Is there a difference, one year after the training, in demonstration of play therapy skills and empathy in the classroom between teachers who were trained and not trained in CTRT?

METHODS

The children in this study attended two early childhood programs located in a Southern urban neighborhood serving a population that experienced poverty, crime, single parenting, teenage parenting, and substance abuse. One of the centers served only children who live in the neighborhood. The other center served, in addition to neighborhood children, children whose mothers lived in a residential treatment center in recovery from substance abuse as an alternative to incarceration. Seventy-one percent of the population received financial support as they moved toward their goal of independent living. Eighty percent of the children in the center were African American, and 58 percent resided in single-family households. The centers served approximately 150 children from birth to pre-kindergarten.

PARTICIPANTS

Teachers were invited to participate in the CTRT training. One teacher described her reason for participating and her selection of a child for the individual play sessions in the following way:

> There were many times I wondered if I was in the right job or whether I was just wasting my time. Being completely honest, it was a low-paying job for the work we did. The play therapy project was a life-changing experience for me. I entered the project as a skeptic. I just wanted something different than being in the stressful classroom all day. This was during a time when I had fourteen 2-year-olds with two assistant teachers. Over half of those kids were labeled as [having] behavior problems, and others had at least one medical diagnosis. My chosen student was a little girl with whom I really didn't have a relationship. She was in my class but she was extremely shy and almost nonverbal. I just remember trying to get her to do different activities or to associate with the other kids only to be met with extreme crying and tantrums. This little girl preferred to be in a corner by herself doing, what looked like to me, absolutely nothing.

The nine teachers who participated in the training sessions were the lead or assistant teachers from the 2-, 3-, and 4-year-old classrooms. The participating teachers included eight females and one male; three were white, five were African American, one was Hispanic; with regard to teaching experience, three had more than three years of experience, two had three years, two had two years, and one had one year; with regard to education, seven were college graduates, one had some college, and one was a high school graduate. For the purposes of comparing teachers' ability to generalize the skills into the classroom setting, a control group of teachers was selected. The teachers in the control group included nine females; three were white, four were African American, one was Hispanic; with regard to teaching experience, five had more than three years experience, one had three years, two had two years; with regard to education, seven were college graduates, one had some college, and one was a high school graduate. The average teacher in the project was an African American female college graduate with at least three years experience teaching in the preschool.

In the first phase of the project, participating teachers selected one child from their classroom with whom they would conduct seven individual play sessions as a part of the CTRT training. The child was selected because of specific behavioral concerns, such as aggression, extreme withdrawal, lack of social or academic skills, or problems with transitions. The children selected to participate in the individual session included six males and three females; the average age was 3.2; eight were African American, and one was white. Each teacher also selected another child from the classroom that exhibited similar characteristics as the child selected for the play sessions. The matched children were nonparticipants and included eight males and one female; the average age was 3.3; all nine were African Americans.

In the second and third phase of the project, 16 teachers who were the lead or assistant teachers from the 2-, 3-, and 4-year-old classrooms participated. Eight of the teachers had participated in the CTRT training the previous year, and eight teachers who had not participated were matched with the participating group on as many demographic points as possible, with particular emphasis on age, ethnicity, educational experience, and work site.

PROCEDURES

The teachers were trained in CTRT during the fall of the first year of the project. During the fall semester, the nine participating teachers met for 10 weeks in a group setting for the training. The training sessions were co-led by an advanced graduate student and a recent counseling graduate currently employed as a school counselor; each of the group leaders had training, supervision, and experience in play therapy. The training followed the 10-week filial training process outlined by Landreth (2006). Participants learned the basic skills of play therapy through live modeling, role-playing as both a child and the counselor, and homework assignments. The first three sessions consisted of teaching the foundations of child-centered play therapy as described by Axline (1947) and Landreth (2006), the appropriateness of toy selection for the playroom, and the following fundamental responses to use in the play sessions: tracking, responding to feelings, responding to the child's effort, returning responsibility to the child, and limit setting. After the third session, teachers practiced these skills with their selected student for 30 minutes each week. The 30-minute play sessions were conducted in a playroom in the school that was equipped with toys in the three categories recommended by Landreth (2006): real life, aggressive, and creative expressive. The play sessions took place one time each week during the school day when a substitute teacher could supervise the other children in the classroom. These individual play sessions continued for seven weeks (sessions 4 to 10).

Immediately following each play session, each teacher met with a counseling graduate student enrolled in a graduate level filial therapy course for 45 minutes of individual feedback. The individual supervision consisted of a review of the videotaped session, a discussion of the teacher's perceptions of the play session, and one specific way to modify the teacher's approach for continued development. During individual supervision, the focus was on the relationship between the teacher and the child in addition to the play therapy skills. The graduate students providing feedback to the teachers modeled the counseling skills being taught as they interacted with them (for example, responding to feelings, responding to efforts, returning responsibility). Rosa shared the following comment about the training:

> I remember the first few weeks in play therapy she would play over in the corner and I would just sit there reflecting what she was doing. It felt like a play-by-play commentary. She didn't even acknowledge I was in the room. I just knew this play therapy stuff was a bunch of junk and there was no way it would work. I'm sure my face reflected this. . . . Then a breakthrough happened in the play sessions with her. It sounds small, but it was an amazing experience for me and my student. I finally learned how to reflect feelings. "You're really confused about how to use that" or "You don't like that toy" would get the little girl to at least look at me. Soon she would smile, shake her head in acknowledgment, or stomp her feet. Finally one day, after a reflection on the frustration she was having with using a toy, the little girl brings it to me and sits it on my lap. "You want me to help you" was greeted with a smile and her pushing the toy further on my lap. I can't remember what the toy was, but I remember how happy she was when I helped her. This was the beginning of our relationship. This same little girl who would never come near me in class now wanted me to tie her shoes.

As this comment shows, during group sessions 4 to 10, teachers discussed their individual play sessions, shared videotaped clips of their work, and received feedback from both the instructors and the other participating teachers. Following the 10-week training when the teachers worked with the individual children to learn the skills, the teachers continued the small group sessions.

Participating teachers met for 13 weeks in a two-hour group to reinforce their skills and to learn to generalize the skills into their classrooms. The play therapy skills were reviewed during the first five sessions. Teachers were reintroduced to the types of play therapy responses, focusing on one technique per group meeting. When reviewing the skills, the goal was for teachers to generalize the use of the skills from the individual play sessions with one child into the classroom setting. Thus, group discussions began to identify appropriate and inappropriate times to use the skills in the classroom, during meal times, and on the playground.

In the group sessions, teachers discussed their successes and challenges when using the skills in their classrooms. Classroom forms were completed by teachers throughout the week, describing the following: the event, the teacher's play therapy response to the event, and the outcome. Feedback was solicited from other group members in hopes of developing an appropriate response to the challenging event. Teachers were encouraged to try the suggestions given by the group and report the outcome in the next session. A sample activity developed to increase the frequency of using play therapy skills, called "I caught you," encouraged teachers to catch their colleagues in the act of successfully using the new skills. At the final session, the teachers reflected upon the year's training and provided feedback about the overall program. Rosa reported that it was difficult for her to learn to use new skills and refrain from her old ways of teaching. She said, "The most difficult skill for me to use in the classroom, for a while, was tracking because when I tracked one child, 13 other children ran over for the attention."

To determine teachers' continued application of the skills one year after the training, eight of the teachers who had the CTRT training from the previous year and a control group of teachers who did not receive training participated in a follow-up study. Each of the teachers conducted one videotaped 30-minute play session with an individual child. Eight children participated in the study. Each child participated in one play session with a teacher in the participating group and one play session with the paired control group teacher. Following the collection of these data, two 45-minute focus groups were conducted with the participating group of teachers in which teachers reflected upon their experiences and what they learned about themselves and the children in their classrooms.

INSTRUMENTS

Children   Both the teacher and the parent forms of the Behavior Assessment Scale for Children (BASC; Reynolds & Kamphaus, 1998) were used to assess the adaptive and problem behaviors of the children in the school setting. The subscales are externalizing problems (aggression, hyperactivity, conduct problems), internalizing problems (anxiety, depression, somatization), school problems (attention problems, learning problems), other problems (atypicality, withdrawal), and adaptive skills (adaptability, leadership, social skills, study skills).

Teachers The Assessment of Child-Centered Play Therapy Skills (ACCEPTS; Post, 2003) was developed to measure the teachers' ability to demonstrate the following play therapy skills and was based on Landreth's (2006) child-centered play therapy skills: following the child's lead, responding to feelings, returning responsibility to the child, responding to the child's efforts, and setting limits. The ACCEPTS was designated I or C, according to whether it was used to assess skills in individual play sessions (I) or in classroom observations (C). To score the ACCEPTS, raters indicated which of the play therapy skills the teachers used in six three-minute time segments. The responses were weighted in a positive direction when the skills were observed (for example, in response to a child's question, "What should I play with now?" the teacher said, "In here, you can decide") and weighted negatively when the teacher responded in a way that did not demonstrate the use of the skills (for example, in response to a child's question, "What should I play with now?" the teacher said, "Why don't you play with the dolls now?"). The rationale for having both positive and negative weights was that using the skills enhances the development of children to accept themselves, understand themselves, assume responsibility for their decisions, and control their behavior; on the other hand, responding to children in the opposite way could potentially prevent or deter the optimal development of children in terms of those same dimensions. The inter-rater reliability for the scale was .88. The content validity of ACCEPTS was .97, based on the ability of graduate students enrolled in a play therapy course to categorize sample teacher responses.

Based on the work of Stover, Guerney, and O'Connell (1971), the Measurement in Empathy in Adult-Child Interaction (MEACI), as modified by Bratton and Landreth (1995), was used to measure the degree of empathy the teacher demonstrated as indicated by communication of acceptance, allowing the child self-direction, and involvement with the child. In this study, the MEACI was designated by an I or C, indicating whether it was used to assess empathy during individual play sessions (I) or classroom interactions (C). Stover et al. (1971) reported reliability coefficients of at least .89 for three of the scales.

Data Analysis

Children   To determine differences between children in the participating group (n = 9) and control group (n = 9) as a result of the individual play sessions that were a part of the CTRT training, four two-way ANOVAs, with one between and one within factor, were used to examine changes from pre-test to post-test on the composite scales on the BASC as scored by the teacher. Two-way ANOVAs were also used to examine changes from pre-test to post-test on the parents' ratings of the BASC composite scales.

Teachers   To determine differences between the participating (n = 9) and nonparticipating (n = 7) teachers in the skills demonstrated in their individual play sessions, dependent *t*-tests were used to examine changes from pre-tests to post-tests on ACCEPTS-I and MEACI-I. Following the group sessions, which continued with participating teachers to help them learn to apply the skills in their classrooms, an independent *t*-test was used to examine differences on the ACCEPTS-C and MEACI-C. Cohen's *d* (1988) was used to determine the effect size and examine the magnitude of difference between the means. All statistical tests used a one-tailed level of significance of .05. A more conservative level of significance was not used because of the small sample size and potential lack of adequate power to detect meaningful group differences.

Teachers: Follow-Up Study   Independent *t*-tests were used to compare the two teacher groups in individual and classroom settings using the ACCEPTS-I, ACCEPTS-C, MEACI-I, and MEACI-C. A Bonferroni correction was used to adjust the significance level so it could control for Type 1 errors on multiple independent *t*-tests between the two groups. Also, themes from the focus group were identified and analyzed using a facilitated discussion process. The themes from the focus groups were examined to determine the experience and learnings of the participants.

RESULTS

Children

The first question addressed differences in children's behavior, as perceived by teachers and parents, between teachers who participated in CTRT and those who did not. There were no statistical significances between or within main effects with regard to children's behaviors; there were, however, three statistically significant interactions: internalizing problems ($F = 3.94$, $p = .03$), behavioral symptoms index ($F = 3.50$, $p = .04$), and adaptive skills ($F = 4.40$, $p = .04$). The effect sizes, as reported using partial η^2, were moderate, ranging from 18 percent to 20 percent of the variance accounted for by the interaction effect. For Internalizing Problems and Behavioral Symptoms Index, the participating group's scores decreased from pre-test to post-test, whereas the control group increased from pre-test to post-test. For the adaptive skills, the participating group's scores increased from pre-test to post-test, while the control group's scores decreased from pre-test to post-test. The teachers did not perceive a difference between children who participated and those who did not participate in externalizing problems. With regard to parents' ratings of the BASC composite scales, no significant interactions were found for any of the scales of the BASC.

TEACHERS

To determine whether a difference existed in the demonstration of play therapy skills and empathy in individual play sessions between teachers trained in CTRT and nontrained teachers, dependent *t*-tests were used to examine changes in teachers' scores from pre-tests to post-tests on ACCEPTS-I. There was a statistically significant increase on the ACCEPTS-I between the pre-test and post-test, indicating an increase in ability to demonstrate play therapy skills in individual sessions with children. Similarly, there was a decrease in the score on the MEACI-I, indicating an increase in the demonstration of empathy. The magnitude of change was quite large for both ACCEPTS-I ($g = 4.1$) and MEACI-I ($g = 1.95$).

Following the 13-week groups with the goal of applying the skills in the classroom setting, an independent *t*-test was used to examine the differences between the participating (n = 9) and control groups (n = 7) of teachers on the ACCEPTS-C. There was a statistically significant difference between the groups (t = 3.83, $p < .01$), such that the participating group had a higher mean demonstration of effective play therapy skills when compared with the control group ($g = 1.76$). Following the training, teachers wrote about their experiences about the training as follows:

- [The training] helped me recognize children as individuals and people. . . . It also helped me to realize the most important goal is helping, not having control.
- [The training] reminded me to see everything from the child's point of view. It helped me to stop and think of the child first.
- Situations that in the past would get me upset or in a tizzy, now my attitude is, "It's not that serious." Then my play therapy skills take over.
- [The training] has helped me empower the children to be involved in decision making and taking responsibility for their actions. There is more of a partnership between the kids and myself.
- I think [the children] realize there is calmness in my spirit. They know that they have a voice and that it matters to me how they feel.
- I am allowing a lot more freedom in play. Before I was a little uptight—not wanting them to be messy. Now they can go much further before I set a limit.
- I definitely pay more attention to the children. What are they feeling? Why are they feeling this way? Instead of reacting to the child, I interact with them.
- It was refreshing to transfer most of the power and responsibility on to the children.
- [The training] has allowed me to view children more as individuals that have feelings instead of as children that need to be managed.

Teachers: Follow-Up Study

The findings indicate that there was a statistically significant difference between the mean scores on the ACCEPTS-I of teachers who participated in the training and those teachers who did not participate (t = 7.56, $p < .013$) one year following the training, such that participating teachers demonstrated play therapy skills more effectively than the nonparticipating teachers. The effect size for the differences between the two groups was large ($d = 4.8$). With regard to demonstration of empathy, the findings indicate that there was a statistically significant difference between the mean scores on the MEACI-I of teachers who participated in the training and those teachers who did not participate (t = -10.53, $p < .013$), such that participating teachers responded more empathically than the nonparticipating teachers. The effect size for the differences between the two groups was large ($d = 6.7$). However, with regard to demonstration of skills and empathy in the classroom, the results indicate that there was no difference between the mean scores on the ACCEPTS-C or MEACI-C of teachers who participated in the training and those teachers who did not participate.

Through the focus groups conducted one year after the CTRT training, the following themes emerged regarding the use of play therapy skills:

- Teachers learned to interact with children in a different way.
- Teachers believed they used the skills in their classrooms.
- Teachers valued children's opinions and feelings more highly.
- Teachers gained a better understanding of the children and made more allowances for "children to act like children."
- Teachers believed that children should have choices and be able to make decisions for themselves.
- Teachers believed that limit setting, especially giving choices, made discipline easier.
- Teachers noted that some skills were hard to use in a classroom because many children wanted their attention at the same time.

One teacher said, "I noticed that at least once or twice throughout the day, I used the training that I learned. I think it is great to know. I'll say something to the kids, and I'm like, yes, that comes from play therapy." Rosa expressed more confidence when she stated:

I feel that I am a much better manager of the classroom. It is a lot easier as compared to prior to the training, whether they (the children) have problems behaviorally or emotionally. I feel much more confident. On a daily basis I feel a lot less stress because I can handle the class in any situation.

These themes echoed the teachers' reactions to the training immediately after the CTRT training the year before (Post, 2003), with one interesting exception. In response to the question of how each teacher's personal view of children had been affected by the training, one teacher said that her view of herself had been transformed, "I think that the training changed my view of myself more than my view of the children."

DISCUSSION

According to the teachers' perceptions, the internalizing behaviors of the participating children decreased from pre-test to post-test, whereas the nonparticipating children's internalizing behaviors increased from pre-test to post-test. The same pattern was evident regarding the adaptive skills, such that the participating group's scores increased from pre-test to post-test while the control group's scores decreased from pre-test to post-test. While the findings are consistent with the findings of Post (1999), which indicated that an intervention may be needed to prevent at-risk children from developing greater problems, they are inconsistent with the findings of Helker and Ray (2009) and Morrison (2006), who found children's externalizing behaviors changed, while internalizing behaviors did not change. Possible explanations for these differences are the different ways that children were identified for the project, the time in the project that children were assessed, or differences in the assessments used to measure change.

Because at-risk children often enter school with disadvantages that have an impact on their readiness to attend and learn in the classroom, these findings present additional evidence that CTRT is one process teachers can use to help vulnerable children become more effective classroom citizens and classroom learners. Perhaps the changes in the children's behaviors were a result of children's behaviors changing in school. An alternative explanation is that the children's behaviors did not change, and the change occurred in the teachers' view of children.

The primary goal of this project was to focus to examine the impact of CTRT training on the teachers, themselves, in both individual play sessions and in their classrooms. The results indicate that teachers who participated in the CTRT were able to demonstrate play therapy skills and empathy with the children in the playroom and in the classroom to a greater degree than nonparticipating teachers. CTRT helped teachers become more responsive, empathic, and understanding of at-risk children. The comments of teachers following the experience showed that the teachers' perceptions about children changed as a result of the training. For example, Rosa reported that the training was important and meaningful to her. She felt pleased with the skills that she learned, felt proud of being able to implement the skills, and shared that her overall view of children changed as a result of the experience. As a result of the experience, her feelings of stress in the classroom decreased, and she had a renewed sense of wanting to work in this preschool setting.

Finally, this study focused on the long-term retention of child-centered play therapy skills of teachers who work with children considered at risk. The results revealed significant differences between trained CTRT teachers and nontrained teachers one year after the training in their play therapy skills and empathy in individual play sessions with a child; teachers, however, did not retain the skills in their classrooms one year later. In spite of the promising results of this research, the study had some limitations that need to be addressed in future research.

The study had several limitations. The sample size was small, and participants were not randomly assigned. Another limitation was that teachers self-selected, and assessed, two children from their classroom. Therefore, teachers were aware of which children were participating in the individual sessions with them for the initial phase of the training. As a result, their ratings of children could have been biased. Another limitation of this study was that the data about teachers' behaviors were collected for only one classroom observation for one hour. Extending the assessment of classroom behavior to a full day or repeated over several days would yield a more accurate assessment of teachers' behaviors in the classroom. A final limitation in the research was that some of the teachers indicated that cultural differences between the group leaders and themselves influenced their ability to be open to the CTRT model. One teacher stated,

> There are differences I've noticed between the ways one culture raises their family compared to how another culture does. Then you learn this new process and the facilitators were white. But, you know, we were all different cultures and you're thinking, well, maybe, this is the way their culture does it and maybe we are coming from a way another culture does it. You had to kind of be really open-minded about the whole process.

This comment indicates that the teacher was conscious of racial differences. What is most interesting about this comment is that while all of the raters in the classroom were White, only one of the two group facilitators was White. The other group facilitator was a biracial, African American and Asian, woman. The implication of this teacher's comment is that factors in addition to race may also be critical, such as issues of consideration of socioeconomic status differences in match between CTRT group leaders and group members. Given these limitations, there is a need for continued research regarding the impact of race and culture in using CTRT.

This current study added to the knowledge base by extending the training process to 13 weeks, rather than the original 10-week training, to help teachers generalizing the skills into the classroom and by focusing on the short- and long-term impact on teachers. However, further research is needed regarding the impact of CTRT. Conducting research with a larger sample and random assignment of both teachers and children would be a valuable contribution. Also, future research could examine the impact of training parents and teachers simultaneously in both preschool and elementary school settings. In addition, future research could provide training that is more in vivo, either with training directly in the classroom or with coaching immediately after in-class observations, similar to the supervision after one-on-one sessions. It would also be useful to explore the impact of providing opportunities for trained teachers to become coaches of their peers to determine whether such an approach would further embed the learning in the trained teachers. What is most positive is that Helker and Ray (2009) and Morrison (2006) have conducted research using CTRT that included more in-class training of teachers to help them generalize the skills into the classroom, adding valuable information to this line of research.

In conclusion, teachers trained in CTRT can help preschool children deemed at risk. Within the safety of the relationship established with a teacher trained in CTRT, school can become a place in which vulnerable children feel more understood, cared about, and accepted. When teachers learn to see the world from the perspective of the children, become more accepting of children, and allow children more freedom and opportunities to become decision makers, schools becomes a better environment for both children and teachers. This is most essential for teachers who work with children deemed at risk—those children who have the greatest risk of failing. These skills can help teachers increase opportunities for growth, awareness, and success for the most vulnerable children in their classrooms. What works for these children changes the future for all of us.

REFERENCES

Adler, A. (1983). *The practice and theory of individual psychology.* Totowa, NY: Rowman & Allanheld.

Albaum, J. S. (1990). *A cost-free counseling model for high risk elementary students* (Report No. CG023092). East Lansing, MI: National Center for Research on Teacher Learning. (ERIC Document Reproduction Service No. ED 327 788).

Axline, V. M. (1947). *Play therapy.* New York: Ballantine.

Baecher, R. E., Cicchelli, T., & Baratta, A. (1989). *Preventive strategies and effective practices for at-risk children in urban elementary schools.* Paper presented at the annual meeting of the American Education Research Association, San Francisco, CA.

Baker, J. (2006). Contributions of teacher-child relationships to positive school adjustment during elementary school. *Journal of School Psychology, 44,* 211–229.

Bratton, S. C., & Landreth, G. L. (1995). Filial therapy with single parents: Effects on parental acceptance, empathy, and stress. *International Journal of Play Therapy, 4,* 61–80.

Bratton, S. C., Landreth, G. L., Kellam, T. L. T., & Blackard, S. R. (2006). *Child parent relationship therapy (CPRT) treatment manual: A 10-session filial therapy model for training parents.* New York: Brunner-Routledge.

Bratton, S. C., Ray, D. C., Rhine, T., & Jones, L. (2005). The efficacy of play therapy with children: A meta-analytic review of treatment outcomes. *Professional Psychology: Research and Practice, 36,* 376–390.

Brown, C. J. (2000). Filial therapy with undergraduate teacher trainees: Child-teacher relationship training (Doctoral dissertation, University of North Texas, Denton, 2000). *Dissertation Abstracts International, 63,* 3112.

Cochran, J. L. (1996). Using play and art therapy to help culturally diverse students overcome barriers to school success. *The School Counselor, 43,* 287–297.

Cohen, J. (1988). *Statistical power analysis for the behavioral sciences* (2nd ed.). New York: Academic Press.

Draper, K., White, D., O'Shaughnessey, T., Flynt, M., & Jones, N. (2001). Kinder training: Play-based consultation to improve the school adjustment of discouraged kindergarten and first-grade students. *International Journal of Play Therapy, 10,* 1–30.

Edlefsen, M., & Baird, M. (1994). Making it work: Preventive mental health care for disadvantaged preschoolers. *Social Work, 39,* 566–573.

Frick-Helms, S. B. (1997). Boys cry better than girls: Play therapy behaviors of children residing in a shelter for battered women. *International Journal of Play Therapy, 6,* 73–91.

Gibbs, J. T. (2003). *Children of color: Psychological interventions with culturally diverse groups.* San Francisco: Jossey-Bass.

Guerney, B. G., Jr. (1964). Filial therapy: Description and rationale. *Journal of Consulting Psychology, 28,* 304–310.

Guerney, B. G., Jr., & Flumen, A. B. (1970). Teachers as psychotherapeutic agents for withdrawn children. *Journal of School Psychology, 8,* 107–113.

Harrison, P. M., & Beck, A. J. (2005). *Bureau of Justice statistics bulletin: Prison and jail inmates at midyear 2004.* Retrieved March 12, 2007, from http://www.ojp.usdoj.gov/bjs/pub/pdf/pjim04.pdf

Helker, W. P., & Ray, D. C. (2009). The impact of child-teacher relationship training on teachers' and aides' use of relationship-building skills and the effect on student classroom behavior. *International Journal of Play Therapy, 18,* 70–83.

Landreth, G. L. (1991). *Play therapy: The art of the relationship.* Muncie, IN: Accelerated Development.

Landreth, G. L. (2002). *Play therapy: The art of the relationship* (2nd ed.). Muncie, IN: Accelerated Development.

Landreth, G. L., & Bratton, S. C. (2006). *Child parent relationship therapy: A 10-session filial therapy model*. New York: Brunner-Routledge.

La Roche, M. (1999). Culture, transference, and countertransference among Latinos. *Psychotherapy, 36*, 389–397.

Morrison, M. (2006). An early mental health intervention for disadvantaged preschool children with behavior problems: The effectiveness of training Head Start teachers in child-teacher relationship training (CTRT) (Doctoral dissertation, University of North Texas, Denton, 2006). *Dissertation Abstracts International, 67*(08).

Myers, G. E., & Gill, C. S. (2004). Poor, rural and female; Under-studied, under-counseled, more at-risk. *Journal of Mental Health Counseling, 26*, 225–242.

Nievar, A. M., & Luster, T. (2006). Developmental processes in African American families: An application of McLoyd's theoretical model. *Journal of Marriage and Family, 68*, 320–331.

Post, P. (1999). Impact of child-centered play therapy on the self-esteem, locus of control and anxiety of at-risk 4th-, 5th-, and 6th-grade students. *International Journal of Play Therapy, 8*, 1–18.

Post, P. (2003). *The assessment of child-centered play therapy skills (ACCEPTS)*. Unpublished manuscript.

Post, P., McAllister, M., Sheely, A., Hess, K., & Flowers, C. (2004). Child-centered kinder training for teachers of pre-school children deemed at risk. *International Journal of Play Therapy, 13*, 53–74.

Ray, D. C. (2006). Evidenced-based play therapy. In C. Schaefer & H. Kaduson (Eds.), *Contemporary play therapy* (pp. 136–157). New York: Guilford.

Reynolds, C. R., & Kamphaus, R. W. (1998). *BASC: Behavior assessment system for children manual*. Circle Pines, MN: American Guidance Service.

Smith, D., & Landreth, G. L. (2004). Filial therapy with teachers of deaf and hard of hearing preschool children. *International Journal of Play Therapy, 13*, 13–33.

Stover, L., Guerney, B. G., Jr., & O'Connell, M. (1971). Measurements of acceptance, allowing self-direction, involvement and empathy in adult-child interaction. *The Journal of Psychology, 77*, 261–269.

Sweeney, D. S., & Skurja, C. (2001). Filial therapy as a cross-cultural family intervention. *Asian Journal of Counseling, 8*, 175–208.

Trostle, S. L. (1988). The effects of child-centered group play sessions on social-emotional growth of four- and five-year-old bilingual Puerto Rican children. *Journal of Research in Childhood Education, 3*, 93–106.

White, J., Flynt, M., & Draper, K. (1997). Kinder therapy: Teachers as therapeutic agents. *International Journal of Play Therapy, 6*, 33–49.

White, J., Flynt, M., & Jones, N. P. (1999). Kinder therapy: An Adlerian approach for training teachers to be therapeutic agents through play. *Journal of Individual Psychology, 55*, 365–382.

CHAPTER 24

An Early Mental Health Intervention for Disadvantaged Preschool Children

MARY O. MORRISON and WENDY P. HELKER

CHILD TEACHER RELATIONSHIP TRAINING: AN EARLY INTERVENTION FOR AT-RISK PRESCHOOL CHILDREN

RATIONALE

Child Teacher Relationship Training (CTRT) emerged from our experiences as classroom teachers and later from our experiences as school counselors and play therapists. As classroom teachers, both of us realized that there were certain children with whom we seemed to naturally be able to have positive relationships; and then there were children with whom we seemed to struggle to connect no matter what we tried. Behavioral difficulties were often associated with the children with whom we had difficulty relating, and we further noticed that often times those same students had difficulty relating positively with their peers. Many times we felt defeated and unsure of how to proceed to keep these same children from disrupting the class, let alone try to cover the required academic material. Using traditional methods of discipline and consequences did not seem to be successful and served to make us feel further frustrated and disconnected from these students. It often seemed that these children needed more than we were trained to provide as teachers, and we often questioned whether these children also needed a more focused mental health approach. As our careers continued and we each chose to move from the classroom into the counseling field, we were introduced to play therapy in our graduate programs. It was through our study of Child-Centered Play Therapy (CCPT) and Child Parent Relationship Therapy/Filial Therapy that we both realized the unique power of a warm, accepting, and genuine relationship between a child and a caring adult as well as the therapeutic principles to address children's mental health. We became excited about how valuable it could be for both teachers and students if teachers were able to learn the principles and skills associated with CCPT and adapt them to use with students in the classroom. We began by first reviewing the literature on child-teacher relationships and the impact on children's early mental health needs. Our findings clearly showed a significant need for early interventions designed to affect student-teacher relationships.

Research indicates that the quality of the student-teacher relationship affects students' social and emotional development, academic achievement, and classroom functioning (Helker, Schottelkorb, & Ray, 2007; Hamre & Pianta, 2001). Positive student-teacher relationships are of primary importance in promoting children's successful adjustment to school, whereas negative student-teacher relationships may exacerbate children's difficulty in adjusting successfully to school. In a comprehensive study of child-teacher relationship effect, Baker (2006) concluded that a positive child-teacher relationship correlated significantly with behavioral and academic indicators of school success across all elementary grade levels and gender. Children who demonstrated social and behavioral problems were especially positively affected by an encouraging child-teacher relationship. Birch and Ladd (1998) indicated that teacher-reported closeness in the child-teacher relationship is positively related to students' academic growth in school as demonstrated by increased student independence and higher visual and language scores on standardized achievement tests. Peisner-Feinberg, Culkin, Howes, and Kagan (1999) concluded through results of their longitudinal study that children who experienced warm student-teacher relationships performed better on thinking, language ability, and math skills when compared to children who did not experience such a warm relationship. Pianta and Stuhlman (2004) investigated different aspects of the child-teacher relationship and found that the interpersonal aspects (relationships with teachers and peers) make a difference in the children's ability to develop competencies in the early years of school. Characteristics of the child-teacher relationship may contribute to the child's ability to build peer relationships as well. Based on results from their study, Howes, Hamilton, and Matheson (1994) suggested that a child's emotional security with his first teacher provides a child positive orientation to peer relationships, and socialization experiences help shape the child's particular behavior with peers.

The results we found while reviewing the literature on children's early mental health needs were equally as powerful. The most recent U.S. Surgeon General's report on the status of children's mental health stated that there is a lack of appropriate mental health services for children, especially for the most disadvantaged families, which was described as a national crisis (United States Public Health Service, 2000). The report further emphasized that "growing numbers of children are suffering needlessly, because their emotional, behavioral, and developmental needs are not being met" (p. 3) and identified several contributing factors: a shortage of mental health professionals specially trained to work with children; a lack of accessible services; and perhaps most salient, the need for early intervention specifically involving caregivers in the delivery of services. The President's New Freedom Commission on Mental Health (2003) reiterated the need for early intervention and emphasized a need for mental health services to be offered in accessible, low-stigma settings such as schools.

Having experienced the challenge of trying to meet the needs of young at-risk children firsthand combined with the reality of the scarce resources available for mental health care for young children, along with our knowledge of the importance of the child-teacher relationship, we set out to try a new approach for working with teachers based on Child Parent Relationship Training (CPRT; Landreth & Bratton, 2006). The development of Child Teacher Relationship Training (CTRT; Bratton, Landreth, Morrison, & Helker, in review) was a natural response to addressing the need for high-quality student-teacher relationships to attend to the mental health needs of young children. The foundation of CTRT/CPRT lies in the basic principles and tenets of Child-Centered Play Therapy (CCPT). Guerney (1964) expanded the ideas of CCPT to include parents as therapeutic agents and titled this new concept *Filial Therapy*.

CHILD PARENT RELATIONSHIP THERAPY (CPRT)

Building on the Guerneys' work, Landreth (1991/2002) developed a more time-sensitive model of filial therapy. Landreth and Bratton (2006) formalized this 10-session model as *Child Parent Relationship Therapy: A 10-Session Filial Therapy Model (CPRT)*. For a more thorough explanation of the CPRT model and research base, please see Bratton's chapter in this text.

ADAPTING THE FILIAL MODEL WITH TEACHERS

Andronico and B. Guerney (1969) first recommended using teachers as therapeutic agents, relying on the idea that the child-teacher relationship is valuable and that teachers are identified as significant people in children's lives. B. Guerney and Flumen (1970) researched this premise and found that teachers were capable of learning CCPT skills and implementing them in play sessions with their students. Several CPRT studies have also shown the effectiveness of the CPRT model with teachers in the school setting (Helker, 2007; Morrison, 2007; Smith & Landreth, 2004) and with pre-service teachers (Brown, 2003; Crane & Brown, 2003).

Kinder Training   Using an approach based on principles and procedures similar to CPRT titled *Kinder Training*, White, Flynt, and Draper (1997), White, Flynt, and Jones (1999), Draper, White, O'Shaughnessy, Flynt, and Jones (2001), and Post, McAllister, Sheely, Hess, and Flowers (2004) researched the effects of training teachers in filial therapy methodology and also demonstrated promising outcomes. While the strength of these studies is limited by the absence of control groups, the results are encouraging. Findings from Kinder Training studies reveal increases in teachers' empathic interactions with students, decreases in child behavior problems, and improvement in early literacy skills.

In the CTRT model, adapted from Child Parent Relationship Therapy (Landreth & Bratton, 2006), a specially trained mental health professional coaches teachers in the basic procedures and principles of Child-Centered Play Therapy (CCPT) based on the philosophy that preschool teachers serve as primary caregivers for their young students and that young children's primary relationships (parents, grandparents, and teachers) are critical to their development and mental health; and such teachers can learn the necessary skills to become change agents for students experiencing social, emotional, and behavioral difficulties.

RESEARCH METHODOLOGY

Using the same subjects, instruments, and treatment, we conducted two studies using the Child Teacher Relationship Training model. Morrison's (2007) study focused on one major research question: Was there a mean reduction in child behavior problems over time (pre- to mid- to post-testing) depending on which treatment children's teachers received? Assessments were administered before intervention, after Phase I, and again after Phase II. Specifically, this investigation was designed to determine the impact of CTRT on internalizing, externalizing, and total behavior problems of clinically referred children when compared to students whose teachers participated in the active control teacher training, Conscious Discipline® (Bailey, 2000).

Helker's (2007) study was conducted during Phase II of Morrison's (2007) study and focused on whether or not teachers were able to generalize CCPT relationship-building skills learned in Phase I with individual children for use in the classroom, and if so, whether teachers could maintain the use of those skills in the classroom over time. Specifically, Helker was interested in the impact that relationship-building skills had on children's behavior compared to children whose teachers received Conscious Discipline® (Bailey, 2000). Furthermore, Helker was curious if a relationship existed between children's behavior and the teacher's use of relationship-building skills.

Structuring the CTRT Model

There is significant planning involved in implementing a CTRT program, including developing a relationship with the school, acquiring space for the playroom, setting up the playroom, and developing a schedule that is appropriate to each unique setting. Morrison and Helker (in press) provide information regarding suggestions in structuring a successful CTRT intervention in a school setting. The following is a description of the research design, participants, instruments, and treatment used in our studies (Morrison, 2007; Helker, 2007).

Selection of Participants

Teacher and child subjects were recruited from one Head Start center in the southwest region of the United States. A total of 24 teachers and 52 children participated in Morrison's (2007) study, and a total of 24 teachers and 32 children participated in Helker's (2007) study (all from the same Head Start Center). There is a difference in the number of child participants in Morrison's (2007) study and Helker's (2007) study because of attrition and because some children began receiving mental health services at school after Phase II, disqualifying them from Helker's (2007) study, which followed children to the end of the school year. All Head Start classroom teacher and aide pairs (12 pairs or classroom teams, n = 24) at the participating school consented to participate in the study. During random assignment of teachers to treatment group, it came to our attention that three teachers were required to attend new teacher in-service, which coincided with the scheduled 2½-day intensive CTRT training. Thus, these three teachers were assigned to the active control group, and the remaining teachers were randomly drawn to participate in the experimental or control treatment. It is important to note that while these three individuals were considered new to the designated role of teacher, two of the three had been teacher aides before finishing their teaching degree and were not new to the Head Start classroom. Children were assigned to treatment based on their teachers' and aides' group assignment. Demographic data regarding teachers' years of experience, education, gender, ethnicity, and age were visually inspected for between-group differences and none were detected.

All children enrolled at the participating Head Start program (n = 188) whose parents provided consent (n = 159) were eligible for participation. Based on teacher ratings, children scoring in the border-line or clinical range on at least one syndrome scale on the Caregiver-Teacher Report Form (C-TRF; Achenbach & Rescorla, 2000) were selected to participate in the study. All subjects were considered economically disadvantaged (Head Start Act, 1981). No subjects were eliminated on the basis of ethnicity or disability. Children's assignment to treatment group was based on their teachers' group assignment. The ethnic makeup sample was representative of the Head Start school's population.

Instrumentation

In both pilot studies, the Child Behavior Checklist–Caregiver-Teacher Report Form (C-TRF; Achenbach & Rescorla, 2000) was used as a primary assessment tool. This particular instrument is widely used in the mental health community to measure problematic child behaviors as identified by teachers and caregivers. For the purpose of this study, the C-TRF was used to qualify children for this study (pre-test), and then given again at mid-point (after Phase I), post-test (after Phase II), and a final time at follow-up (10 weeks after the conclusion of Phase II) to examine treatment effects. The C-TRF is composed of eight syndrome and six DSM-oriented scales, as well as three domain scores: internalizing problems, externalizing problems, and total problems. To screen children for the study, teachers completed a C-TRF on all children whose parents gave consent to participate. Children who qualified for the study scored in the borderline or clinical range on at least one scale of the C-TRF.

To determine whether teachers are able to learn the relationship-building skills and use them in the classroom setting, an additional assessment tool, the Child Teacher Relationship Training-Skills Check-list (CTRT-SC; Helker, Bratton, Ray, & Morrison, 2007, as cited in Helker, 2007) was used. The CTRT-SC was created using the Play Therapy Skills Checklist, originally developed by the Center for Play Therapy (Ray, 2004) as a guide. The CTRT-SC is an observation form designed to identify whether responses teachers make to children in the classroom can be classified as relationship-building skills or are responses that are not designated as relationship-building skills (Helker & Ray, 2009).

TREATMENT

The 12 teacher-and-aide pairs in the experimental group received Child Teacher Relationship Training. The 12 teacher-and-aide pairs in the active control group received training in Conscious Discipline® (Bailey, 2000). Treatment for experimental and active control groups extended approximately 18 weeks. All aspects of training for both groups were provided as part of teachers' regularly scheduled school day; therefore no additional after-school time was used to implement this intervention.

Experimental Group Treatment Child Teacher Relationship Training (CTRT) is an adapted model of Child Parent Relationship Therapy (CPRT); therefore, protocol and curriculum from the *Child Parent Relationship Therapy (CPRT) Treatment Manual* (Bratton et al., 2006) were used in this study with minor adaptations to accommodate the Child-Teacher Relationship Training examples, classroom setting, and school schedule. CTRT treatment was conducted over two phases of training, referred to as CTRT Phases I and II. Consistent with the CPRT model, teacher-aide dyads were divided into two groups of six for weekly training and supervision to promote interaction and provide individual attention to participants within the group. Teachers and classroom aides were paired together; there were therefore three classrooms represented in each group. CTRT training, supervision, and coaching were provided by advanced doctoral counseling students with extensive training and supervised experience in play therapy, filial therapy, and CPRT methodology. Both CTRT supervisors were also certified school counselors (Morrison, 2007).

During Phase I, teachers were taught core CTRT principles and skills, including allowing the child to lead, reflective listening, reflecting content, recognizing and responding to children's feelings, therapeutic limit setting, building children's self-esteem, facilitating creativity and spontaneity, facilitating decision making, returning responsibility, and structuring. Phase I training content is equivalent to the curriculum covered in the CPRT 10-session model outlined in the *CPRT Treatment Manual* (Bratton et al., 2006). We focused on structuring training in a way that used the teachers' and aides' time most efficiently. Therefore, we provided intensive training during in-service days at the beginning of the school year and held the weekly one-hour supervision meetings during teachers' and aides' planning period each week. According to the CTRT model, 2½ days of intensive didactic instruction covers the equivalent of the content of the first five sessions in the CPRT manual. Following this intensive training, teachers and aides selected one child of focus to practice the CTRT skills with in seven weekly 30-minute play sessions. Consistent with the CPRT model, teachers and aides choose a designated 30-minute time block and specific day to conduct their play sessions; consistency of this appointment is critical to the model. Sessions were videotaped in Phase I and viewed during the weekly one-hour supervision time. During supervision in Phase I, supervisors provided didactic and experimental practice of skills that are presented in sessions 5 through 10 in the CPRT Manual (Bratton et al., 2006) and adapted for the school setting. Supervisors provided specific feedback regarding teachers' and aides' use of skills demonstrated in their recorded play sessions, as well as encouragement and support, and helped teachers and aides understand children's expression of experiences and feelings during the play session. Consistent with the CPRT model (Landreth & Bratton, 2006), the weekly child-teacher play sessions and weekly supervision provided a controlled setting for teachers and aides to focus and practice their skills before attempting to generalize their skills to everyday use. In fact, teachers and aides were specifically instructed not to practice CTRT skills in the classroom during this phase so they could ensure successful integration before using their newly acquired skills in the more difficult setting of their classroom (Morrison, 2007).

The focus of Phase II was to assist teachers and aides in generalizing their use of CTRT skills with an individual child in the playroom to use with small groups of children in the natural classroom setting. To facilitate this transition, individual play sessions were discontinued and replaced with Child Teacher Relationship-Time (CTR-Time) in the classroom. Supervisors worked with teachers and aides to establish a daily time in the classroom in which children were allowed to direct their own play at centers such as dramatic play, blocks, manipulatives, home center, and so on. During a 15-minute portion of this time, teachers or aides with modeling and coaching from the supervisor were asked to practice using CTRT skills with small groups of children. Concurrently, the other teaching partner focused on general classroom management, and then they switched roles to allow for both teaching partners the opportunity to have CTR-Time with students. It is essential that teachers and aides used this specifically structured time to practice using skills to avoid overwhelming teachers and aides and encourage successful implementation of the new skills. As part of the supervision process, the CTRT supervisor spent several weeks modeling and coaching how to transition the use of relationship-building skills with a small group of children in the classroom while the teachers and aides watched and participated as comfortable (Morrison, 2007).

As CTR-Time continued over the course of 10 weeks, modeling decreased as teachers and aides became more proficient in using CTRT skills, eventually using the skills independently of the supervisor. Also during Phase II, teachers, aides, and supervisors continued to meet for weekly, one-hour supervision sessions and focused on more advanced skills, such as group reflection skills, advanced limit setting, and choice giving (Bratton et al., 2006). The supervisors continued to support the teachers and aides and address the challenges, questions, and difficulties associated with transitioning from individual play sessions to the classroom setting. At the completion of the 10-week Phase II of training, the supervisor's role shifted. Weekly supervision sessions and in-classroom modeling were discontinued but were offered to teachers and aides on an as-needed basis (Morrison, 2007).

Active Control Treatment   Conscious Discipline® is a teacher-training program widely used in early childhood settings. Curriculum includes

Conscious Discipline®: 7 Basic Skills for Brain-Smart Classroom Management (Bailey, 2000) and Conscious Discipline® DVDs (Bailey, 2004). Conscious Discipline® is a relationship-based community model attending to both the child and the adult in the relationship. Bailey trains adults to be pro-active rather than reactive in working with children while in conflict. The focus of this approach is to build character, relationships, and social skills, which are believed to be more meaningful than a traditional compliance-based discipline model. In the present study, the participating school's educational specialist, a designated Conscious Discipline® trainer who held a master's degree in early childhood education, conducted training for the active control group. Teachers and aides met for training for one day before the start of school and, in a similar format to the experimental group, continued to meet throughout the study to receive further training and support in implementing Conscious Discipline® into their classrooms. While training was typical of what is traditionally received in Conscious Discipline® (Bailey, 2000), we were unable to directly control for the frequency, intensity, or integrity of the training. Hence, we made the decision to designate this treatment an active control rather than a comparison treatment (Morrison, 2007).

DATA COLLECTION

The primary instrument used in both studies was the Child Behavior Checklist-Caregiver-Teacher Report Form (C-TRF; Achenbach & Rescorla, 2000); thus the same data collection procedures were used. Prior to teachers completing the C-TRF on students, consent was obtained from teacher and aide subjects and from parents of child subjects. Spanish-speaking research assistants and consent forms written in Spanish were provided to parents as necessary. To ensure the integrity of data collection, substitutes were provided in each classroom while teachers completed the C-TRF in a quiet room free from distraction. Researchers were present at all times during data collection to answer any questions and ensure consistency in data collection methods. The C-TRF was administered before treatment, mid-point (at the conclusion of CTRT Phase I), and post-test (at the conclusion of CTRT Phase II) and at follow-up (10 weeks after the conclusion of Phase II).

In Helker's (2007) study, the CTRT skills checklist (CTRT-SC) was used to observe teachers' implementation of CTRT skills in the classroom. Doctoral students with advanced training in Child-Centered

Play Therapy who were familiar with checklist terms conducted the observations. Using the interval agreement approach (Kennedy, 2005), raters established inter-rater agreement on the CTRT-SC at three distinct points during the study (76 percent before the study, 93 percent at the mid-point, and 88 percent at the end of the study). Using the CTRT-SC, teachers and aides were observed at the beginning of CTRT Phase I, at the end of CTRT Phase I (mid-point of the CTRT intervention), at the end of the CTRT Phase II (conclusion of CTRT intervention), and at follow-up (10 weeks following the completion of the CTRT intervention).

DATA ANALYSIS

Morrison (2007) computed a two-group-by-three repeated-measures split plot ANOVA for each dependent variable to determine whether the children in the Child Teacher Relationship Training (CTRT) group and the active control group performed differently across time (three points of measure). Dependent variables included the pre-, mid-, and post-test C-TRF ratings from the externalizing, internalizing, and total problem scales. To avoid the risk of an inflated experiment-wise Type I error, a more conservative alpha level of .025 was used to interpret statistical significance of results (Armstrong & Henson, 2005). ηp^2 was used to assess the magnitude of the treatment effect in order to better understand the practical significance, or therapeutic value, of the treatment (Kazdin, 1999). The following guidelines proposed by Cohen (1988) were used to interpret ηp^2 effect sizes: .01 = small effect, .06 = medium effect, and .14 = large effect.

In Helker's (2007) study, a one-way between-groups analysis of covariance (ANCOVA) was conducted to compare the experimental group's ability to demonstrate the use of relationship-building skills with the active control group's ability to demonstrate the use of relationship-building skills in the general classroom. A one-way repeated measures analysis of variance (RM-ANOVA) was conducted to address whether the experimental group was able to learn relationship-building skills and maintain the use of those skills in the classroom over time (Helker & Ray, 2009).

Helker (2007) used an ANCOVA to compare experimental group children's externalizing behavior scores with children in the active control group's externalizing behavior scores. An ANCOVA was also used to do the same comparison for the children's scores on both the internalizing behavior problems as well as the total behavior problems scales. Correlation coefficients were calculated to address whether a relationship exists between the frequency of teachers' and aides' use of relationship-building skills in the classroom and the decrease of children's externalizing, internalizing, and total problems scores. ηp^2 effect sizes using Cohen's (1988) interpretations were also computed to measure practical significance (Helker & Ray, 2009).

RESULTS AND DISCUSSION

Morrison's (2007) study was designed to determine the impact of CTRT on internalizing, externalizing, and total behavior problems of clinically referred children when compared to students whose teachers and aides participated in the active control training, Conscious Discipline® (Bailey, 2000). Helker (2007) investigated if the teachers and aides could learn the CTRT skills and maintain them over time when compared to the active control group. Helker also wondered if children's behavior would be affected as a result of the model over time (at the follow-up of the conclusion of Morrison's study) and if there was a relationship between children's behavior and the teachers' and aides' use of the CTRT skills in the classroom when compared to children in the active control group.

Results of Morrison's (2007) study indicated that CTRT is a viable treatment option in addressing the mental health needs of young children with behavioral problems. Results for the dependent variable, externalizing problems, revealed a statistically significant interaction effect of time (pre-, mid-, post-test) by group membership, $F(2, 49) = 6.902, p = .002, \eta p^2 = .22$. These findings reveal that CTRT demonstrated a large treatment effect ($\eta p^2 = .22$) on children's externalizing behavior problems when compared to children whose teachers and aides participated in the active control group. Furthermore, children in the CTRT group demonstrated a statistically significant reduction in target behavior over the three points of measure. These results are important because of the difficulty teachers and aides have in working with children with externalizing behavior problems and are therefore the most common reason for mental health referrals for young children (Brinkmeyer & Eyberg, 2003; Keiley, Bates, Dodge, & Pettit, 2000). Webster-Stratton and Reid (2003) further speculated that externalizing problems, specifically related to conduct disorders, are established in the preschool years and without treatment increase in severity, giving further support to the impact CTRT can have on children's mental health.

Results for the dependent variable, internalizing problems, revealed no statistically significant interaction effect of time (pre-, mid-, post-test) by group membership, $F(2, 49) = 2.501$, $p = .092$, $\eta p^2 = .09$. Findings indicate that while not statistically significant, CTRT demonstrated a moderate treatment effect $(\eta p^2 = .09)$ for children's internalizing behavior problems when compared to children in the active control group. The impact of CTRT on internalizing problems can be seen in teachers' anonymous written feedback regarding their experience. "One of my students only began talking after CTR-Time began—I don't think he would have spoken had it not been for CTR-Time." Another teacher reported, "There has been a larger impact and much more noticeable difference with my quiet and withdrawn students." These comments are noteworthy as internalizing behavioral problems often go unnoticed by teachers and are associated with being shy or quiet and the assumption that children will outgrow these difficulties (Keiley et al., 2000).

Results on the dependent variable, total problems, revealed a statistically significant interaction effect of time (pre-, mid-, and post-test) by group membership, $F(2, 49) = 5.094$, $p = .01$, $\eta p^2 = .17$. These findings indicate that compared to the active control group, children in the CTRT group demonstrated a statistically significant decrease in total problems, with the magnitude of the effect of the CTRT treatment considered large $(\eta p^2 = .17)$. Young children often display signs of co-morbidity, making it difficult to assign a single diagnosis (Achenbach & Rescorla, 2000); therefore, these results are valuable in responding to the child's overall mental health needs.

Statistical analyses from Helker's (2007) study revealed teachers and aides in the treatment group were able to learn and use CTRT relationship-building skills in the classroom. Results indicate a statistically significant difference in the experimental group's demonstration of CTRT skills compared to the active control group $(F (1, 21) = 44.44$, $p < .01$.) at the end of CTRT Phase II. Findings also indicate a large effect size $(\eta p^2 = .68)$ (Cohen, 1988). At follow-up, 10 weeks after the completion of the CTRT intervention, the experimental group's demonstration of the use of relationship-building skills in the classroom remained at a statistically significantly higher level than the control group $(F (1, 21) = 16.55$, $p < .01$.). Results also indicated a large treatment effect $(\eta p^2 = .44)$ (Cohen, 1988). These results indicate that teachers and aides are able to learn and implement the CTRT skills in the general classroom.

To determine whether the teachers and aides in the experimental group maintained their use of CTRT skills in the classroom, a one-way repeated measures ANOVA was conducted to compare their scores on the CTRT-SC at all four data collection points. Results indicated there was a significant effect for time (Wilks's Lambda = .13, $F(3, 9) = 19.81$, $p < .01$, $\eta p^2 = .87$). The effect size of .87 is large (Cohen, 1988). These results are noteworthy in that the teachers and aides not only learned the relationship-building skills but implemented the skills in their classroom and maintained the skills 10 weeks after the conclusion of the CTRT intervention. These results indicate that teachers believed these skills to be helpful enough to implement them in their daily interactions with students.

Results of Helker's (2007) study suggest that the CTRT program may be an effective intervention for enhancing student-teacher relationships. These results can further be illustrated by several CTRT participants' responses when asked to provide anonymous written feedback regarding their experiences participating in CTRT. One teacher wrote, "I am more patient, taking into consideration the way I see things and the children's view, too." Another commented, "I have learned to let the children make their own choices," and a third stated, "It made me stop and reevaluate some of my ideas about classroom relationships." These participants' perceptions about their roles with their students changed as a result of participating in the CTRT program. When teachers and aides begin to view their roles with their students with less power and control, a foundation for more positive child-teacher relationships can be built (Dollard, 1996).

Results regarding whether teachers' and aides' demonstration of relationship-building skills in the classroom affected students' behavior indicated that students in the treatment group made statistically significant improvement ($F(1, 29) = 4.76$, $p = .037$, $\eta p^2 = .14$) in externalizing problems between pre-test (time 1) and post-test (time 3) as compared to students who were in the active control group. Practical significance indicates a large treatment effect ($\eta p^2 = .14$). No statistically significant difference was found between the groups at follow-up testing (Time 4) ($F(1, 29) = 1.06$, $p = 0.31$, $\eta p^2 = .04$); however, children maintained the behavior improvement shown during the treatment period (time 1 to time 3).

Excerpts from CTRT participants' anonymous responses also demonstrate how significantly some students' classroom behavior changed. The following are comments that teachers made regarding changes in student behaviors:

He has greatly improved in his ability to manage frustration. He is no longer as aggressive as he was when he gets frustrated.

She has completely turned around. She is independent and willing to try new things.

I've noticed an increase in his self-confidence. He's very independent now.

Teachers and aides in the active control group reported no changes in student behavior either positively or negatively.

Results of the one-way ANCOVA revealed no statistically significant differences between the experimental and active control groups' scores on internalizing problems at post-testing (time 3) $F(1, 29) = 1.27, p = .27$, $\eta p^2 = .04$, or at follow-up testing (time 4) $F(1, 29) = 1.70$, $p = .20$, $\eta p^2 = .06$. No statistically significant differences were found between the experimental and active control groups' scores on total problems at post-testing (time 3) $F(1, 29) = 3.08$, $p = .09$, $\eta p^2 = .10$, or at follow-up testing (time 4) $F(1, 29) = .67, p = .42, \eta p^2 = .02$. The effect size from pre- to post-testing (time 3) was moderate (.10) (Cohen, 1988).

The final question that Helker (2007) was curious about is whether there was a relationship between teacher-aide dyads' frequency of use of relationship-building skills and a decrease in students' behavior problems. A Pearson product-moment correlation coefficient was calculated to answer this question. A statistically significant relationship was found between teachers' and aides' most frequent use of relationship-building skills (observation 3) and a significant decrease in students' externalizing behavior (time 3) $(r = .41, n = 32, p < .05)$. The r^2 effect size was calculated at .16, which is large according to Cohen's (1988) guidelines. This means that as the teachers and aides increased their use of relationship-building skills in the classroom, there was a decrease in students' externalizing behaviors (such as aggression and hyperactivity). These findings are important because externalizing behaviors are typically difficult and challenging for teachers in regard to classroom management, discipline, and instruction (Birch & Ladd, 1998). Externalizing behavior problems are also believed to contribute to problematic and conflictual interactions and relationships with teachers and peers and may inhibit children's abilities to form close relationships in the classroom (Birch & Ladd, 1998). Therefore, these analyses are encouraging because they demonstrate that when teachers and aides used CTRT relationship-building skills with children who exhibit externalizing behavior problems, these problems decreased.

The relationship between teacher-aide dyads' demonstration of relationship-building skills in the classroom (as measured by the CTRT-SC) and students' exhibition of internalizing problems (as measured by the C-TRF) at observations 2, 3, and 4 was investigated and no statistically significant relationship between the two variables was demonstrated.

The relationship between teacher-aide dyads' demonstration of relationship-building skills in the classroom (as measured by the CTRT-SC) and students' exhibition of total problems (as measured by the C-TRF) at observations 2, 3, and 4 was also investigated using Pearson product-moment correlation coefficient. No statistically significant relationship between the two variables was demonstrated.

The results of Morrison's and Helker's studies indicate support for the use of the CTRT intervention in a preschool setting and further suggest the need for a larger, randomized controlled study in multiple sites. Teachers and aides were able to not only learn and implement the relationship-building skills into their classroom but also to maintain the use of the skills at follow-up. Results indicate that students' externalizing and total behavior problems improved during the treatment period. Results of the analyses indicate there is a strong correlation between the decreases in children's externalizing behavioral problems and the teachers' and aides' high use of CTRT skills in the classroom, giving strong support to the CTRT intervention. The administrators at the participating Head Start center were so pleased with the changes in the students and teachers that they invited the researchers to return the following year and train the control group teachers and aides, and administrators have continued to request CTRT training for all new teachers and aides each year. Recent feedback from the principal at the participating school indicated that since CTRT had been implemented, there had been a significant reduction in office referrals by teachers, from several a week to less than one per week (personal communication with Dr. Sue Bratton, April 2009). The anonymous feedback provided by the teachers in their evaluation of the CTRT intervention provided support for their positive experiences in learning and implementing these skills. One teacher stated, "This training was invaluable. I believe all teachers should have access to this information." Another teacher reported, "I have increased my knowledge and awareness in several areas. Therefore, I truly think that I have become a more competent teacher."

While further research is needed to substantiate study findings, teacher and staff feedback add support to the statistical findings and suggest that CTRT is a viable intervention to target at-risk children's behavior.

LIMITATIONS AND RECOMMENDATIONS

It's important to consider how these studies could be improved, as well as how future research can build on the results of our studies. We believe it would be helpful to conduct these studies with a greater sample size and multiple sites in order to increase the power of the statistical measures. A larger sample would also increase the ability to generalize the results more broadly. Objective raters of the children's behavior change would be a strong addition to this study, as having the participating teachers rate the change in children's behavior is a significant limitation. Given the current method of data collection, it is hard to determine whether the children's behavior changed or whether the teachers' perceptions changed, although it can be argued that if the teachers' perceptions changed in a positive way, the intervention would be considered successful. However, it is important to note that teachers in the active control training group were exposed to a similar philosophy regarding the importance of the child-teacher relationship and the impact of children's underlying needs on behavior, and those teachers did not report the degree of change reported by the experimental group. Using an assessment tool that measures variables from the child's perspective or parent's perspective would add an interesting dimension to the research. Using an assessment instrument that specifically measures the child-teacher relationship to determine the impact of CTRT on a specific child-teacher relationship may yield concrete and interesting results. Because of the timing of the study, teachers had to complete the C-TRF on students at the beginning of the school year, and it is possible they did not have enough time to accurately rate students' behavior and some behaviors exhibited by students could have been due to adjusting to the new school year.

CONCLUSION

The emotional and mental health needs of young children often go unnoticed and are therefore rarely addressed (United States Public Health Service, 2000). The child-teacher relationship is clearly a powerful tool in the life of a young child and can be used to make significant changes in the child's academic success as well as emotional well-being (Hamre & Pianta, 2001). Child Teacher Relationship Training significantly affected the externalizing behavior problems of young children. These results are noteworthy, given the current focus in child psychopathology literature on the devastating effects of externalizing problems (Webster-Stratton & Reid, 2003). Child Teacher Relationship Training has demonstrated promising results in these studies to be an effective intervention to attend to the mental health needs of clinically referred children in a preschool setting.

REFERENCES

Achenbach, T. M., & Rescorla, L. A. (2000). *Manual for the ASEBA preschool forms & profiles.* Burlington, VT: University of Vermont, Research Center for Children, Youth, & Families.

Andronico, M. P., & Guerney, B. G., Jr. (1969). The potential application of filial therapy to the school situation. In B. G. Guerney, Jr. (Ed.), *Psychotherapeutic agents: New roles for non-professionals, parents and teachers* (pp. 371–377). New York: Holt, Rinehart & Winston.

Armstrong, S. A., & Henson, R. K. (2005). Statistical practices of IJPT researchers: A review from 1993 to 2003. *International Journal of Play Therapy, 14*(1), 7–26.

Bailey, B. A. (2000). *Conscious discipline.* Oviedo, FL: Loving Guidance.

Bailey, B. A. (Author) & Loving Guidance, Inc. (Publisher). (2004). *Conscious Discipline®Live DVD Series* [DVD] Available from https://www.becky bailey.com/store.cfm?showproduct=0&prod_id=161.

Baker, J. (2006). Contributions of teacher-child relationships to positive school adjustment during elementary school. *Journal of School Psychology, 44*, 211–229.

Birch, S. H., & Ladd, G. W. (1998). Children's interpersonal behaviors and the teacher-child relationship. *Developmental Psychology, 34*, 934–946.

Bratton, S. C., Landreth, G. L., Kellam, T. L. T., & Blackard, S. (2006). *Child parent relationship therapy (CPRT) treatment manual: A 10-session filial therapy model for training parents.* New York: Brunner-Routledge.

Bratton, S. C., Landreth, G. L., Morrison, M. O., & Helker, W. P. (in review). *Child teacher relationship training (CTRT) treatment manual.* New York: Brunner-Routledge.

Brinkmeyer, M. Y., & Eyberg, S. M. (2003). In A. E. Kazdin & J. R. Weisz (Eds.), *Evidence-based psychotherapies for children and adolescents* (pp. 204–223). New York: Guilford.

Brown, C. (2003). Filial therapy training with undergraduate teacher trainees: Child-teacher relationship training (Doctoral dissertation, University of

North Texas, Denton, 2000). *Dissertation Abstracts International, A, 63*(09), 3112.

Cohen, J. (1988). *Statistical power analysis for the behavioral sciences* (2nd ed.). New York: Academic Press.

Crane, J. M., & Brown, C. J. (2003). Effectiveness of teaching play therapy attitudes and skills to undergraduate human services majors. *International Journal of Play Therapy, 12,* 49–65.

Dollard, N., Christensen, L., Colucci, K., & Epanchin, B. (1996). Constructivist classroom management. *Focus on Exceptional Children, 29*(2), 1–12.

Draper, K., White, J., O'Shaughnessy, T. E., Flynt, M., & Jones, N. (2001). Kinder training: Play-based consultation to improve the school adjustment of discouraged kindergarten and first-grade students. *International Journal of Play Therapy, 10,* 1–30.

Guerney, B. G., Jr. (1964). Filial therapy: Description and rationale. *Journal of Consulting Psychology, 28,* 303–310.

Guerney, B. G., Jr., & Flumen, A. B. (1970). Teachers as psychotherapeutic agents for withdrawn children. *Journal of School Psychology, 8,* 107–113.

Hamre, B. K., & Pianta, R. C. (2001). Early teacher-child relationships and the trajectory of children's school outcomes through eighth grade. *Child Development, 72,* 625–638.

Head Start Act. (1981). Pub. L. No. 97-35, 635-645.

Helker, W. P. (2007). The impact of child teacher relationship training on teachers' and aides' use of relationship-building skills and the effect on student classroom behavior. *Digital Dissertations,* DAI-A 68/02, August 2007.

Helker, W. P., & Ray, D. C. (2009). Impact of child teacher relationship training on teachers' and aides' use of relationship-building skills and the effects on student classroom behavior. *International Journal of Play Therapy, 18*(2), 70–83.

Helker, W. P., Schottelkorb, A. A., & Ray, D. C. (2007). Helping students and teachers connect: An intervention model for school counselors. *Journal of Professional Counseling: Practice, Theory, and Research, 35*(2), 31–45.

Howes, C., Hamilton, C. E., & Matheson, C. C. (1994). Children's relationship with peers: Differential associations with aspects of the teacher-child relationship. *Child Development, 65,* 253–263.

Kazdin, A. E. (1999). The meanings and measurement of clinical significance. *Journal of Consulting and Clinical Psychology, 67,* 332–339.

Keiley, M. K., Bates, J. E., Dodge, K. A., & Pettit, G. S. (2000). A cross-dominate growth analysis: Externalizing and internalizing behaviors during 8 years of childhood. *Journal of Abnormal Child Psychology, 28*(2), 161–179.

Kennedy, C. (2005). *Single-case design for educational research.* Boston: Allyn and Bacon.

Landreth, G. L. (1991). *Play therapy: The art of the relationship.* New York: Brunner-Routledge.

Landreth, G. L. (2002). *Play therapy: The art of the relationship* (2nd ed.). New York: Brunner-Routledge.

Landreth, G. L., & Bratton, S. C. (2006). *Child parent relationship therapy: A 10-session filial therapy model.* New York: Brunner-Routledge.

Morrison, M. (2007). An early mental health intervention for disadvantaged preschool children with behavior problems: The effects of training Head Start teachers in child teacher relationship training (CTRT). *Digital Dissertations*, DAI-A 67/08, February 2007.

Morrison, M. O., & Helker, W. P. (in press). Child teacher relationship training: Using the power of the child-teacher relationship as a school-based mental health intervention. In A. Drews & C. Schaefer (Eds.), *School-based play therapy* (2nd ed.). Hoboken, NJ: John Wiley & Sons.

New Freedom Commission on Mental Health. (2003). *Achieving the promise: Transforming mental health care in America.* Final report (DHHS Publication No. SMA-03-3832). Rockville, MD: U.S. Department of Health and Human Services.

Peisner-Feinberg, E. S., Culkin, M. L., Howes, C., & Kagan, S. L. (1999). The children of the cost, quality, and outcomes study go to school (Executive Summary). Retrieved May 15, 2008, from http://www.fpg.unc.edu/~ncedl/PDFs/CQO-es.pdf.

Pianta, R. C., & Stuhlman, M. W. (2004). Teacher-child relationships and children's success in the first years of school. *School Psychology Review, 33,* 444–459.

Post, P., McAllister, M., Sheely, A., Hess, K., & Flowers, C. (2004). Child-centered kinder training for teachers of pre-school children deemed at-risk. *International Journal of Play Therapy, 13,* 53–74.

Ray, D. C. (2004). Supervision of basic and advanced skills in play therapy. *Journal of Professional Counseling: Practice, Theory, & Research, 32,* 29–40.

Smith, D. M., & Landreth, G. L. (2004). Filial therapy with teachers of deaf and hard of hearing preschool children. *International Journal of Play Therapy, 13,* 13–33.

U.S. Public Health Service. (2000). *Report of the Surgeon General's conference on children's mental health: A national action agenda.* Washington, DC: Author.

Webster-Stratton, C., & Ried, M. J. (2003). The incredible years parents, teachers, and children training services: A multifaceted treatment approach for young children with conduct problems. In A. E. Kazdin & J. R. Weisz (Eds.), *Evidence-based psychotherapies for children and adolescents* (pp. 224–240). New York: Guilford.

White, J., Flynt, M., & Draper, K. (1997). Kinder therapy: Teachers as therapeutic agents. *International Journal of Play Therapy, 6,* 33–49.

White, J., Flynt, M., & Jones, N. P. (1999). Kinder therapy: An Adlerian approach for training teachers to be therapeutic agents through play. *Journal of Individual Psychology, 55,* 365–382.

CHAPTER 25

A Qualitative Study of Parents' Perceptions of Filial Therapy in a Public School

YUEHONG CHEN FOLEY*

"PLAY INTERVENTION"

In January 2005, I received a surprise phone call from a Title I public school principal. She said her school had about 1,350 students, but 7 *percent* of them were disruptive in classrooms and were escorted to the office at least once a week even though various school interventions were ongoing. She obtained my contact information from the county and hoped I would conduct filial therapy training in her school on Saturdays to 12 parents whose children reached 15 discipline referrals in three months.

The principal could arrange only four sessions because of a financial constraint, and the parents were not committed because of a lack of trust in the school service, but she would beg them to come. She asked me to not use the word *therapy* and instead named the program in the school as *play intervention*. She had been amazed by the improvement in

---

Acknowledgment: Special thanks to Ms. Susan M. White, Ms. Tamara Frazier, the teacher baby-sitters, and parents for their generous support to the success of this research project. Yuehong Chen Foley is the founder and president of Responsible Child, LLC, and part-time school counselor in Gwinnett County Public Schools. Correspondence regarding this article should be addressed to info@responsible child.com, or Maria_ChenFoley@gwinnett.k12.ga.us.

disruptive children after they played with a substitute counselor. She asked the substitute counselor and me to meet and provide play training with the parents who agreed to come. The substitute counselor and I reviewed the filial therapy training materials that I have been using for two years and decided to teach parents reflective listening, empathy, encouragement, and limit setting through hands-on play training and live supervision in a group format, with each parent and child every session. We each led a separate group of six parents on Saturdays from 10 A.M. to noon in a classroom while the children were playing structured activities with the principal in the media center. The parents practiced their skills with their child for 10-minute sessions during the parent group, received positive feedback from the leader and group members, shared home parenting struggles, and brainstormed behavior intervention strategies.

Later, they invited their adult family members into the sessions, spoke highly of the experience and the effectiveness, and requested that the principal find additional funding for the filial play program. The principal told me, "I never heard parents being so enthusiastic about a school program! Each of them came to me so excited about the training experience and results. They loved it and wanted more of it! And their children's behaviors improved at home and school. Amazing[ly], they stopped disrupting the classroom after four filial play sessions!" These positive results of filial therapy led to an ongoing play therapy and filial therapy program in this public school.

After I completed my doctoral degree in 2005, I was hired as a behavior interventionist by this school to work with disruptive students so they could stay in the classroom to learn. I started an intensive play intervention with children during the school hours, consulted and coached teachers to use play therapy skills in their classrooms, and provided filial play training on Saturdays with the parents whose children were most disruptive in classrooms. My principal interviewed the teacher and parent participants after each 10-week training program was completed. After she was promoted in the school district, I continued filial play training in the evenings and school hours and conducted parent interviews and research projects. I conducted five filial therapy groups each year between August 2005 and May 2008. I review in this chapter relevant background literature, describe the methods of one qualitative research study of parents' perceptions of filial therapy in my school in 2007, and discuss the results and implications.

CHILDREN'S BEHAVIOR CHALLENGES

Compared to previous generations, children currently experience poverty, family disruption, and inadequate parenting more prevalently and suffer from insecurity, confusion, low self-esteem, and lack of self-efficacy (Wagner, 1994). When entering elementary school, many children struggle with respecting people, following the rules, or accomplishing the tasks (Walker, Stiller, Severson, & Golly, 1998).

Children's self-concept and social development are strongly affected by parenting styles (Adler, 1927); their early values, beliefs, and behavior patterns that originated within their families (Axline, 1947) persist into adulthood (Adler). A misbehavior issue is not solely a child's problem, but a result of discouragement from and inadequate relationships with the significant adults in the child's life (B. Guerney, 1964; L. Guerney, 2000). Their schooling outcome and life satisfaction are associated with the quality of parent-child relationships (Bowlby, 1969; Walker et al., 1998). Negative parenting approaches such as parental criticism and demands on children strongly associate with their mutual psychological distress and contribute stress to the parent-child relationship (Clarke, 1996; Roberts, 1990).

Unfortunately, many parents struggle with building a respectful and nurturing relationship with their young children as well as setting appropriate boundaries (Landreth & Bratton, 2006). A misbehaving student needs appropriate structure, encouragement, and empathy to improve self-confidence and competence in handling conflicts. Since parents are the most important caregivers in their children's lives, a slight amount of change in parental attitude and behaviors create a greater impact on parent-child-relationship and behavioral improvement than any professional could (Landreth & Bratton). It is beneficial to improve parenting competency and confidence by training parents to become therapeutic change agents for their own children (B. Guerney, 1964).

It is essential for children to have a safe place to act out the feelings and experiences that are unacceptable to them and to modify their responses to the real world, enhance their self-concept, and cumulate opportunities for positive effects and feedback from the environment (Guerney, 2000). However, children under 11 years of age have not developed verbal skills to fully express their feelings and thoughts; thus, toys and play are their communication methods (Axline, 1947; Landreth, 2002).

FILIAL THERAPY

Filial therapy is an educational model that trains parents to practice child-centered play therapy skills with their own children (B. Guerney, 1964; L. Guerney, 2000). My motivation for conducting filial therapy in the school setting was to reduce discipline referrals and increase classroom stay time of the disruptive students; increase their social skills and coping resources, improve their parents' parenting efficacy and school involvement; and advocate filial therapy as an educational component in schools. Previous research consistently indicated that filial therapy improves behaviors, attitudes, and relationships of parents and children (Landreth & Bratton, 2006; Ray, Bratton, Rhine, & Jones, 2001). There is a scarcity of parents' voices, however, to report the effectiveness of filial therapy (Foley, Higdon, & White, 2006; Landreth & Bratton, 2006) in school settings. The purpose of my research is to investigate parents' perceptions of filial therapy effectiveness and their suggestions to make it more effective in the school setting.

RESEARCH METHODS

PARTICIPANTS

Parents of students with five or more discipline referrals in one month were invited to filial play training on Saturdays by my principal, teachers, and me. I also sent a flyer home introducing my job responsibility, filial therapy skills and benefits, and course schedules. The participants in this study were seven parents who volunteered to join a group interview after attending 10 sessions of filial therapy. Mr. T was an African American father of second-grade daughters who were twins experiencing daily sibling rivalry. Mr. and Mrs. D were a Hispanic couple with one kindergarten boy and one pre-K daughter who experienced sibling rivalry, anger outbursts, and frequent crying. Mr. and Mrs. W were a newlywed Caucasian couple with one fourth-grade son and one second-grade son with sibling rivalry and severe emotional and behavioral problems at home and school. Mrs. H was an African American mother with a fourth-grade daughter, a second-grade son, and a pre-K son with sibling rivalry and constant aggression verbally and physically. Mrs. A was an African American mother with a pre-K son and a fourth-grade son who had frequent suicidal thoughts and power struggles with adults. All of the students in this group were on free or reduced lunch. Parents' ages ranged from 26 to 45 years, and their education ranged from high school to some college.

FILIAL THERAPY GROUP LEADERS

I was one co-leader; I was raised in China, speak fluent English, and I hold a doctoral degree and a Licensed Professional Counselor credential. At the time of the intervention, I had three years of extensive training and supervised practice in play therapy and filial therapy in the United States. I received 30 minutes of individual supervision every week from a licensed professional counselor while conducting filial therapy. My co-leader was the in-school suspension manager who holds a bachelor's degree in criminal justice, received 20 hours of play therapy in-service at my school, and worked with me closely using play therapy skills with disruptive students for a full year in 2006.

FILIAL THERAPY INTERVENTION

The filial therapy training was provided on Tuesdays from 5:30 P.M. to 7:30 P.M. in spring 2007. We adapted Landreth's (2002) description of 10 weekly 2-hour group sessions and incorporated the parents' suggestions from previous filial therapy groups to focus on step-by-step practice. All training meetings were audiotaped, and the play sessions were videotaped for supervision. The parents stayed in the school conference room where there was a TV connected to the video camera in the playroom. All the children were playing in the front hall area and were supervised by three teachers who were receiving behavior intervention coaching from me. Each parent participant selected one of their children to play with in the first four group training sessions, and then played with all two to three of their children in the fifth to tenth group training sessions. Each mini-play session was 15 minutes in the playroom. The group watched it on TV in the conference room simultaneously and then waited for the parent to return and start the discussion. I videotaped all the play sessions for group discussion, supervision, and research purposes with parents' permission and gave them each a copy of their own mini-play sessions to review at home upon their request. At the end of each session, the co-leaders and parents used five minutes to verbally share one thing they learned or appreciated in the group experience and one skill they were planning to practice for a full week until the next session.

Following Landreth's (2002) model, the first session was used for introduction and instruction. My co-leader and I took turns teaching the basic concepts of play therapy and importance of positive parenting styles on child development. One parent who previously completed this training came in to share hers and her child's success in this program, and some parents were motivated while others were doubtful about it. Then I introduced parental stress management tips and the therapeutic skills (nonjudgmental reflective responding, empathy, encouragement, limit setting, linking) for the group to practice throughout the 10-week training. When introducing each skill, my co-leader and I took turns role-playing a therapist responding to a misbehaving child. The parents recalled specific responses from the therapist, discussed the reasons and results of such responses, and shared personal reactions. The parents visited the playroom and discussed the rationale of using certain toys for play. Then we encouraged the parents to notice one positive behavior of their child each day and verbalize their appreciation to that child before the next session.

In the second session, the co-leaders took turns demonstrating 15-minute play sessions with four of the participants' children while their parent was in the playroom. The leaders instructed the group that the player parent will walk with the co-leader to the front hallway and say to the invited child, "We are going to play for 15 minutes in the playroom." The parent was instructed to look at the child all the time and listen to the therapist playing with the child. While the other parents watched the session on TV, they were encouraged to write down the therapist's responses and the child's reactions. After the parent and therapist return to the group, the discussion focused on the specific skills used, the child's reactions, and the player parent's impressions. The observer co-leader shared her positive notes and observations about the player leader and parent first, followed by the player leader sharing appreciations of the child and parent, and then group sharing. This process was repeated until four mini-play sessions were conducted. During group discussions, the co-leaders immediately affirmed the parents' responses that aligned with play therapy principles, paraphrased some sentences to support their efforts in practicing therapeutic skills in interaction, and encouraged the individuals to modify their responses accordingly. The leaders highlighted the common strengths of the group members' sharing. Parents were encouraged to tell each child one positive observation of the child and one self-affirmation or positive self-disclosure daily.

In the third session, three parents took turns conducting 15-minute play sessions with one leader whispering responses to them. As the parent gradually increased accurate responses, the leader reduced whispering. During the group discussion, the observer co-leader shared encouragements to the player parent and leader first, followed by the player leader and parent's sharing and the group sharing of positive feedback. Parents continued to modify responses during interaction and to discuss the play skills used in their language. The leaders linked the strengths of the players and group sharing to the play skills. Three parents practiced play in the fourth session using the same format. Parents were encouraged to continue daily appreciations of self and each child based on their efforts in self-care and self-control and positive changes in attitudes and behaviors.

In the fifth session, three parents conducted 15-minute sibling play sessions with two or three children and one leader in the playroom. Before playing, the leaders instructed the group about the linking skill, role-played, and asked the players to say one sentence to one child followed by one sentence to another, and then point out their commonality or differences. The parent and leader took turns to respond to the siblings' play, and occasionally, the leader whispered to the parent what to say when the parent was struggling. As the parent increased responses, the leader stopped whispering. In the group discussion, the leaders provided encouragements to the player parent, emphasized responding to each child in turn, pointing out their common strengths and growth areas, and encouraged parents to continue positive responses to each child daily.

In the sixth to tenth sessions, the sibling play training followed the same format as the fifth session. Parents took turns viewing a videotape on therapeutic limit setting by Dr. Garry Landreth (Center for Play Therapy, 1997). Each parent began 30-minute weekly home play sessions with their child in the sixth session and continued till the end of training. Parents provided verbal report of their home play sessions to compare with their playroom play practice. The group discussion after each sibling play session highlighted the parents' improvement in play therapy skills and the children's play theme changes. Parents also shared personal applications of these skills in family routine structuring, home behavior choices and consequences, and parental self-care and self-control in their community and work settings.

RESEARCH PROCEDURES

Interview Questions   This research intended to investigate parents' perceptions of the effectiveness of filial therapy training. I was interested in learning what changes occurred in parenting skills through the training that improved the parent-child relationship and the child's behavior. In addition, I was curious what suggestions parents have for filial therapy to be more effective in a school setting. Specific interview questions included:

- Have you noticed any changes in your parenting attitude and behavior as a result of the filial therapy experience?
- Have you noticed any change in your children's behaviors?
- What are your most frequently used skills, most improved skill, and most challenging skill in filial therapy?
- What are your suggestions to make filial therapy more effective in our school?

Data Collection and Analysis I used grounded theory methodology in data collection and analysis because it uses the researcher as the primary instrument for collecting data in the natural setting to understand the meaning of participants' shared information (Lincoln & Guba, 1985). It requires the researcher to collect, analyze, and comprehend the data, ask for clarification in the real context, and identify themes in the inquiry process (Strauss & Corbin, 1990). I followed the general interview guide approach (Patton, 1990) to provide topics, explore, and ask for specific examples that will support me to develop a fuller comprehension of the participants' perceptions of filial therapy experience.

One week after the last training session, my co-leader and I conducted and audiotaped the group interview with the seven parents. We used recursive analysis method (member checking during interview) to increase the internal validity by reflecting the participants' sharing, probing for clarification and examples, summarizing the common and unique points of each participants' sharing, and asking for feedback about his or her understanding before proceeding to the next question. I transcribed the data, analyzed them, recognized themes, and identified parents' personal changes leading to children's changes, and the sustainability of the skills parents acquired through filial therapy. Two weeks later, we conducted the follow-up group interview with the same parents. In the group interview, my understandings and interpretations of the findings were checked with the participants. Transcription of both interviews was coded by me and two other doctoral students independently. All three of us completed qualitative research courses. Two of us cross-checked the coding and interpretations from the three coders; then I discussed the findings with my co-leader and the participants. They confirmed the accuracy of the data and interpretations. This constant comparison method enabled the accuracy of findings to enhance the internal validity, credibility, and trustworthiness of the data (Lincoln & Guba, 1995; Strauss & Corbin, 1990).

RESULTS AND DISCUSSION

All seven parents in the interview reported positive changes in the parent and child attitudes, behaviors, and relationships. Specifically, they reported that parenting competence and confidence increased, their stress decreased, their parent-child relationship was more positive and cooperative, and child behaviors and sibling relationships improved. These findings support previous research results of the 10-week filial therapy program (Foley, Higdon, & White, 2006; Landreth & Bratton, 2006). The following is a discussion of the themes that emerged from participants' responses to questions of perceptions of parents' personal change, perceptions of children's changes, most challenging and most frequently used skill, and suggestions for how to make the filial play program be more effective in the school.

PERCEPTIONS OF PERSONAL CHANGES

Six parents reported that they felt more patient, calm, and aware of their parenting attitudes and actions as a result of attending filial therapy training. They reported new realization of how negative they had been and increased efforts in using positive statements, specific and clear choices, and consequences. They expressed satisfaction with their children's respectful responses and responsible behaviors.

MRS. D: Before this class I didn't realize how negative I was when giving them attention; it was only going to make them argue, not doing it, ignore me . . . now I put it in a positive way, I catch their attention, and they start doing things quickly . . .

MRS. H: You showed me and my family a lot that I didn't know about. It really helps us to help our kids without screaming, and they listen to you a lot without having to change your voice. I now speak with more confidence when I'm talking to them, without raising my voice or anything. It has helped!

One father used to ask his children "why" when he encountered a misbehavior and realized asking "why" the child behaved the way she did was not going to solve the problem. Thus, he changed his way of speaking. He caught himself being negative to his children and had the courage to change and apologize to the children:

MR. T: I think it changed how I speak to them, like saying positive things. Like before, this is my experience. I say, "Why did you do that? Why?" But after a couple of these classes, I started to look and change how I should say things. At times I want to go to the negative, but I knew I should not say that (chuckle). I think one time, things started and it was upsetting me so my daughter reminded me "Daddy, you should be positive, positive!" (Group laugh) Kids catch me in the negative things, and I started saying, "Oh, I am sorry. I was mean."

One husband's sharing suggested that his wife was not only applying the newly practiced skills to the children but was also teaching him how to do it:

MR. D: I came to a couple of these classes and I changed a lot. I noticed their behavior changed. I haven't tried to use these words a lot, but my wife has been helping me to learn a lot.

Mrs. W was advised by her son's private counselor that he would not be able to control himself because of attention deficit disorder, so it was wrong for her to hold him accountable for things like bringing home his agenda and homework or using self-control. However, through filial training, she was able to raise expectations and see her children's cooperative responses in taking responsibility for chores and academic assignments. She shared:

MRS. W: Well, it's been very enlightening all the way around. I have raised my expectations for both children. I think that they have gained different expectations for themselves, just being able to believe that I can raise my expectations and that not being unrealistic or unreasonable has been very beneficial. I feel less stress, I feel my buttons are not easily pushed, and I just think the relationship all the way around is a lot more satisfactory, more hopeful.

Her husband echoed that both sons were getting along, which reduced parenting stress, and helped them raise the expectation for them to improve in school.

MR. W: The changes in the relationship skills were just recognizing the different ways of communicating with kids, letting them know they have choices to make, giving them those consequences, I think it's been very helpful to me. As far as stress levels in the house, when you are constantly worried about them fighting or something like that, it's always an issue. They are relating so well with each other now, my wife said earlier, it's just so good that we can let them play and not having to worry about them yelling, screaming, and getting into a fight or something like that. They are doing well there. Hopefully it's showing up in the schoolwork, too, getting all the stuff done at school, that's the next-most important place. They're doing well at home, and they just need to do well at school.

The parents' shift from negative comments and control to positive responses and appreciations of their children seemed to reduce the parents' feelings of guilt and helplessness, buffer their overwhelmed emotions and stress, and improve their self-concept and relationship with the children. Their efforts to speak and act positively appeared to facilitate the personal growth and change for themselves and their children. This supports the premise that children's problems in part result from parental lack of knowledge and skill (Guerney, 1964). This also supports the premise that a slight change in parental attitude and behaviors would create a greater impact on parent-child-relationship and behavioral improvement than a counseling professional could (Landreth & Bratton, 2006).

PERCEPTIONS OF CHILDREN'S CHANGES

Parents reported observing more patience, cooperativeness, responsiveness, and responsibility in their children at home. They noticed that their children were applying the same play skills and language in self-talk and interactions, such as encouragements, choice giving, limit setting, and self-discipline. Their children's positive changes sometimes motivated the parents' self-awareness and continuous adjustments.

MRS. H: It makes them think a lot. I noticed my children, even with the four-year-old, he says, "You need to give me a little time to think about what I have to choose." Three or four minutes later he chose whatever I wanted him to choose. Kids calmed down more. He tried to stay close to everybody and say, "Thank you," and "I appreciate everybody's help," and remind me "Whatever I do, I have two choices. If I don't do it, I know the consequences." It helped a lot. It's taken a lot of stress away from me, very much so. They improved more in classroom, he listens to the teacher more, so far he is improving (smile). The other day my little four-year-old told his dad, "If you choose to promise to buy me a toy and then not buy it, you choose for me to feel very disappointed with you. I would rather you don't say you are going to buy me something at all." (Group laugh and applause.)

Mr. W: I had a lot of concerns with both boys interfacing with each other being so equal in age, and when we had an incident beforehand, I expect that they are bound to fight at some point. Now they are playing so respectfully together and in occasions they would raise their voices with each other, but it's so easy to rein them back in now. You know we were concerned about them playing together unsupervised. Of course, now we can continue to do what we have to do, and they are having independent play in their own environment. So it is giving a lot of control back to us. In the mornings, I am getting them prepared for school, just being able to get myself ready sometimes is a challenge. I think this helped me in that area, too.

Mrs. W: I think what I see is a responsiveness in both of them that we just didn't expect that we didn't have to solicit it, or support it, or encourage it, and just the fact that their listening skills, their ability to control themselves, makes everything in the house a little more pleasant; and just learning that we can give simple choices so that, if they are misbehaving to control us or control their environment or control each other, then we are giving them back a certain amount of control and self-esteem. I think even when people like themselves more, then they like each other. Giving back some control makes it easier to gain responsiveness out of them. It is just very pleasant, very helpful. And honestly when I first came here, I wasn't hopeful, and I know I don't have to give up, and I know I have skills to be a good parent.

Although parents noticed positive changes in children's sibling relationships and behaviors, they were aware that more improvement could be achieved. They were ready to make ongoing efforts in parenting style adjustment and personal growth to support children's continuous social development.

Mr. D: I saw a little bit of change between the two children. They get along. They do encourage each other.

Mrs. D: I also noticed they try to interact openly, there is still a little sibling rivalry like "Don't talk to me! Leave me alone!" We are working on that a little bit more, having them share, play along independently or together without a parent having to tell her, "Oh, you shouldn't do that." For my stress level, I think coming to the class showed me that it's okay to let her cry. It used to get to me, but now it's much better. I ignore her a little when she cries, and I am trying to get my husband to not push his button when she is crying or when my son is crying. In Hispanic culture sometimes, it's like "Little boys shouldn't cry, you need to be tough." I am teaching my husband a little bit that it's okay for our son to cry. He has feelings like everybody else. If he wants to cry, let him cry.

MR. T: We don't want the kids to think that "Daddy is just for May. Mommy is just for June." But sometimes it went like that. Sometimes it's too difficult for me, even with my wife, to handle those situations. May wants to cling to Daddy and June to Mommy. What I want to do is to try to change. One time May came to me, I asked her to ask Mommy. She didn't want to. It's so difficult for her to ask Mommy because she is so clingy to me. I tell her, "You just go and ask." Sometimes she just changes her mind. It's so hard to change their thinking . . . but we are working on it.

MOST FREQUENTLY USED SKILLS

Sharing appreciations and giving choice were identified as the most frequently used skills. As two parents were sharing, the group laughed and nodded.

MRS. W: If you choose . . .
(Group laughs.)
MRS. D: I think for me, it is the appreciation. It is important to appreciate, and I see my children being nicer to each other and appreciate themselves, like we do appreciations at the end of each session.

MOST IMPROVED SKILL

Limit setting and encouragement were identified as the most improved skill.

MRS. D: Limit setting. I learned a lot and improved a lot in it. Like, in the past, I would allow many things to pass and make my kids comfortable, but now I know it's more important for them to take responsibility.
MRS. W: I thought I was good at limit setting before, but now I would have to re-evaluate myself in doing it. Now I re-evaluated and put

some things to work, and realized many things that I didn't even think of.

Mr. W & Mrs. D: Encouragement. We know the concept. I just need more specific words how to encourage.

Most Challenging Skill

Limit setting and thinking about appropriate responses to children were identified as the most challenging skill.

Mr. W: Probably the most challenging for me is still coming up with that "If you choose to do this" and then having that instant "Okay, what's the consequence?"
(Group laugh.)
Mrs. W: What you are saying is challenging is thinking before we speak, which is probably most challenging for our kids most of the time learning to think before they speak and to be able to relate what's going to come out of your mouth to what action you are about to take, and how to fix others.
Mr. D: I think the challenge for me is changing the way that I talk to them. Everything is kind of challenging for me. But I hear my wife, she does and says things in a certain way, it's hard to change my way in talking to them, but I will try, you know, it's helping a lot. It is challenging to have the words and the way to talk to them.
Mrs. D: My challenge is still to not baby them anymore, and stick to [the] consequence[s], and not allowing accidents. "Oh, it's an accident." That's fine. I am trying to say, "You know you did it one time, it is an accident. Then you do it again, there is a consequence." Of course, they will whine "It's an accident," but I am trying to stick to what I said, "Here is the consequence."

Suggestions for School Filial Play Program to Be More Effective

Promoting a positive perception of filial training and providing it for more parents were suggested by parents as ways to help the program be more effective.

Mrs. H: I don't know how the kids know of Ms. Chen Foley. Yesterday I was telling one neighbor, "Oh, we've been coming to see Ms. Chen Foley." The very first question is that, "Are your children that bad? What is going on in your house?"
(Group chuckling.)

Mrs. H: So I had to explain to them what is going on in the school with filial play. Still, she is, like, "Children who see Ms. Chen Foley have some issues. Your children? I don't see issues. Why do you have to join it?" I said, "It's okay. There is nothing going on. Just to help us to be happier.

Group: Yeah, definitely!

Mrs. H: We told the neighbor, "We are not that bad, really." My second-grade son had to tell other kids about that. Yesterday he told me, "I told the kids seeing Ms. Chen Foley is not all that bad. We are not bad. She is helping us to be good and learn there. But still, they don't believe me." If you can train them and just change things a little, that will help. Also, I hope the training time will be a little bit longer next time.

Group: Yeah. Good suggestion.

Mr. W: I learned a lot here, and it really helped my family to blend. If I had one suggestion, I knew it is not necessarily possible, but if similar groups of students can be together, it may make them more involved in their classroom because all parents can benefit from this program. So if you could have half of the students in this, you probably wouldn't have to explain the situation. If every child could have an interface with her, you know, that will be great! That will be a more ideal situation even if it's once a month.

Mrs. W: I will certainly be willing to take a phone call from another parent. If someone asks me, "What do you think of the school filial training?" I will be more than happy to tell them I feel more competent as a parent now, even though I have been a parent for 24 years; before that, I was parented by very old-fashioned controlling "If you don't do as I say I am going to kick your butt." I carried over some of those skills and didn't have a lot of education. Everybody wants to be a better parent, but not everybody wants to put the effort into it. But honestly, what was offered to me, I was desperate to receive. I want my children to feel good about themselves. This program helped!

CONCLUSION

This study indicates the 10-week filial therapy training is effective with the racially diverse and economically disadvantaged parent group. The participants improved their self-awareness, nonjudgmental acceptance of their children, and consistency in using encouragements, structuring, and limit-setting skills. They believe these changes reduced their stress, secured a more positive parent-child relationship, and resulted in their children's improvement of cooperation, responsibility, and respect. From 2007 to 2009, these parents periodically updated me in the hallway or cafeteria that their children continued to behave and solve problems appropriately at home and received positive notes from teachers, and they were grateful that no more disciplinary referrals or complaints required their immediate appearance in the school so they were able to keep their jobs!

The parents' reports of generalizing play therapy skills in daily life during the filial therapy training suggest that they value these skills in daily life and were eager to apply them to outside play sessions. Future filial therapy trainers may continue to focus on parents' skill-practice in the play session and use parents' real-life cases in group discussion to further reinforce skill transfer and confidence. Adding more time for parents to share and analyze their responses in daily interactions and to brainstorm more practical strategies is desirable to support their mastery of encouragement and choice-giving techniques in real-life situations.

The parents' suggestions to improve filial therapy effectiveness in the school have important implications. Providing play training to a full classroom or including more parents from the same classroom will reduce the participants' stress from defending their self-image or explaining their situations to the community. Future trainers could show a short video introduction of filial therapy to parents at the registration times and arrange training meetings during parents' lunch hours or during the evening or weekend hours. Their willingness to advocate the program to other parents is valuable in increasing parent involvement in the school community. Inviting the successful trainees to talk to a new group was proved to be helpful. Future research could explore how to make filial therapy more conducive to the larger group of parents in the same classroom or grade level, to connect with the school curriculum, and to improve parent involvement.

There are some limitations of this study. One is that the sample size is small, and three parents were tardy for two sessions because of their work schedules; so the results may not be representative of other parents who attended 10-week filial therapy. Future studies could recruit a larger group and adjust the course time to improve attendance and yield a more confident result. The fact that the researcher is the trainer at the same time might have caused researcher bias and members' pleasing report. Future research may use an interviewer who was not involved in the training group to increase objectivity in participants' report. Follow-up interviews with the participants may explore parents' opinions on how to improve the group training format, hands-on practice, videotaping, and live supervision so they can sustain the play skills and home play sessions and to what extent filial training resulted in their children improving behaviorally, socially, and academically.

REFERENCES

Adler, A. (1927). *Understanding human nature* (W. B. Wolfe, Trans.). New York: The World Publishing Company.

Axline, V. M. (1947). *Play therapy: The inner dynamics of childhood*. Boston: Houghton Mifflin.

Bowlby, J. (1969). *Attachment*. New York: Basic Books.

Center for Play Therapy, & Landreth, G. (Producer). *Child-centered play therapy: A clinical session* [Videotape]. United States of America: Center for Play Therapy. (Available from the Center for Play Therapy, University of North Texas, P.O. Box 311337, Denton, TX 76203–1337.)

Clarke, E. J. (1996). *Effects of conflict on adult children's relationship to parents: A multi-dimensional approach to parent-child conflict*. Doctoral dissertation, University of Southern California, Los Angeles.

Foley, Y. C., Higdon, L., & White, J. F. (2006). A qualitative study of filial therapy: Parents' voices. *International Journal of Play Therapy, 15*, 37–64.

Guerney, B. G., Jr. (1964). Filial therapy: Description and rationale. *Journal of Counseling Psychology, 28*, 304–310.

Guerney, L. (2000). Filial therapy into the 21st century. *International Journal of Play Therapy, 2*(9), 1–17.

The importance of play. Retrieved March 9, 2009, from http://www.centerforcreativeplay.org.

Landreth, G. L. (2002). *Play therapy: The art of the relationship* (2nd ed.). New York: Brunner-Routledge.

Landreth, G. L., & Bratton, S. C. (2006). *Child parent relationship therapy*. New York: Routledge.

Lincoln, Y. S., & Guba, E. G. (1985). *Naturalistic inquiry*. Newbury Park, CA: Sage.

Patton, M. Q. (1990). *Qualitative evaluation and research methods*. Thousand Oaks, CA: Sage.

Ray, D. C., Bratton, S. C., Rhine, T., & Jones, L. (2001). The effectiveness of play therapy: Responding to the critics. *International Journal of Play Therapy, 10*(1), 85–108.

Roberts, R. E. L., III. (1990). *Intergenerational affection and psychological well-being: Implications of the changing salience of work and family over the adult life course*. Unpublished doctoral dissertation, University of South California, Los Angeles.

Strauss, A. L., & Corbin, J. M. (1990). *Basics of qualitative research: Techniques and procedures for developing grounded theory* (2nd ed.). Thousand Oaks, CA: Sage.

Wagner, W. G. (1994). Counseling with children: An opportunity for tomorrow. *The Counseling Psychologist, 22,* 381–401.

Walker, H. M., Stiller, B., Severson, H. H., & Golly, A. (1998). First step to success: Intervening at the point of school entry to prevent antisocial behavior patterns. *Psychology in the Schools, 35,* 259–269.

FUTURE RESEARCH DIRECTIONS FOR PLAY THERAPY

CHAPTER 26

Evidence-Based Standards and Tips for Play Therapy Researchers

JENNIFER BAGGERLY

A S EVIDENCED IN the other chapters in this book, play therapy research has made substantial progress in the new millennium. Play therapists have come a long way from Phillips's (1985) indictment of play therapists simply "whistling in the dark." At the same time, play therapy research must continue to meet current evidence-based treatment (EBT) standards, which are criteria that mental health and medical professionals use to evaluate the rigor of research studies (Silverman & Hinshaw, 2008). Certainly, some controversies about evidence-based treatments do exist, such as developmental considerations, matching patient values, ensuring cultural competence, effectiveness in nonclinic settings, and using professional judgment (APA, 2008; Chambless & Ollendick, 2001). Because of these controversies, the 2005 APA policy statement on evidence-based practice in psychology recommends "the integration of the best available research with clinical expertise in the context of patient characteristics, culture, and preferences" (p. 1). Yet, if play therapy is to be viewed by mental health professionals, agency directors, principals, insurance companies, and judges as a viable treatment approach for children with specific problems, then play therapy researchers must exert due diligence in designing studies that meet evidence-based criteria (Baggerly & Bratton, 2010). In fact, the Association for Play Therapy research committee recognized the need for well-designed experimental outcome studies and developed a research strategy (available at http://www.a4pt.org/download.cfm?ID=12466) to encourage such research.

EVIDENCE-BASED CRITERIA

Although there are many views of evidence-based criteria, one well-known standard for determining evidence-based psychological treatments was developed by Chambless et al. (1998) and is listed in Table 26.1. According to Chambless et al., for play therapy to meet criteria as a well-established treatment, "at least two good between-group design experiments" are needed. This statement begs the question, "What is a good study?" As is discussed next, a good study entails:

- Comparison group receiving an EBT preferably, or at least a placebo psychotherapy
- Randomized assignment
- Adequate sample size
- Reliable and valid measures of specific problem with blind administration and scoring
- Treatment manuals implemented with fidelity checks
- Therapists appropriately trained and supervised in treatment approach
- Specific client characteristics: diagnosis or presenting problem, age, and culture
- Appropriate statistical analysis
- Problems or limitations addressed
- Detailed description for replication by independent teams

In fact, these criteria were used recently by the Association for Play Therapy research committee to award a research grant. Table 26.2 presents the APT research grant-scoring sheet as a reference for future researchers.

Comparison Group   Comparing play therapy treatment to a recognized evidence-based psychological treatment for a specific diagnosis or problem is the preferred research design. Findings that demonstrate play therapy is equal or superior to an EBT will elevate play therapy. How do you identify a specific evidence-based psychological treatment to use as a comparison group? Peer-reviewed journal publications are one reliable method. For example, in the *Journal of Clinical Child and Adolescent Psychology,* Silverman and Hinshaw (2008) list current EBTs for children and adolescents by presenting problem, such as traumatic symptoms, anxiety, depression, and so forth. Although there are a plethora of books touting evidence-based approaches, it may be difficult to identify which books are considered valid and reliable by most leaders in the field. Another reliable method of identifying EBTs is obtaining professional

Table 26-1
Criteria for Evidence-Based Psychological Interventions

Division 12 Task Force criteria (Chambless et al., 1998), Group A

Well-established treatments

I.   At least two good between-group design experiments must demonstrate efficacy in one or more of the following ways:

   A. Superiority to pill or psychotherapy placebo, or to other treatment.

   B. Equivalence to already established treatment with adequate sample sizes.

   OR

II. A large series of single-case design experiments must demonstrate efficacy with:

   A. Use of good experimental design *and*

   B. Comparison of intervention to another treatment.

III. Experiments must be conducted with treatment manuals or equivalent clear description of treatment.

IV. Characteristics of samples must be specified.

V.   Effects must be demonstrated by at least two different investigators or teams.

Probably efficacious treatments

I.   Two experiments must show that the treatment is superior to waiting-list control group.

   OR

II. One or more experiments must meet well-established criteria IA or IB, III, and IV above, but V is not met.

   OR

III. A small series of single-case design experiments must meet well-established treatment criteria.

Promising interventions

I.   There must be positive support from one well-controlled study and at least one other less well-controlled study.

   OR

II. There must be positive support from a small number of single-case design experiments.

   OR

III. There must be positive support from two or more well-controlled studies by the same investigator.

Note: This information is quoted from Chambless & Ollendick, 2001, p. 689.

Table 26-2
APT Research Grant-Scoring Sheet

---

1. Does proposal use a randomized controlled play therapy study?

   Points: 0 No, 1 Partially, 2 Yes

2. Does proposal use play therapy in which play is emphasized as a primary ingredient of the treatment, that is, in which play is the principal means for facilitating expression, understanding, and mastery of experiences?

   Points: 0 No, 1 Partially, 2 Yes

3. Does proposal provide treatment to children ages 11 and younger?

   Points: 0 No, 1 Partially, 2 Yes

4. Does proposal provide evidence that the sample size is large enough to achieve statistical significance as determined by power analysis (for example, 30 in treatment group, 30 in control group)?

   Points: 0 No, 1 Partially, 2 Yes

5. Does proposal provide treatment that targets a specific diagnosis (for example, ADHD, Major Depressive Disorder, PTSD), symptom (for example, nightmares, disruptive classroom behavior), or problem (for example, parent-child communication deficits, high parental stress)?

   Points: 0 No, 1 Partially, 2 Yes

6. Does proposal use standardized assessment instruments with sound validity and reliability for the specific diagnosis, symptom, or problem?

   Points: 0 No, 1 Partially, 2 Yes

7. Does proposal use a manualized protocol that clearly and systematically describes treatment in detail so that another mental health professional trained in the principles and procedures of the specific play therapy approach could implement the treatment?

   Points: 0 No, 1 Partially, 2 Yes

8. Does proposal designate as its Principal Investigator a Registered Play Therapist (RPT) or Registered Play Therapist-Supervisor (RPT-S) who has demonstrated the necessary education and training in the proposed play therapy treatment to implement the protocol?

   Points: 0 No, 1 Partially, 2 Yes

9. Does proposal ensure that treatment integrity and fidelity are carefully and systematically monitored through regular checklists, supervision, and audits?

   Points: 0 No, 1 Partially, 2 Yes

10. Does proposal ensure that data collection and scoring are conducted by independent or blind assessors and that means of collection assures the integrity of data?

    Points: 0 No, 1 Partially, 2 Yes

11. Does proposal use investigators who have an established and successful research history as evidenced by previous research studies, publications, and so forth?

    Points: 0 No, 1 Partially, 2 Yes

12. Significance: Does this study address an important problem? If the aims of the application are achieved, how will scientific knowledge or clinical practice be advanced? What will be the effect of these studies on the concepts, methods, technologies, treatments, services, or preventative interventions that drive this field?

    Points: 0 No, 1 Weak, 2 Okay, 3 Good, 4 Strong

13. Approach: Are the conceptual or clinical framework, design, methods, and analyses adequately developed, well integrated, well reasoned, and appropriate to the aims of the project?

    Points: 0 No, 1 Weak, 2 Okay, 3 Good, 4 Strong

14. Approach: Does the Principal Investigator acknowledge potential problem areas and consider alternative tactics?

    Points: 0 No, 1 Weak, 2 Okay, 3 Good, 4 Strong

15. Innovation: Is the project original and innovative? For example, does the project address an innovative hypothesis or critical barrier to progress in the field?

    Points: 0 No, 1 Weak, 2 Okay, 3 Good, 4 Strong

16. Investigators: Are the investigators appropriately trained and well suited to carry out this work? Is the proposed work appropriate to the experience level of the Principal Investigator and other researchers? Does the investigative team bring complementary and integrated expertise to the project (if applicable)?

    Points: 0 No, 1 Weak, 2 Okay, 3 Good, 4 Strong

17. Environment: Does the scientific environment in which the research will be conducted contribute to the probability of success? Does the proposed study benefit from unique features of the scientific environment, or subject populations, or employ useful collaborative arrangements? Is there evidence of institutional support?

    Points: 0 No, 1 Weak, 2 Okay, 3 Good, 4 Strong

18. Protection of Human Subjects from Research Risk: Does the proposal provide a benefit-risk assessment for the human subjects?

    Points: 0 No, 1 Weak, 2 Okay, 3 Good, 4 Strong

19. Diversity & Equity: Does the proposal consider subjects from both genders and diverse racial and ethnic groups as appropriate for the scientific goals of the research? Does it evaluate plans for the recruitment and retention of subjects?

    Points: 0 No, 1 Weak, 2 Okay, 3 Good, 4 Strong

20. Budget and Period of Support: Is the budget description realistic and justified according to the aims and methodology of the project?

    Points: 0 No, 1 Weak, 2 Okay, 3 Good, 4 Strong

    Total Points: Range 0 to 58

associations' lists that were reviewed by a committee. A few professional associations that offer EBT recommendations are:

- APA Division 53, Society of Clinical Child and Adolescent Psychology at http://www.effectivechildtherapy.com
- The Society of Clinical Child and Adolescent Psychology and Network on Youth Mental Health at http://sccap.tamu.edu/EST/index_files/Page624.htm
- National Child Traumatic Stress Network at http://www.nctsnet.org/nctsn_assets/pdfs/effective_treatments_youth_trauma.pdf
- National Registry of Evidence-Based Programs and Practices at http://nrepp.samhsa.gov

Once a suitable EBT has been identified for a comparison group, researchers must ensure that therapists with proper training and supervision are available to implement the particular treatment, as is discussed next.

A comparison group could also receive a non-EBT or a psychotherapy placebo in which children, parents, and teachers believe they are receiving treatment but participate in an activity that is not considered to be therapeutically effective. For play therapy research studies, a psychotherapy placebo could be an untrained volunteer watching a child play with random nontherapeutic toys in a small room. Ray, Chapter 8 (this book), used a reading mentoring as a comparison group, which could be considered a psychotherapy placebo. A non-EBT or psychotherapy placebo is usually considered less desirable than an EBT as a comparison group but is still better than a wait-list control group because it helps rule out the threat to internal validity of change occurring simply due to children receiving extra attention.

Randomized Assignment   Participants should be randomly assigned to either the play therapy treatment group or the comparison group. Random assignment controls for threats to internal validity by allowing participants with individual differences (for example, severity of problem or motivation) to be equally assigned to either group. This procedure prevents numerous biases, such as children who are more motivated being assigned to the treatment group. Random assignment gives more power for the statistical analysis so that any change after the experiment can be attributed to the play therapy intervention rather than to chance. Common methods of randomly assigning participants include using the "randomly select cases" function in SPSS or SAS or simply rolling dice, with even numbers being assigned to play therapy and odd numbers being assigned to the comparison group.

Adequate Sample Size   The proper number of participants, or the sample size, must be determined for a research design. Although positive change may have occurred for most of the participants, many times statistical significance will not be achieved simply because there were not enough participants. Researchers are encouraged to conduct a power analysis to determine the needed sample size to achieve statistical significance at the .05 confidence interval and a large effect size. Statisticians or power analysis programs (Faul, 2008) can help researchers conduct a power analysis. Sample sizes vary depending on the type of statistical analyses (for example, ANOVA or MANCOVA) and the number of measures (dependent variables) that are being used and may range from as few as 20 in each group to as high as 60 in each group.

Reliable and Valid Measures   Well-recognized assessment measures with sound reliability and validity are essential for a good research study. The assessment instrument must measure the specific presenting problem related to the research question. For example, if the research question is "Does child-centered play therapy significantly decrease depression in preschool children when compared to cognitive therapy?" then it is better to have a designated scale, such as the children's depression inventory (Kovacs, 1992), rather than a subscale of a more general instrument, such as the depression subscale of the Child Behavior Checklist (Achenbach, 1991). One of the best ways to identify well-recognized assessment instruments is to consult peer-reviewed journal articles on the specific topic. Instruments should be administered and scored by personnel trained in the assessment and who are blind to the participants' assignment to the treatment or the comparison group.

Treatment Manuals   Play therapy researchers need a clear, detailed description of the principles and procedures of a specific type of play therapy treatment. An introductory book of play therapy in general will not suffice. Rather, the play therapy treatment approach must be specified (for example, child-centered, Adlerian, Jungian, cognitive behavioral, and so forth), and a treatment manual should be followed. To date, treatment manuals have been published for both Child-Centered Play Therapy (Ray, 2009) and the Filial Therapy model of Child Parent Relationship Therapy (Bratton, Landreth, Kellam, &

Blackard, 2006). Such treatment manuals facilitate the integrity of play therapy and filial therapy by emphasizing play as the "primary ingredient of the treatment; that is, in which play is the principal means for facilitating expression, understanding, and mastery of experiences" (APT, 2009, p. 7). Fidelity checks to ensure the treatment manual is implemented correctly can be accomplished by having therapists complete session checklists and hiring trained, independent reviewers to randomly view videotaped sessions.

Therapists Trained and Supervised Appropriate training in a specific treatment of play therapy and the comparison intervention usually entails more than attendance at a one-day workshop. Ideally, therapists would have completed a graduate course in play therapy or the comparison intervention, extensive reading, and supervised practice in a particular treatment approach. Many comparison treatments require certification or at least a certificate in training so therapists can appropriately implement the treatment. Ongoing supervision by a supervisor trained in the treatment approach should be provided throughout the study. Qualifications of supervisors and therapists should be reported in the research manuscript.

Specific Client Characteristics Participants in the study should meet specific inclusion and exclusion criteria, including age and a particular diagnosis or presenting problem. It is not enough to say the participants had behavior problems. Rather, the studies must have targeted the same diagnosis or presenting problem, such as preschool children ages 3 to 6 years old with traumatic symptoms who meet clinical levels of trauma on the trauma symptom checklist for young children (Briere, 2005). Participants' gender, race, ethnicity, language, and socio-economic status should also be reported. What may be effective for Caucasian boys from upper-middle-class families may not necessarily be effective for Mexican-American girls from limited-income migrant families, even though they may have the same diagnoses of depression. Also report that parents' consent on an institutional review board approved informed consent was obtained for each participant.

Appropriate Statistical Analysis Data analysis is a dynamic process. A researcher may plan to conduct a particular statistical analysis, such as repeated measures ANOVA, but find after reviewing the pre-test data that an ANCOVA is needed. Statisticians are helpful allies throughout the research project and should be consulted before, during, and after data collection. Play therapy researchers should provide detailed descriptions of analyses, report effect sizes, and use a more stringent alpha level to avoid a Type I error (Baggerly & Bratton, 2010).

Problems or Limitations Addressed Common problems such as participant recidivism or changes in the treatment location should be anticipated, addressed, and described. Incentives to participants, either financial or social, can help reduce recidivism. Proper infrastructure, such as support staff and well-equipped private facilities at the treatment location, will help ensure success. Official approval and buy-in from the highest authority (for example, agency director or superintendent) to the line staff (for example, residential workers and teachers) will be invaluable in preventing research challenges. Since every study has limitations, a clear discussion of them will prevent readers from being suspect of the integrity of a study.

Detailed Description for Replication by Independent Team If play therapy researchers follow the preceding recommendations and report them in detail, then replication of the study by other independent teams will be facilitated. Some play therapy researchers may erroneously believe that since one study on a particular problem was already completed, then replication is not needed. Yet, the EBT standards, as defined by Chambless et al. (1998), clearly state that at least two good between-group design experiments are needed to demonstrate efficacy. Therefore, play therapy researchers are encouraged to consider replicating and improving studies described in this book.

TIPS FOR SUCCESS

In addition to following the EBT criteria discussed earlier, there are several other tips for success in conducting good play therapy research studies. First, form a research team of fellow therapists, a statistician, experienced research consultants, and administrators or staff at the treatment location. Ask team members to partner with you in developing and implementing a good between-group design that meets the EBT criteria. Meet with the team often to problem-solve barriers and celebrate successes. Second, conduct a thorough literature review on the topic to identify common client characteristics, assessment instruments for the target population, comparison group

476 Future Research Directions for Play Therapy

alternatives, and potential problems and solutions. Third, develop clear research questions that are related to the research design and assessment instruments. Some research questions such as "How does play therapy help children after their parents' divorce?" are not specific enough. A better research question is "Does child-centered play therapy significantly decrease the revised children's manifest anxiety scale total scores of elementary children whose parents' divorced when compared to children receiving cognitive behavior therapy?" After conducting the study, report the data and answer the specific research question. Finally, write a research manuscript in a timely fashion, and disseminate research results by submitting the manuscript to a peer-reviewed journal, such as the *International Journal of Play Therapy*, the *Journal of Counseling and Development*, *Professional School Counseling, Social Work, School Psychology Quarterly, Journal of Counseling Psychology*, or *Journal of Clinical Child and Adolescent Psychology*. Many play therapy researchers find it helpful to have a co-author with an established record of peer-reviewed publications to prepare the manuscript according to stringent journal requirements. A published article with a co-author is better than data in a file!

WHERE ARE WE NOW?

Now that the direction is clear toward a good between-group design, also known as well-controlled randomized clinical trials (RCT), we must answer "Where are we now?" in establishing play therapy as an evidence-based treatment. Ray and Bratton's discussion in Chapter 1 of this book clearly answers the question. As a brief review, a careful review of recent studies shows increased rigor in play therapy research designs over the past 10 years. Also, numerous studies meet the criteria of Chambless et al. (1998) for:

- Random assignment to play therapy treatment or evidence-based comparison group (for example, CCPT was compared to Second Step by Schumann, Chapter 11)
- Treatment manuals or clear detailed descriptions of treatment (for example, the CPRT treatment manual [Bratton, Landreth, Kellam, & Blackard, 2006] was used by Ceballos, Chapter 20)
- Inclusion and exclusion criteria for a specific population (for example, only Head Start children in borderline or clinical range were included by Morrison and Helker, Chapter 24)

- Reliable and valid assessment measures (for example, the behavioral assessment system for children [Reynolds & Kamphaus, 1992] was used by Garza (Chapter 10) and Child Behavior Checklist Teacher Report Form [Achenbach & Rescorla, 2000] was used by Smith, Chapter 22)
- Appropriate data analyses (for example, ANOVA and effect size were reported by Ray, Chapter 8)

Thus, more and more, play therapy researchers are intentionally and systematically meeting these evidence-based treatment standards. Also, several play therapy researchers (for example, Bratton, Gil, and Schottelkorb) are currently implementing separate studies that meet all of the aforementioned criteria for play therapy to be recognized as a well-established treatment.

Although the research studies described in this book do not meet Chambless et al. (1998) criteria for well-established treatments, several do meet criteria for probably efficacious treatments. For example, Ray, Chapter 8, demonstrated that CCPT was superior to an active control group with co-morbid ADHD conditions, controlling for most internal validity threats such as maturation, rater bias, and attention. Schumann, Chapter 11, demonstrated that CCPT was statistically equal to the evidence-based Second Step guidance curriculum for children with aggressive behavior problems. Thus, CCPT may be considered a probably efficacious treatment or at least a promising intervention for elementary-age schoolchildren with behavior problems. Also, since filial therapy with minority populations (Glover, Yeun, Sheely, Ceballos, Chapters 16 to 19) has been shown to be more effective than wait-list controls, it may be considered a probably efficacious treatment or at least a promising intervention as well.

Finally, Chambless et al. (1998) states that a small series of single-case designs meet criteria for probably efficacious treatments. In response, play therapy researchers have intentionally and systematically increased the number of studies using single-case designs. For example, Schottelkorb, Chapter 12, conducted a single-case analysis of five elementary school students with ADHD who received CCPT and found that three of the five children improved their on-task behavior. Garofano-Brown, Chapter 13, conducted a single-case analysis of three developmentally delayed preschool children who received CCPT and found increases in children's development and decreases in their behavior problems after CCPT. These and future single-case designs will aid in establishing CCPT as a well-established treatment.

CONCLUSION

We conclude that play therapy researchers have made steady progress in building a firm foundation of play therapy research since the new millennium and continue to do so. Play therapists and mental health professionals should be encouraged that several play therapy and filial therapy studies appear to meet EBT criteria for probably efficacious treatments. In addition, several independent play therapy researchers are currently conducting play therapy studies that meet criteria for well-established treatments. Finally, it is important to remember that a lack of current randomized clinical trials (RCT) does not mean a treatment is ineffective. Rather, it means the treatment has not yet been tested in RCT and that more research is needed.

All play therapists can contribute to play therapy research by collaborating on well-controlled randomized treatment studies as described earlier, conducting single-case analyses, or contributing to the APT Foundation research fund. Play therapy research has a bright and hopeful future of being recognized as a well-established treatment.

REFERENCES

Achenbach, T. M. (1991). *Manual for the child behavior checklist and 1991 profile.* Burlington, VT: University Associates Psychiatry.

American Psychological Association. (2005). *APA Policy Statement on Evidence-Based Practice.* Retrieved September 18, 2009, from http://www2.apa.org/practice/ebpstatement.pdf.

American Psychological Association (APA) Task Force on Evidence-Based Practice for Children and Adolescents. (2008). *Disseminating evidence-based practice for children and adolescents: A systems approach to enhancing care.* Washington, DC: American Psychological Association.

Association for Play Therapy (2009). *Play therapy research grant application.* Available at http://www.a4pt.org/download.cfm?ID=27697.

Baggerly, J., & Bratton, S. C. (2010). Building a firm foundation in play therapy research: Response to Phillips (2010). *International Journal of Play Therapy, 19(1),* 26–38.

Bratton, S. C., Landreth, G. L., Kellam, T. L. T., & Blackard, S. (2006). *Child parent relationship therapy (CPRT) treatment manual.* New York: Routledge.

Briere, J. (2005). *Trauma symptom checklist for young children: Professional manual.* Lutz, FL: Psychological Assessment Resources.

Chambless, D. L., Baker, M., Baucom, D. H., Beutler, L. E., Calhoun, K. S., Crits-Christoph, P., et al. (1998). Update on empirically validated therapies, II. *Clinical Psychologist 51(1),* 3–16.

Chambless, D. L., & Ollendick, T. H. (2001). Empirically supported psychological interventions: Controversies and evidence. *Annual Review of Psychology, 52*, 685–716.

Faul, F. (2008). *G*Power. Version 3.0.10.* University of Kiel, Germany.

Kovacs, M. (1992). *Children's depression inventory manual.* Los Angeles: Western Psychological Services.

Phillips, R. D. (1985). Whistling in the dark? A review of play therapy research. *Psychotherapy: Theory, Research, & Practice, 22*, 752–760.

Ray, D. C. (2009). *Child-centered play therapy treatment manual.* Royal Oak, MI: Self-Esteem Shop.

Silverman, W. K., & Hinshaw, S. P. (2008). The second special issue on evidence-based psychosocial treatments for children and adolescents: A 10-year update. *Journal of Clinical Child & Adolescent Psychology, 37*(1), 1–7.

Society of Clinical Child and Adolescent Psychology & Network on Youth Mental Health. (n.d.). *Evidence-based treatment for children and adolescents.* Retrieved June 9, 2009, from http://sccap.tamu.edu/EST/index_files/Page624.htm.

Author Index

Abidin, R., 126
Abidin, R. R., 105, 110, 115, 117, 148, 149, 156, 160, 215, 236, 301, 313, 326, 342, 343, 359, 365, 366
Abner, M., 373
Achenbach, T. M., 106, 110, 111, 167, 197, 213, 214, 235, 301, 342, 343, 347, 348, 359, 362, 363, 364, 377, 397, 432, 436, 439, 473
Ackerman, B., 106
Adler, A., 411, 449
Airasian, P., 253, 254
Ajamu, A., 340, 341, 342, 344, 349
Albaum, J. S., 410
Albee, G., 373
Alexander, E. D., 374
Alfaro, E., 355
Allan, J., 73
Allen, J., 391
Allin, H., 5
Altbach, P., 357
Alvarez, R., 357
American Counseling Association, 3
American Psychiatric Association, 147, 160
American Psychological Association, 210, 211, 212, 467
American Psychological Association Task Force on Evidence-Based Practice for Children and Adolescents, 469

American School Counselor Association, 194, 195, 392
Ames, L., 231
Andres-Hyman, R., 177, 178, 189, 357, 358
Andronico, M., 324, 393
Andronico, M. P., 430
Anes, L., 177, 178, 189, 357, 358
Armstrong, S., 112, 153
Armstrong, S. A., 251, 261, 392, 437
Asbrand, J., 17, 19, 24
Asbrand, J. P., 88, 96, 97
Association for Play Therapy, 250, 470, 472, 474
Axline, V. M., xiv, 28, 72, 96, 138, 205, 251, 252, 262, 379, 392, 414, 449
Ayers, W., 6, 8, 173

Baecher, R. E., 410
Baggerly, J., 7, 15, 17, 18, 20, 25, 250, 271, 287, 290, 340, 341, 467, 474
Bailey, B. A., 431, 433, 436, 438
Bailey, D. F., 358
Baird, M., 410
Baker, B., 232, 244
Baker, J., 410, 428
Baker, M., 290, 468, 469, 475, 476, 477
Baker, S., 231
Baker, S. B., 193
Balkin, R. S., 251, 261, 392
Balvanz, J., 39, 41, 42
Bamara, M., 355

Subject Index